Flyfisher's Guide to™
New Mexico

Fishing Titles Available from Wilderness Adventures Press, Inc.™

Flyfishers Guide to™

Flyfisher's Guide to Alaska

Flyfisher's Guide to Arizona

Flyfisher's Guide to the Big Apple

Flyfisher's Guide to California

Flyfisher's Guide to Chesapeake Bay

Flyfisher's Guide to Colorado

Flyfisher's Guide to Colorado's Lost Lakes
and Secret Places

Flyfisher's Guide to Connecticut

Flyfisher's Guide to Eastern Trophy Tailwaters

Flyfisher's Guide to the Florida Keys

Flyfisher's Guide to Freshwater Florida

Flyfisher's Guide to Idaho

Flyfisher's Guide to Mexico

Flyfisher's Guide to Montana

Flyfisher's Guide to Michigan

Flyfisher's Guide to Minnesota

Flyfisher's Guide to Missouri & Arkansas

Flyfisher's Guide to Nevada

Flyfisher's Guide to the New England Coast

Flyfisher's Guide to New Mexico

Flyfisher's Guide to New York

Flyfisher's Guide to North Carolina & Georgia

Flyfisher's Guide to the Northeast Coast

Flyfisher's Guide to New England

Flyfisher's Guide to Oregon

Flyfisher's Guide to Saltwater Florida

Flyfisher's Guide to Southwest Montana's
Mountain Lakes

Flyfisher's Guide to Tennessee

Flyfisher's Guide to Texas

Flyfisher's Guide to the Texas Gulf Coast

Flyfisher's Guide to Utah

Flyfisher's Guide to Virginia

Flyfisher's Guide to Washington

Flyfisher's Guide to Western Washington Lakes

Flyfisher's Guide to Wisconsin & Iowa

Flyfisher's Guide to Wyoming

Flyfisher's Guide to Yellowstone National Park

On the Fly Guide to™

On the Fly Guide to the Northwest

On the Fly Guide to the Northern Rockies

Best Fishing Waters™ Books

California's Best Fishing Waters

Colorado's Best Fishing Waters

Idaho's Best Fishing Waters

Montana's Best Fishing Waters

Oregon's Best Fishing Waters

Washington's Best Fishing Waters

Micro SD Cards with GPS Waypoints

Montana's Fishing GPS Maps

Colorado's Fishing GPS Maps

Washington's Fishing GPS Maps

Anglers Guide to™

Complete Anglers Guide to Oregon

Angler's Guide to the West Coast

Saltwater Angler's Guide to Southern California

Field Guide to™

Field Guide to Fishing Knots

Fly Tying

Go-To Flies™

Flyfishing Adventures™

Montana

Trout Adventures™

North America

Flyfishing Northern New England's Seasons

Flyfisher's Guide to™

New Mexico

Van Beacham

Wilderness
Adventures
Press, Inc.™

Belgrade, Montana

Flyfisher's Guide to™

Published by Wilderness Adventures Press, Inc.™
45 Buckskin Road
Belgrade, MT 59714
866-400-2012
Website: http://store.wildadv.com
email: books@wildadv.com

Second Edition

Printed in the United States

ISBN 978-1-932098-82-2 (8-09206-98822-4)

DEDICATION

This book is dedicated to my father, William Frank Beacham, who always found time to take me fishing, and my mother, Jo Ann, for letting us go as often as we did. Through fishing, my father taught me patience, acceptance, understanding, and how to listen and follow my instincts. His direction helped me to catch a lot of fish and achieve my dream of doing what I love for a living—flyfishing. His passing is what gave me the inspiration to complete this project so that others may experience what flyfishing in New Mexico has meant to me, and the three generations of Beachams before me.

Thanks Dad. I hope the fishing is as good in heaven as it is here in the "Land of Enchantment."

William Frank Beacham
August 23, 1928–January 11, 2002

The charm of flyfishing is that it is the pursuit of that which is elusive, yet attainable; a perpetual series of occasions for hope.

Author unknown

An angler tries his luck on the Red River in March.

Table of Contents

ACKNOWLEDGMENTS

So many people helped me with this book that I couldn't possibly remember them all here, but they are mentioned throughout the book. First, I want to thank John Marmaduke and Allen Vaongevalle of Hastings Books for referring me to Chuck Johnson at Wilderness Adventures Press. Chuck was incredibly patient with me, as I worked to complete the book during some really trying times. When I embarked on this project I had no idea how much time it would take to research and write everything, and I was trying to keep my head above water in my guiding business during the worst drought in my lifetime. Without editor Darren Brown's help in getting this thing wrapped up, I'd still be at it.

I also want to thank all the contributors to this book, whose help I couldn't have done without—knowledgeable, professional anglers like John Tavenner, owner of Sandstone Anglers on the San Juan River; Jarrett Sasser, owner of High Desert Angler in Santa Fe. And there wouldn't even be a Southeast Region in the book if it weren't for Winston Cox in Ruidoso. A special thanks goes to legendary Norm Abie, the guru of the Rio Penasco and a walking flyfishing encyclopedia, who passed away just before the first edition of this book. We're going to miss you, Norm.

The Southwest Region wouldn't have been possible without the contribution of author Dutch Salmon, owner of Hi Lonesome Books. Thanks Dutch, for the great insight on a virtually unknown fishery. Thanks also to Bob Widgren, co-owner of Los Pinos Rods, who saved my ass again by coming up with the material on Elephant Butte Lake just in the nick of time for the first edition and again for this revision with his important contribution on tiger muskie fishing on Quernado and Bluewater lakes. Ed Adams of Ed Adams Flyfishing fills in an important gap left in the first edition with his unique insight to the mystery of successful flyfishing for giant northern pike in the mighty Rio Grande Gorge.

I also want to thank my friends and people that work for me, who all helped in so many ways. My buddy Bruce McClymond called every day and told me to get my ragged ass out of bed and get crackin' on the book so we could start fishing together again. And all my guides took up the slack when I was unable to guide because I was doing research or writing.

Thanks to Colleen Tretter, who painstakingly assembled all the hub city information in this book and helped Neal Ogden revise it all again for this edition, and what a great

job they did. Thanks also to my new dearest best friend, Kelly Haukebo, for her loving support. But perhaps more than anyone else, I need to thank Jack and Stephanie Woolley for holding down the fort while I wrote this book. My business would not have made it without you guys.

The author high-sticking on the lower Red River. (Stephanie Woolley)

FOREWORD

Van Beacham has compiled a wonderful book about flyfishing in New Mexico. His lifelong passion for the sport of flyfishing is evident throughout this very informative book. I have spent many days fishing with Van, and have been fortunate to experience his onstream compassion for everything and anything that has to do with flyfishing. His book brings the reader into his world, and if you pay attention it will become your world, too.

Van was born in Santa Fe, New Mexico, and started fishing with his father and grandfather when he was four years old. He has been fishing and/or guiding in northern New Mexico ever since. Van currently owns and operates The Solitary Angler in Taos.

You will find virtually everything you need to know about flyfishing in New Mexico within these covers, including where, when, and how to fish every nook and cranny of the state, along with what's hatching and how to match it.

Enjoy the book, enjoy New Mexico, and most important, enjoy flyfishing!

Jack Woolley
Manager, The Solitary Angler

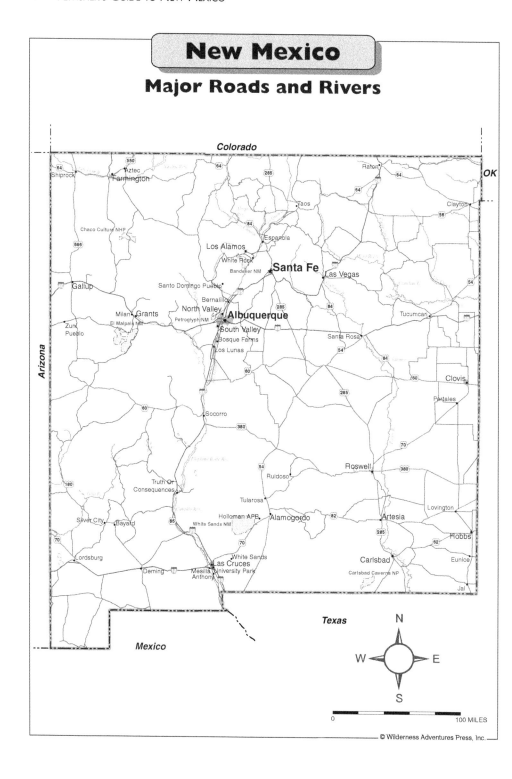

New Mexico
Major Roads and Rivers

New Mexico Facts

New Mexico is a beautiful state, rich in history, culture, art, and natural resources.

New Mexico was the 47th state, joining the union on January 6, 1912
Capital: Santa Fe
Largest City: Albuquerque
Area: 121,593 square miles; the fifth largest state
Population: 2,086,046 (2012 estimate)
Major Industries: Mining (potash, copper, silver, uranium), oil, natural gas, tourism
Highest Point: Wheeler Peak—13,161 feet above sea level
Lowest Point: Red Bluff Lake—2,817 feet above sea level
Bordering States: Arizona, Colorado, Oklahoma, Texas, Utah
Bordering Country: Mexico
Nickname: Land of Enchantment
Fish: Rio Grande cutthroat trout
Tree: Piñon (*Pinus edulis*)
Flower: Yucca (*Yucca glauca*)

Other Facts
- More than 25,000 Anasazi sites have been identified in New Mexico by archeologists.
- One quarter of New Mexico is forested, and there are seven national forests, including the 3.3-million-acre Gila National Forest, the nation's largest.
- The word "Pueblo" is used to describe a group of people, a town, or an architectural style. The Pueblo people of the Southwest have lived in the same location longer than any other culture in the nation.
- Since New Mexico's climate is so dry, three-quarters of the roads are left unpaved.
- Taos Pueblo is located 2 miles north of the city of Taos. It is the oldest continuously occupied community in the United States.

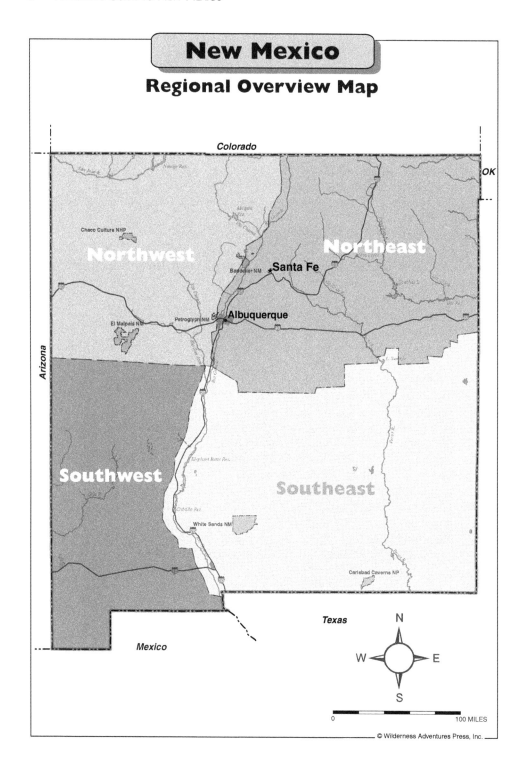

New Mexico
Regional Overview Map

© Wilderness Adventures Press, Inc.

STATEWIDE ANGLING INFORMATION

Regular License Year: April 1–March 31; 24 hours a day all year long. Gamefish may be taken in all waters open to angling.

New Mexico Department of Game and Fish
P.O. Box 25112
Santa Fe, NM 87504-5112
1 Wildlife Way, Santa Fe, NM 87507
www.wildlife.state.nm.us

To receive information in the mail: 1-800-862-9310
Public Affairs (general information): 505-476-8000
TDD (hearing and speech impaired): 505-476-8143
Fisheries Management: 505-476-8055
Law Enforcement: 505-476-8066
Conservation Services: 505-476-8101
Fax (licenses/procurement/payment): 505-476-8137

Northwest Region
3841 Midway Place NE
Albuquerque, NM 87109
505-222-4700

Northeast Region
215 York Canyon Road
Raton, NM 87740
575-445-2311

Southwest Region
2715 Northrise Dr.
Las Cruces, NM 88011
575-532-2100

Southeast Region
1912 W. Second Street
Roswell, NM 88201
575-624-6135

The best description of most fishable water in New Mexico is "pocket water."

ABOUT FLYFISHING IN NEW MEXICO

The information in this book is based on my own experience and that of other anglers who've fished here over the last 46 years, when we had normal or above normal water flows. It's important to note that until about 10 years ago, New Mexico had been in a very wet, 30-year cycle. But from about 1998 until 2005, New Mexico, along with much of the West, suffered from an extended drought, and some of our streams and lakes definitely took a beating. From 2005 to the present (2010), we have been averaging above normal precipitation again and things have improved dramatically, although not fully. Still, depending on future conditions, some may not resemble anything like the descriptions in this book, so it's always important to check local conditions before heading out.

New Mexico is rich in angling diversity even though it's the second driest state in the country. Every region offers excellent flyfishing for coldwater and warmwater species. From high-mountain lakes and streams to remote desert canyons and gorges, there is something here for every angler to enjoy.

Opportunities abound year-round. Northern New Mexico is situated at the southern end of the Rocky Mountains, and southern New Mexico also has some very intriguing high mountains. In between is a high desert where the cold water becomes warm. Many of these high desert areas offer great winter flyfishing, and in some of the "cusp" areas there are different species active at different times of the day and/or year.

For instance, in the Rio Grande Gorge, the best trout fishing is during fall, winter, and early spring, while late spring and summer is best for smallmouth bass and northern pike. (Pike are also active in late winter and early spring, and trout will feed furiously in the middle of summer during late-evening and nighttime hatches.)

Not only does our southern latitude provide mild winter temperatures and lots of sun, but our high alpine areas offer mild summer temperatures, as well. So when it's too hot in the gorge, it's just right in the mountains. Hatches also occur year-round, and some of the best dry-fly fishing in the state can be found on the legendary "Special Trout Waters" of the San Juan River. In the dead of winter, you can find solitude, hatches, and rising fish on a little-known spring creek in southeast New Mexico known as the Rio Penasco.

The information here is divided into four regions, and there is a special section on private waters because some of the best flyfishing is on private property. In recent years, a lot of these fisheries have been protected, developed, and opened to the public for a fee. Because many of New Mexico's streams are small, there is also a special section on flyfishing tactics for these waters.

There are detailed maps of the majority of the lakes and streams in the state, with parking areas, campgrounds, access points, and river miles highlighted on each. At the end of each fishery, there are "Stream Facts," which offer concise summaries of the waters described. There's also a list of important agencies, campgrounds, and outfitters for easy reference.

In the hub city information at the end of each section, you'll find all the resources you need to plan a visit. My hope is that you'll be able to arrange your next flyfishing trip entirely from this book. If you can't, write me about what you think I need to include in the next revision.

SMALL-STREAM FLYFISHING

When most people think of flyfishing the Rocky Mountain West, they probably imagine themselves standing hip deep in a broad western river, casting 30 to 40 feet of line into a deep riffle or pocket they can't reach by wading. Or floating down a big river in a drift boat, pounding the banks with a big attractor and anticipating the slashing attack of a wild trout. But the reality is that the majority of western flyfishing water is in the form of small streams and creeks, most of which have yet to be discovered by all but the most adventurous anglers.

You see, all those big rivers actually start high in the Rockies as tiny creeks born from melting snow and underground springs. All you have to do is look at a good map of any part of the Rockies and you'll see that there are thousands of small streams and creeks, most teeming with trout. Yet about 80 percent of the anglers I meet are fishing on the big rivers, usually floating, and rarely getting out of the boat. I like floating and fishing from a drift boat as much as anyone because it allows me to reach places I otherwise can't, even if it's just the other side of the river. But there is a lot of other water to explore.

Things have changed over the years as flyfishing has become popular and somewhat of an industry. Gone are the days when you are the only angler on the river. Today, on some rivers, boats wait in line to fish the next hole, and other boats and anglers are never out of view. It certainly isn't a solitary experience. And for an angler like myself, who learned to flyfish on New Mexico's waters in the early sixties, the main reason for going fishing has always been to get away from everything and be alone with nature. I certainly don't fish for the social aspects, and I don't know why anyone would want to fish where everyone else is fishing, although in a way I'm glad most anglers don't mind it. As long as those anglers are pounding the famous waters—providing good business for the guides, outfitters, and fly shops near those rivers—they won't be pounding the more sensitive, fragile small streams and creeks.

I accept the fact that it's all relative and that what used to seem like a lot of fishing pressure to me may seem like almost no pressure to someone who just started flyfishing. For example, I used to get upset if I saw even one other angler on a 5-mile stretch of the Rio Grande near Pilar during the caddis hatch. Now I'm happy to find a riffle that's not being fished. As the sport gets more popular, I get more used to seeing other anglers on "my" water. Also, I have to accept the fact that I have been part of the reason flyfishing is more popular in New Mexico, since I have been guiding anglers for over 20 years and writing about flyfishing for 15 years.

Most of the best flyfishing in this country is on the many tailwaters, below dams, which are not natural rivers. Before tailwaters were created, there was very little flyfishing pressure in the West. Indeed, about 80 percent of the angling pressure in this region today is on about 20 percent of the fishable water. Tailwaters have created a whole new breed of flyfishers and are, in my opinion, the single most significant reason for the explosion in the industry. Most guides, outfitters, and fly shops exist because of tailwaters.

If we all had to guide on strictly wild freestone streams many guides would be out of business. Not only are they unpredictable compared to tailwaters, which makes guiding more difficult, but many beginning anglers don't have the time or the patience to fish streams that don't consistently produce. Let's face it, when you're learning and you only have a few days a year on the water, you want to go where you have the best chance of catching lots of fish. That means hiring a guide and going to one of the best rivers, usually a tailwater.

Even my business, The Solitary Angler, which specializes in "quality flyfishing without the crowds," has changed considerably since the days when I started guiding. When I go fishing I like to hike into the Rio Grande Gorge and fish for wild browns and cuttbows, yet my guides and I take the majority of our guided trips to one of three small tailwaters in the region because we know clients will usually catch more fish there.

On the Rio Grande, a wild freestone river, we know that the chances of catching few or no trout are often pretty good. The San Juan River, a famous New Mexico tailwater, has more guides operating on the first 4 miles of river below Navajo Dam than the rest of the state combined.

More and more, though, anglers are beginning to move away from the big tailwaters and the crowds in search of solitude and a more natural experience. This new angling population is concerned less with how many fish they catch or how big the fish are. If they can wade in a stream in a natural setting, without too many people, and catch a few wild trout on a fly they're happier than floating a famous river and catching big fish with a bunch of other people.

Small streams and creeks provide the best opportunities for such anglers. They're also better for beginning flyfishers to learn on because it isn't necessary to cast far, and there are endless chances to succeed since you're constantly moving and fishing new water. Each riffle, pool, pocket, and run is different, offering a new challenge in casting technique, presentation, drift, reading the water, and, hopefully, landing and releasing a trout.

Another thing that's easier to understand on small streams is trout behavior. On big rivers, it's hard to know what trout are doing unless they're actively feeding. But on creeks and small streams, the trout's world is in plain view, just like an aquarium. You can observe fish in their natural habitat—feeding, competing, resting, spooking, and even spawning. Also, you can usually sight fish, increasing your chances of catching the larger fish. Learning how to flyfish on small streams and creeks will also make you better at fishing larger waters.

Defining Small Streams and Creeks

In defining a small stream or creek in New Mexico you must first put into perspective the difference in water size here compared to waters in Colorado, Wyoming, Montana, Idaho, and Utah. To explain, I'll tell you a fish story about a fellow guide I know named Rick from Jackson Hole, Wyoming. He came to New Mexico to ski Taos and check out the winter fishing I'd been telling him about. I took him to the Red River, at its confluence with the Rio Grande, the first day. After walking almost a mile and a half down the Gorge to the confluence he looked at the two rivers and said, "Is that the Rio Grande? And that's the Red River? You call these rivers?"

Nodding, I said, "What do you mean? Other than the San Juan, the Rio Grande Gorge is the largest and most important river in the state, and the Red River is the largest tributary of the Gorge."

He shrugged his shoulders and said, "In Wyoming, we call these creeks."

"I know," I said, "but this is New Mexico and, trust me, these are rivers."

We rigged up with double nymphs and headed down to the first pool in the Red River, where I immediately spotted a big cuttbow and pointed it out to him. His first cast was perfect, as was his drift, and the big buck took the small nymph. He lifted the rod and went for the reel with his left hand. Before I could say anything the fish ripped downstream so he let go of the reel, allowing the fish to run downstream into the rapids at the confluence—where it broke him off.

"Son of a bitch!" he said. "That was as big as anything I've hooked in the big rivers up north."

I laughed and told him, "Next time, don't use your reel. Strip the fish in and hold tight with a bent rod and try to keep it in the pool where you hooked it. You can't let big trout run downstream like that in these fast, boulder-strewn rivers or they'll get you every time."

He looked at me as he gathered his limp line and mumbled, "Right."

New Mexico streams are diminutive compared to streams in the northern Rockies for three reasons. First, we simply don't get as much precipitation as those northern areas. Second, our winters are shorter and our atmosphere is drier so we have more moisture loss due to sublimation and evaporation. Finally, we're the only state west of the Mississippi that doesn't have an instream flow bill so there's great strain on our waterways due to consumptive use.

Where there are feeder creeks in the central Rockies, we have tiny creeks and seeps. Where they have major rivers, we have medium-sized rivers like the Rio Grande and Rio Chama. So even though the lower Red River may be a small stream compared to other rivers, it isn't considered one here, although some of the techniques talked about here are valuable on streams of any size. Larger rivers should be broken down and looked at as several small streams running parallel to each other. No matter how big the river, you can only fish one drift line at a time, unless you're stripping streamers across currents.

So what is a small stream in New Mexico? If you can't cast or throw a rock across it, then it's not a small stream. In this context, a small stream is a stream or creek whose average summertime flow is less than 30 cfs. Depending on the grade, a stream with this flow is about 15 to 20 feet wide, although it could be as wide as 30 or 40 feet in slow pools or beaver ponds. Most streams in New Mexico are small streams, and even some of the main rivers run less than 30 cfs during fall and winter or during drought conditions. Many fishable creeks in New Mexico are 5 cfs or smaller—only about a foot or two wide.

A typical small stream in New Mexico.

In Wyoming I wouldn't even look at creeks this size, and they probably wouldn't contain very many, if any, catchable-sized fish. In New Mexico, however, we have healthy fish populations in very tiny creeks, and sometimes these waters hold trout up to 18 inches. This is primarily due to our mild, short winters. Our creeks don't usually suffer from winterkill. The shorter winters also translate into longer growing seasons and more abundant aquatic insect populations.

This is what makes our small streams and creeks so special; they are very productive for their size. Try one of the hundreds of such waters in New Mexico and you'll see what I mean.

Equipment and Tackle

As with any sport, different conditions require different equipment, tools, and techniques. When fishing a large river or lake, where long casts into the wind are often necessary, a 9-foot, 6-weight, fast-action rod is recommended, but when you're fishing a small, brushy stream where short casts are the norm you need a short, light-action rod like a 7- to 8-foot, 2- to 4-weight.

This is where most visiting anglers make their first mistake. They bring the wrong equipment and tackle for the small streams they'll be fishing in New Mexico. In order to be effective on small streams, you need the right stuff. It's a hard part of my job, explaining to these anglers that the two thousand dollars worth of fine rods and reels they have won't do them much good where we're going to fish. Next, I have to explain that they don't need their four-hundred-dollar chest waders, either. We offer rental equipment at my fly shop for this very reason, but usually the anglers stick with their own stuff the first day. Then we get to a creek and on the first cast the fly is snagged in a tree, so I hand them one of my rods and they end up using it the rest of the day. By lunch they're burning up in their chest waders, wishing they had breathable hip waders like mine.

Small streams here come in two sizes: small and tiny. Rods should range from about a 6½-foot, 2-weight to an 8-foot, 5-weight with light to medium action. You want to be able to feel the rod flex, even when casting just your leader and a couple of feet of line. Also, the lighter action is more forgiving when you try to land large fish in small water. And small fish actually feel like monsters on the end of your line. If you can only bring one rod for the small streams of New Mexico, I'd recommend an 8-foot, 4-weight. It's large enough when you need power for casting in the wind or fighting large trout, yet delicate enough to deliver a short cast without disturbing the water's surface.

I like double-taper floating lines 90 percent of the time. They perform well, deliver the fly delicately, and after a season or two you can turn them around and use the other end. It's like getting two lines in one. If I'm fishing wide-open meadows or slow water where I might need to make longer casts in a stiff wind, then I use a weight-forward line or a WindCutter line by Rio Products to punch through the wind with accuracy.

I use a light disc-drag reel, but I almost never need it to fight the fish on small streams. Stripping line in is imperative if you want complete, precise control of the fish, yet I still see even very experienced anglers using their reel to fight the fish on small streams.

In most cases, leaders should be 6 to 12 inches shorter than the rod you're using. Long leaders are very difficult to cast and handle on the water. I generally use an 8-foot, 4-weight rod with a 7½-foot tapered leader, usually 5X unless I'm streamer fishing, in which case I use 3X. Sometimes I'll add a dropper about 12 inches long so I can fish with a dry fly on top and a nymph below.

One of the nice things about flyfishing small streams and creeks is that it doesn't have to be a big production. You can get by with a lanyard or fishing shirt with big pockets and a couple of spools of tippet (3X and 5X), a fly box with an assortment of flies, and a few tools like clippers and hemostats. Throw in some floatant, indicator yarn, and a spool of ribbon lead, and you're set.

Hatches and Fly Selection

The big question most novice anglers ask is "What fly do I use?" Well, the fish in small streams and creeks will eat the food that's most available to them. Despite popular belief, hatches do occur on small streams, and even tiny creeks. Sometimes prolific hatches of midges, mayflies, caddis, and small stoneflies will come off, especially on streams with flows between 20 and 30 cfs. The tiny creeks have hatches too, but other than midges they aren't generally as prolific. Beaver ponds on any small stream produce a wide variety of aquatic insects.

Of course, terrestrials are present on all streams, but the smaller the stream the more important they become to the trout. These terrestrials tend to inhabit the riparian zone near the water, and smaller waters usually have a greater percentage of brush and grass hanging over the water. Smaller creeks tend to have less aquatic insects, so terrestrials are a significant source of protein, especially during non-hatch periods. And trout are more likely to see a terrestrial as soon as it hits the water, so most get eaten quickly.

In some situations, matching the hatch may be imperative, but any good-floating, medium-sized attractor will usually take trout on the surface. And if they won't come to the top, a small dark beadhead nymph on a dropper will usually do the trick.

My favorite dries include olive Elk Hair Caddis, size 14 to 18; Ginger Duns, size 16 to 20; Parachute Adams and Parachute Blue-Winged Olives, size 14 to 20; Griffith's Gnats, size 16 to 22; Stimulators and Terminators, size 12 to 16; Parachute or Dave's Hoppers, size 10 to 16; and Black and Cinnamon Ants, size 14 to 18. For nymphs, I use regular and beadhead Hare's Ears, Pheasant Tails, Prince Nymphs, Copper Johns, and Golden Stone Nymphs, size 12 to 20; red and green midge larvae and midge pupae, size 16 to 22; and a variety of small Woolly Buggers, size 10 to 14.

Small-Stream Techniques

Certain techniques will ensure you have an enjoyable and successful day of fishing on small streams. In addition to having the right equipment, you must change your approach. Flyfishing these streams involves stalking, spotting, and hunting skills, along with the traditional skills related to casting, presentation, and drift. The most important thing to remember is that less everything is almost always better—less line, less leader, less power, less distance, less effort, less line on the water, and a less powerful hook-set.

Once rigged, approach the water slowly, using anything you can to hide your body, such as brush, trees, and grass. You should always work upstream for the obvious reasons. Fish face upstream in the current so they can keep their equilibrium and keep water flowing through their gills, as well as to look for food drifting downstream. If you were to fish downstream it would be difficult to keep every fish in the stream from seeing you through the crystal-clear water. If you were to wade it would muddy up the water downstream, alerting trout to your presence.

Fishing upstream allows you to creep very close to the prey before casting because trout can see in front, to the side, and up, but not to the back. If you're quiet and move slowly with stealth you can easily get within one or two rod lengths of a trout on most small streams. This makes it easier to cast without hanging up in the brush and to get a good drift.

Sneak up as close as possible and use a "hi-stick" technique when nymph fishing fast pocket water.

On brushy streams that are 20 to 30 feet wide, wading along the edge is the best approach. It provides the best angle for casting and for not being spotted by fish. Wade to just below the riffle, pool, or hole that you intend to target and scan the area for fish rising, flashing or just holding in the clear water. Whether you see any fish or not, plot out in your mind how you're going to fish the pool. Unless you spot a particular trout you want to catch, fish the run methodically and cover the water thoroughly.

Position is everything on small streams. Sometimes one step can make all the difference in whether or not you can hit your target with the fly or get the right drift. Remember, less is better, so the less distance there is between you and the target, the less line you need to put on the water, which affects your drift. It also means that you must set the hook very lightly, with just a twitch, or you could end up in the trees if you miss the strike.

As mentioned earlier, the most common mistake anglers make when fishing small streams is using equipment that is too heavy. Even if they have light stuff, they try to cast way too far. They think that if they don't have 20 or 30 feet of line out, they aren't flyfishing. Nothing could be further from the truth.

A short cast of only 5 feet of line and your leader requires just as much skill as a long cast. Often I'll tell a client to move a couple of steps closer to the target, and they'll reply that they can cast to it from where they are. I explain to them that I know they can make long casts, but that long casts don't catch fish, good drifts do. Everything is much tighter on small streams, so a 30-foot cast could mean that your fly is in one pool while your line is drifting through the pool below, causing all kinds of uncontrollable drag on your fly, not to mention spooking every fish in the pool. And if it's very brushy long casts translate to more time tangled in the bushes, leading to frustration and tension.

Once you're in position with the right equipment, you need to make delicate and accurate casts with as little false casting as possible. False casts spook fish, and there's a greater chance you will end up in the bushes. Most anglers want to cast too hard, which doesn't work, so they keep casting harder and pulling out more line until they're completely out of control.

Keep just a few feet of line out past your rod tip and keep another 2 or 3 feet in your line hand. Keep your arm low with your elbow bent but locked, and use only your wrist when casting, regardless of what you may have learned on larger streams or from other anglers. Keep the casting arc at 90 degrees like usual, snapping only your wrist back and forth. On your final delivery cast, let the remaining 3 or 4 feet of line shoot out through your rod guides before landing on the water. This will allow you to get more distance, while staying out of the bushes.

Once the fly, leader, and line are on the water, immediately transfer the line in your non-rod hand to the front forefinger of your rod hand and begin stripping the line in at the same speed the fly is moving through the current, thus keeping all slack out of the system. Fish methodically from one side of the run to the other, then slowly creep up to the base of the next run and repeat the process. Try to keep your forward and back casts right in the middle of the stream, away from the brush.

Too much brush sometimes makes it impossible to make a back cast so you may have to use a roll, flip, or bow cast for those hard-to-get-to places under overhanging branches. To perform a roll cast, just lift your rod tip to the back-cast position with enough line hanging out to get to the target, and then do a forward cast. The line will roll out in front of the rod tip and straighten. A flip cast is a hybrid of a short roll cast and a bow cast. Just hold the tippet or fly in your non-rod hand and as you come forward let the leader go.

For a bow cast, hold the fly or tippet in your non-rod hand and bring the rod tip up to the forward-cast position in the right angle for getting to the target without hitting nearby branches. The rod should be flexed about 30 or 40 percent at this point, just like a bow. When everything is ready, let go of the fly or leader and the rod will send the fly and leader forward to the target. When fishing very short line in tight quarters, try to keep your casts very short (only 2 or 3 feet of line beyond your rod tip) and all your line and most of your leader off the water during the drift. I call this technique "dabbling," although it's often referred to as "dapping." Either way, less is better.

Many small streams and creeks in New Mexico meander through wide-open meadows where casting more line is feasible, but you still should try to get as close as possible before casting so you can get an optimum drift. Pools can be longer in slower water, so longer casts may be necessary. In such cases, try to make your false casts over the bank (not the water).

Adding a dropper of about 12 to 24 inches to your dry fly, depending on the average depth of the stream, with a regular or beadhead nymph will get you close enough to the bottom for effective nymphing. The dry fly is not only a legitimate offering, but a strike indicator, as well. If a fish takes the nymph the dry fly will go under, indicating a strike. You must keep your indicator fly dry by false casting in between casts and/or applying floatant. I like the powder stuff to keep it floating high. If it sinks you've tied on too heavy a nymph, too small a dry fly, or you're getting too much drag in your drift.

If the water you're fishing is so deep or fast that you aren't getting to the bottom with the dry-dropper, then go with one or two nymphs with some lead just above the top fly. Attach a small amount of visible yarn (not enough to float the nymphs) on the leader and trim it short. It should be about a foot out of the water when the weight is ticking along the bottom and all the slack is out. If you keep hanging up, even with no slack in the system, you probably have on too much lead. Keep adjusting the indicator and the weight until you're ticking the bottom unimpeded with a tight line and with the indicator about a foot or two above the water.

When "hi-stick" nymphing, the indicator is actually a depth indicator more than a strike indicator. If you're ticking along the bottom and hang up on a shallow spot or rock, take notice of where your indicator is in relation to the water's surface. On the next drift through you'll know that you have to strip some line in and/or lift a little higher when you come to the shallow spot. Strikes are detected through a combination of watching the indicator and feeling the line with the forefinger of your rod hand. If a tick becomes a talk, set the hook.

Nymphing a small pool.

A strike is more abrupt than just the normal ticking of the bottom or the slow, dead feeling of a snag. Still, set the hook on everything because if it's the bottom you have to get the fly up anyway. I tell all my clients, "Set everything, there is no bottom!" The most common mistake anglers make when hi-sticking is thinking every bump is the bottom instead of a fish.

Streamers also work well on small streams, especially in pocket water. I use small Woolly Buggers with a bead at the head for weight. Usually, I'll add a little lead about 12 to 18 inches above the fly to get it down quick in the fast, boiling pockets. On small streams, most of the action you put on the streamer is done with the rod itself. Make short casts and let the fly sink, strip the line until the end of the fly line is near the rod tip, and then start rotating and/or jigging the rod tip through the remainder of the riffle, pool-pocket, or hole. This is a great way to cover the water and search for fish when there is no hatch or when fishing a stream for the first time.

No matter what technique you use to hook trout on small streams and creeks, you should avoid using your reel to land the fish. Instead, try to get in the habit of stripping your line in to land the fish. If you have a lot of line out, you may have to reel up some slack so it doesn't pile around your feet. Generally, though, you shouldn't have that much line out anyway if you're following the "less is better" rule.

If you're using the fishing techniques described above you should already have line control during the drift, with the line hanging off the forefinger of your rod hand, while stripping the slack in with your non-rod hand. If you get a strike, don't jerk, just twitch your wrist up. With a short, tight line, that's all it takes to hook a trout.

Once the fish is hooked, apply pressure and hold the line tight against the cork, causing the rod to bend, and strip in as much slack as possible. It's important to note that the traditional "rod tip up" method is not the standard on most small streams and creeks. Rather, "rod bent" is what's important. Of course, raising the rod will bend the rod, which is the whole reason for keeping your rod up. However, on many small streams you have tight quarters, obstacles, undercut banks, and things the fish can wrap around, so precise control is imperative.

You may not be able to raise your rod due to branches overhead. And if the fish is heading under a bank or brushpile you may have to angle your rod to the right or left, while keeping the rod bent, to turn the fish before it wraps you around something and breaks off. The bent rod is the key to landing fish, especially big fish on small water. The expensive rods now available perform well under these conditions. They're like shock absorbers, and when properly used it's hard to break even 6X tippet because most of the weight is absorbed by the flexing rod. The largest brown trout I ever caught was on Culebra Creek with a 2-weight rod and 6X tippet. I never let the 8- or 9-pound brown have more than 5 feet of line, and I kept the rod bent almost double the entire time.

Letting fish run in small water will spell disaster more often than not. If a large fish heads downstream and a bent rod won't turn it, you must move with it, trying to keep it from taking too much line. If there aren't any nearby obstacles and the fish is pulling so hard you think it may break off, it's okay to let some slack slide through your finger. But as soon as you catch up with the fish get the excess line back in. Wear the fish down quickly with a bent rod and short line before landing it.

When the fish is temporarily worn down (not exhausted) and you have only about a rod length of line and leader beyond the rod tip, the trout's head will come slightly out of the water and its belly will be up. When a trout is belly up it loses its equilibrium and will just lie there and cooperate. Gently grip the trout (with your palm) on its back near the dorsal fin and hold it belly up and completely submerged. When the fish is belly up and completely under water it can breathe and won't fight you as much.

Place your rod under your armpit or between your legs to free up your rod hand. Don't squeeze the fish; just support its weight in your palm and remove the barbless hook with a pair of hemostats or your fingers. All the while, the fish should be comfortably breathing under the surface. Once the hook is removed, just turn the fish right side up, support its weight under the belly with one hand, and with the other hold the fish around the base of the tail and wriggle it back and forth until it swims away on its own.

I do not recommend using a net. Even though the jury may still be out on the best way to catch and release trout with minimal harm, I can tell you that in my many years of experience I've seen or tried many techniques for releasing trout on small streams.

What I've found is that, despite popular belief, fighting a fish until it's worn down enough to easily handle in the water does not harm it as much as bringing it in before it's tired and then wrestling with it in a net, out of the water, where it can't breathe.

Also, when a fish is out of the water, whether in a net or not, its weight is not being supported by the buoyancy of the water, which puts extreme, unnatural stress on the fish and its organs.

Standard bag-style nets make it almost impossible to handle the fish and remove the hook under the water, as the net collapses around the fish and its gills. This forces the angler to take the fish out of the water. Another common occurrence is that when using a double-hook rig the second hook gets tangled in the net, making it more difficult to release the fish and taking away from your fishing time.

The bottom line is that what exhausts and kills fish is not the fight on the end of the rod, but the fight after it's caught and out of the water. The longer it's out of the water, the less its chance for survival. Try landing fish in slow, shallow water near the bank without a net using the techniques described above and soon you'll be releasing fish in seconds without ever removing them from the water. Most of the fish you catch in small streams and creeks are too small to use a net on anyway. You'll find that a net just gets in the way on small, brushy streams, as it hangs up in the branches and brush before coming loose and whacking you upside the head or in the middle of the back several times a day. I have a collection of nets that I found in the bushes after they were pulled from the vests of anglers.

If you must use a net, use one that's friendly to fish. Of course, on large streams and lakes or in boats, where you're catching big fish and a net isn't in the way all the time, a good catch-and-release net or a rubber, non-collapsible net is great to have.

Flyfishing small streams and creeks can be very frustrating for some anglers, but they add so many elements to the sport that you won't find on larger rivers. If you treat the frustrations as challenges and use the right gear and techniques to overcome them you will find that they open up a whole new world of opportunities for wild, quality flyfishing without the crowds, not just in New Mexico, but anywhere there are small streams.

Working a run on the Middle Fork of the Gila River. (Jan Haley)

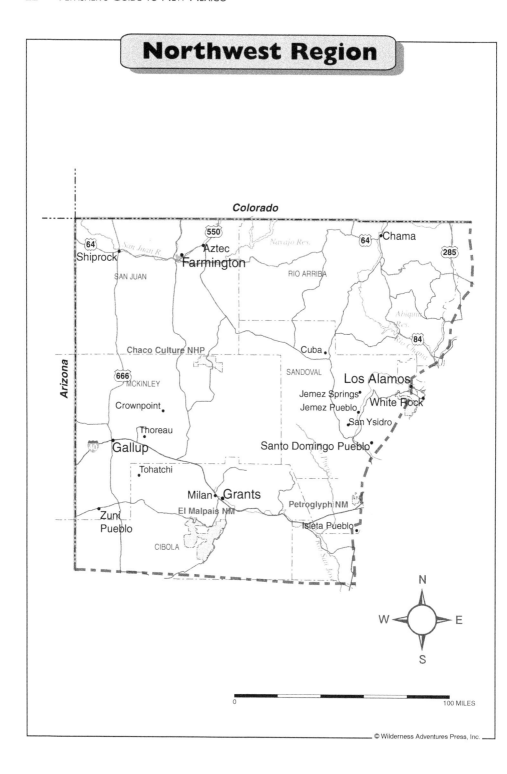

Northwest Region

Colorado

San Juan R.

Navajo Res.

550
64 Shiprock
Aztec
Farmington
64 Chama
285

SAN JUAN

RIO ARRIBA

Abiquiu Res.

84

Chaco Culture NHP

Cuba

84

Arizona

666 MCKINLEY

SANDOVAL

Los Alamos

Jemez Springs
Crownpoint
Jemez Pueblo
White Rock

Thoreau

San Ysidro

40 Gallup

Santo Domingo Pueblo

Tohatchi

Milan Grants

Petroglyph NM

Zuni
Pueblo

El Malpais NM

Isleta Pueblo

CIBOLA

N
W E
S

0   100 MILES

Northwest Region

Northwest New Mexico provides a wide variety of year-round flyfishing opportunities. The San Juan Mountains store millions of acre-feet of water in their high, icy snowfields, which give birth to three of New Mexico's finest rivers: the San Juan, the Rio Chama, and the Rio de Los Pinos.

Farther south, the Jemez Mountains harbor a wealth of small streams loaded with rainbows and wild brown trout. The streams are crystal clear most of the time and run through a combination of beautiful alpine meadows and spectacular canyons and gorges, where magnificent waterfalls plunge into deep, emerald-green pools. Rising trout can be caught in the Jemez region every month of the year.

THE SAN JUAN RIVER AND NAVAJO RESERVOIR

Navajo Lake is located in the hills of northern New Mexico and southern Colorado at an elevation of 6,100 feet. The lake is well known for its abundance of trophy brown and rainbow trout, and sizable large and smallmouth bass, northern pike, and carp aren't uncommon.

Navajo Dam is one of the largest earthen dams in the world, creating a lake 35 miles long. There are many remote coves for camping, as well as campsites provided by the Park Service. The marina has 190 covered slips and 40 in the open. Summertime temperatures reach 85 to 100 degrees, although it can be quite cool at night.

The dam impounds water from three major drainages and regulates the flow of the San Juan River, providing flood control in a region that experiences flash floods on a regular basis. The unplanned result of the dam is the San Juan River tailwater, one of the finest fisheries for trophy rainbow trout in the world.

Three separate recreation sites comprise Navajo Lake State Park. Pine River, the most developed area along the lake, includes a visitor's center with interpretive exhibits and a nicely developed campground. Sims Mesa is across the lake, accessible by NM 527. The San Juan River Area below the dam is where most flyfishers opt to camp, so they can fish the river early and late in the day. The park has numerous facilities, including 246 developed sites, electric and full hook-ups, RV dump station, restrooms with running water, showers, marina, and a playground.

On the San Juan River below the dam there is really just one activity—flyfishing for huge and abundant trout. This is one of the most popular flyfishing destinations in the country, but that wasn't always the case. A couple of years after the river below Navajo Dam first opened to the public, my father read the so-called restrictive regulations, the first of their kind in New Mexico, which stated that angling was restricted to the

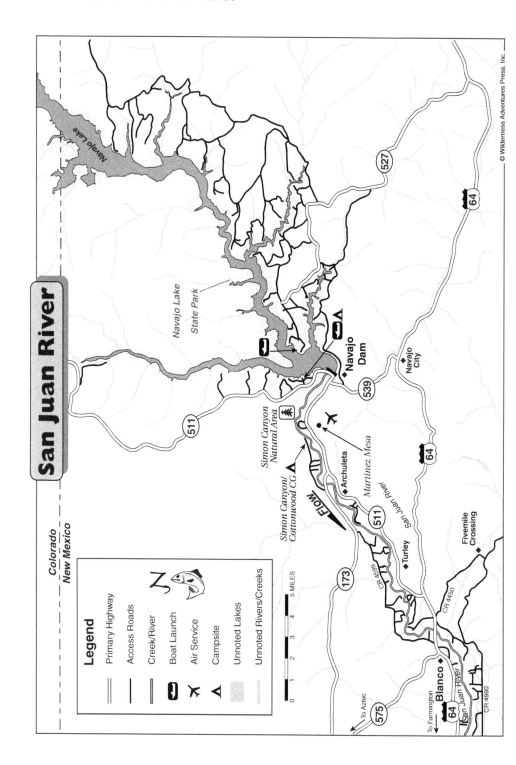

San Juan River

Navajo Lake

Navajo Lake
State Park

Colorado
New Mexico

Navajo
Dam

Navajo
City

Simon Canyon
Natural Area

Simon Canyon/
Cottonwood CG

FLOW

Archuleta

Martinez Mesa

Turley

San Juan River

Fivemile
Crossing

Blanco

San Juan River

To Aztec

To Farmington

527

64

539

511

64

173

511

CR 4599

CR 4450

CR 4990

575

64

Legend

Primary Highway
Access Roads
Creek/River
Boat Launch
Air Service
Campsite
Unnoted Lakes
Unnoted Rivers/Creeks

0 1 2 3 4 5 MILES

use of artificial flies and lures only, with a daily bag limit of four trout over 14 inches. At the time, the regular limit was 16 per day and 32 in possession.

Not realizing the importance of tailwaters at the time, he said, "I don't know why anyone would drive all that way to fish a muddy old river that looks like it could hardly support a trout."

My father paid no attention to this water in the first few years after the dam's completion because the San Juan really was just a muddy old river with mostly catfish, carp, suckers and squawfish, and only a few browns. But the dam had created a new river that looked like a giant, cold, crystal-clear spring creek, flowing at a consistent 42 degrees year-round.

By the time I was 10 years old, in 1968, I noticed the regulations had changed to four fish over 16 inches, then in 1970 it was two over 16. By 1972, I convinced my oldest brother, Bill, to take me to the San Juan to figure out what the deal was. We drove over one Friday night and slept on the riverbank. Back then, you could drive right up to the river.

We woke to find a muddy river just like the one my dad had described, but we were several miles below the dam and it had rained the night before (the lower river usually gets murky after a good rain). We continued upstream to the dam, where we found gin-clear water and big trout everywhere. Before my brother could get rigged, I tied on a size 14 Double Hackle Peacock and raced down to cast to a rising rainbow about 16 inches long. The fly drifted into his lane and he gulped it down.

Five minutes later I landed the silvery rainbow buck, which was so fat that it looked more like a football with fins than a trout. It was the first of over 40 trout up to 22 inches that we caught that day. We broke several off, and kept increasing our tippet strength until we were using 2X. They definitely weren't leader shy, and some of them actually rattled from all the snails in their bellies.

We only saw only one other angler that day, an illegal baitfisherman, but we didn't care because everywhere you looked there were fish. The river was full of great habitat for snails, scuds, and aquatic worms, and there were midges by the billion.

Silty weed beds, especially in the side channels, provided plenty of rich food through the 1970s, as the San Juan gained fame as a great fishery. Modern nymph fishing with snails, scuds, giant San Juan worms, and leeches using lead and strike indicators was pretty much innovated on the San Juan River. The river bred some of the finest nymph fishers anywhere, and the techniques continue to evolve as the fishery changes.

In the early eighties, the dam was in need of repair so they drew the reservoir down by running huge amounts of water through for a couple of years. The scouring flows changed the character of the river dramatically, washing out silt beds and revealing rock and gravel. Many of the snails and scuds disappeared, only to be replaced by an increase in midges and Baetis. At the same time, fishing pressure increased dramatically.

Since the repair, flows have decreased steadily due to water projects, squawfish studies, drought, and other reasons. All this has led to smarter, fussier fish and a lot more angling competition. Gone are the days of 3X tippet and size 14 nymphs. Now it's size 22 to 28 midge patterns and 6X or 7X fluorocarbon tippet.

When I first started guiding anglers here in the early eighties, the river received very little fishing pressure except in a couple of popular areas. Few other guides worked the river, and no one had written any articles or shot any videos yet; drift boats were unheard of. A guide that worked for me, John Tavenner, and I used to fish and guide on the river a lot during the winter. We became "nymph-o-maniacs," so to speak, and John became completely addicted to the San Juan. I eventually lost his services, and he's now the head guide for his own company, Sandstone Anglers.

John has a reputation among his peers as one of the finest and most innovative anglers on the river. He agreed to help me provide the best information on fishing the San Juan River. Here's what he wrote about this special water.

The San Juan is rated as one of the top five rivers in the country, so crowds are common on weekends and during the peak season (May through October).

Fishing the Tailwater

(Contributed by John Tavenner)

The San Juan River is the best known and most popular fly fishing destination in New Mexico. This tailwater fishery has one of the largest fish populations per mile in the lower 48 states. It is also a year-round fishery and offers anglers fantastic fishing opportunities every month of the year.

The water released below the dam remains a bone-chilling 42 degrees or less. The 4 miles below the dam were one of the first Special Trout Waters in the United States, with tackle and bag restriction to preserve the fishery. Now days, this 4-mile stretch is catch and release only with single barbless hooks and a maximum of two hooks. In the Special Trout Waters, there are between 5,000 and 10,000 fish per mile with an average size of 14 to 20 inches. Because of the biomass in the river, an average fish will weigh about 1 to 4 pounds!

In recent years, the river has changed. We experienced a severe drought between 2000 and 2004. The river lost some insect habitat and gained more habitat for different types of insects. The fish have adapted well, although the fish population may not be as great as it once was. The population is still very impressive. There is now a much greater brown trout population than we ever had. The Donaldson rainbows planted here in 2005 and 2007 are reproducing as well. While the river is still enhanced with a new strain called Triploid rainbows, most fish planted here are in the 3- to 5-inch range. This is to insure that they survive whirling disease. The new Triploid rainbows are known for their fast growth rates and to be a hard-fighting fish.

In the last few years, stream improvements have been added to the river. These have taken place below Simon Canyon to the end of the Special Trout Waters. Other stream improvements have been added in the area around Cottonwood Campground and the Village of Navajo Dam. The additions in the Special Trout Waters have helped in many ways. It created excellent spawning areas, fish habitat and kept the river cleaner. The insect hatches are starting to recover from the drought, and the fish are successfully spawning with the new gravel the river had received at that time. And we are receiving better summer flows that have helped the river since 2005 in keeping this area free of sand and silt from Simon Canyon flash flooding.

In 2008, the San Juan River was to receive funding from the State of New Mexico for habitat work and stream improvements. But before the contractors could bid on it, the funding was lost due to budget shortfalls. State Game commissioner Jim McClintic and the game commission were in favor of a special use stamp for fishing the Special Trout waters on the San Juan River. A bill was drafted but was eventually shelved. Several small interest groups intent on giving the river bad publicity and blaming the gas industry and a national organization who's intent was to have the San Juan fund other projects on separate rivers led to this.

Thankfully everything is not as bad as it seems and the San Juan still amazes me. According to NMGF Biologist Mark Wethington, the fish are as fat and healthy as they have ever been since this kind of data has been collected. My catch rates are as good today as any time that I've guided this river Since the 1980s. I've had to change the way that I fish since then, and the flies are smaller, but the fishing is still excellent.

It's a good idea to fish with a guide here, at least on your first trip. A guide can help tie on the incredibly small flies and can also show you the techniques that catch fish. Many seasoned anglers are frustrated and/or skunked on their first visit to this great river, but a good guide can teach a total beginner to hook 20 fish a day. For those do-it-yourselfers, here are a few pointers.

One thing to keep in mind is that the fish are literally located from bank to bank. So start close to any shoreline and fish your way toward the middle. This is true throughout the Special Trout Water. These fish aren't afraid of anglers; in fact, they will actually follow you around, feeding on the larvae, nymphs, and worms that get dislodged from the river bottom as you wade.

To put it mildly, they've been schooled. This activity on the part of the fish can be very frustrating, since it's unlawful to disturb the stream bottom in order to attract trout, which is locally known as the "San Juan Shuffle." Walking in the river is considered disturbing the stream bottom, making it against the law to try to catch the fish directly downstream of where you or someone else is standing. So the idea is not to get into those situations. Stay well back from the spot you are fishing and cast into it. Only move forward after you have worked an area thoroughly.

Here is a small list of patterns that work well. The primary food source is midges, and you will have two different classes of midges: small or very small. For the larger ones, you should have red and orange larva size 18 to 22; pupae are a dark gray, brown or olive in a size 20, or a long-shank size 22. Some flash on or behind the thorax on the pupa works best on both sizes. For the smaller version, you will need olive, cream and orange larva size 20 to 24, and pupa that are gray, dark gray or olive size 22 to 28. The larger midges are more common below Texas Hole, while the smaller are common everywhere. Baetis are also common, although for only a short period during the day. Look for fish in fast water in the afternoons with size 20 to 22 Thread-body Baetis, RS-2, or Foam-wing Baetis.

Small micro-egg patterns in yellow, gold, cream, and pink on size 18 to 22 hooks work well, especially when cuttbows and rainbows are spawning. Fish these flies on 5X to 7X fluorocarbon tippet.

Fighting these large fish can be very difficult on the light tackle required to hook them. Try leaving the heavy rods at home and stick with 8½- to 9-foot, 4- or 5-weight rods. This will help protect the fragile tippets and flies. Use disc-drag reels and don't palm the reel. Set the drag loose but not so loose that it backlashes when line is pulled off the reel aggressively. And let the reel do the work. Once the drag is set, leave it alone; don't try to adjust it in the middle of a fight. Always let the fish run when it wants to. If you try to stop it, you'll lose the fish. Instead, use the rod to steer the fish away from trouble and toward the bank. Keep the rod bent all the time, as this will wear the fish down sooner.

The best technique for fishing the San Juan is a slack-line presentation. This works well for both nymphs and dries. With nymphs, cast quartering mostly upstream and mend your line accordingly. Leave as much slack as is manageable, as the currents, especially those caused by weeds, can cause micro-drag. Hi-stick nymphing can work

John Tavenner shows off a healthy cuttbow. (Monica Tavenner)

in pocket water and around the heads of fast riffles, particularly if the water is off-color, but will often cause micro-drag in slow water.

Rig your nymphs with 12 to 18 inches of 5X or 6X tippet and add a micro shot above the knot. Place your indicator (poly-yarn indicators are used by almost every guide on the river) the same distance from the weight as the depth of water you are fishing. Use polarized glasses to locate fish and then adjust your weight and indicator for each situation. Remember, if you're using the recommended flies and not getting results, the most likely remedy is probably adjusting your rig, presentation, or drift—not changing flies.

Another important tip is to set the hook when your indicator makes even the slightest deviation from a natural float. Strikes often go unnoticed, even by the most experienced nymph fisher, so training your eyes to see fish when they move toward your fly or when they open their mouths will increase your hook-up ratio.

Very late in the evenings and early in the mornings, try streamers such as Woolly Buggers and Rabbit Leeches in size 6 to 12 in white, gray, black, brown, and olive. These also work very well for night fishing, which is legal here. Just remember that when fishing it night it pays to never fish alone and to stick to water you are already familiar with. Scout out where you want to night fish while it's still light. The fish will patrol the banks, so you don't have to get very far into the water. After dark can be a good time to catch some really large fish.

With dry flies, a downstream slack-line presentation is the best choice. Rising fish here are very picky about presentation and have great vision. These fish rise so slowly that an upstream presentation will often be pushed out of the path by the fish's nose. A great technique is to position yourself above a rising fish and then cast quartering downstream, making your fly land upstream of, and a few feet beyond, the fish. Purposely drag the fly back upstream by raising the rod tip. Pull it into the same drift line as the rising fish, then drop the rod tip slowly to the water and let the fly drift naturally to the fish. This way the fish will see the fly before anything else. Good reach casts and curve casts are also valuable for getting the fly to the fish first.

Recommended dry flies would include midge clusters and Griffith Gnats in sizes 12 to 20. The midges can be so numerous that the flies will cluster up along seams and in back eddies. Some clusters can be the size of a quarter at certain times of the year. Very small parachute dries, size 24 or 26 can work when fish are taking singles. When they are eating something small, fish a tandem dry-fly rig with a fly you can see. Baetis dries should include Parachute Adams, size 22 to 24, dark olive Sparkle Duns size 22, any realistic mayfly pattern in a gray to dark gray size 22. During parts of the spring and throughout the summer, terrestrials can work very well along the banks. We have a carpenter ant fall in the summer months and a black ant size 10 to 14 works well. Hoppers in August and September work well along the banks.

Now that we have discussed some of the basics of how to fish the San Juan, let's take a look at the river from top to bottom. The regulations for the Special Trout waters are artificial flies and lures only, single barbless hook. No more than two flies are allowed. The first quarter mile below the dam is known as the Catch-and -Release(C&R) area, as this was originally the only portion of river that was catch and release only (now the entire 4 miles of Special Trout waters are catch and release). The first 200 yards of river have been closed to the public since 9/11. The old C&R area starts below the big island near where the water is released from the dam and continues to the two large poles on each side of the river that used to hold up a large cable. The C&R run is defined by a large flow on the south side of the river. A broad riffle with many channels and drop-offs takes up about three-quarters of the river. There is an island on the north side, with a small channel running down the north bank. The flows converge at the bottom of the island and form a fast chute.

Because of the regulations there are a lot of very large trout here, but midges provide the only insect hatches (the water is too cold for anything else). I use size 20 to 26 midges almost exclusively in this area.

A happy client with a huge rainbow. (Rick Heathe)

You can also take fish on San Juan Worms, egg patterns, and small gray scud patterns.

The run below the poles is called the Cable Hole.

The Cable Hole is composed mostly of a fast, deep channel on the north side, and several side channels on the south side. As the channels converge, they form the run known as the Upper Flats. This is a long, slow pool with several islands on the north side and a deep channel running down the middle. A shallow ledge runs across the river where the channels meet, forming a slight riffle drop-off at the beginning of the Upper Flats.

Most of these two runs are classic midge water, slow moving with a weedy bottom. The midge population here is phenomenal. On some days, the midges will be crawling all over everything, including you. The same flies that work in the catch-and-release area upstream work here. You can also expect good dry-fly fishing, especially on cloudy days.

To access the Catch and Release, Cable Hole, and Upper Flats, take NM 511 toward Navajo Dam. A quarter-mile before reaching the dam you should see the Bureau of Reclamation's headquarters. The parking lot is on the west side of the building, and a trail leads to the river.

Downstream from the Upper Flats, the river branches into a maze of side channels on the south side and a big, deep channel on the north side. The side channels, also known as the Braids, are the most heavily fished section of the river, mainly due to the handy parking in the San Juan Point parking lot (also known as the Texas Hole parking lot). Several runs have names here: the Kitty Hole, Audi's Run, and the Sand Hole, which is also known as the Beaver Run.

The main channel on the north side is often referred to as the Back Bowls. You can usually find more solitude on this side. The Back Bowls have a very heavy flow, with a lot of big rocks and deep drop-offs. Baetis mayflies start to show up here, and they'll continue to hatch downstream. Of course, midges, worms, eggs, and scuds are also effective.

The Back Bowls and the braided channels all meet to form the famous Texas Hole. The run is nearly a half-mile long, with a fast, deep channel at the top, slow and deep at the bottom. The Texas Hole could easily harbor the most fish of any single run on the San Juan, with anywhere from 5,000 to 10,000 fish present.

This is also the launch area for people floating the Special Trout Water. Because most people launch in the morning hours, the Texas Hole has heavy boat traffic at this time. Throw in all the wade fishers and it can be a real zoo. If you want to wade this area, I'd recommend trying the afternoon hours. No permit is required to float this section, but every boat must have life jackets. Shuttles can be arranged at various locations in the village of Navajo Dam. There are several take-outs available, so let the shuttle drivers know where you plan to stop.

Below the Texas Hole the river splits yet again. The channels on the south side of the river offer some good fishing, especially with midges. The main channel forms several large pools known as the Upper Chutes. The bottom of the Upper Chutes is an area known as Steady Rock, with a large flow along some big boulders. Below this, a shallow ledge runs across the river and forms Jack's Hole, which is the start of a section called Three Island Run.

The area from the Upper Flats to Three Island Run can be accessed from the San Juan Point parking area off NM 511. The turnoff is near the Catholic Church on the north side of the road.

Three Island Run routinely produces some of the largest fish on the river. The same flies that work in the Texas Hole will do fine here. Downstream, the river narrows as it passes through an area known as the Hell Hole and then pours into a broad shallow riffle known as the Lower Flats. The south channel enters here and then splits again into another channel at the bottom of the Lower Flats. The two side channels and the Lower Flats form a section that is well suited to the wading flyfisher. The lower side channel is an excellent choice for anglers who want to catch brown trout.

Where the south channel branches off, the main river narrows and forms a long, deep pool known as Lunker Alley. The slow water at the bottom of Lunker Alley is an excellent dry-fly area, while the backwater eddies near the top offer good nymph-fishing opportunities.

A V-shaped run below Lunker Alley signals the start of Baetis Bend. Here, the river makes a left turn followed by a right. The lower south channel reenters at the bottom of Baetis Bend. There are several good riffle-drops in Baetis Bend, with an island at the top and a good ledge in the middle. Mostly flat water, Baetis Bend offers some excellent dry-fly fishing. Fish rise here almost daily, especially to its namesake hatch. Midges, SJ Worms, egg patterns, and scuds all work here.

To access the river from Hell Hole to Baetis Bend, look for a left turn a half-mile past the Simon Point parking area. You'll see a big parking area by a natural gas well.

Below Baetis Bend the river makes a slow, lazy arc to the left through an area known to the guides as Death Row, due in part to the slow flows and strong canyon winds you encounter while floating. This is good streamer and dry-fly water, but anglers do quite well on nymphs too, although the flow barely moves. At the bottom of Death Row you'll find an impressive mushroom-shaped rock formation on river right called E.T. Rock. Below this, there's another flat with a deep channel on the south side of the river known as the Cannon Run. This run has produced a lot of really big fish over the years, and there are a lot of browns here.

At the end of the Cannon Run a ledge traverses the river and forms Simon Canyon Run, where a large wash enters the river on the north side. There are many drop-offs and ledges among the weed beds that thrive in this run. From here downstream, the aquatic insect life becomes more diverse in the summer months. This includes caddis (*brachycentrus*) and Pale Morning Duns, size 16 to 18. These insects can really turn the fish on from June through September, and anglers have a shot at some terrific dry-fly action.

Below Simon Canyon Run is a long dredged run known as the Lower Chute. This spot can also produce some very large fish. My personal best fish on the river came from here, a 26½-inch cuttbow with an amazing 16½-inch girth.

Below this run the river makes a slow bend to the right and forms a run known as Duranglers Corner (named after the fly shop on the hill on river left). It has a very good nymphing riffle at the top and slows down at the bottom of the run, providing excellent dry-fly opportunities.

To access the section from Cannon to Duranglers, look for the Simon Point turnoff on NM 511, near Duranglers Fly Shop and 2½ miles from the village of Navajo Dam.

Below Duranglers Corner another ledge forms the final run of the Special Trout Water—Last Chance. A broad, shallow riffle carries a good population of trout, especially at the head of the run. Baetis is the main hatch from Simon to the end of the Special Trout Water, but midges, SJ Worms, and egg patterns produce well, too. To access this area, look for the parking lot along NM 511, a half-mile before the Duranglers shop. This is also the take-out for anglers floating the Special Trout Water.

Since the San Juan is the finest year-round fishery in the country lets take a look at the fishing on the river month by month.

January: This is the month to escape the crowds, and still see plenty of wildlife and experience some fantastic fishing. The trout in the San Juan spawn during the winter, which means the big fish are very active. The largest fish I've had a client land came during this month. It's one of the best months to catch a 20-plus-inch fish. Hatches are still present, and you can even get some excellent dry-fly fishing. This is winter fishing at its best, but be prepared for any weather conditions. High temperatures 30s to 50s, lows 0 to 20s.

February: Another excellent month to escape the crowds, especially during the week. Fish are still spawning, just not as much. Hatches can still be good enough to have some dry-fly activity. We usually see a warming trend by now, although you should still be prepared for winter fishing. High temps 30s to 60s and lows 10s to 30s.

March: Spring breaks increase the number of fishermen, but still far less than what you will see during the summer and fall. Weekdays are still uncrowded and the fishing is very good. Midge hatches are increasing and so are the Baetis mayflies. Fish are still spawning and big fish are still active. The weather can still be unpredictable, so be prepared. High Temps 40s to 60s and lows 20s to 30s.

April: This is the start of spring here and the insect activity is increasing, which gets the fish feeding better. The spawning is about over, and we will start fishing more of the insects that the San Juan is best known for. We start to see larger midges during April, nicknamed the Big Mac, and the fish will key in on this abundant food. High temps are 40s to 70s and lows 30s to 40s, but you can still have snow.

May: The only issue with May is that this is typically when they will increase flows in the river, producing the spring run-off. For a person planning a guided fishing trip, check with us as we will know when the river will be rising, and other than the day they will be increasing flows, fishing should be very consistent. In high water, we do all of our fishing from the boat because it is the only practical way to access the river. Usually this also means uncrowded fishing since there will be very few wading anglers once the flows get above 1,500 cfs. On a normal year, the river will be at peak flows by Memorial Day weekend (5,000 cfs). High temps 60s to high 80s and lows 40s to 50s.

June: The flows in the river will start to fall in June. This is always dependent on how much snow the mountains got during the winter. On a normal year, the flows in the river will be at or below 1,000 cfs by the middle of the month. Once this happens, we experience the best fishing of the year for the next month. The hatches explode!

Midges, Baetis and even Caddis and PMDs will be present. By mid-month, the lower San Juan River will be starting to rock, and this section offers the best dry-fly fishing of the season. June is also when we have a chance to see our Flying Ant fall. It's an inch-long black Carpenter Ant, and it happens with the first good rain shower of the summer. It's a one- or two-day event, but the fish will still eat them for several months afterwards. This is also the time to fish the hatches on the lower San Juan. High temps are 70s to upper 90s and lows are 50s and 60s.

July: One of the best months of the year to fish. Hatches are peaking, Baetis in the upper river and Caddis and PMDs in the lower river. The lower San Juan has fantastic dry-fly fishing and you can literally fish a size 12 dry fly all day long and have a fantastic time. Toward the end of the month the hatches start to taper off, but the first few weeks are spectacular. Water will be gin clear and you will see active fish swimming in the upper river. High temps are 70s to upper 90s and lows are 50s and 60s.

August: The Baetis hatch is over until the fall, but the midge activity is very good. The Big Macs are abundant and the fish will suspend and feed on the rising pupa with vigor. This is also a good month for fishing terrestrials, such as hoppers and ants. Fishing these large dries close to the banks can produce some fun fishing. People will be heading back to school, so the summer crowds thin out until mid-September. High temps are 70s to upper 90s and lows are 50s and 60s.

September: The insect activity increases as the month goes on and we will usually start to see Baetis by the end of the month. By mid-month, we will see an increase in the number of people, which usually means the start of our fall season, which is our most popular time to fish. Weather starts to cool off and become more fall like. High temps 60s to 80s and lows 40s to 50s.

October: Our most popular month of the year, and just taking one look around you see why. No other month offers the beauty that October does, and by mid-month our fall colors are in full swing. The weather is perfect and the fishing is as good as it gets once again. Baetis are in full swing and dry-fly fishing is excellent once again. Fish are feeding like there is no tomorrow, bulking up for the winter. By the end of the month, we could have snow, so be prepared. Highs are 60s to 70s and lows 20s to 40s.

November: My favorite month to fish. Maybe our best dry-fly month. Hatches are outstanding, clumping midges and baetis produce a lot of risers and the brown and rainbow trout start their spawning during this month. The fish in the San Juan tend to be winter spawners due to the lack of change in our water temperature. They tend to respond to the change in daylight more, and after the first full moon phase this month, they will be hot and heavy into spawning. If you know the spawning areas then you will see lots of activity. The crowds of the fall thin out considerably, especially during the week. Bad weather can happen this month so be prepared. High temps are 40s to 70s and lows 20s to 40s.

December: You could fish all day and not see another fisherman, especially during the week. The hatches are still very good and dry-fly fishing is a very good possibility. And the spawning is in full swing. Winter fishing conditions are the norm, but if you have the correct clothing, you might have a incredible day of fishing. Don't hesitate to fish in December, you won't be disappointed! High's 30s to 40s lows 0 to 20s.

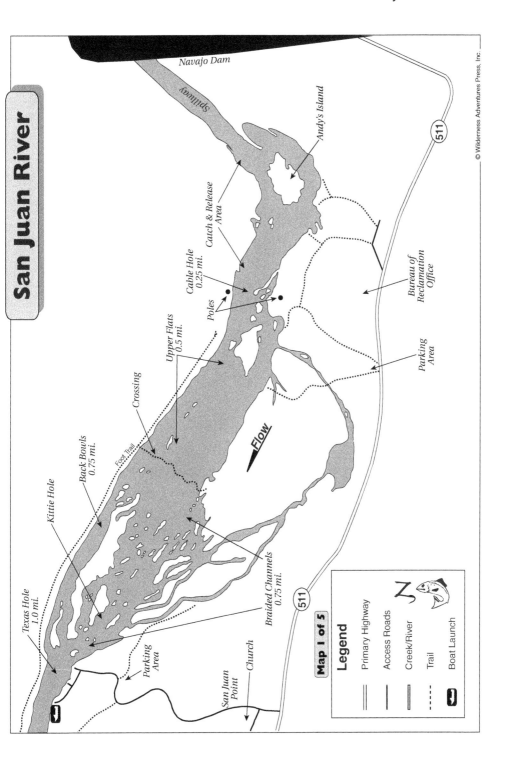

San Juan River

Navajo Dam

Spillway

Andy's Island

Catch & Release Area

Cable Hole
0.25 mi.

Poles

Upper Flats
0.5 mi.

Crossing

Foot Trail

Back Bowls
0.75 mi.

Kittie Hole

Texas Hole
1.0 mi.

Parking Area

San Juan Point

Church

Braided Channels
0.75 mi.

Flow

Bureau of Reclamation Office

Parking Area

511

511

Map 1 of 5

Legend

N

Primary Highway

Access Roads

Creek/River

Trail

Boat Launch

© Wilderness Adventures Press, Inc.

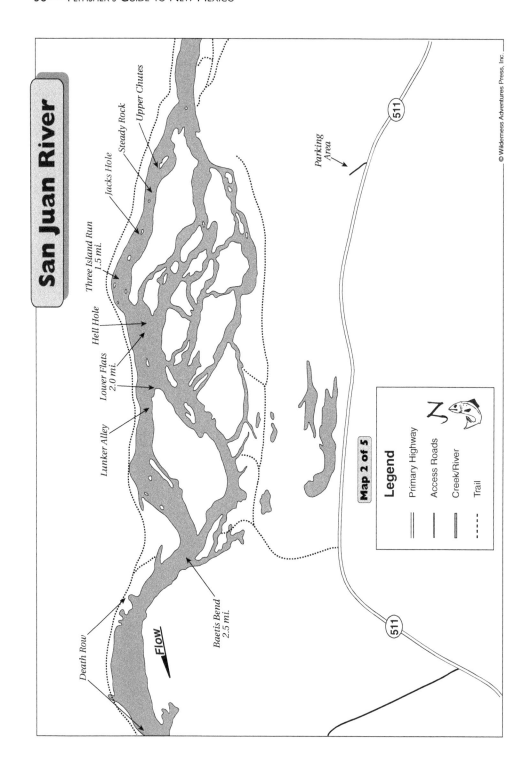

San Juan River

Upper Chutes

Steady Rock

Jacks Hole

Three Island Run
1.5 mi.

Hell Hole

Lower Flats
2.0 mi.

Lunker Alley

Death Row

Flow

Baetis Bend
2.5 mi.

Parking
Area

511

511

Map 2 of 5

Legend

Primary Highway

Access Roads

Creek/River

Trail

© Wilderness Adventures Press, Inc.

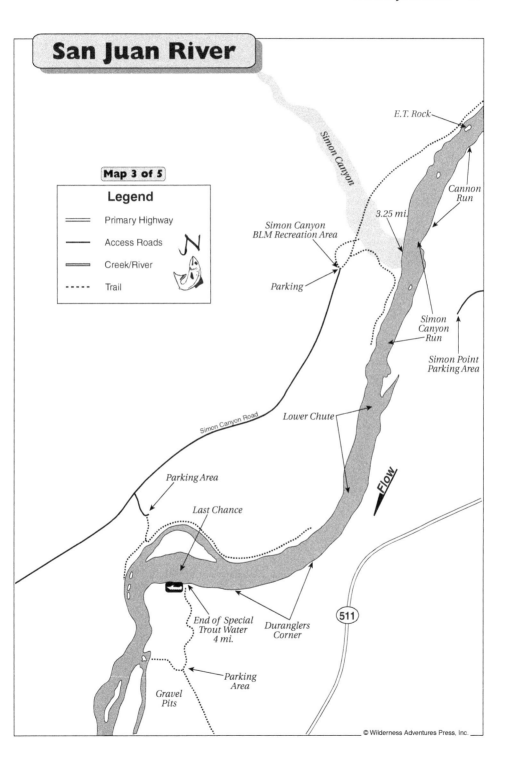

San Juan River

Map 3 of 5

Legend

═══ Primary Highway

─── Access Roads

═══ Creek/River

----- Trail

N

Simon Canyon

E.T. Rock

Cannon Run

3.25 mi.

Simon Canyon
BLM Recreation Area

Parking

Simon
Canyon
Run

Simon Point
Parking Area

Simon Canyon Road

Lower Chute

Flow

Parking Area

Last Chance

End of Special
Trout Water
4 mi.

Duranglers
Corner

511

Parking
Area

Gravel
Pits

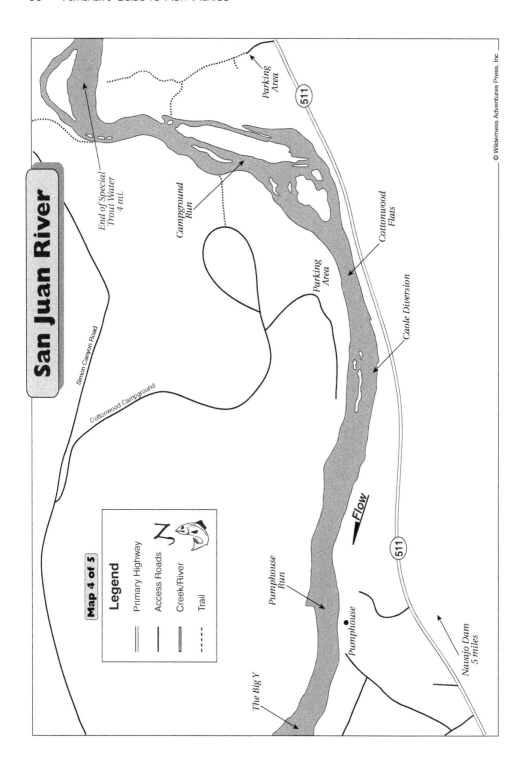

San Juan River

Map 4 of 5

Legend

|||| Primary Highway

—— Access Roads

▬ Creek/River

···· Trail

End of Special Trout Water 4 mi.

Campground Run

Simon Canyon Road

Cottonwood Campground

Parking Area

Cottonwood Flats

Caole Diversion

Parking Area

511

511

Flow

Pumphouse Run

Pumphouse

The Big Y

Navajo Dam 5 miles

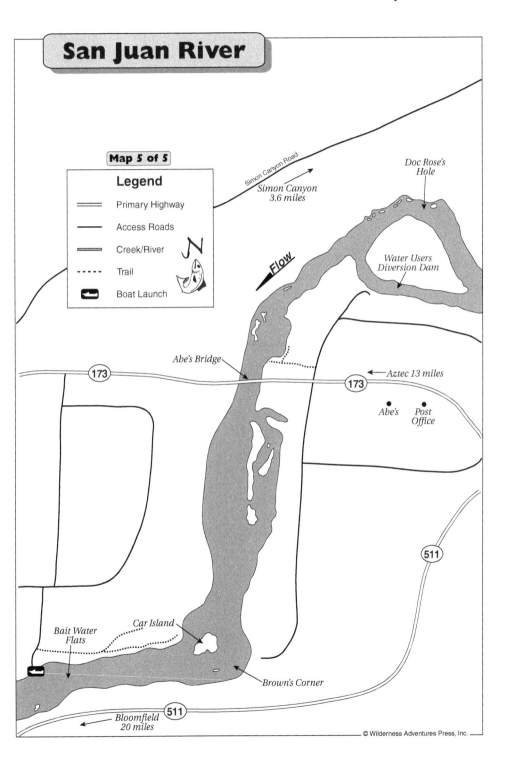

San Juan River

Map 5 of 5

Legend

═══	Primary Highway
──	Access Roads
══	Creek/River
----	Trail
▬	Boat Launch

N

Simon Canyon Road

Simon Canyon
3.6 miles

Doc Rose's
Hole

Flow

Water Users
Diversion Dam

Abe's Bridge

173

173

Aztec 13 miles

Abe's

Post
Office

511

Bait Water
Flats

Car Island

Brown's Corner

Bloomfield
20 miles

511

© Wilderness Adventures Press, Inc.

The Middle San Juan

(Contributed by John Tavenner)

The river doesn't end with the Special Trout Water. There are about 12 more miles in which you can find some quality fishing. The next few miles of river to the village of Navajo Dam is regularly stocked with trout, and you are allowed to keep five fish of any size, with no tackle restrictions. The look of the river remains the same: large pools with riffles and slow, deep areas at the tails of the runs. The average fish is a little smaller, 8 to 14 inches, but their numbers are very good and they fight aggressively. If you want to get away from the crowds, this is a good section to try.

Flies for this section include size 20 egg patterns in pink and chartreuse; SJ Worms; Pheasant Tails, size 16 to 20; Prince Nymphs, size 16 to 18; and Woolly Buggers, size 8 to 10. Don't be surprised if you tie into a decent-sized trout down here, as fish over 25 inches are caught in this section every year.

The Lower San Juan

(Contributed by John Tavenner)

A boat is required to fish the lower San Juan River. The float is 8 miles through an area that is almost entirely on private land. You can launch at the village of Navajo Dam and be nearly alone on the river right away. The water laws of New Mexico are such that you can't touch the stream bottom or banks because landowners own the river bottom. You can't even anchor or get out of the boat to fish. So this is strictly a float section, and with 8 miles of river to cover, it takes nearly all day.

If you prefer wading, Soaring Eagle Lodge is located about 2 miles downstream of the village of Navajo Dam. Soaring Eagle leases 1.5 miles of the river on the Jacques Ranch and offers pay-to-play fishing on this wonderful piece of water. Only six anglers a day are allowed and the fee is currently $75 per rod.

The lower San Juan is quite different in that the fish are all wild; no stocking takes place in this section. More browns are present than rainbows. The fish population is not as strong as in the upper sections, but it's still very good. There is also a diverse insect population, with many types of caddis, mayflies, and even some Golden Stoneflies. These hatches only occur during the months of June and July, but they enable the angler to fish larger flies (size 10 to 16) than in the upper sections. Terrestrials (size 8 to 18) such as hoppers and ants work well in the late-summer months. So do streamer patterns (size 4 to 8), especially sculpin imitations.

The take-out is a little difficult to find, and you'll need a four-wheel drive if you are trailering your boat. Scout out the take-out before you fish, as it's easy to pass by. For first-timers, a guide can be very helpful on this float. Hit this water when the fishing is good, and you'll have a memorable trip.

To find the San Juan from Farmington, take NM 64 east to Blanco. Turn left on NM 511, and it's 8 miles to the village of Navajo Dam and 13 miles to the dam itself. Continue up the dam to reach Navajo Reservoir. From Albuquerque, take I-25 north to the NM 550 exit at Bernalillo. Take NM 550 until Bloomfield, turn right on NM 64 to Blanco, and follow the above directions from there. From Durango, Colorado, take Highway 550 south to Aztec. Turn left on NM 173 and go 18 miles to the village of Navajo Dam. NM 173 dead-ends at NM 511.

Camping is available at Cottonwood Campground, a state park facility on the north side of the river above the village of Navajo Dam, off CR 4280. You can also camp at the Bureau of Land Management recreational area at Simon Canyon on CR 4280. To access these campgrounds, take NM 173 west from Navajo Dam, cross the bridge and follow the signs. There is also a wonderful campground and marina near the dam on Navajo Reservoir. RV hook-ups can be found at the state park campgrounds, as well as at the village of Navajo Dam.

Navajo Reservoir

(Contributed by John Tavenner)

The reservoir behind the dam has many side canyons and river inlets to explore. It has close to 1.8 million acre-feet of water in storage when full, with more than 200 miles of shoreline. The dam was constructed where the Los Pinos and the San Juan Rivers met. The Piedra, another major tributary, joins the lake above there.

John Tavenner reeling in a hefty trout. (Monica Tavenner)

Navajo Reservoir contains a wide variety of fish for anglers to pursue. The warmwater species tend to be the most popular with flyfishers. Starting in late spring, smallmouth bass move into shallow water and supply the best action. The state record of 6.5 pounds was caught here recently, and there's a good population of bass up to 4 pounds. Look for them near rocky structure. A variety of poppers, Clouser Minnows, crayfish patterns, and even Woolly Buggers will take smallies.

Largemouth bass are also found in Navajo. Although not as common, the lake record is a whopping 14 pounds. Look for bucketmouths around trees and other structure. The same bass flies work well for largemouths, but streamers are usually best.

Northern pike are another fun warmwater fish in Navajo, and they can be found on shallow flats in the spring. Due to our southern latitude, these toothy leviathans can grow upwards of 30 pounds, so use a steel leader and fish rabbit-strip flies such as Bunny Leeches and Double Bunnies for the best success. There's also an abundance of crappie around the fallen timber, and small, bright Woolly Buggers can produce some nice fish.

Carp are growing in popularity here. These fish are plentiful and willing to take dry flies. Cicadas, large ants, crickets, and hoppers will take these fish. Look for carp at the mouths of bays and in the brackish water at the ends of canyons. Some anglers roll their eyes when talk turns to catching carp, but after they hook a 7- or 8-pounder on a fly they realize what great sport it really is.

In late fall, at the mouths of the rivers that enter Navajo, you can find big brown trout and kokanee salmon moving up to spawn. Navajo can produce some sizeable browns, with the lake record exceeding 20 pounds. Use large streamers for the browns and red or pink flesh flies for the salmon. Large streamers on sinking lines might someday produce a state-record brown in Navajo.

Stream Facts: San Juan River

Season
- Year-round.

Special Regulations
- The first 250 yards of river are designated catch and release.
- The next 3.5 miles is designated Special Trout Water, with a daily bag limit of one trout over 20 inches. After keeping a trout you must leave the STW.
- Catch-and-release area and STW: Only artificial flies and lures with single barbless hooks may be used.
- Disturbing the stream bottom (San Juan Shuffle) intentionally or unintentionally and fishing the wake or drift line below is illegal.

Trout
- Rainbow, cuttbow, and brown trout averaging 16 to 20 inches, some larger.

River Miles
- Dam and C&R—0 to .25
- Cable Hole—.25
- Upper Flats—.50
- Back Bowls, braided channels—.75
- Texas Hole—1
- Three Island Run—1.5
- Lower Flats—2
- Baetis Bend—2.5
- Simon Canyon—3.25
- End of Special Trout Water—4
- Town of Navajo Dam, start of lower river—7
- Soaring Eagle Lodge—9
- Take-out on lower river—15

River Characteristics
- Riffles, pools, flats, and some pocket water. Numerous side channels away from the main flow, sometimes braided with islands separating them. The river bottom is composed of small to medium-sized bedrock, sandstone, and gravel, with silt and weed beds mainly in the channels. Occasional boulders and logs are scattered about. The riverbanks are covered with willows, grasses, and some cottonwood trees. The water is cold, around 42 degrees year-round. Neoprene waders or breathable waders with plenty of layers underneath are recommended, especially during winter months.

River Flows
- Winter: 250 to 500 cfs
- Spring: 250 to 5,000 cfs
- Summer: 5,000 to 500 cfs
- Fall: 1,000 to 250 cfs

Campgrounds
- Developed campgrounds are available at Navajo Lake State Park, with power, running water, showers.
- Below the dam, camping can be found at Cottonwood Campground on the north side of the river above the village of Navajo Dam, off CR 4280.
- Undeveloped camping at the BLM recreational area at Simon Canyon on CR 4280.

Maps
- *New Mexico Atlas & Gazetteer,* page 14; BLM Area Map: Farmington; USGS Quadrangle Maps: Navajo Dam, Archuleta
- *San Juan River* 11x17 flyfishing map by Wilderness Adventures Press. Includes GPS for all access points, hatch chart and description.

Agencies

- New Mexico State Parks Division, P.O. Box 1147 Santa Fe, NM 87504; 1-888-NMPARKS
- Navajo Lake State Park, Park Manager Doug Bryant, 1448 NM 511 #1, Navajo Dam, NM 87419; 505-632-2278
- The Navajo Lake State Park can provide maps and a list of outfitters permitted to operate on public lands.

Outfitters

- Sandstone Anglers, John and Monica Tavenner, 83 CR 2929, Aztec, NM 87410; 505-334-9789, www.sandstoneanglers.com
- High Desert Angler, 460 Cerrillos Road, Santa Fe, NM 87501; 505-988-7688, 1-888-988-7688, www.highdesertangler.com
- Float-n-Fish Fly Shop (guide service and kick-boat rentals and shuttles) located on the San Juan River
- Duranglers on the San Juan, 1003 Highway 511, Navajo Dam, NM; 505-632-5952
- Chris Guiekema, Resolution Lodge and Guide Service, Navajo Dam, NM; 1-888-328-1858
- Born-n-Raised, Inc., located at Abe's Motel & Fly Shop, Navajo Dam
- Soaring Eagle Lodge and Fly Shop, P.O. Box 6340, #48 CR 4370, Navajo Dam, NM 87419; 1-800-866-2719
- Rick Hooley, Rocky Mountain Anglers, Navajo Dam, NM; 505-632-0445
- San Juan Troutfitters, Farmington, NM; 505-324-8149
- Rizuto's San Juan River Lodge and Fly Shop, 1796 Hwy. 173, Navajo Dam, NM 87419; 1-800-525-1437

JICARILLA LAKES/NAVAJO RIVER

The Jicarilla Lakes are located west of Chama, New Mexico, on the Jicarilla Indian Reservation. The lake sizes and species present vary, but there are rainbows, cuttbows, browns, bluegills, smallmouth bass, and even catfish. The Reservation also has several miles of the Navajo River, which has wild browns and rainbows. (See Private Waters for a map and further details on this unique fishery.)

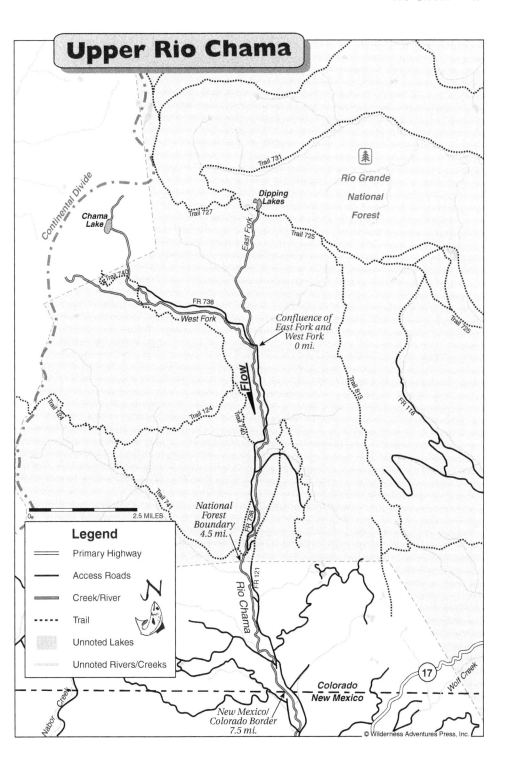

Upper Rio Chama

Continental Divide

Trail 731

Rio Grande

Dipping Lakes

Chama Lake

Trail 727

National

Trail 725

Forest

East Fork

Trail 740

FR 738

West Fork

Confluence of
East Fork and
West Fork
0 mi.

Flow

Trail 124

Trail 124

Trail 740

Trail 813

FR 118

Trail 725

2.5 MILES

Trail 741

National
Forest
Boundary
4.5 mi.

FR 738

FR 121

Rio Chama

Legend

═══	Primary Highway
──	Access Roads
═══	Creek/River
····	Trail
▦	Unnoted Lakes
▤	Unnoted Rivers/Creeks

Nabor Creek

Colorado
New Mexico

17

Wolf Creek

New Mexico/
Colorado Border
7.5 mi.

© Wilderness Adventures Press, Inc.

this is, my theory is that most of the big fish migrate up to the headwaters from the middle Chama Valley, where the river gets very low due to irrigation needs starting in early summer and lasting through September. In the middle valley, there are always plenty of big fish early in the year, but once the river gets low and warm, usually mid- to late June, it's as though they disappear. Meanwhile, at about that same time, the headwaters become fishable after spring runoff.

One major problem with the headwaters is that roads and logging in the area, as well as the nature of the soil itself, have created unstable land within the upper Chama Basin. So when heavy rains occur, the river can remain murky and unfishable for days, especially if the rain triggers mudslides. The best time to fish the headwaters is from just after runoff, usually late June or early July, through mid-October, when the water starts cooling considerably.

When it's clear, the upper Chama is a delight to fish. Terrestrials work well since the fish are very opportunistic this high up. Hatches do occur, especially in the beaver ponds, and you should try to match the hatch if the trout refuse your terrestrial. Dropping a nymph about 18 inches below your dry fly can also produce excellent results. Use at least 4X tippet so you can apply a lot of pressure to prevent large fish from taking you under a bank or log and breaking off.

The terrain of the upper Chama is rugged and access is by foot only from the end of the Forest Service road. I wear breathable hip waders and a good quality wading boot with non-skid rubber soles for traction. I recommend an 8-foot rod for a 4- or 5-weight line in this area.

To get to the headwaters of the Rio Chama from the town of Chama, go north on SR 17 for about 6 miles, turn left on FR 121, and follow it about 6 miles to the Rio Grande National Forest boundary.

Below the Forest Service boundary, the Rio Chama runs through private property for about 8 miles before entering the Edward Sargent State Wildlife Area, where anglers will find about 6 miles of excellent fishing for wild browns and holdover rainbows 12 to 16 inches, with some larger.

The problem with this section is difficult access and the rugged nature of the river and its banks. Although SR 17 parallels the river, there's private land between the road and the water, so all access is at the bottom of the wildlife area. Access to the river is available from the bridge on SR 17 just north of the town of Chama or from the dirt road that takes you into the wildlife area.

From downtown Chama, go north on SR 17, turn west on First Street, and go two blocks, then turn north on Pine Street, which turns to dirt as you enter the wildlife area. Just past the entrance there is a small parking area, and it's about a half-mile hike down to the river. Camping is allowed in designated areas within the wildlife area. A USGS topographic map, BLM edition (Chama quadrangle), is invaluable in finding the roads in the Sargent Wildlife Area.

Once on the river, stay in it or close to it because the canyon sides are steep and the brush and forest are so thick that walking with a rod is difficult at best. This section has plenty of nice riffles, pools, deep holes, overhanging banks, and some channels

Fishing the stonefly hatch on the middle Chama.

around islands.

There are good hatches in this section of the Rio Chama, including large Salmonflies and Golden Stoneflies starting in late June and lasting through early July. I match them with a #10 to #14 Gold Stimulator or Bird's Stonefly. Caddisflies hatch from late May through mid-August, and PMDs hatch throughout the month of July. Hoppers and ants work well during August and September, especially with a nymph dropper. Late September and October produce some good Baetis hatches at times, and streamers work well throughout the fall.

Also within the wildlife area are the Rio Chamita and Nabor Creek. The Rio Chamita is loaded with small cutthroats, browns, and rainbows, and Nabor Creek and the small reservoir that feeds it have native Rio Grande cutthroats. Both streams are small, but fishing can be very productive. Fishing them in conjunction with the Rio Chama can be a good way to spend a day.

Access to the creeks on the Sargent Wildlife Area is good. There are information signs at the entrance, and the road follows the Rio Chamita upstream for 5 or 6 miles to its confluence with Nabor Creek. From the confluence, there are a couple of miles of fishable water on Nabor Creek upstream to the reservoir.

Special regulations apply to all waters within the Sargent Wildlife Area. Only artificial flies and lures with a single barbless hook may be used. On all waters except Nabor Creek, the daily bag and possession limit is two trout any length. On Nabor Creek and reservoir all fishing is catch and release only.

Middle Rio Chama

From the Sargent Wildlife Area boundary downstream for about 25 miles, the Rio Chama runs through a beautiful valley of mostly private property. There is a 4-mile-long NMDGF easement about 2 miles south of the town of Chama, which is heavily stocked and fished by baitfishers. Nevertheless, it can provide some good flyfishing for holdover rainbows and wild browns, some to 18 inches. If you go during the week and are willing to walk a little you can escape the crowds and find some excellent flyfishing at times. The best time to fish the G&F easement is just before runoff (mid-April through early May) and just after (late June through mid-July).

Some of the private areas can be accessed if you politely ask the owners, but for the most part this area is off limits.

Below this 25-mile stretch, the Rio Chama enters the Rio Chama State Wildlife Area.

To get to the RCSWA from Chama, go south about 14 miles on US 64 and then turn right on NM 112 (El Vado Lake Road) just past Los Ojos. Follow it about 6 miles to the entrance of the wildlife area, which is marked by a large sign on the right. The first three dirt roads to the right provide the best access to the river, and primitive camping is available at Cottonwood Flats and other areas up and down the river. Four-wheel drive is recommended because when it rains the *caliche* (clay) roads turn to slime.

There are over 8 miles of river in the RCSWA, and most of it is remote hike-in fishing, providing solitude and a chance to catch some nice wild browns and holdover rainbows that average 12 to 16 inches and some big browns that exceed 20 inches. The middle 4 miles of the river run through an awesome gorge, where deep pockets and holes hold even more large browns. To access the gorge section, turn right off US 64 just before Los Ojos on NM 95 and follow it to Heron Reservoir and the dam. From the dam, follow the marked trail down Willow Creek to the river.

This is wild river flyfishing at its best. During the summer and early fall, I usually fish upstream of the Willow Creek outflow from Heron Reservoir because sporadic water releases for irrigation can make the river murky.

There are solid hatches in the wildlife area, and dry-fly fishing can be very good at times. Nymph fishing is also productive, especially preceding a hatch. Just before runoff in mid-April, nymph fishing the deep pockets, pools, and riffles with caddis larvae and large brown stonefly nymphs can be deadly.

One time in the late seventies, I took a friend of mine to the water above Willow Creek. He was using salmon eggs and worms with his Zebco 33 spinning rod, and I was using an old-fashioned rig my dad showed me when I was a small boy, which consisted of three snelled wet flies attached to a level leader using loop-to-loop connections. I had on a Double Hackle Peacock, a Hare's Ear Nymph, and a wet-style Willow Fly (actually a wet caddis). This was traditional wet-fly fishing, before lead and indicators. You simply cast out and slightly downstream and let the flies drift down through the current, slightly submerged, and then swing up with a tight line, feeling for a strike.

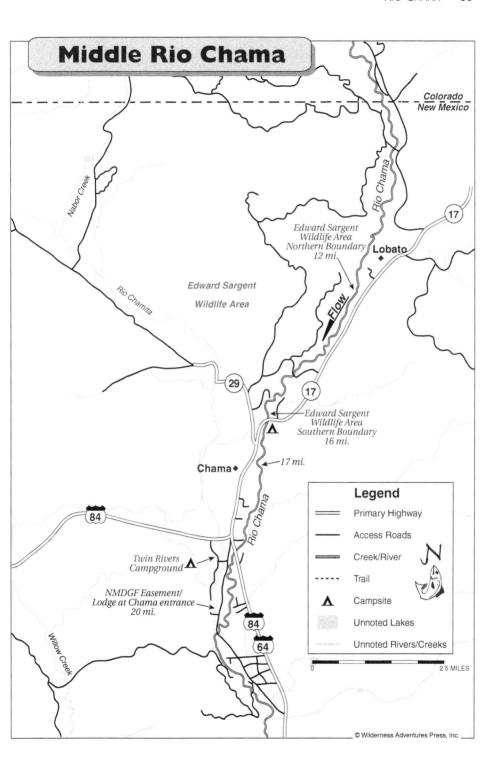

Middle Rio Chama

Colorado
New Mexico

Nabor Creek

Rio Chama

17

Edward Sargent
Wildlife Area
Northern Boundary
12 mi.
Lobato

Rio Chamita

Edward Sargent
Wildlife Area

Flow

29

17

Edward Sargent
Wildlife Area
Southern Boundary
16 mi.

17 mi.

Chama

84

Rio Chama

Legend

══════	Primary Highway
─────	Access Roads
═════	Creek/River
- - - -	Trail
▲	Campsite
▦	Unnoted Lakes
	Unnoted Rivers/Creeks

Twin Rivers ▲
Campground

NMDGF Easement/
Lodge at Chama entrance
20 mi.

Willow Creek

84

64

0   2.5 MILES

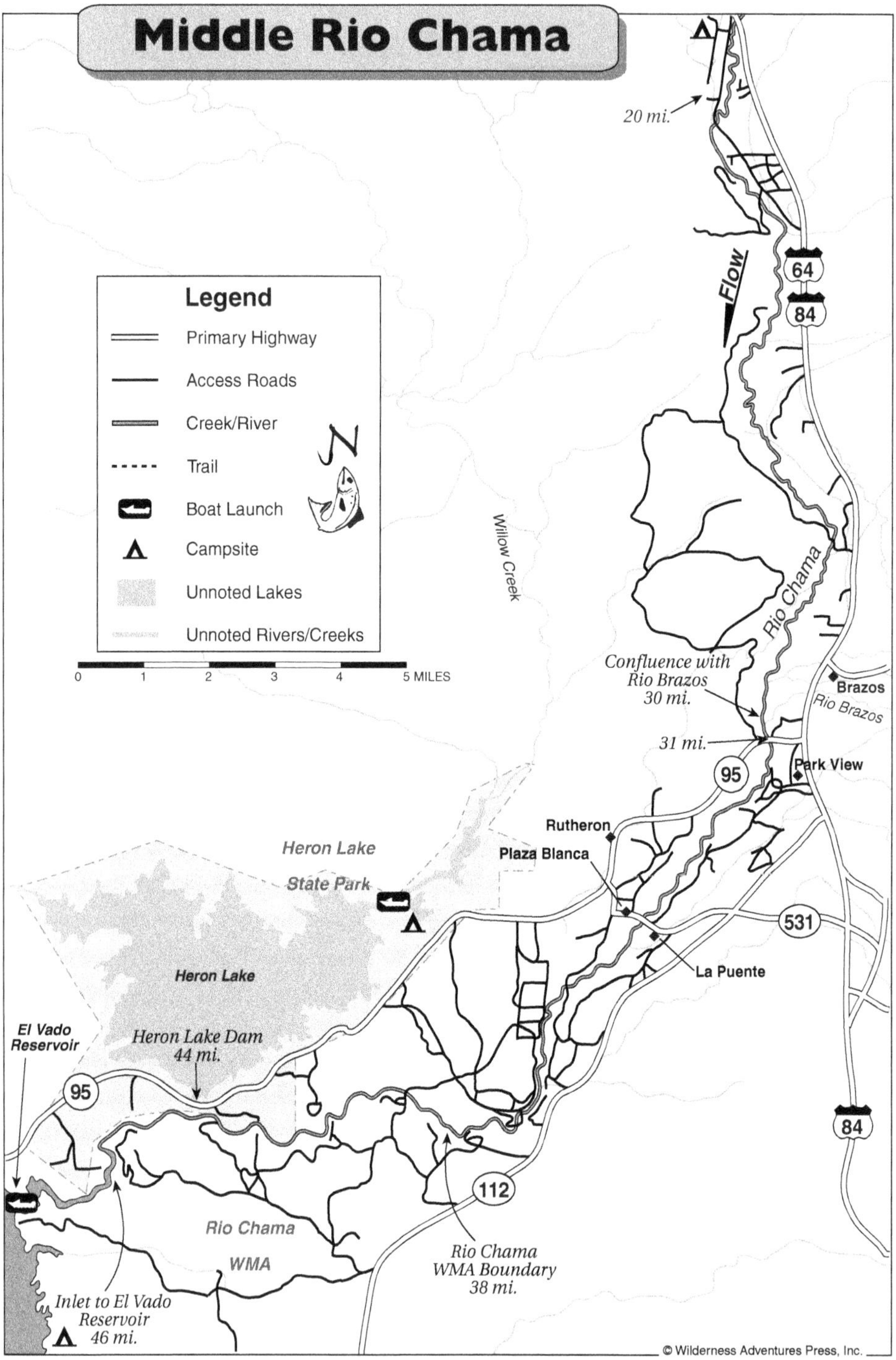
Middle Rio Chama
Legend
Primary Highway
Access Roads
Creek/River
Trail
Boat Launch
Campsite
Unnoted Lakes
Unnoted Rivers/Creeks
0
1
2
3
4
5 MILES
20 mi.
Flow
64
84
Willow Creek
Rio Chama
Confluence with Rio Brazos 30 mi.
Brazos
Rio Brazos
31 mi.
95
Park View
Rutheron
Plaza Blanca
Heron Lake
State Park
531
La Puente
Heron Lake
El Vado Reservoir
Heron Lake Dam 44 mi.
95
84
112
Rio Chama
WMA
Rio Chama WMA Boundary 38 mi.
Inlet to El Vado Reservoir 46 mi.
© Wilderness Adventures Press, Inc.

My buddy watched in dismay as I caught and released over 40 wild browns between 12 and 20 inches, including one double, while he caught one pale stocked rainbow about 10 inches long on a salmon egg. The next day he went down to the local sporting goods store and bought a fly rod, and we went back to the river the next week. I didn't do as well because I was helping him most of the time, but we both caught fish and he became an avid flyfisher, eventually tying his own flies and wrapping his own rods.

The first significant hatches in this area are the caddis and large Golden Stoneflies, which start hatching during runoff and continue through June and into July. I like using large Bird's Golden Stoneflies and Stimulators during the day, unless I'm not getting results, in which case I change to a double-nymph rig with a caddis larva or pupa on top and a large gold or brown stonefly nymph on bottom. I adjust my lead and indicator according to the depth and speed of the current and fish the faster, deeper riffles and holes.

By mid-July PMDs start hatching, but they aren't consistent. I match them using a Wulff-style or Parachute Ginger Dun. The evenings in July can be excellent, with various mayfly hatches and sometimes multiple caddis hatches, as well as spinners, hitting the water until dark. When there's a good hatch and sipping fish, it can take a while to fish some of the large pools. Mornings and evenings are best for dry-fly fishing, while midday is better for nymph fishing. Late evening and after dark, large mouse patterns skittered across the surface can result in some ferocious strikes from large browns and rainbows.

This brown was deceived by a Bird's Golden Stonefly.

A couple of miles below Willow Creek is the inlet area where the Chama enters El Vado Reservoir. The actual inlet varies depending on how high the reservoir is. SR 95 runs right by the inlet area, and a couple of side roads just before the inlet provide access to the river. Float-tubing the inlet, especially after sunset or on cloudy days, can be fun using a variety of flies, but during early summer my favorite choice is a size 14 or 16 Griffith's Gnat with a size 16 red midge larva dropper.

Starting in late September, kokanee salmon begin running up the Chama to spawn. These fish are enjoyable to catch, especially early in the migration before they turn pink. The closer you can get to the inlet, the greater the chance of getting the kokanees while they're still silver and actively eating. I use a double-nymph rig with a small golden egg on the top and a red or pink and white flesh fly on the bottom. Salmon will take the egg occasionally, but mainly they eat the flesh fly out of aggression.

If you find a pod of kokanees anywhere in the RCSWA, look for rainbows staging right below them. The rainbows will shred your egg if they're in there. When fishing over kokanee, the strikes are usually just little pecks, and their deformed mouths are very toothy and bony so it's important to set the hook hard on anything and everything that resembles a strike.

In October, the stream-bred browns begin spawning, and they can be found up and down the river, but the water gets very cold so the best fishing is at midday. I use large streamers most of the time, but sometimes an imitation golden micro-egg will produce better than anything else.

The upper 2.9 miles of the Rio Chama within the RCSWA is managed as a Special Trout Water and special regulations apply. Use only artificial flies and lures with a single barbless hook. The daily bag and possession limit is two trout any length.

Heron Lake and El Vado Reservoir

Heron Lake and El Vado Reservoir are man-made reservoirs within the RCSWA managed by the state parks. There's good access to both lakes via dirt road, and both have boat ramps. Heron has a no-wake regulation, which has made it very popular with anglers, windsurfers, and sailors. Both lakes have developed and primitive camping on their shores.

Heron Dam releases water into the Rio Chama through Willow Creek just upstream from El Vado Reservoir. It covers about 5,500 acres and gets most of its cold water from the San Juan/Chama water project, which involves piping water from the west side of the Continental Divide in Colorado's San Juan watershed (the Navajo River) to the east side of the Continental Divide into New Mexico's Rio Chama watershed via Willow Creek. From there it flows into El Vado Reservoir via the Rio Chama.

Heron Lake has cutthroat, rainbow, brown, and lake trout, but kokanee salmon are the most abundant fish. For the flyfisher, spring and fall are the best times to fish for trout because the lake stratifies in the summer, making it difficult for the trout and salmon to survive in shallow water. There are dozens of coves on Heron Lake, all of which have cruising trout during spring and fall. Fishing from shore is possible, but float-tubing is the best way to fish the coves.

Trout can often be seen rising during spring and fall midge hatches, and thrashing rises occur during evening caddis hatches in late May and early June. In the fall, try stripping large streamers for cruising or spawning lake trout.

El Vado Lake is a wake lake, and consequently has water skiers and boaters everywhere during the summer months. Like Heron, spring and fall are best except at the inlet, which has the most consistent flyfishing on the lake.

There's good access to most of El Vado, and a state park is located on the northeast shore. There's a full-service campground, which has plenty of campsites with bathrooms and outhouses, water, a boat ramp, marina, and gravel airstrip. To get to the state park, take SR 112 west from Tierra Amarilla and go about 12 miles to the gravel road marked by a sign to El Vado Lake State Park. The road leads to the middle of the state park on the east shore. Continuing on SR 112 will take you to the dam, where you can access the lake from either side via gravel roads. There is a motel, restaurant, and convenience store near the east side of the dam and some cabins at El Vado Ranch on the Rio Chama just below the dam. There's also a nice RV park and convenience store called El Vado Lake RV Resort a couple of miles below the dam.

The upper Chama is quite small.

Stream Facts: Upper and Middle Chama River/Heron and El Vado Reservoirs

Season
- Year-round.
- Upper Chama: Late June through mid-October.
- Middle Chama: Year-round but best just before and after runoff.
- Heron and El Vado Reservoirs: Year-round but too cold and icy December through March.

Special Regulations
- Sargent Wildlife Area: All waters within the area are artificial flies and lures only with a single barbless hook. On all waters within the area (except Nabor Creek and Nabor Lake) including Rio Chama, Rio Chamita, and Sexton Creek the daily bag and possession limit is two trout any length. Catch and release only is allowed on Nabor Creek and Nabor Lake.
- Rio Chama Wildlife Area: From the northern boundary of the Rio Chama Wildlife Area downstream 2.9 miles as posted, artificial flies and lures with a single barbless hook only may be used. The daily bag and possession limit is two trout any length.

Trout
- Upper Chama: Wild browns and some rainbows 12 to 16 inches, some larger and small brookies in the forks.
- Middle Chama: Wild browns and holdover rainbows 14 to 18 inches, some larger.
- El Vado and Heron: Rainbows, kokanee salmon; a few browns and lake trout in Heron.

River Miles
- Confluence of East Fork and West Fork—0
- Rio Grande National Forest boundary—4.5
- New Mexico/Colorado border—7.5
- Edward Sargent Wildife Area northern boundary—12
- Edward Sargent Wildife Area southern boundary—16
- Village of Chama—17
- NMDGF easement/Lodge at Chama entrance—20
- Confluence with Rio de Los Brazos—30
- NM 95 to Heron Lake State Park—31
- Rio Chama Wildlife Area boundary—38
- Heron Lake dam—44
- Inlet to El Vado Reservoir—46 to 47

River Characteristics
- Upper Chama: Small freestone creek gathering volume at the forks. Meandering stream through a combination of willows, brush, and meadows with many deep holes, pools, and undercut banks.
- Middle Chama: Medium-sized freestone river running through a valley with cottonwoods, willows, and alders. Numerous nice riffles, pools, holes, channels around islands. Wildlife area is in a flat-bottom canyon and has more pocket water.

River Flows
- Winter, summer, and fall: 40 to 100 cfs
- Spring runoff: 60 to 1,000 cfs

Campgrounds
- Primitive campground at the end of FR 121 at the Rio Grande National Forest boundary.
- Developed campgrounds with toilets and water at Heron Lake State Park and El Vado Lake State Park.
- Primitive camping available at the Rio Chama Wildlife Area.

Maps
- *New Mexico Atlas & Gazetteer,* page 15; U.S. National Forest Rio Grande National Forest; BLM Taos Resource Area Map (Chama); USGS Quadrangle Maps: Earchulera Creek, Chama Peak, Chama NM, Brazos, Tierra Amarilla, Heron Reservoir

Agencies
- BLM Taos Resource Area, 224 Cruz Alta Road, Taos, NM 87571
- USFS, Rio Grande N.F., Supervisor's Office, 1803 West Hwy 160 Monte Vista, CO 81144; 719-852-5941
- NMDGF, P.O. Box 25112, Santa Fe, NM 87504; 505-476-8000

Outfitters
- The Solitary Angler, 204B North Pueblo Road, Taos, NM 87529; 1-866-502-1700, www.thesolitaryangler.com
- Ed Adams Flyfishing, P.O. Box 428, Questa, NM 87556; 575-586-1512
- Taylor Streit Fly Fishing Service, P.O. Box 2759, Taos, NM 87571; 575-751-1312

UPPER AND MIDDLE RIO CHAMA MAJOR HATCHES

Insect	J	F	M	A	M	J	J	A	S	O	N	D	Time	Flies
Midges													M/A/E	Red & olive midge larva #16–#20; olive, gray, black and zebra midge pupa #18–#24; Disco Midge #18–#24; Mating Midge #14–#20; black & gray Midge Clusters #10–#16; Griffith's Gnat #16–#22; Snowfly #16–#26
Caddis													Larva-M Pupa-M/A/E Adult-A/E	Green & olive caddis larva #12–#16; Double Hackle Peacock #12–#16; La Fontaine's Caddis Pupa #12–#18; Van's Rag Pupa #10–#18; olive, tan & gray Elk Hair Caddis #12–#20; olive, gray & peacock Fluttering Caddis #10–#18
Baetis													M/A	Dark olive Hare's Ear #16–#22; Pheasant Tail #16–#22; Van's Rag Fly dark olive #16–#22; Lawson's BWO Fan-Wing Emerger #16–#22; Olive Parachute #16–#22; Olive Comparadun #16–#22
Salmonfly, Golden Stonefly													M/A	Black & brown stonefly #6–#10; Salmonfly #6–#12; Orange Stimulator #6–#10
PMDs, PEDs													M/SF	Light Hare's Ear #12–#18; Pheasant Tail #12–#20; Van's Rag Fly light olive #14–#20; Lawson's Fan-Wing Emerger #14–#22; PMD, PED #12–#20; Ginger Dun #14–#20; parachute ginger, light olive #14–#20

Hatch Time Code: M = Morning; A = Afternoon; E = Evening; D = Dark; SF = Spinner Fall

The Lodge at Chama (Chama Land and Cattle Company)

The Lodge at Chama is a deluxe sprawling private ranch located adjacent to the village of Chama. There are over 13 lakes and miles of crystal-clear streams to fish, all teeming with trout. The accommodations are remarkable and service is impeccable. (See page 374 in Private Waters for details on this magnificent ranch.)

Rio de Los Brazos

The Rio de Los Brazos is a major tributary of the Chama River, and it offers some of the best stream fishing in New Mexico, especially for large brook trout, although there are plenty of nice browns and rainbows, as well. It boasts excellent dry-fly fishing from its headwaters down through the Brazos Meadows and finally into the Brazos Box. Except for a short stretch of NMDGF access below the box canyon, virtually the entire watershed is private. But there are several commercial operations on this splendid freestone stream. (See page 380 in Private Waters for further details on this river.)

THE RIO CHAMA BELOW EL VADO RESERVOIR

The Rio Chama below El Vado Reservoir is a large—for New Mexico—tailwater river with excellent flyfishing opportunities for hefty wild browns and some holdover rainbows. As a boy, I fished this fabulous river with my father on many occasions. We used to stay in an old cabin on El Vado that a friend of his owned. We rarely fished the reservoir; instead, my father could hardly wait to get on the Chama below the dam. It was his favorite place to flyfish for big browns. The water was cold, clear, and rich, and at that time, no one else seemed to realize what a great fishery it had become since the dam was built.

I was only seven years old the first time I fished there. My dad rigged me with a wet fly of some kind and said, "Throw it out there and let it swing through the current, then pick it up and do it again." He moved up toward the dam, while I cast and retrieved with the 9-foot bamboo rod he was letting me use.

No sooner was he positioned and casting than I hooked a giant fish that leapt twice. I yelled and he came running back to help. He saw it and said I had a damn carp on, so I started hauling it in rapidly until it jumped again and he said "It's not a carp, it's a brown, quit horsing him!" I got excited and carefully played the fish to the edge. My dad estimated him at over 5 pounds, by far the biggest fish I'd ever seen. He was finally coming in, and I had him right up to the bank when he suddenly flopped back into the water, fleeing as my father grabbed at him. I thought I was going to die when he got away.

I caught many more browns below El Vado over the next 12 years before moving to Wyoming. After returning and starting my guide service, I came back to the great river in 1986 to do a fishability study for the BLM. The dam was being repaired and new gates were installed that were designed to flush silt from the bottom of El Vado.

Since then, the river seems to rarely run clear except during late fall, winter, and early spring. Nevertheless, it remains the best fishery in the state for large browns.

In recent years, an angling buddy who guides for me from time to time has been lunker hunting on the Chama below El Vado. Mark Cowan is the most tenacious flyfisher I've ever known, with extraordinary skill in finding fish where few others can. If Mark isn't working, chasing fish in Alaska, or running his bonefish operation in Xcalac, Quintana Roo, Mexico he's likely fishing on the Chama below El Vado. With the changes that have taken place since the dam was rebuilt, I asked Mark to contribute some of his knowledge about the fishery.

Fishing Below El Vado

(Contributed by Mark Cowan)

After a one-hour hike that involved several precarious river crossings, my clients John and Gene were happy to finally begin casting. Sweaty and still huffing, they quickly tossed streamers into the water. Gene immediately landed a 19-inch brown in its Halloween colors, but on this river that wasn't something to get overly excited about. The large swirl we spotted in the tailout above us was more like what we'd come to find.

Gene's third cast in the area of the boil produced a violent strike that led to a five-second hook-up. The fish was big—really big—and it had escaped with a serious head shake. Just above the tailout was a deeper run with large boulders and a single snag on river left. I had hooked and lost a big fish in this run the previous spring and suggested that John do a little exploring with his size 4 Woolly Bugger. John already had experience with this fishery and knew how to cover the very murky water.

After five or six casts, his call of "I got one, boys!" rang through the canyon. The fish held deep—no spectacular runs or big leaps. By the way his 6-weight was leaning into the 3X leader, I could tell the fish was large, but it wasn't acting like the other large browns we'd landed. After ten minutes or so with little progress, it was obvious he was tied to a nice fish, but poor water clarity prevented us from seeing more than a foot below the surface.

When he was able to bring the fish to within about 15 feet, I took the large Brodin net off John's clip and prepared to do my guide thing. The fish finally came up out of the depths, only showing us its tail. It resembled a small shovel, and I quickly realized that the net wouldn't help us much. Five minutes later John worked the fish into the shallows and I tailed it, much like you would a salmon. The big brown measured 26 inches, and with its healthy girth probably weighed 8 pounds or more, the largest trout John had caught in moving water. The day continued with a number of "smaller" fish landed, and all would have been huge in any other stream system.

This section of the Chama River is just below El Vado Dam, a man-made reservoir created to store irrigation water for farmers along the Rio Grande near Albuquerque, and for the city's domestic use. The upper Rio Chama, Tierra Amarilla Creek, and the San Juan Chama diversion project, which transfers water from the Colorado River via aqueduct for irrigation purposes, all help fill El Vado.

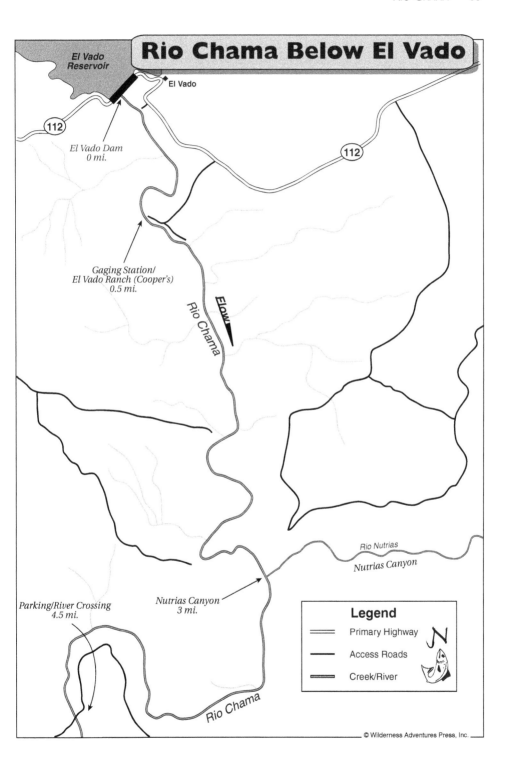

Rio Chama Below El Vado

El Vado Reservoir

El Vado

112

El Vado Dam
0 mi.

Gaging Station/
El Vado Ranch (Cooper's)
0.5 mi.

112

Rio Chama

Flow

Rio Nutrias

Nutrias Canyon

Parking/River Crossing
4.5 mi.

Nutrias Canyon
3 mi.

Rio Chama

Legend

═══	Primary Highway
──	Access Roads
▭▭▭	Creek/River

N

The Chama below the dam is not a classic tailwater, as irrigation and domestic demands cause wild fluctuations in water flows. These can range from 200 to 1,000 cfs in a single day. The result is almost constant murkiness. As I'm writing this description, the flow is 197 cfs, and the historic range for the same day is a low of 7.6 cfs and a high of 731 cfs. The average is 166, a good fishable flow. Due to low reservoir levels and siltation in El Vado, the river has almost always been off-color over the last three years.

Part of the problem is that the latest modification of the dam involved designing the outflow gates so they flush silt—which builds up rather quickly—from the bottom of the reservoir. But if you are lucky enough to find it marginally clear in the spring or fall, and at flows of 200 cfs or less, you can have the most memorable trout fishing experience of your life.

On one fine April day with the water at 200 cfs and an acceptable greenish color, I landed six fish from 22 to 25 inches. Two of these were large rainbows, which is unusual. The 20 or so browns I caught that day from 14 to 19 inches were almost a nuisance as I made cast after cast with my Soft-Hackle Streamer, looking for the real trophy. The 20 pound, 4 ounce New Mexico state record came from this section of river.

This is wild brown trout country, and these fish are at the top of the food chain. Several times a year the NMDGF stocks the river upstream with good numbers of catchable-sized rainbows. I think that some of the larger browns anticipate this offering and feast on stockers up to around 10 inches.

David Ballard fishes an evening hatch on the Rio Chama below El Vado Reservoir at El Vado Ranch (formerly Cooper's).

The river has no regulations other than the standard bag limits imposed on most New Mexico trout streams. Locals fish here with everything from Rapalas to big nightcrawlers.

This stretch of the Rio Chama can be divided into three basic sections. What I call Section One runs from the gaging station just below the dam to about ⅓ mile below El Vado Ranch. This fishery is essentially put and take, with bait the name of the game for most anglers. In spite of fairly easy access, though, the area doesn't see a lot of use, and a flyfisher can do well if rainbows up to 16 inches or so are the quarry.

Section Two extends roughly another mile downriver, basically from just below El Vado Ranch to just above the Rio Nutrias Canyon confluence. Browns outnumber the stocked rainbows here, but the lack of catch-and-release angling is evident in the numbers of fish caught. Regardless, in a typical day, an experienced flyfisher can land quite a few fish, some of which will be over 20 inches.

Section Three extends from just above the Nutrias Canyon confluence downriver about another mile. This is the most difficult section of river to reach, so it holds the greatest number of large browns.

The Chama is Woolly Bugger country, and a flyfisher would do just fine by bringing only black Woolly Buggers, size 4 and 6 and tied with lots of hackle. Most of us are too insecure to go to a river with only one pattern in two sizes, so Soft-Hackle Streamers in black, black/olive, brown, and brown/cream round out the streamer selection. A Double Bunny Leech will also work well on the largest browns.

Other important flies include small leeches (size 8 and 10) in brown, gray, and black, and Beadhead Pheasant Tail Nymphs in size 16 and 18. In the fall, you may see a significant number of fish up to 16 inches rising in the tailouts. These fish are usually feeding on Baetis emergers and adults. Your favorite Baetis imitations in size 18 and 20 will work here. In the early fall, and on the rare occasion when the water is very low and somewhat clear, grasshoppers slapped along the bank can produce some big fish.

Even in murky water, if you walk slowly along the bank you'll sometimes see noses poking up in the foam lines and along obvious seams along the cutbanks. A small, dark parachute with a beadhead dropper will often take these fish. In the spring, egg patterns work well for the rainbows, and in late fall, the same flies will work on browns and rainbows.

To reach the fishery, drive about 14 miles southwest on SR 112 after exiting US 84 as it leaves Tierra Amarilla, heading north to Chama. This will put you at El Vado Ranch, which offers modest cabins and day parking at $3.00 per vehicle. Your best shot at the river's trophy fish is to hike downriver from here for a mile or two. You'll be hiking within the BLM-managed Chama Wild and Scenic River easement. You will certainly stumble over rocks as you gaze at the awe-inspiring beauty of the canyon. You enter BLM land about 3 miles downstream, still within the incredible canyon. Your explorations will only be limited by your fitness level.

Other access is difficult at best, so most anglers opt for the above. But here is a brief description of other choices for those of you who own beefy four-wheel drives and good topographic maps.

From US 84, travel 10.3 miles southwest on SR 112. On the left you will see an unlocked steel gate. Turning left through the gate puts you on private land, but the road itself is a public access route. Stay on the main road. You will drive across (through) the Rio Nutrias, and after a total distance of about 6 miles you come to an old ranch house, where you literally drive through the front yard. Immediately after the ranch house you'll cross a cattle guard and turn right.

Now you are on a rough BLM road that will eventually carry you to the river's edge near Puerto Chiquito, an arroyo just upstream. Again, stay on the main track, as the surrounding land is private. The fishing from here upriver is good, and during a long day you should be able to fish to the Rio Nutrias Canyon confluence and back. I must warn you, though, that this vehicle access route is difficult in good weather, and can be impossible in wet or snowy weather. It's also easy to get trapped if rainstorms bring the Rio Nutrias to flood stage. Pay attention to the weather and get back to pavement quickly if things deteriorate.

In the lower part of Section Three, there is a series of hot springs, which are nice for a soak if you have time. These same springs warm the water and make for some good early-spring fishing just downriver.

The river is rocky here, and because you often cannot see the bottom, wading can be treacherous. Large boulders scattered throughout the stream offer good holding areas for the wild browns, and the river has excellent terrain variation, with good tailouts, riffles, pocket water, and deep seams.

The most popular method in the area is classic streamer fishing, with a cast slightly upstream and an immediate mend upstream, which allows the fly to get down quickly. Retrieve in a series of 6-inch strips. It's critical to get your fly down fast. I believe the fish strike from lateral-line detection as much or more than from sight, so your fly must push a lot of water and be near the fish. Often, adding an erratic wiggle/twitch as you lift the fly will trigger the strike. Expect to lose a fair number of flies to the many rocks, and know that the fish will use the rocks to their advantage when hooked.

This is not a river where you need to concentrate on hatches, but count on caddis in the spring and several types of mayflies in early fall. Midges are present year-round. In the fall, pumped-throat samples from the fish almost always reveal tiny Baetis nymphs (size 20 to 22). Also, when you touch the bellies of these fat fish, you'll often feel a fairly large baitfish and/or crayfish. Undoubtedly, crayfish make up a large part of the brown trout's diet here.

Standard nymphing with a floating indicator is also an effective way to fish the river, especially in the better-defined riffles. A large upper fly with a small Pheasant Tail or similar beadhead below is the ticket. When nymphing, you must "farm" the water, methodically working rows a foot or so wide until you've covered all the water. With the low visibility, this is the only way you'll locate the trophy you are seeking without turning to streamers.

A word on the current drought: As of late 2003, this river system is in its third year of a significant drought. River flows are micro-managed by the Bureau of Reclamation, which tries to keep the endangered silvery minnow alive downstream while supplying the city of Albuquerque with sufficient domestic water. The low reservoir level causes more water to be released from the bottom of the dam, which creates the almost constantly murky conditions. This situation is not likely to change until the drought subsides and the reservoir is able to store more water.

Amazingly, in 2003, the Bureau of Reclamation considered cutting off the flow of the river entirely, and in response the NMDGF encouraged fishermen to keep all fish caught. Fortunately, the order was rescinded and the fishing "free for all" never really happened.

Below Section Three, the Rio Chama isn't much of a trout fishery as it continues through the Wild and Scenic canyon for another 25 miles before reaching Abiquiu Reservoir. There are plenty of browns (including a few real big ones), but the water is usually much murkier due to numerous arroyos that dump tons of silt and clay into the river. If you have a good boat, fishing the inlet to Abiquiu can be spectacular at times, especially when the browns are running in the fall. Below Abiquiu is another excellent tailwater section of the Rio Chama.

Stream Facts: The Rio Chama Below El Vado Reservoir

Season
- Year-round, but March/April and October/November are the best months due to lower water flows and better clarity. Average flows in the summer months may go over 800 cfs, and several commercial rafting companies use the river at this time. Fishing at these flows is difficult at best.

Special Regulations
- No tackle restrictions; regular New Mexico fishing regulations apply.

Trout
- Wild browns and stocked rainbows.

River Miles
- El Vado Dam—0
- Gaging station/El Vado Ranch (Cooper's)—0.5
- Nutrias Canyon—3
- Parking/river crossing—4.5

John Griffith with a huge brown caught about 4 miles below El Vado Dam. The Chama has the largest browns in the state, including some over 20 pounds. (Mark Cowan)

River Characteristics
• A medium to large tailwater with freestone characteristics and wildly fluctuating water flows. The water is often off-color and is best fished at flows at or below 200 cfs. Terrain is excellent, with good riffles, tailouts, pocket water, cutbanks, and deep seams. This entire section of river is within the beautiful Chama Wild Rivers Area and associated canyon.

River Flows
• Spring and fall: generally 200 cfs or less
• Summer: from 300 to 1,200 cfs, with the largest flows mid-week
• Contact the Bureau of Reclamation for daily stream flow conditions (505-462-3586)

Campgrounds
• Nearby camping is very limited. The nearest developed campgrounds and RV parks are located in Chama, about 20 miles away. There is primitive camping within the Rio Chama State Wildlife Area that adjoins the west side of El Vado Reservoir. For more information, call El Vado Lake State Park at 575-588-724.

Cabins and Motels
• El Vado Ranch (575-588-7354) is the nearest lodging opportunity, located on the river just below the dam. There are 10 modest cabins fully furnished with kitchens. The base rate is $78 per night. A small grocery store is onsite, and fishing licenses are sold here.

Maps
• *New Mexico Atlas & Gazetteer,* page 16; BLM Taos Resource Area Map (Chama); USGS Quadrangle Map: El Vado, Navajo Peak, Laguna Peak, Echo Amphitheater, Ghost Ranch

Agencies
• BLM Taos Resource Area, 224 Cruz Alta Road, Taos, NM 87571
• Santa Fe National Forest Jemez Ranger District, P.O. Box 150, Jemez Springs, NM 87025; 505-829-3535
• NMDGF, P.O. Box 25112, Santa Fe, NM 87504-5112; 505-476-8000

Outfitters
• The Solitary Angler, 204B North Pueblo Road, Taos, NM 87529; 1-866-502-1700, www.thesolitaryangler.com
• Ed Adams Flyfishing, P.O. Box 428, Questa, NM 87556; 575-586-1512
• Taylor Streit Fly Fishing Service, P.O. Box 2759, Taos, NM 87571; 575-751-1312

MAJOR HATCHES, RIO CHAMA BELOW EL VADO & ABIQUIU RESERVOIRS

Insect	J	F	M	A	M	J	J	A	S	O	N	D	Time	Flies
Midges	■	■	■	■	■	■	■	■	■	■	■	■	M/E	Red & olive midge larva #16–#20; olive, gray, black and zebra midge pupa #18–#24; Disco Midge #18–#24; Mating Midge #14–#20; black & gray Midge Clusters #10–#16; Griffith's Gnat #16–#22; Snowfly #16–#26
Caddis				■	■	■	■	■	■	■			Larva-M Pupa-M/A/E Adult-A/E	Green & olive caddis larva #12–#16; Double Hackle Peacock #12–#16; La Fontaine's Caddis Pupa #12–#18; Van's Rag Pupa #10–#18; olive, tan & gray Elk Hair Caddis #12–#20; olive, gray & peacock Fluttering Caddis #10–#18
Baetis		■	■	■	■	■	■	■	■	■	■	■	M/A/SF	Dark olive Hare's Ear #16–#22; Pheasant Tail #16–#22; Van's Rag Fly dark olive #16–#22; Olive Parachute #16–#22; Olive Comparadun #16–#22
Golden Stonefly						■	■						M/A	Black & brown stonefly nymph #8–#14; Gold Stimulator #8–#16
Tricos							■	■	■	■			M/SF	Trico nymph #18–#22; Lawson's Fan-Wing Emerger #20–#24; parachute Trico #18–#22; Comparadun Trico #18–#22
PMDs, PEDs							■	■	■	■			M/SF	Light Hare's Ear #12–#18; Pheasant Tail #12–#20; Van's Rag Fly nymph light olive #14–#20; Lawson's Fan-Wing Emerger #14–#22; PMD, PED #12–#20; Ginger Dun #14–#20, parachute ginger, light olive #14–#20

Hatch Time Code: M = Morning; A = Afternoon; E = Evening; D = Dark; SF = Spinner Fall

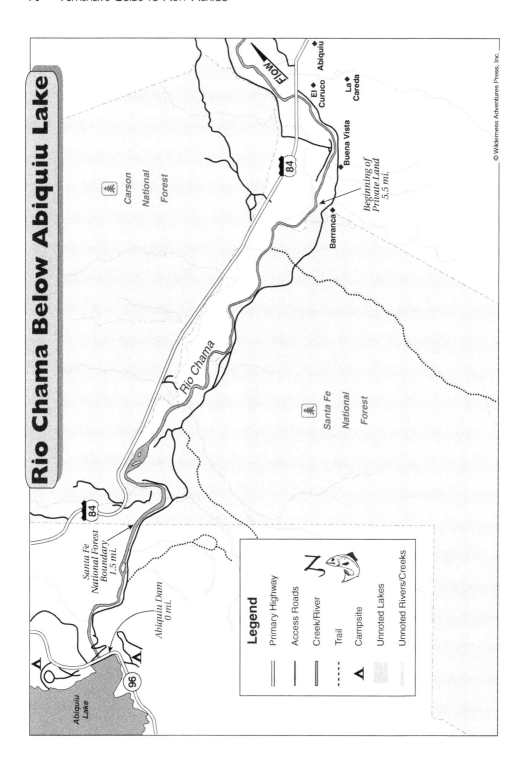

Rio Chama Below Abiquiu Lake

FLOW

◆ Abiquiu

El ◆
Curuco

La ◆
Careda

■ Buena Vista

84

Barranca ◆

Beginning of
Private Land
5.5 mi.

Carson
National
Forest

Rio Chama

Santa Fe
National
Forest

84

Santa Fe
National Forest
Boundary
1.5 mi.

Abiquiu Dam
0 mi.

96

Abiquiu
Lake

Legend

═══	Primary Highway
───	Access Roads
▐	Creek/River
- - -	Trail
▲	Campsite
▒	Unnoted Lakes
～～	Unnoted Rivers/Creeks

Abiquiu Reservoir

After flowing 30 to 35 miles through the Wild and Scenic River canyon, the Rio Chama enters Abiquiu Reservoir, the third in a series of dams in the watershed. Abiquiu Lake is located 61 miles north of Santa Fe at the junction of NM 96 and US 84 in northern New Mexico. This U.S. Army Corps of Engineers lake is part of a comprehensive plan for flood and sediment control in the Rio Chama–Rio Grande Basin. Construction of the project began in September 1956, and it was completed in February 1963. At a 340 feet above the streambed, Abiquiu Dam is the tallest earthen dam in the state.

The 5,200-acre lake offers excellent flyfishing for smallmouth bass. There are also some stocked rainbows and a few browns, which can be caught in early spring and late fall, but smallies up to 3 pounds are the primary target. Largemouths, crappie, perch, and walleye may bend your rod here, too.

Since it's a storage reservoir for Albuquerque, water levels in Abiquiu fluctuate greatly, and so does the fishing, but there's always one species or another willing to cooperate. Crappie are active in April, and shortly after that the smallmouth action heats up. Both species will hit Beadhead Woolly Buggers with a little Flashabou in various colors, size 6 to 12. Crappie, smallmouths, and largemouths will stay active close to shore through July, when they seem to drift farther out. Crappie can be found in shallow water during their spawn in May and June, making them easy prey for the flyfisher.

It's best to fish Abiquiu with a boat so you can get from spot to spot quickly. If nothing happens after a few casts, just move on. Once you find fish, you can expect plenty of action. I like to cast near structure, ledges, flats, and near shore, slapping the water intentionally to get their attention. Then I make quick, short strips with short pauses in between, which imparts a lot of action to the Woolly Bugger. Sometimes fish will short-strike, but if you keep stripping they'll often hit the fly again with more enthusiasm.

There's also some great trout opportunities at the inlet where big browns and rainbows congregate at times to feed and stage before they move up the Chama River to spawn. The browns spawn in the late fall, starting when the leaves turn and the rainbows spawn sporadically from February through May.

Whatever time of the year, look for risers first and match the hatch. If there's no hatch try any type of streamer or a damsyl nymph stripped slowly near the inlet where there is some current. Or try nymphing the current with a double nymph rig using an egg on top and a standard nymph on the bottom.

The Rio Chama Below Abiquiu Reservoir

When I first discovered this lowest part of the Rio Chama in the late sixties, the quality trout fishery was still in its infancy. Before the completion of Abiquiu Dam in 1963, this part of the Chama was always coffee-colored, and trout were hard to come by. But the new tailwater was a rich, clear, green color, and I remember driving down below the dam with my father as he marveled at the clear water. We proceeded to catch our limit of fat 12- to 18-inch rainbows and browns using wet flies. It remained one of the best-kept secrets in northern New Mexico for quite some time. But by the early eighties flyfishing clubs, guides (like me), and general word-of-mouth had put it on the angling map. Soon after it was discovered, though, authorities decided to upgrade the dam.

Originally, flood control at Abiquiu Dam involved temporarily capturing water during peak drainage seasons and slowly releasing it at predictable and reliable flows. It was not until 1986, when the Corps entered into a water supply contract with Albuquerque to store up to 200,000 acre-feet of water, that it retained a storage pool.

During the upgrade construction, there were several careless disasters, from spills of cement and leaking transformers that were buried near the river to the deliberate dewatering of the river, cutting flows drastically and causing great fluctuations. The dam was redesigned to flush silt, so during high flows it now runs murky instead of with the previous steady, clear flows.

Without better water-flow management, the river may never achieve its potential as a great tailwater, yet when flows are less than 300 cfs it can still be quite good—and it's improving. Fishing can be good at any time of the year if the water is clear and/or low. It's managed as Special Trout Water, with a daily bag and possession limit of two trout, although with no tackle restrictions (unfortunately). Grazing has been eliminated on the public land, and structures have been repaired. Hatches are improving, but now we're in the midst of a drought. Once the drought ends, it will be interesting to see how much the fishing improves.

The river has nice runs, riffles, pools, and some pocket water. About a mile below the dam there are some wide pools and islands, forming channels. Cottonwoods, willows, and brush are on the banks and islands, but they rarely interfere with casting. Wading isn't difficult, although the bedrock and larger boulders can be quite slimy, so felt soles and chest waders are recommended.

The best access is along a road below the dam on the southwest side of the river. It follows the river for about 2½ miles, and there are several parking areas and one picnic area. Where the road leaves the river, you can park and walk downstream as far as you care to fish. Just stay on the southwest side, because the northeast side becomes private after a short distance.

Stoneflies, caddis, mayflies, and midges all hatch in the tailwater, providing year-round food. By mid-May large Golden Stoneflies begin hatching, and evening caddis hatches can bring some fish to the surface. But except during fall or spring Baetis hatches, when the river is clear, this is mainly a nymph or wet-fly river. Bumping caddis larvae, stonefly nymphs, and dark olive Hare's Ear Nymphs (beadhead and regular) along the bottoms of deep riffles and pools can produce good action. Use a standard or "hi-stick" nymph technique to get to the bottom, and set the hook when there's any deviation in the drift.

There is a decent hatch of Pale Morning Duns in July, as well as other mayflies, which I match with a thorax-style, poly-wing Ginger Dun, size 16. I also like to add a light Beadhead Hare's Ear about 18 inches below the dry fly. Evening spinner falls combined with a caddis hatch can bring trout to the surface to feed heavily, providing some of the best dry-fly fishing of the year.

Since the rebuilding of the dam, and through the ensuing drought, the NMDGF has been stocking more rainbows than before. Now there are some hefty holdover 'bows that tend to feed on dries better than the browns, especially during Baetis hatches. Look for them working in the foam lines and at the heads of riffles during a hatch.

In the fall, about November 1, the browns start running, and they become quite active. This is the best time to catch a big brown using any kind of marabou or bunny-type streamer. Strip the fly actively at the base of pools, where they tail out just before entering the next riffle. Also, try the heads of riffles and around any rocks. Several long runs near the dam attract browns, and they can stack up at this time. A long cast and quick upstream mend allow you to strip in an oval path, which often turns some nice fish.

Winter ends the browns' spawning season, but midges begin hatching on a daily basis, and Baetis continue to show up on nice days. Fish between 8 and 12 inches will come to the surface at times, providing decent winter dry-fly opportunities. Look for rises in the flats and foam lines, but if they aren't rising, dredge the bottom near the tails of riffles with a red midge larva and a Pheasant Tail Nymph, size 18 to 20.

The Rio Chama below Abiquiu is a unique tailwater river with good access, and when conditions are right it can produce some nice fish. Drastic changes in flow and silt continue to have a negative impact here, but the fishery shows good resiliency, providing decent flyfishing year-round.

The Rio Chama below Abiquiu Dam has good winter fishing for rainbows and browns from 12 to 20 inches.

Stream Facts: Rio Chama Below Abiquiu Reservoir

Season
- Year-round.

Special Regulations
- Special Trout Water (STW): Daily bag and possession limit is two trout, no tackle restrictions.

Trout
- Wild browns and holdover rainbows running 12 to 15 inches, some larger.

River Miles
- Abiquiu Dam—0
- Santa Fe National Forest boundary—1.5
- Beginning of private land on southwest side—5.5

River Characteristics
- Large tailwater below Abiquiu Dam with long wide runs, riffles, pools, deep holes, and some large boulders.

River Flows
- Winter and fall: 50 to 250 cfs
- Spring runoff and summer: 250 to 1,000 cfs

Campgrounds
- Abiquiu Lake has developed campsites with toilets, water, and tables.

Maps
- *New Mexico Atlas & Gazetteer,* page 15; Santa Fe National Forest Map; BLM Taos Resource Area Map (Abiquiu); USGS Quadrangle Maps: Cannones, Abiquiu

Agencies
- BLM Taos Resource Area, 224 Cruz Alta Road, Taos, NM 87571
- Abiquiu Lake COE, P.O. Box 290, Abiquiu, NM 87510; 505-685-4433
- Santa Fe National Forest Jemez Ranger District, P.O. Box 150, Jemez Springs, NM 87025; 505-829-3535
- NMDGF, P.O. Box 25112, Santa Fe, NM 87504-5112

Outfitters
- The BLM, Taos Resource Area, and the Carson Nation Forest, Questa Ranger District, can provide information, including maps and a list of outfitters permitted to operate on public lands. These include:
- The Solitary Angler, 204B North Pueblo Road, Taos, NM 87529; 1-866-502-1700, www.thesolitaryangler.com

- Ed Adams Flyfishing, P.O. Box 428, Questa, NM 87556; 575-586-1512
- Taylor Streit Fly Fishing Service, P.O. Box 2759, Taos, NM 87571; 575-751-1312
- High Desert Angler, 460 Cerillos Road, Santa Fe, NM 87501; 505-988-7688, 1-888-988-7688, www.highdesertangler.com

Wearing down a nice brown on a mild December day.

HOPEWELL LAKE

Located near the top of the southern extension of the San Juan Mountains, halfway between Taos and Chama on US 64, Hopewell Lake offers the flyfisher a shot at wild brook trout and stocked rainbows in a high-alpine setting. Hopewell is small, but in a region with so few public lakes, it's an important stillwater for float-tubers. Access is easy, it's relatively close to Taos or Chama, and it's beautiful and productive. But despite all this, it doesn't get that much pressure, except on weekends and holidays.

Ice-cold melting snow provides water for the man-made lake, which stays cool even in the middle of summer. At an elevation of 9,750 feet, the season is short, with ice-out occurring around the end of April most years and cold weather setting in around the middle of October. Afternoon showers are common during the summer months, which helps to keep the air fresh, cool, and crisp.

Typical high-mountain lake patterns work well at Hopewell. Among my favorites are red midge larvae, size 16 to 20; red Slight Leeches, size 14 to 18; Olive Marabou Damsels, size 8 to 14; Marabou Dragon Nymphs, size 6 to 10; Peacock Snails, size 12 to 16; assorted Woolly Buggers; Callibaetis spinners, size 14 to 18; Griffith's Gnats, size 16 to 22; midge pupae, size 16 to 22; Blue Damsel Parachutes, size 8 to 14; and assorted beetles, ants, and hoppers.

The lake doesn't have many special features, but the inlet and weeds on the east end, near the inlet, and around the dam are good areas in which to start. Submerged weed beds are scattered around the lake, and fish tend to cruise around and through them. There are also a few shelves extending out from shore, with steep drops where fish congregate.

Ice-out is a great time to hit the lake because the fish start getting active as the water begins to warm and the first midge hatches come off. Brookies move to the inlet and some go up Placer Creek during runoff to feed on nymphs and worms that get washed down. Stripping nymphs, shrimp, or Woolly Buggers near the inlet can be very effective. I also like to use a double-nymph rig with a floating indicator set about 4 to 6 feet above the flies. I tie on a red midge larva, size 16 or 18, and a midge pupa, size 18 or 20, and cast near weed beds and slowly retrieve the line, watching the indicator closely. Takes are usually subtle, so strike even if there is only a slight hesitation in the indicator.

Another key time is during the summer Callibaetis hatches, which occur from mid- to late June through July. Just before noon, the spinners start hitting the water near shore, and fish will cruise very close, sipping them in. This is fun fishing. Try casting to cruising sippers with a size 18 Callibaetis spinner pattern on 6X tippet. Around sunset, micro-caddis hatches sometimes bring fish to the surface, and midges hatch every evening, adding to the dry-fly action.

In the fall, brookies stack up near the inlet before migrating upstream to spawn. This is the best time to catch them, as they feed aggressively in order to fatten up before spawning. They'll attack Woolly Buggers, nymphs, and even dry flies when in this mode. Holdover rainbows also move in to feed on lost eggs the brookies lay.

Make sure you layer up when fishing Hopewell, especially during ice-out and in the fall or any time you're float-tubing, because you may run into cold, windy weather. In summer, warm, sunny days and afternoon thunderstorms are the norm. Get out of the water and take cover in your car during these storms. I use the 14-second rule. If I see lightning, I count until I hear the thunder. If I hear it before 14 seconds, I'm out of there in a flash.

Placer Creek, the stream above the lake, is small but has a decent population of wild brookies. It's very narrow, and a 7½-foot, 2-weight rod is perfect. Standard attractors like a Royal Trude or Rio Grande King will bring fish to the surface.

The fishing is a little better below the dam because there is more nutrient-rich water coming out of the bottom of the reservoir. You'll find brookies, browns, and holdover rainbows here. The first half-mile or so is open, then the creek plunges into a narrow, deep canyon for about a mile before opening up again. There's a nice 1.5-mile stretch worth fishing before the creek joins the Rio Vallecitos. Standard patterns work well, and a dry-dropper rig with a high-floating dry and a Beadhead Hare's Ear or Pheasant Tail can be deadly.

There is a developed Forest Service campground at the lake, which has recently been upgraded, and there are plenty of picnic tables and bathrooms. Primitive camping is available just below the dam.

The ease of access, beautiful scenery, lake and stream fishing, and variety of fish make Hopewell Lake a great destination. I often stop to fish here on my way to or from the Chama River or Rio de Los Brazos.

Lake Facts: Hopewell Lake and Placer Creek

Season
- Year-round, but the lake freezes by mid-November.

Trout
- Wild brookies and stocked rainbows in the lake and in Placer Creek above the lake. Wild brookies and browns and stocked rainbows in Placer Creek below the lake.

Lake Characteristics
- Fourteen-acre lake with an oval shape and a steep angle from shore (except at the inlet) and a few shelves. Some weed beds, especially near the inlet.

Campgrounds
- Hopewell Campground has developed sites with bathrooms and 32 units.

Maps
- *New Mexico Atlas & Gazetteer,* page 15; Carson National Forest Map; BLM Taos Resource Area Map; USGS Quadrangle Maps: Burned Mountain

Agencies
- Carson National Forest, Tres Piedras Ranger District, P.O. Box 38 Tres Piedras, NM, 87577; 575-758-8678

- USFS Supervisor's Office, 208 Cruz Alta Road, Taos, NM 87577; 575-758-7200
- NMDGF, P.O. Box 25112, Santa Fe, NM 87504-5112

Outfitters
The Carson National Forest Supervisor's Office can provide information, including maps and a list of outfitters permitted to operate on public lands. Outfitters include:
- The Solitary Angler, 204B North Pueblo Road, Taos, NM 87529; 1-866-502-1700, www.thesolitaryangler.com
- Ed Adams Flyfishing, P.O. Box 428, Questa, NM 87556; 575-586-1512
- Taylor Streit Fly Fishing Service, P.O. Box 2759, Taos, NM 87571; 575-751-1312

A dry-dropper rig like the one this angler is fishing works well on the Rio Vallecitos.

RIO VALLECITOS

The Rio Vallecitos is a medium-sized stream located in the north-central part of the state, about 30 miles north of Espanola. To get there, head north on US 285 from Espanola about 23 miles to NM 111, where you turn left and go another 6 miles to La Madera. Keep following NM 111 up the Rio Vallecitos.

There's a patchwork of public and private property along the river, with over 10 miles of public water on the lower Vallecitos. But it's not obvious where the public water is until you get above Canon Plaza, about 16 miles north of La Madera, so a Carson National Forest map is essential in identifying the public land. The upper Vallecitos and Placer Creek are really just small creeks below Hopewell Lake, but they add another 6 or 7 miles of remote and fishable water.

The Rio Vallecitos becomes the Rio Ojo Caliente just a few miles below La Madera and eventually dumps into the Rio Chama about 35 miles downstream, but all the fishing is in the Vallecitos itself. Ojo Caliente is famous for its hot springs at the Ojo Caliente Mineral Springs, where there are deluxe accommodations. If you want to combine some of the best private hot springs anywhere with some great stream fishing, or if you're married and your wife doesn't fish, this is the place for you.

The Rio Vallecitos is fishable just before runoff (mid-March through April) and after (early June through October). The lower part of the river runs through a beautiful valley punctuated by rugged narrow canyon sections. Hispanic culture still flourishes here, and ranchers grow alfalfa, grass, and cattle. Small villages are scattered throughout the valley, and some landowners are accommodating to anglers that ask politely for permission. I always offer a gift like a homemade pie, a ham, or even a six-pack of beer.

The first good public stretch begins about a mile north of the village of Ancones. This section runs through a narrow canyon, with the Ortega Mountains to the west and the Mesa de la Jarita to the east. Mostly 8- to 16-inch browns occupy this stretch, and it's the best area for a chance at a fish larger than that.

Stoneflies and caddis are prevalent here in June, and there are lots of boulder-strewn pockets and deep holes to fish. I use a large Stimulator with a medium-sized golden stone nymph dropper during the day. If that doesn't stir up any action, I switch to a double-nymph rig with a caddis larva on top and a stonefly nymph on bottom. Woolly Buggers stripped through the pockets and deep holes can also be productive. Once the sun drops behind the canyon wall, I change to a caddis on top, usually a size 14 or 16 olive Elk Hair Caddis. There are multiple caddis hatches at times, so you may have to match the right hatch. The action can be fast and furious during these hatches, with every brown in the river feeding on top. Caddis continue to hatch into August, when it starts getting a little warm.

About a half-mile above the end of the canyon there's another mile or so of public water. Here, the river slows down and opens up into the valley, and the deep pools and long foam lines are a pleasure to fish with a dry fly or a dry-dropper combo. The same flies work here, but add some mayflies to the mix.

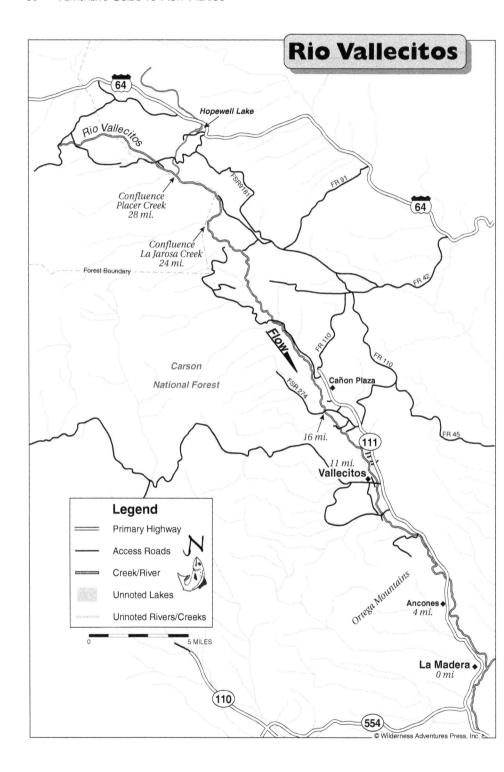

Rio Vallecitos

Rio Vallecitos

Hopewell Lake

Confluence
Placer Creek
28 mi.

Confluence
La Jarosa Creek
24 mi.

Forest Boundary

FSR 9181

FR 91

FR 42

Flow

FR 110

FR 110

Carson

National Forest

Cañon Plaza

FSR 274

16 mi.

FR 45

11 mi.
Vallecitos

111

Ortega Mountains

Ancones
4 mi.

La Madera
0 mi

Legend

═══	Primary Highway
───	Access Roads
▬▬▬	Creek/River
▒	Unnoted Lakes
	Unnoted Rivers/Creeks

N

0   5 MILES

110

554

© Wilderness Adventures Press, Inc.

Meadows, and it offers the best fishing in this high-country portion of the Los Pinos. Above the meadows, the creek narrows a bit and the grade is steeper with less holding water, but there are still some good pockets that hold fish.

Some good hatches come off in the upper meadows, especially near the inlet to the reservoir, where midges and Callibaetis hatch regularly. An Adams Irresistible, size 16, is my favorite fly during the summer months, except for evening midge hatches, when I fish the reservoir for cruising sippers with a Griffith's Gnat, size 16 or 18, and a large size 16 midge pupa dropper. The lake midges are huge, and the pupae are about a half-inch long. Float-tubing the reservoir in early morning and late evening, when it's not as windy, can be very productive for large rainbows, browns, and brookies, but I usually opt to fish the creek.

Below the reservoir, the Los Pinos tailwater runs through a beautiful canyon for about 1.5 miles before opening up into the lower Trujillo Meadows near CO 17. The canyon has a great combination of riffles, pools, and deep pockets, and it holds some really nice browns, although they're temperamental as hell. When there is a hatch, they feed selectively and when there isn't they have to be hauled up from the bottom with a nymph or streamer. The entire river below the reservoir is one of the most hatch-oriented streams I've ever fished, and the hatches are excellent.

To access the upper Trujillo Meadows, the reservoir, and the canyon below from Chama, New Mexico, take NM 17 north for about 12 miles to a road on the left, marked FR 118 to Trujillo Meadows Reservoir and Campground. There are developed and primitive sites at the campground.

To get to the lower Trujillo Meadows, just stay on CO 17 north for another 4.5 miles to FR 116 on the left, which is four-wheel drive only. Drive about a mile and park at any pullout. There aren't any trails, so it's about a half-mile hike downhill across rugged terrain to the river.

The lower Trujillo Meadows used to have excellent fishing for 12- to 16-inch browns, but the river is right next to CO 17 and anglers discovered it in the eighties. The average fish size is now about 8 to 12 inches, and the numbers are also down. The area where the river crosses the highway is private, but for years people have fished it like public water. It was recently posted, and the owners have been cracking down so don't fish it without permission. It will surely improve the fishing if they keep trespassers out.

About a mile below CO 17 the river is joined by the North Fork near the village of Los Pinos, where it enters private property for the next 3 miles. The fishing gets good again below there, but access is difficult, with no developed roads or trails into the river until you get to the old train station at Osier.

The best access to Osier is from Antonito, Colorado. Take CO 17 towards Chama, New Mexico, for about 11.5 miles and turn left on FR 103 and follow it another 18 miles to Osier. From Osier, take the rough road down to the river and park. You can then fish upstream through 5 miles of remote, beautiful water that includes riffles, long pools, and beaver ponds punctuated by rugged stretches of pocket water. There are one or two pieces of private property that you might have to go around now that houses are starting to go up. Some of the terrain is very rugged, but the fishing is worth it. Wild browns average 12 to 16 inches, with some to 20 inches, and there are tons of 8- to 12-inch fish.

From Osier downstream about 1.5 miles, the Los Pinos is nice and open and offers decent access to broad riffles and pools that are easily waded. Some anglers actually take the famous Cumbres & Toltec Railroad (an old narrow-gauge steam-engine train) from Antonito, Colorado, or Chama, New Mexico, and get off at Osier Station and hike down to the river to fish and camp. When they're finished, they hike back up to the station and take the train back out. It makes for quite an adventurous trip back in time.

The Los Pinos enters New Mexico about 1.5 miles below Osier and plunges into a narrow, steep, rugged canyon known as Toltec Gorge. The canyon is almost inaccessible for the next couple of miles, so I don't recommend it unless you have access through private property at the bottom end of the gorge. You must have permission from the owners, and the only way in is from far downstream in New Mexico. Unfortunately, getting permission is next to impossible, so in effect, the river from the upper end of Toltec Gorge downstream about 10 miles is off limits to all except a few lucky anglers. For them, the fishing is fantastic, with lots of wild browns up to 18 inches or more.

After entering New Mexico, the river picks up several small creeks that add a significant amount of water, and by the time it flows back into the Carson National Forest it's quite large for a New Mexico stream, about 30 to 40 feet wide in most places.

The author fishing dries during an afternoon hatch of Blue Duns on a classic pool on the Rio de Los Pinos near Osier, Colorado.

Access to the New Mexico side of the Los Pinos is via US 285. From Taos, take US 64 west about 26 miles to Tres Piedras, and turn right (north) on US 285. Drive about 5 miles past the Colorado border and start looking for County Road C on your left, which is marked by a road sign. Turn left and go about a mile to the stop sign, and then turn left again on the paved road, following it up a hill and around a corner to where it makes a hard turn to the left toward the village of Ortiz.

At this point, look for a gravel road on the right that heads almost straight on; just bear right onto this road. Stay on this road for just a few miles southwest to the Colorado–New Mexico border, where you'll see the Los Pinos on your left. Follow the road for about 2.5 miles through private property until you enter the Rio de Los Pinos State Wildlife Area, marked by a sign. There's about 3.5 miles of roadside access in the state property, with some developed and primitive campsites.

Continuing up the dirt road past the wildlife area will lead you through about a mile of private water before you hit the entrance to the Carson National Forest where FR 284 turns primitive. The road parallels the river for the next 2 miles, after which water becomes private again.

The road continues to follow the river for about half a mile before heading up the side of the mountain for 2.5 miles, where it intersects FR 75. Turn left on FR 75 and go about .75 mile to its intersection with FR 103 at the Colorado border. Turn left yet again and follow the road and signs approximately 15 miles through awesome high country with panoramic views of the Toltec Gorge to Osier and the upper Los Pinos in Colorado.

From the lower Trujillo Meadows down through Toltec Gorge and into New Mexico, the Los Pinos hatches are basically the same. In April, pre-runoff hatches include Little Brown Stoneflies, Baetis, and caddis. At other times, tight-line nymphing along the bottom or stripping streamers can be very productive.

Starting in early June, after runoff has peaked, the large Salmonfly hatch is already in full swing in the lower reaches, and the hatch progresses upstream over the next couple of weeks. Golden Stoneflies begin next, overlapping the Salmonflies in late June, along with hatches of Blue Duns, Gray and Green Drakes, PMDs, Ginger Duns, and incredible evening hatches of caddis. In fact, the river has so many good hatches that trying to figure out what to use can be overwhelming at times.

Once, I was fishing a pool on the New Mexico portion of the river during the beginning of a caddis hatch. Trout were boiling at the head of the pool so I tied on a caddis that looked just like the dark olive–bodied naturals. After several good drifts and no strikes I observed the rises a little closer and realized they weren't thrashing the surface for emerging caddis at all, but were sipping something smaller.

I tied on a Ginger Quill because Ginger Duns had been hatching earlier in the day and connected with a 16-inch holdover rainbow on the first cast. I didn't have to pump her throat because she was stuffed to the gills with Ginger spinners. They were actually coming out of her mouth. I trimmed the bottom hackle off my fly so it sat flush on the water and ended up having one of those evenings we all dream about.

Whether venturing into the remote areas of the Los Pinos, to the water near Osier, or even when driving right up to the edge of the river in New Mexico, you'll find a variety of water types, magnificent scenery, excellent hatches, and lots of trout without huge crowds of anglers. There are numerous long pools up to 10 feet deep, with broad riffles at their heads and long foam lines at their tails. There is an abundance of overhanging brush, undercut banks, logjams, and boulder-strewn pockets. The banks are covered in cottonwoods, willows, alders, roses, and pine trees, but there's still plenty of room to cast.

I recommend an 8½- to 9-foot, 3- to 5-weight for this water. Wading isn't difficult, but the boulders can be slick, so use caution. Hip boots are usually sufficient, but waist or chest waders are better because there are many deep areas. I usually wade up the side opposite the best water and stay close to the edge, casting straight upstream on the side I'm wading in, then working my way across until I cover all the feeding lanes, paying close attention to the opposite bank.

The Los Pinos is a classic dry-fly stream, and fish will generally rise during hatches, but this isn't always the case. I've seen the river covered with bugs and nothing feeding on the surface, particularly when the sun is on the water. Other times, like during stonefly season, there's hardly anything on the water but you'll see thrashing rises from time to time and fish will readily take a large Stimulator on the surface. When they won't come to the surface, a nymph fished in the deep riffles and seams can produce good action.

For flies, I stick to the usual matches for the various hatches. Starting in early June, I use large dark stonefly nymphs, size 6 to 10; caddis larvae, size 12 to 16; large Salmonfly dries, size 4 to 10; or Elk Hair Caddis, size 12 to 18. As the water drops later in June, I start using golden stone nymphs, size 12 to 16; Bird's Stoneflies, size 12 to 16; Terminators and Stimulators, size 12 to 16; PMDs, size 16 to 20; Blue Quills and Duns, size 12 to 18; Ginger Quills and Duns, size 14 to 18; Green Drakes (Wulffs or parachutes), size 12 to 14; and Adams Irresistibles and Parachute Adams, size 12 to 18. By late July, I add terrestrials like Parachute Hoppers, size 10 to 14; black, cinnamon, and two-tone ants, size 14 to 18; and black and brown Beadhead Woolly Buggers, size 8 to 14.

The highlight of the Los Pinos for me is late June and early July, when PMDs and/or Blue Quills start in the morning and Salmonflies and Golden Stoneflies continue through midday. Occasionally, large Brown or Green Drakes will hatch, followed by afternoon mayfly hatches and ending with blizzard hatches of caddis after the sun leaves the water, resulting in a feeding frenzy in every riffle and pool. It's possible to land a hundred fish on such days, but I'm not that greedy anymore. Now I catch a few and take a break, then move and catch some more, eat lunch, catch some more, then break until the evening frenzy.

The Los Pinos fishes best just after runoff, roughly late June through July, when there seems to be good flows, consistent hatches, and cool temperatures. By August, flows are low, temperatures high, and the hatches are restricted to mornings and evenings. Some fish can be taken on terrestrials or with nymphs, but I usually avoid the Los Pinos in August unless we're getting good cloud cover and regular afternoon showers.

The Special Trout Water can be very productive in early summer.

One fly that works well in August is a Cinnamon Ant, size 14 or 16. Bob Widgren, owner of Los Pinos Rods in Albuquerque, turned me on to this pattern 20 years ago. Bob is the foremost expert on the Los Pinos and knows its many moods. One day, I was fishing on my own and couldn't catch anything. I had some looks but no takers. I was driving to another spot and sipping a beer when I ran into Bob and his wife, Lee, and asked how they were doing. He responded that they'd done well on the surface, including a couple of 16-inch browns. I asked what he was using and he gave me his classic huge grin and said, "A cinnamon ant." He showed me one, just a standard hair body with a furnace hackle. Luckily, I had something very similar with me, and I started picking up fish right away. Sometimes it *is* the fly.

Things cool off by mid-September, and late-season Baetis hatches and even some hoppers, ants, and evening caddis will bring fish to the surface. If they won't feed on top, try standard nymphing techniques in the heads of riffles and pools or strip a Woolly Bugger through the riffles, pools, and pockets. By the end of October, the Rio de Los Pinos starts getting very cold, but a few pre-spawn browns can be found in the middle of the day in the tails of riffles and pools. Stripping streamers in front of the protective and competitive browns will force them to lash out for your fly.

The Rio de Los Pinos is one of the premier dry-fly streams in the Southwest. The combination of varied water types, consistent hatches, magnificent scenery, solitude, and splendid flyfishing provide an experience that is hard to match.

Stream Facts: Rio de Los Pinos

Season
- Year-round, but fishing is only possible from April through October. Best fishing is just after runoff, usually mid-June through July and September through October.

Special Regulations
- From FR 284 and 87A 2.5 miles upstream to private land: Use only artificial flies or lures with single barbless hooks. Daily bag limit: two fish any length.

Fish
- Wild brown trout from 8 to 18 inches, stocked and wild rainbows 8 to 16 inches, some larger. In and above Trujillo Meadows Reservoir, add wild cuttbows 8 to 18 inches and brookies 6 to 14 inches.

River Miles
- Trujillo Meadows Dam—0
- Lower Trujillo Meadows bridge on CO 17—2
- Osier Station Road—7.5
- Colorado–New Mexico state line—8.5
- Upper boundary of Special Trout Water—17
- Lower boundary of Special Trout Water—19.5
- Upper boundary of Rio de Los Pinos State Wildlife Area—20
- Lower boundary of Rio de Los Pinos State Wildlife Area—24
- New Mexico-Colorado border—28

River Characteristics
- Above Trujillo Meadows Reservoir: Small freestone stream winding through open meadows with good undercut banks and deep holes for the first 1.5 miles. Above the upper Trujillo Meadows it gets narrower, faster and brushier with good pocket water.
- Below Trujillo Meadows Reservoir: The first 1.5 miles below the reservoir is medium-sized and has deep holes and pocket water. Lower Trujillo Meadows has medium-sized water winding through willows and meadows, with some good riffles, pools, and undercut banks. Some bank erosion due to overgrazing. Toltec Gorge has a unique combination of riffles, deep pools and holes, beaver ponds, and fast pocket water. Stream bank varies from sheer rock to open meadows and cottonwood forest. River bottom has gravel, medium and large boulders, and some silt at the tails of pools and along the banks.

Campgrounds
- There is developed (no electric or water) and primitive camping in the Rio de Los Pinos Wildlife Area in New Mexico and in the Special Trout Water.
- There is primitive and developed camping with water and bathrooms at Trujillo Meadows Reservoir in Colorado.

Maps

- *New Mexico Atlas & Gazetteer,* pages 15 and 16; *Colorado Atlas & Gazetteer,* pages 89 and 90; Carson National Forest Map; Rio Grande National Forest Map; USGS Quadrangle Maps: Toltec Mesa, Bighorn Peak, Los Pinos

Agencies

- USFS Supervisor's Office 208 Cruz Alta Road, Taos, NM 87571; 505-758-6200
- Carson National Forest, Tres Piedras Ranger District, P.O. Box 38, Tres Piedras, NM 87577; 575-758-8678
- NMDGF, P.O. Box 25112, Santa Fe, NM 87504-5112

Outfitters

The USFS Supervisor's Office can provide information, including maps and a list of outfitters permitted to operate on public lands. Outfitters include:

- The Solitary Angler, 204B North Pueblo Road, Taos, NM 87529; 1-866-502-1700, www.thesolitaryangler.com
- Ed Adams Flyfishing, P.O. Box 428, Questa, NM 87556; 575-586-1512
- Taylor Streit Fly Fishing Service, P.O. Box 2759, Taos, NM 87571; 575-751-1312

A nice brown caught in the Special Trout Water on the New Mexico side of the Los Pinos. (Cathie Hughs)

RIO DE LOS PINOS MAJOR HATCHES

Insect	J	F	M	A	M	J	J	A	S	O	N	D	Time	Flies
Caddis			▓	▓	▓	▓	▓	▓	▓				Larva-M Pupa-M/ A/E Adult-A/E	Green & olive caddis larva #12–#16; Double Hackle Peacock #12–#16; La Fontaine's Caddis Pupa #12–#18; Van's Rag Pupa #10–#18; Lawson's Caddis Emerger #12–#18; olive, tan & gray Elk Hair Caddis #12–#20; olive, gray & peacock Fluttering Caddis #10–#18
Craneflies				▓	▓	▓	▓	▓					Larva-M/E	Cranefly larva peacock, gray, or dark olive #6–#16; Taylor Streit's Poundmeister #6–#14
Green, Gray Drakes							▓	▓					M/A/SF	Olive Hare's Ear #10–#14; Green & Gray Drake #10–#14; Green & Gray Paradrake #10–14; Green Drake spinner #12–#14
Ginger, Yellow, Blue & Mahogany Duns						▓	▓	▓	▓				M/E	Light, dark & olive Hare's Ear #12–#18; Pheasant Tail #12–#18; light, dark, pink & ginger Hair-Wing Duns or Cahills #12–18 or the same in parachutes
BWO				▓	▓				▓	▓	▓		M/A/SF	Dark olive Hare's Ear #16–#22; Pheasant Tail #16–#22; Van's Rag Fly dark olive #16–#22; Lawson's BWO Fan-Wing Emerger #16–#22; Olive Parachute #16–#22; Olive Comparadun #16–#22

RIO DE LOS PINOS MAJOR HATCHES (cont.)

Insect	J	F	M	A	M	J	J	A	S	O	N	D	Time	Flies
Salmonfly, Golden Stonefly						█	█						M/A	Black & brown stonefly #6–#10; Golden Stone Nymph #10–#14; Elk Hair Salmon Fly #6–#12; Orange & Gold Stimulators #6–#14; Terminator #12–#16
PMDs, PEDs					█	█							M/SF	Light Hare's Ear Nymph #12–#18; Pheasant Tail #12–#20; Van's Rag Fly Nymph light olive #14–#20; Lawson's Fan-Wing Emerger #14–#22; PMD, PED #12–#20; Hair-Wing or PW Ginger Dun #14–#20, Parachute ginger, light olive #14–#20
Terrestrials					█	█	█	█	█				M/A	Para-hoppers tan, yellow #8–#14; Bees #12–#14; Cinnamon Ant #14–#18; Lady Bug #16–18; black & peacock beetles #12–#18

Hatch Time Code: M = Morning; A = Afternoon; E = Evening; D = Dark; SF = Spinner Fall

CRUCES BASIN WILDERNESS

The Cruces Basin Wilderness is where the headwaters of the southernmost fork of the Rio de Los Pinos originate. A small wilderness area, the Cruces Basin is only about 27 square miles, but it drains from an immense highland known as the Brazos Ridge. There are over six creeks loaded with wild brookies in the upper reaches, and Beaver Creek has both brookies and browns in the lower reaches.

From its confluence with the Los Pinos, Beaver Creek extends upstream for 3 miles, where it divides into several small creeks. The creeks, with names like Cruces, Diablo, Escondido, and Lobo, are small but very fishable. Situated high (between 9,000 or 10,000 feet) in the Cruces Basin Wilderness, the creeks run through mostly meadows and willows broken up by some narrow stretches with trees, brush, and rock. There are tons of beaver ponds on all the creeks and small riffles and pools between them, providing plenty of opportunities to catch brook trout that average 8 to 10 inches, with a few whoppers stretching to 13 or 14 inches.

I once got a 16-inch trophy in a big beaver pond on Cruces Creek. This is the one place where I usually keep a couple of fish for dinner when I'm camping out. The pink meat on a wild brookie cooked over an open fire is hard to beat, and they're actually overpopulated in some of the beaver ponds, so some harvesting is good. I never keep a brown, though, since they are scarcer and grow larger.

Any attractor, size 12 to 18, fished on the surface will usually produce more brookies than you can count. This is a great place to take kids with enough energy to make the trek into the wilderness area. The area is also fairly open so long casts aren't necessary. Camping is great, with astounding panoramic views. Wildlife is plentiful—including elk, deer, bear, and beaver.

From the trailhead at the end of FR 572 it's only a little over a mile to the confluence of the other creeks and Beaver Creek. Below the confluences, Beaver Creek has a decent flow and is fishable for about a half-mile before plunging into a narrow, rugged canyon with sheer cliffs on both sides of the river. Access here is difficult at best and should never be attempted alone. There's better access from the confluence of the Los Pinos, but this requires permission from the landowner.

To get to the Cruces Basin Wilderness from Taos, take US 64 west to Tres Piedras and turn north on US 285. Go about 10 miles and turn left on FR 87, an improved dirt road. Follow the signs about 21 miles to FR 572. Turn right and follow it about 2 miles to the end of the road and the trailhead.

Cruces Basin Wilderness

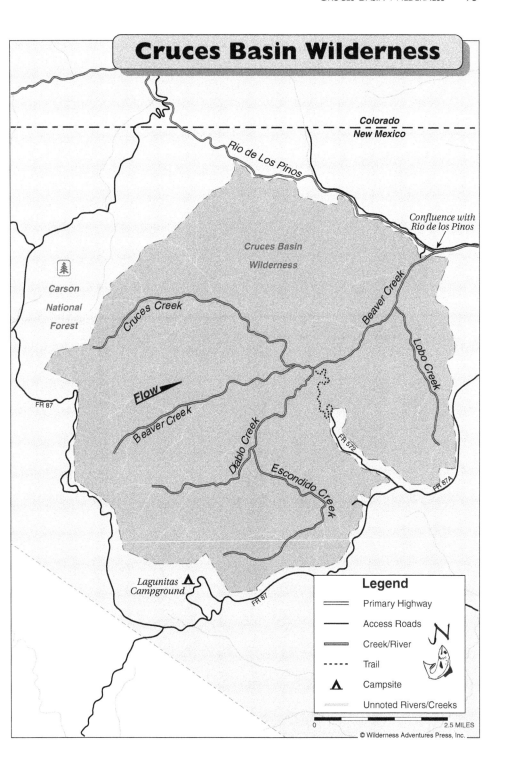

Colorado
New Mexico

Rio de Los Pinos

Confluence with
Rio de los Pinos

Cruces Basin
Wilderness

Beaver Creek

Carson
National
Forest

Cruces Creek

Lobo Creek

Flow

FR 87

Beaver Creek

Diablo Creek

FR 572

Escondido Creek

FR 87A

Lagunitas ▲
Campground

FR 87

Legend

Primary Highway

Access Roads

Creek/River

Trail

▲ Campsite

Unnoted Rivers/Creeks

0   2.5 MILES

© Wilderness Adventures Press, Inc.

Stream Facts: Cruces Basin Wilderness

Season
- Year-round, but fishable from mid-May through October.

Trout
- Brookies, browns, and some rainbows in lower Beaver Creek.

River Characteristics
- High mountain creeks running through meadows and willows with numerous beaver ponds and winding stretches with undercut banks. Lower Beaver Creek plunges into a 3-mile-long box canyon with deep holes, plunge pools, and fast pocket water.

River Flows
- Winter, summer, and fall: creeks average 3 to 5 cfs; Beaver Creek averages 23 cfs
- Spring runoff: creeks average 12 to 25 cfs; Beaver Creek averages 60 to 125 cfs

Maps
- *New Mexico Atlas & Gazetteer,* page 15; Carson National Forest Map; BLM Taos Resource Area Map; USGS Quadrangle Maps: Toltec Mesa

Agencies
- Carson National Forest, Forest Supervisor's Office, 208 Cruz Alta Road, Taos, NM 87571; 575-758-6200
- NMDGF, P.O. Box 25112, Santa Fe, NM 87504-5112

Outfitters
The Forest Supervisor's Office can provide information, including maps and a list of outfitters permitted to operate in the Cruces Basin Wilderness. Outfitters include:
- The Solitary Angler, 204B North Pueblo Road, Taos, NM 87529; 1-866-502-1700, www.thesolitaryangler.com
- Ed Adams Flyfishing, P.O. Box 428, Questa, NM 87556; 575-586-1512

JEMEZ AREA STREAMS

The Jemez area streams are unique because they offer a variety of flyfishing opportunities within a relatively small region. From canyon pocket water on the Rio Guadalupe or East Fork to the spring-creek headwaters of the Rio San Antonio on the newly acquired Valles Caldera National Preserve (VCNP), the Jemez region has something for anglers of all ages and levels of experience. There's always somewhere to wet a line at any time of the year, even during spring runoff and winter. The region's watersheds hold rainbows, browns, cutthroats, and brookies, and there are great hatches on all the streams.

Because of its proximity to metropolitan Albuquerque, as well as the entire central New Mexico region that includes Santa Fe, Espanola, and Los Alamos, the Jemez Mountains get tons of visitors. Hikers, bikers, hunters, sightseers, historians, artists, and anglers all share the streams, lakes, trails, and terrain. Yet it's quite easy to find solitude, especially if you fish weekdays or outside the summer months, or if you're willing to drive over rugged dirt roads and hike a little.

The area's geology is volcanic in nature. The rocks and soil erode easily during runoff or summer thunderstorms, causing turbidity in the streams. It can take days for the lower reaches of the streams to clear up after a good thunderstorm, but if you keep going upstream or move to another stream you can usually find clear water. The lower reaches of streams like the Jemez River have layers of clay, ash, and sandstone in the substrate and surrounding canyon walls, which turn the waters a yellow or rusty color after a good rain.

The Rio San Antonio starts as a spring on the Valles Caldera National Preserve (VCNP).

During spring, each stream runs off differently depending on the sun, elevation, snowpack, and size of the watershed. By March, the lower Rio San Antonio, lower Jemez River, lower Guadalupe, and Rio Cebolla are the first to turn muddy, but the East Fork of the Jemez from its confluence with the Jemez upstream to the boundary of the VCNP may remain clear and very fishable, even with dry flies.

As the snow in the VCNP and Bandelier National Monument begins to melt, the East Fork gets murky, but the Rio Cebolla starts to clear. By the end of April, the upper San Antonio clears up, but the Jemez and Guadalupe are still high and murky. The runoff usually ends by mid- to late May, and fishing remains good on all the streams until the midsummer heat waves hit in July and August.

Much of the Jemez region is part of a giant caldera and ancient volcano that includes over 200,000 acres of the Santa Fe National Forest, 32,000 acres of the Bandelier National Monument, and 89,000 acres of the Valles Caldera National Preserve, formerly the Baca Grant. There are campgrounds throughout the national forest, most near a stream or lake. Over 9 miles of Special Trout Water on three streams in the national forest and several miles of heavily regulated and intensely managed water on the Rio San Antonio and East Fork of the Jemez River within the VCNP make the Jemez region very accommodating to the flyfisher.

Most of the streams are small, more like creeks, and some are tiny, especially in the headwaters. But they are fertile and hold good populations of wild fish in addition to rainbows, which are heavily stocked near the more popular areas. Most fish are in the 8- to 12-inch range, but there are larger fish in some of streams that have deep holes. Hatches are prolific at times, and they run the entire gamut from tiny midges and Baetis to larger caddis and stoneflies, not to mention terrestrials such as hoppers, beetles, and ants.

All the streams can be fished with a 7- to 8-foot, 2- to 5-weight rod, 7½-foot leaders, and 5X or 6X tippet. For waders, I like breathable stocking-foot hip waders with a hiking style wading boot that has hard rubber soles. Pant or chest waders would only be necessary in a few spots. It should be noted that while fishing on the VCNP waters, waders are not allowed in order to prevent whirling disease. Of course, that means you have to wade wet.

Two of the most significant streams, the Rio San Antonio and the East Fork of the Jemez River, both emanate from the VCNP, which was known as the private Baca Land Grant Location 1 until 2000 when it was purchased by the public.

The Valles Caldera National Preserve

On July 25, 2000, the American people purchased approximately 89,000 acres of the Baca Ranch in northern New Mexico. The Valles Caldera Preservation Act designated these spectacular lands as the Valles Caldera National Preserve, a unit of the National Forest System. The Act also created the Valles Caldera Trust to manage the Preserve.

The Valles Caldera Preservation Act established the Preserve to "...protect and preserve the scientific, scenic, geologic, watershed, fish, wildlife, historic, cultural, and recreational values of the Preserve, and to provide for multiple use and sustained yield of renewable resources within the Preserve" consistent with Valles Caldera Preservation Act.

A unique public land management approach was developed for the Preserve. The Valles Caldera Trust (the Trust), a wholly owned government corporation, will manage the Preserve and a nine-member Board of Trustees will govern the Trust. The Board is made up of the Forest Supervisor of the Santa Fe National Forest, the Superintendent of Bandelier National Monument, and seven individuals with a variety of skills.

Fishing on the Preserve is conducted under the rules and regulations of the NMDGF. The Game and Fish Commission may change the rules in any given year, so check with the state or the VCNP before fishing here.

Highlights of the program include:
- Limited numbers of anglers assigned to stream stretches to assure solitude and wildlife-viewing opportunities.
- Smaller bag limits than most other nearby waters.
- Restricted angling methods to better conserve the fishing resource.

Long term, the Trust will seek to develop diverse fishing opportunities, including the possible creation of ponds accessible to children and physically challenged people along with more physically demanding and adventurous wild stream fishing. Studies were being done to determine if native Rio Grande cutthroat trout could be reintroduced in the Rio San Antonio, which is an idea I was against, especially with the region suffering from severe drought at the time. Fortunately, they determined, for now anyhow, not to reintroduce them.

The wild browns that now thrive in the Rio San Antonio do so because they are well-suited for the conditions there. Sediment loading from overlogging and the nature of the soil, which has a large amount of volcanic ash, make it inhospitable for cutthroats. Also, browns are fall spawners, ensuring better natural reproduction than the spring-spawning native cutts. A global warming trend that has caused most New Mexico streams to run at warmer temperatures and lower than average levels the last 10 years makes this water better suited for browns. The East Fork, on the other hand, already supports a wild rainbow population, indicating it may be possible to successfully reintroduce Rio Grande cutthroats there.

An online reservation system allows interested participants to log on to www.vallescaldera.gov to plan their trips or they can call the preserve to make reservations. You will be allowed to select a "beat," or section of river, for your use that day. The online reservation system allows you to pay via credit card and obtain a printed permit prior to coming out to the preserve, where you will have to check in. You may reserve a specific day from their monthly calendar, and choose from the list of available sections for that day. Reservations are nontransferable.

When the VCNP first opened the Rio San Antonio to fishing in July 2003, reservations were granted on a first-come, first-served basis. Less than four months later, they were already forced to go to a lottery system because of the unbelievable popularity of the fishery. Like me, everyone has been looking over that fence into

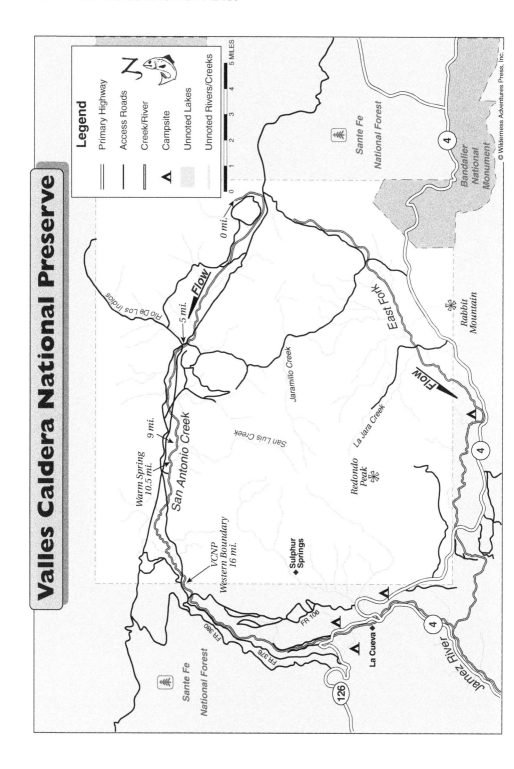

Valles Caldera National Preserve

Legend

	Primary Highway
	Access Roads
	Creek/River
▲	Campsite
	Unnoted Lakes
	Unnoted Rivers/Creeks

0 1 2 3 4 5 MILES

Rio De Los Indios

Flow

0 mi.

5 mi.

Warm Spring 10.5 mi.

9 mi.

San Antonio Creek

VCNP Western Boundary 16 mi.

Sulphur Springs

Jaramillo Creek

San Luis Creek

East Fork

Flow

La Jara Creek

Redondo Peak

Rabbit Mountain

Santa Fe National Forest

Bandelier National Monument

4

4

4

FR 106

La Cueva

FR 380

FR 376

126

Jemez River

Santa Fe National Forest

© Wilderness Adventures Press, Inc.

the immense Valle Grande for years, dying to fish the untouched waters for virgin trout. Now they could, and the race was on to be among the first lucky anglers to test their skills on the wild trout. Originally, there were 13 "reaches" on the San Antonio and they were booked full through the end of the season within a week or two of its opening to reservations online. Eventually, they modified everything and now they are back to taking reservations on a first-come first-served basis and letting people select their "reach". There are now only four "reaches" on the Rio San Antonio but they are much longer. Reaches 1 & 3 allow up to four anglers per day and "reaches" 2 & 4 allow up to six anglers per day. Another great change is that you can now access the preserve in your own vehicle, after checking in and you must check out as well.

If you don't have Web access, you can call the Valles Caldera Trust office to make a reservation. But the website is the best method for making a reservation quickly.

- Online reservations can be made at www.vallescaldera.gov.
- Toll-free phone: 1-866-382-5537 (business hours only).
  - All visitors must check in at the headquarters prior to entering the perserve. To get there from Los Alamos, take Hwy 4 west to mile marker 39 and turn right at the gate and follow the road for two miles to the preserve.
  - Only artificial flies with a single barbless hook may be used
  - Rio San Antonio – Reaches 1 & 3 allow up to four anglers per dayand reaches 2 & 4 allow up to six anglers per day.
- The Valles Caldera Trust encourages catch and release
- Anglers may take up to 5 fish on Rio San Antonio.
  - East Fk. of the Jemez River - Remote hike-in fishing where 10 anglers per day are allowed.
  - East Fk. of the Jemez River - Catch and release only
- The Preserve's current fee schedule for fishing or just entering the property for any reason is a $35 entrance fee per person per day. No discounts for kids.
- To prevent the spread of whirling disease, nets, waders and felt-soled wading boots are not allowed. Nets can be rented from the preserve.
- Remember that prices, regulations, and management strategies can change at any time, so check the website or call for current information.

Rio San Antonio on the VCNP

The Rio San Antonio begins high up near the eastern rim of the Valles Caldera. At its head, the Rio San Antonio is nothing more than a pipe stuck in the ground with a large natural spring spewing out of it that forms the first pool, which has several small brown trout.

From there, the San Antonio winds its way west through what is known as the Valle Antonio for about 16 miles, picking up water from several springs and small tributaries along the way. The Valle Antonio is a giant, lush (except during drought) meadow surrounded by mountains and hills, which are remnants of the volcano. Deposits of obsidian, pumice, and other minerals dot the landscape, and some end up in the creek bottom.

The VCNP opened the Rio San Antonio to the public on a limited basis in July 2003. They divided the creek into 11 beats (sections), which are all between ½ mile and 1½ miles long, depending on how much fishable water they have. Each beat supposedly provides enough fishable water for two anglers for about five hours. Of course, that depends on the angler and how good the fishing is that day. As discussed earlier, the beats are reserved on a lottery system accessed online or by calling the VCNP.

At its widest point, the Rio San Antonio within the VCNP is only about 10 feet across, except during runoff or after a rainstorm. In fact, in the upper 4 or 5 miles you can jump across it in many places. It has an incredible population of wild browns that average 6 to 10 inches, and some of the deeper runs have browns up to 13 or 14 inches, along with the occasional 16-inch whopper.

In a normal year, when there's plenty of water, a decent small-stream angler can catch over 50 browns in a day. But during low flows they spook more easily, so one to three fish per run is all you can expect. When the stream opened in July 2003, average anglers were catching 30-plus fish a day, even though we were suffering from a major drought. Within a month, the catch rate dropped by half due to continued pressure on the little gem. It just goes to show that even with catch-and-release practices, fragile fisheries can only handle so much pressure before the trout become wise to what's going on. Authorities may have to further limit use in the future if they want to minimize impact on the fishery. Still, it's much better than turning the public loose on the little creek, as is the case on most public lands. A fishery this fragile wouldn't maintain its quality for one season without limits on the number of anglers per day.

If you're lucky enough to be assigned a beat through the lottery system, you and the other anglers will meet at the entrance gate in the morning, where a VCNP host gives an orientation and supplies every angler with a walkie-talkie, and then takes you by van to your beat. There are no trees since you're in the middle of a giant meadow, so make sure to bring a good hat, sunscreen, and a rain jacket in addition to enough food and water for the day. And you can't run to the car for tackle or more flies, so make sure you have everything you need before boarding the van in the morning.

The Rio San Antonio is one of those little creeks where you can finally use that little 7-foot, 2- or 3-weight bamboo or graphite rod that the local fly shop sold you, even though you thought you'd never need it. Casting these slight rods is a delight, and the little browns feel like monsters as they run, jump, and try like hell to take you under a grassy undercut bank.

When using a lightweight rod, don't overpower your cast. They are the equivalent of a putter in golf, with which you just tap the ball. Use only your wrist to cast, maintaining a 90-degree casting arc, and be delicate. Using your arm or too much power just destroys the smooth energy of the rod. Always fish upstream—creep slowly and keep a low profile, sometimes crawling to the base of a pool. Watch your shadow, making sure it doesn't touch the water, and make all false casts away from the water you're fishing.

Through the entire 16 miles, the creek's character is pretty much the same except

The Rio San Antonio within the VCNP is broken up into 11 beats. You must make reservations well in advance to fish here.

that it gains volume downstream. About 3 to 10 feet wide, it winds through tall grass and wildflowers, which create good overhang along the banks. There are some deep holes and undercut banks, especially at the bends, where larger browns can hide when they aren't out feeding in the flow.

Spotting fish is usually easy, except after heavy thunderstorms, which can cause the little creek to swell and run murky, sometimes for days. Usually, though, the afternoon showers aren't heavy enough to muddy the creek, and they cool things off for you and the fish. The browns also tend to spook less and feed on dries better when it's cloudy. Be particularly cautious about lightning during thunderstorms. If you see lightning anywhere within the caldera, it's too close for comfort. Crouch down well away from where you place your rod.

For flies, hoppers or a large black ant are my favorite non-hatch choices. Blue-Winged Olives (Baetis) hatch in spring and fall, and a micro-caddis hatch starts in late June and lasts through July. Unfortunately, the best part of the hatch happens near dusk, long after the VCNP host picks you up. Gray Duns hatch on cloudy afternoons in July and August, and Little Yellow Sallies appear in late June through July, although they aren't usually very abundant.

In the lower 3 or 4 miles of the Rio San Antonio, larger caddis (*Rhyacophilia*) and some small dark-brown stoneflies show up. Small Parachute Adams and olive, gray, and ginger parachutes, size 16 to 20; olive and peacock Elk Hair Caddis, size 14 to 18; Green Weenies (green caddis larvae), size 14 to 18; olive, natural, and dark Hare's Ear Nymphs, size 14 to 18; and Pheasant Tail Nymphs, size 14 to 18, are all flies that work here, but keep in mind that the fish will become fussier as they see more flies on this uniquely managed fishery. Be prepared for the day that 6X and 7X tippets and exact imitations become the norm on this magnificent little spring creek.

Stream Facts: Rio San Antonio on the VCNP

Season
- May through October (check for current closures).

Special Regulations
- The Valles Caldera Trust encourages catch and release, but anglers may take up to two fish; anglers must release fish larger than 13 inches.
- Anglers may catch and release until two fish are bagged, but must quit fishing if they have two fish in possession.
- To prevent the spread of whirling disease, waders and felt-soled wading boots are not allowed.
- Remember that prices, regulations, and management strategies can change at any time.
- Fees: $10.00 entrance fee for adults and a rod fee of $10.00 per adult angler per day. Children 15 years of age and younger $5.00 entrance fee and a rod fee of $5.00. Groups of four qualify for a discount of 20 percent off the total.

Trout
- Browns 8 to 12 inches, some larger.

River Miles
- Headwater spring—0
- Rito De Los Indios—5
- San Luis Creek—9
- Warm Spring—10.5
- VCNP western boundary—16

River Characteristics
- Spring creek flowing through grassy meadows. Starts out tiny, picking up water all the way to the boundary. Lower 5 miles are the best for larger browns.

River Flows
- Winter, summer, and fall: 3 to 15 cfs
- Spring runoff: 30 to 100 cfs

Campgrounds
- Las Conchas, East Fork, Jemez Falls—developed with toilets and water.

Maps

- *New Mexico Atlas & Gazetteer,* page 23; Santa Fe National Forest Map; USGS Quadrangle Maps: Jemez Springs, Redondo Peak

Agencies
- Santa Fe National Forest Jemez Ranger District, P.O. Box 150, Jemez Springs, NM 87025; 505-829-3535
- NMDGF, P.O. Box 25112, Santa Fe, NM 87504-5112
- Valles Caldera National Preserve, 1-866-382-5537; VCNP can provide a list of registered outfitters

East Fork Jemez River on the VCNP

The East Fork of the Jemez River originates as several seeps and springs in the southeastern corner of the Valles Caldera National Preserve, locally known as the Valle Grande. The springs get their water from the Sierra De Los Valles and surrounding peaks, remnants of the ancient volcano's rim. As the East Fork meanders downstream through the Valle Grande, a gigantic meadow surrounded by 9,000-foot peaks, it is reminiscent of the small spring creeks of Yellowstone National Park or southwestern Montana.

After picking up enough water to be called a creek, it continues its gentle, winding course for about 3 miles to its junction with Jaramillo and La Jara Creeks, at least doubling its flow. From there, it continues southwest for 2 miles, where it's pinched between the foothills of Redondo Peak to the northwest and Rabbit Mountain to the

The East Fork of the Jemez originates as several small springs on the eastern boundary of the VCNP.

southwest. The creek has scoured a 1½-mile-long canyon over the centuries, changing the character of the stream dramatically before it leaves the VCNP at its southern boundary with the national forest.

There are a total of around 4 or 5 miles of fishable water on the East Fork within the Preserve, of which only the lower 3 miles have enough water for practical fishing, especially during drought. On the upper 2 or 3 miles, the creek is so skinny that getting your fly in the water is a difficult task. And forget about it in a stiff breeze.

There are fish here, though, and even farther up in good years, but the tall grass along the banks cover a large portion of the 2-foot wide serpentine channel. Dabbling a fly in the open areas can produce wild rainbows 9 to 12 inches long that have somehow established themselves over the years, apparently from the days when it was a private ranch.

The astounding spacious beauty and solitude of the VCNP are reason enough to sign up for a beat on the Rio San Antonio or East Fork. Wildlife is abundant, and it's not uncommon to hear elk bugling in the distance or see an eagle fly overhead while fishing a clear spring creek for wild brown or rainbow trout, all under the rim of an ancient volcano.

Lower Rio San Antonio

The first 3 miles of the Rio San Antonio, from where it leaves the western boundary of the VCNP, resembles the upper section except that the valley narrows until it becomes a canyon just downstream of San Antonio Hot Springs. The first 2 miles of the San Antonio, from the boundary downstream as posted, is designated Special Trout Water (STW). Only artificial flies and lures with a single barbless hook may be used, and all fish must be immediately released. No trout may be in your possession.

Don't expect the quality of experience that you'd get while fishing your own beat on the VCNP just upstream, but on the plus side, you don't have to sign up for a lottery or pay any money. And there is more water to fish. Access is easy via an improved dirt road, and campers fill the parking lot at the end of the road. Tents line the riverbanks for a half-mile up and downstream of the parking area during peak season, especially on weekends. Luckily, the majority of these folks come to enjoy the hot, therapeutic spring water flowing out of San Antonio Hot Springs, not to fish.

The STW does attract a fair number of anglers, though, so avoid weekends and try late spring, early summer, and fall, when fishing is best and crowds are least. Especially during low runoff years, midday fishing in the summer can be slow due to warmer water temperatures.

The same flies recommended in the VCNP section of the river work here, but caddis and stoneflies are more prolific. The Rio San Antonio begins to change character as it turns south, transforming from a spring creek to a freestone stream, with more flow from runoff and springs, a steeper grade, and an increase in the number and size of boulders. Stream improvements at several locations provide nice pools and riffles in which to drift a fly.

If the wild browns and stocked rainbows won't come for a dry, try dropping a beadhead nymph or caddis pupa off the dry. One of the most common mistakes I see anglers make is not setting the hook every time the dry fly, or indicator, goes under during an otherwise good drift.

Just after runoff in late spring, this stretch fishes well as the trout feed on larvae and nymphs with reckless abandon after the long winter. There's usually great flow and the water may be a little off-color, so you can get closer to the fish. Nymph fishing with a green or olive caddis larva and a Beadhead Pheasant Tail Nymph can produce excellent results. Either standard or hi-stick nymphing can be very effective. As water levels drop with the arrival of summer, standard nymphing is the preferred method in order to prevent spooking trout. Drift the nymphs through the riffles and heads of pools, as well as around boulders and along undercut banks.

Pale Morning Duns come out on summer mornings and Ginger Duns hatch in the afternoon, but the fish generally don't pay much attention to the latter until the sun goes down and the spinners hit the water. Imitate them with a Ginger Quill, size 16 or 18. Fish at the heads of riffles, where the adults are popping up and down on the water's surface, laying eggs, taking off, and then dying and falling back to the water where trout are eager to devour them. August brings morning Tricos, but you must be out very early to catch the action. The trout usually stop feeding on them by the time most anglers hit the water. The first and last two hours of light are best at this time of year.

Access to this section of the San Antonio is from La Cueva, located on NM 126 near the intersection of NM 4 and 126. From the intersection, go west on NM 126 for about 3 miles and turn right on FR 376. Follow this for about 5 miles to the San Antonio Hot Springs parking area and the river. Go upstream to fish the STW.

A short hike downstream will get you into the first remote canyon stretch of the Rio, where brush and rugged terrain keep most people from venturing very far down. For the hardy, solitary angler, this is a great stretch. Browns and some nice holdover rainbows inhabit this 4-mile canyon. Riffles, pools, and boulder-strewn pocket water, combined with spring creek–type features, provide some great flyfishing.

I usually hike downstream along the old road 2 or 3 miles and fish back up. I use my old Sage 7-foot, 11-inch light-line with a DT4F line and rarely have more than 2 or 3 feet of line out beyond my rod tip. I walk along the bank and sometimes in the water, holding line and leader off the water most of the time and following the fly with my rod tip, plucking fish out of every likely spot.

Over 30 years ago, when you could drive along the river, I remember going fishing up here for the first time with a friend of mine, Bob Bowker. We drove as far as we could in his '63 International Travel-All and parked. I had a Joe's Hopper tied to the end of my 7 feet of level 8-pound test, and I walked up to the first little pool where I saw a nice fish rise. I crept to the river's edge, hiding behind some tall grass, then flipped my fly in near the head of the pool and let it drift a couple of feet into the brown's feeding lane. He sucked my fly down, tugging, jumping, and trying to take me

A flyfisher enjoying an afternoon of dry-fly fishing below San Antonio Hot Springs in the Santa Fe National Forest.

under the bank, but I kept my yellow Eagle Claw fiberglass fly rod bent and eventually battled the 16½-inch buck into submission. It would end up being the largest fish bagged that day. Whenever I'm asked if I've fished the Rio San Antonio, I still think of that fish.

The lower end of this stretch can be reached by parking at the trailhead where FR 132 heads north. It's located where the Rio San Antonio crosses the road near San Antonio Campground. Observe the "no trespassing" signs just upstream of the parking area. There's about a mile of decent water right near the campground where rainbows are regularly stocked, but expect competition from spin- and baitfishers.

Below the campground, there are about 1½ miles of private water flowing through the village of La Cueva, where there are cabins, ponds, and a convenience store. At the bottom end of the village is the La Cueva Campground and the beginning of a 3½-mile stretch from hell that ends at the confluence with the East Fork of the Jemez River near Battleship Rock Campground.

NM 4 parallels the Rio all the way, and numerous pullouts provide easy access, but the river itself is as treacherous as it is beautiful, with steep banks, boulder-strewn whitewater, plunge pools, and waterfalls. The habitat is excellent for producing the largest browns in the river, and pressure is generally light except near the campgrounds (Dark Canyon, Indian Head, and Battleship Rock).

From just below La Cueva Campground downstream about 1½ miles to Spence Hot Springs, the river is steep, fast, and littered with giant boulders that you occasionally have to climb over or around. I use breathable, stocking-foot hip waders and a durable hiking-style wading boot with special rubber soles designed for water and land. They're the best soles I've found for combination hiking/wading.

Stay along the river's edge, entering the water only to reach a distant pocket. Keep casts short except in some of the large plunge pools, where a longer cast to the head of the pool may be required to catch the wild browns and occasional holdover rainbows that average 10 to 13 inches (some over 16 inches). My personal best was an 18-inch buck, caught one evening during a caddis hatch. Three inches of him was head and jaw, but he put up a good fight, trying to take me under his favorite boulder several times before giving up.

In addition to the insects found farther upstream, this stretch has a healthy stonefly population. Large Salmonflies start hatching in May when the river is usually still high. In low-water years, it will already be clearing by then. The river is quite fishable by late May, when the hatch is in full swing.

Dark stonefly nymphs, size 8 to 12, fished deep can produce excellent results. Tight-line nymphing is the best technique for fishing the fast, deep pockets and pools, but if there are flies on the water or in the air I immediately switch to a Bird's Stonefly, size 10 or 12. If they won't take the dead-drifted fly try skittering or skipping it on the surface a few times, and be ready for vicious strikes. When you do get a strike, don't do anything until the fish takes it under; then just lift, don't set the hook hard. Fight the fish with a tight line and avoid letting it run by keeping a bent rod at all times. If a big trout gets downstream of you in this fast water, it's over.

Caddis also hatch in the evening during June, July, and even August, providing good dry-fly action.

The last 1½ miles of the Rio San Antonio from Spence Hot Springs downstream to the confluence with the East Fork has some of the best flyfishing on the river. The pools are a little larger, the fishing is a little easier, and the aquatic insects are plentiful. Various stoneflies, caddis, and mayflies are present, and surface fishing is usually good from May through November, except during spring runoff and after torrential downpours in the summer. Elk Hair Caddis, Golden Stoneflies, Terminators, Humpies, parachute mayflies, and other attractors all work well. To avoid other anglers, I usually park about ¼ mile above Battleship Rock Campground and fish upstream toward Spence Springs.

From its spring creek headwaters to the fast freestone pocket water near Spence Springs, the Rio San Antonio offers excellent flyfishing nine months a year. Most of it is open to the public, and there are plenty of campgrounds and access points. Despite the relatively easy access, you can still find productive areas to fish alone. Not bad for a stream so close to the largest metropolitan area in the state.

Stream Facts: Lower Rio San Antonio

Season
- May through November.

Special Regulations
- The first 2 miles of the San Antonio, from the boundary downstream as posted, is designated Special Trout Water (STW). Only artificial flies and lures with a single barbless hook may be used, and all fish must be immediately returned to the water. No trout may be in your possession.

Trout
- Browns and some rainbows 8 to 12 inches, some larger.

River Miles
- Forest Service/VCNP boundary—0
- Bottom of STW—2
- San Antonio Hot Springs—2.5
- San Antonio Campground—6.5
- La Cueva Campground—8.5
- Dark Canyon Campground—9.5
- Spence Springs—10
- Indian Head Campground—11
- Battleship Rock Campground—12

River Characteristics
- The upper 3 miles is a small spring creek running through meadows. The middle changes to freestone, with faster water running through a narrow canyon. The lower river is rough and rocky, with deep holes, plunge pools, and boulder-strewn pocket water, yet easy access.

River Flows
- Winter, summer, and fall: upper—15 to 25 cfs; lower—20 to 30 cfs
- Spring runoff: upper—25 to 100 cfs; lower—30 to 200 cfs

Campgrounds
- San Antonio, La Cueva, Dark Canyon, Indian Head, and Battleship Rock all have developed facilities, toilets, and water.

Maps
- *New Mexico Atlas & Gazetteer,* page 23; Santa Fe National Forest Map; USGS Quadrangle Maps: Seven Springs, Jemez Springs

Agencies
- Santa Fe National Forest Jemez Ranger District, P.O. Box 150, Jemez Springs, NM 87025; 505-829-3535
- NMDGF, P.O. Box 25112, Santa Fe, NM 87504-5112

Outfitters
The Jemez Ranger District can provide you with a list of qualified outfitters permitted to operate in the Santa Fe National Forest. Outfitters include:
- The Reel Life, Sanbusco Market Center, 500 Montezuma Ave., Santa Fe, NM 87501; 505-995-8114, 1-877-733-5543
- High Desert Angler, 460 Cerillos Road, Santa Fe, NM 87501; 505-988-7688, 1-888-988-7688, www.highdesertangler.com

The lower Rio San Antonio has plenty of wild browns from 8 to 14 inches.

The Lower East Fork of the Jemez River

From where the East Fork leaves the southern boundary of the Valles Caldera downstream to its confluence with the Rio San Antonio near Battleship Rock, there are about 11 miles of water, mostly within the Santa Fe National Forest. Several access points along NM 4 provide good coverage from top to bottom. This section flows through a tight canyon with breathtaking views of volcanic cliffs lined with pines, firs, and spruce abbreviated by occasional grassy meadows full of wildflowers. In 1990 this rare and awesome stretch of water was designated a Wild and Scenic River.

The East Fork is between 10 and 25 feet wide, and most of the time you're in a narrow canyon with cliffs or brush right up to the riverbank. This means you have to stay in the water much of the time, especially at many of the bends, where crossing is required. Hip boots or, in the summer, just wading boots are sufficient for the East Fork. The stream has slicks, riffles, pools, pockets, holes, undercut banks, and waterfalls (which create some nice swimming holes).

Wild browns and a strain of wild rainbows, as well as stocked rainbows, inhabit

the East Fork. Dry-fly fishing can be excellent, and a dry-dropper combo will almost always produce trout up to 16 inches in the deeper holes. The area has become very popular in recent years among hikers, bikers, and anglers, and it's not uncommon to see people even after walking a mile from your vehicle. Most won't be fishing, though, so you can usually find some unfished water, especially in the lower canyon.

From the boundary of the VCNP downstream about 1½ miles to Las Conchas Campground, there's a nice stretch of fly water that doesn't get a great deal of pressure due to the difficult nature of the trail upstream of the campground. A short walk up usually weeds out most anglers.

The East Fork of the Jemez varies from high meadows to rugged canyons with waterfalls that drop over 40 feet.

The water is clear and, except in the faster flows near boulders, the wild rainbows and browns can be difficult to fool. Much like on the VCNP, the trout will spook easily, especially during low-water conditions. Light tippets, delicate casts, and drag-free drifts are necessary to catch the trout, which average 8 to 12 inches. There are many riffles and pools and some undercut banks where the river opens up a little bit in narrow meadows. Try small olive and peacock caddis, size 16 to 18, and olive or gray parachutes, size 16 to 20. If you don't get a rise, try dropping a dark Beadhead Hare's Ear or Pheasant Tail Nymph, size 18, off the dry fly.

NM 4 crosses the river less than a half-mile downstream, and there is a small parking area here. A short hike downstream will get you away from the baitfishers and picnickers and into a beautiful meadow section of the Fork. I usually walk about 2 miles to the where the meadow narrows down to a tight canyon, at the beginning of the upper East Fork Box. From there, I fish back toward the parking area through the meadow.

There are plenty of browns and a few rainbows eager to take your fly early in the morning and again late in the evening. During late spring and fall, fishing can be good most of the day, especially if Baetis are hatching. If they are, try an Olive Dun, size 18; otherwise, use a caddis pattern, Stimulator, or hopper with a nymph or caddis larva trailer.

If you are the adventurous type, try the East Fork Box just downstream from the end of the meadow. Rugged, rocky, and nearly impossible to wade, the Box requires a lot of scrambling and climbing, sometimes on all fours, up and down cliffs to get to the deep, gin-clear pools at the base of magnificent cascades and waterfalls. Some of these pools hold nice fish. The last time I fished the Box, I caught over 50 trout, several over 12 inches, and I had over 20 strikes in a couple of the larger pools. Try the same flies mentioned above, but if you're not getting good dry-fly action, try stripping a Woolly Bugger, size 10 to 14, through the deep holes and pockets. Don't be surprised if you turn some browns up to 16 or even 18 inches.

The west end of the Box can be accessed about 4 miles downstream, where NM 4 crosses the Fork. Walk upstream from the parking area through the meadow for about 10 minutes to beat the crowds and start fishing the riffles, pools, and foam lines that are loaded with 10- to 12-inch browns and a few rainbows. You'll come to the VCNP boundary after about a half-mile, and a trail will lead you over the ridge and into the west entrance to the Box.

From the NM 4 river crossing downstream to Jemez Falls there is a lovely, quiet 1½-mile stretch offering excellent dry-fly fishing from May through November. The best access is about three-quarters of a mile past the river crossing, where you turn left on FR 133 to Jemez Falls Campground. Park in the day-use lot and follow one of several trails over the edge, upstream of the falls.

The pools are picturesque, with waterfalls, lush riverbanks, and an abundance of shade cast by trees and the canyon walls. The canyon comes right to the river's edge in some areas, but most pools are shallow along the shore, so moving upstream is not very difficult. Fish rise regularly to various hatches, especially in the shady areas.

The hardest part of fishing here is paying attention to your fly when there are so many beautiful things to look at all around you. The sights and sounds in this volcanic canyon are fascinating.

From Jemez Falls downstream to its confluence with the Rio San Antonio, there are about 3 more miles of great dry-fly fishing. Several waterfalls plunge into deep holes compressed by the canyon walls in the first mile, creating almost unfishable conditions. Unless you are an expert rock climber who has ropes to repel down the sheer cliffs, you need to be willing to scramble around the rim looking for game trails down to the bottom of the canyon, which may only allow you to fish one or two pools before you hit another dead end.

It's far better to follow NM 4 to Battleship Rock Campground, where the Rio San Antonio joins the East Fork. From the day-use parking area, follow the East Fork upstream toward the hot springs. A 10-minute walk will get you away to solitary fishing, and you'll find a nice variety of water, including some deep holes with decent browns and a few rainbows. There's a lot of brush, though, so keep casts short. Caddis, Stimulators, and hoppers with droppers work well here when fish are taking dries. In the fall, try black or black and brown Woolly Buggers.

The first 1½ miles from the confluence up to the hot springs is actually fishable in the winter, and on nice sunny days you might catch some fish. Try small nymphs, micro-eggs, and Woolly Buggers stripped slowly through the deeper holes.

The East Fork offers excellent dry-fly fishing nine months out of the year, combined with some of the prettiest water and some of the most spectacular scenery in the state. If you're willing to walk a little you can escape the crowds and catch rainbows and browns that average 10 to 12 inches, with some to 16 inches.

Stream Facts: East Fork Jemez River

Season
• April through November.

Trout
• Wild browns and rainbows and stocked rainbows 8 to 12 inches, some larger.

River Miles
• Boundary of Forest Service and VCNP—0
• Las Conchas Campground—1.5
• NM 4 bridge—6.5
• Jemez Falls Campground—8
• Lower Jemez Falls—9
• East Fork Hot Springs—10.5
• Confluence with Rio San Antonio—12

River Characteristics
- The East Fork combines meadows and canyons, slick glides and undercut grassy banks, plunge pools, waterfalls, and boulder-strewn pockets. Much of the stream requires short to long hikes over sometimes rugged terrain, especially near the falls.

River Flows
- Winter, summer, and fall: 10 to 20 cfs; flash floods up to 200 cfs
- Spring runoff: 25 to 150 cfs

Campgrounds
- Las Conchas, developed with toilets.
- East Fork, developed with toilets and water.
- Jemez Falls, developed with 51 sites, toilets and water.
- Battleship Rock, developed with toilets and water.

Maps
- *New Mexico Atlas & Gazetteer,* page 23; Santa Fe National Forest Map; USGS Quadrangle Maps: Redondo Peak, Jemez Springs

Agencies
- Santa Fe National Forest Jemez Ranger District, P.O. Box 150, Jemez Springs, NM 87025; 505-829-3535
- NMDGF, P.O. Box 25112, Santa Fe, NM 87504-511

Outfitters
The Jemez Ranger District can provide you with a list of qualified outfitters permitted to operate in the Santa Fe National Forest. Outfitters include:
- The Reel Life, Sanbusco Market Center, 500 Montezuma Ave., Santa Fe, NM 87501; 505-995-8114, 1-877-733-5543
- High Desert Angler, 460 Cerillos Road, Santa Fe, NM 87501; 505-988-7688, 1-888-988-7688, www.highdesertangler.com

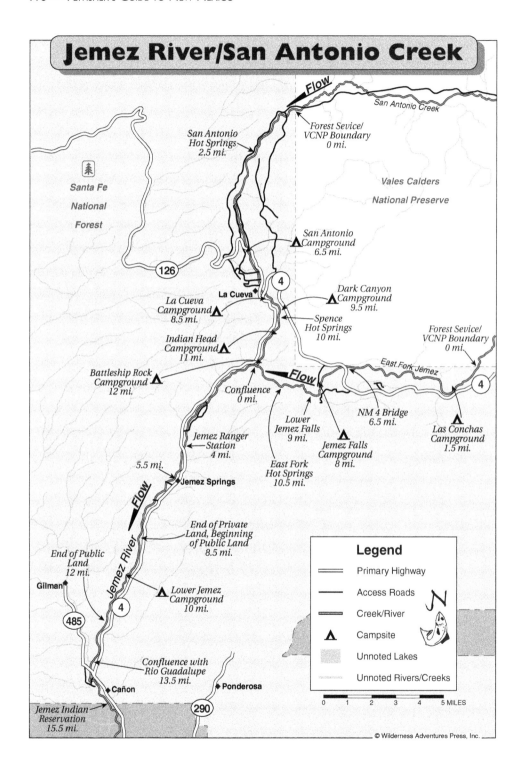

Jemez River/San Antonio Creek

Flow

San Antonio Creek

Forest Sevice/
VCNP Boundary
0 mi.

San Antonio
Hot Springs
2.5 mi.

Vales Calders
National Preserve

Santa Fe

National

Forest

San Antonio
Campground
6.5 mi.

126

La Cueva

Dark Canyon
Campground
9.5 mi.

La Cueva
Campground
8.5 mi.

Spence
Hot Springs
10 mi.

Forest Sevice/
VCNP Boundary
0 mi.

Indian Head
Campground
11 mi.

East Fork Jemez

Battleship Rock
Campground
12 mi.

Flow

4

Confluence
0 mi.

NM 4 Bridge
6.5 mi.

Lower
Jemez Falls
9 mi.

Las Conchas
Campground
1.5 mi.

Jemez Ranger
Station
4 mi.

Jemez Falls
Campground
8 mi.

5.5 mi.

East Fork
Hot Springs
10.5 mi.

Flow

Jemez Springs

End of Private
Land, Beginning
of Public Land
8.5 mi.

End of Public
Land
12 mi.

Legend

Gilman

Jemez River

Flow

Lower Jemez
Campground
10 mi.

Primary Highway

Access Roads

Creek/River

Campsite

Unnoted Lakes

Unnoted Rivers/Creeks

N

485

4

Confluence with
Rio Guadalupe
13.5 mi.

Cañon

Ponderosa

0   1   2   3   4   5 MILES

Jemez Indian
Reservation
15.5 mi.

290

© Wilderness Adventures Press, Inc.

The Jemez River

The Jemez River begins at the confluence of the Rio San Antonio and the East Fork of the Jemez River near Battleship Rock. From Battleship Rock downstream about 15 miles to the confluence of the Rio Guadalupe, the Jemez is a year-round fishery. Below that, it loses quality as a trout fishery and enters Indian land where fishing is not allowed.

The majority of the 15-mile stretch is also private, significantly limiting the amount of accessible water on the Jemez. There is public access just below Battleship Rock for a short distance, about ½ mile of public water between Soda Dam and the village of Jemez Springs, and about 3 or 4 miles of public water (off and on) between the village of Jemez Springs and the confluence with Rio Guadalupe. The Forest Service District Office is located on the north end of Jemez Springs, where anglers can get maps, information on camping, fire restrictions, and area closures.

The Jemez runs through a rusty-colored sandstone canyon. Cottonwoods, alders, and willows line the banks, creating shade, undercut banks, and great habitat for trout. The river is approximately 15 to 30 feet wide, and the river bottom has pebbles, bedrock, silt, sand, and clay, with some larger boulders and downed logs that provide plenty of sheltering lies for larger trout. During runoff (March through mid-May) and after summer cloudbursts, the river runs off-color, making flyfishing impossible for a day or two. When this happens I just move up to a headwater stream above the runoff.

Stoneflies begin hatching in May, and fishing can be quite good on large dry flies with nymph droppers. If they're taking the dry fly often, I remove the dropper so I can cast tighter into the banks and under overhanging brush, where the larger browns tend to hide. Because this area is the first place anglers can fish coming from Albuquerque—and because NM 4 runs right next to the water—the river receives a lot of pressure, especially from baitfishers. The state stocks the area heavily and regularly.

By summer, caddis and mayflies are hatching regularly and evening dry-fly fishing during the feeding frenzy can be quite good. Midday fishing is very slow, so I usually go upstream to the headwaters or just take a break and have some lunch and a cold beer.

Fall fishing on the Jemez can be quite good as the water temperatures cool off. Browns and rainbows will generally take hoppers, Stimulators, caddis, and parachute mayflies. By late fall, streamers, assorted nymphs, and golden micro-eggs usually start to produce because the wild browns start running in preparation for their spawn.

Because of the lower altitude and numerous springs that enter the river, the Jemez River offers solid winter flyfishing. The river remains ice-free and snow rarely sticks around very long. Midges hatch all winter long, and on warm days there will be a few Baetis out. Later in the winter, occasional weak caddis hatches will bring trout to the surface, particularly in the slower pools. Nymph fishing with small flashback nymphs, pupae, and bright midge larvae can also be very productive for wild browns and rainbows (which are stocked all winter long). Drop these flies in the deeper pools, holes, and riffles.

Access to the Jemez River from Albuquerque is via I-25 to US 550 west to San Ysidro. Then take NM 4 to the Santa Fe National Forest boundary and the confluence of the Rio Guadalupe and the Jemez River. From Los Alamos, drive west on NM 4 for 33 to 40 miles. NM 4 parallels the Jemez for its entire length, and several pullouts and the lower Jemez Campground provide good access.

The Jemez River only has a few miles of fishable water, but it's the largest of the Jemez area streams and it provides year-round flyfishing. Try it some fall, winter, or spring day; you won't regret it.

Stream Facts: Jemez River

Season
• April through November.

Trout
• Wild browns from 8 to 14 inches, some to 18 inches; stocked rainbows 8 to 12 inches, some larger holdovers are present.

River Miles
• Confluence of the East Fork and Rio San Antonio—0
• Jemez Ranger Station—4
• Jemez Springs—5.5
• End of private land, beginning of public land—8.5
• Lower Jemez Campground—10
• End of public land—12
• Confluence with Rio Guadalupe—13.5
• Jemez Indian Reservation—15.5

River Characteristics
• The Jemez is medium-sized, approximately 15 to 30 feet wide, with good cover and holding lies. During runoff (March through mid-May) and after summer cloudbursts, the river may run off-color temporarily. Move up to a headwater stream at these times.

River Flows
• Winter, summer, and fall: 25 to 40 cfs
• Spring runoff: 50 to 200 cfs

Campgrounds
• Battleship Rock, developed with toilets and water.

Maps
- *New Mexico Atlas & Gazetteer,* page 23; Santa Fe National Forest Map; USGS Quadrangle Maps: Jemez Springs, Ponderosa

Agencies
- Santa Fe National Forest Jemez Ranger District, P.O. Box 150, Jemez Springs, NM 87025; 505-829-3535
- NMDGF, P.O. Box 25112, Santa Fe, NM 87504-5112

Outfitters
The Jemez Ranger District can provide you with a list of qualified outfitters permitted to operate in the Santa Fe National Forest. Outfitters include:
- The Reel Life, Sanbusco Market Center, 500 Montezuma Ave., Santa Fe, NM 87501; 505-995-8114, 1-877-733-5543
- High Desert Angler, 460 Cerillos Road, Santa Fe, NM 87501; 505-988-7688, 1-888-988-7688, www.highdesertangler.com

The lower Jemez is the largest stream in the area and offers year-round fishing, except during runoff and after heavy thunderstorms.

JEMEZ AREA STREAMS MAJOR HATCHES

Insect	J	F	M	A	M	J	J	A	S	O	N	D	Time	Flies
Caddis													Larva-M Pupa-M/A/E Adult-A/E	Green & olive caddis larva #12–#16; Double Hackle Peacock #12–#16; La Fontaine's Caddis Pupa # 12–#18; Van's Rag Pupa #10–#18; Lawson's Caddis Emerger #12–#18; olive, tan & gray Elk Hair Caddis #12–#20; olive, gray & peacock Fluttering Caddis #10–#18
Craneflies													Larva-M/E	Cranefly larva peacock, gray or dark olive #6–#16; Taylor Streit's Poundmeister #6–#14
Gray Drake													M/A/SF	Olive Hare's Ear #10–#14; Green & Gray Drake Hair-Wing (Wulff style) #10–#14; Green & Gray Paradrake #10–#14; Gray Drake spinner #12–#14
Ginger, Yellow, Blue & Mahogany Duns													M/E	Light, dark & olive Hare's Ear Nymph #12–#18; Pheasant Tail Nymph #12–#18; light, dark, pink & ginger Hair-Wing Duns or Cahills #12–#18 or the same in parachutes
Baetis													M/A/SF	Dark olive Hare's Ear Nymph #16–#22; Pheasant Tail #16–#22; Van's Rag Fly Nymph dark olive #16–#22; Lawson's BWO Fan-Wing Emerger #16–#22; Olive Parachutechute #16–#22; Olive Comparadun #16–#22

Hatch Time Code: M = Morning; A = Afternoon; E = Evening; D = Dark; SF = Spinner Fall

JEMEZ AREA STREAMS MAJOR HATCHES (cont.)

Insect	J	F	M	A	M	J	J	A	S	O	N	D	Time	Flies
Salmonfly, Golden Stonefly, Yellow Sally					█	█							M/A	Black & brown stonefly nymph #6–#10; Elk Hair Salmon Fly #6–#12; Golden Stonefly Nymph #12–#16; Orange & Gold Stimulators #6–#16; Terminator #12–#16
Little Brown Stonefly			█	█									M/E	Dark Brown Hare's Ear #12–#16; Brown Elk Hair Caddis #12–#16
PMDs, PEDs							█	█					M/SF	Light Hare's Ear Nymph #12–#18; Pheasant Tail #12–#20; Van's Rag Fly Nymph light olive #14–#20; Lawson's Fan-Wing Emerger #14–#22; PMD, PED #12–#20; Hair-Wing or PW Ginger Dun #14–#20, Parachute ginger, light olive #14–#20
Terrestrials						█	█	█	█				M/A	Para-hoppers tan, yellow #8–#14; Dave's Hoppers #6–#14; Bees #12–#14; black & two-tone ants #14–#18; black & peacock beetles #12–#18

Hatch Time Code: M = Morning; A = Afternoon; E = Evening; D = Dark; SF = Spinner Fall

RIO CEBOLLA, RIO DE LAS VACAS, AND RIO GUADALUPE

The Rio Guadalupe gets its water from springs and snowmelt coming from the Rio Cebolla and Rio de Las Vacas watersheds. The Rio de Las Vacas and its main tributary, Rito Penas Negras, combine to provide several miles of quality, yet difficult, flyfishing for small, wary browns and Rio Grande cutthroats.

Rio Cebolla

I was only 17 years old the first time I fished the Rio Cebolla. I was with a bunch of my cronies on a fishing trip to Fenton Lake. For them, fishing meant sitting on the shore of a lake next to a spinning rod loaded with bait, eating junk food, and drinking beer. This was just before the days of float tubes, and I didn't care too much about flyfishing for stocked rainbows with an army of baitfishers, so I worked my way around to the dam.

I peered over the edge and saw a beautiful little creek flowing through a lush, green meadow. I scrambled down to the first little pool, where I saw a couple of nice browns. I stayed wide as I walked down below them, then turned and crept back up to the base of the pool. I had a size 16 Adams on my leader, and using a bow cast, I flipped the fly to the top of the little pool. No sooner had it hit the water than the race was on to see which brown was going to get it. The smaller of the two won, and soon I had the fat 13-inch in the creel.

The next cast produced the other brown, a 15-inch buck that was as fat as it was long. I walked downstream about a half-mile and fished my way back up, catching nice browns in every bend of the creek, and one big rainbow, until I had my limit. Back at camp, most of my buddies were napping or eating. Only one was still fishing, and all they'd caught between them was a couple of stockers. I'll never forget the expressions on their faces when I dumped my creel into the 5-gallon bucket. The 16 browns between 12 and 18 inches nearly filled it. We had a great fish fry that night.

I do miss the days when there were so few anglers that you didn't worry about catch and release. Thank God we practice it now, though, or streams like this would be ruined—just like many others have been, due to lack of special regulations and too much harvesting of wild trout. To repay my debt, several years later I helped the Sangre de Cristo Flyfishers club lobby the NMDGF to get special regulations implemented on this little gem. It was during this time that I realized I had actually been trespassing on private land that day in 1975. Public land doesn't start until about a mile below Fenton Lake. I'm sure it's well posted these days.

The first regulations started with a mile of water located about 3 miles below the lake, where a daily bag limit of two trout over 12 inches was instituted. That's now been eliminated, and a stretch of catch-and-release water has been added in the headwaters above Seven Springs Hatchery. Even though it's the same creek above the lake, the fishery is nowhere near as good as it is below Fenton. The average fish in the new STW is about 9 to 11 inches, while the average fish in the old STW below Fenton Lake was 12 to 15 inches.

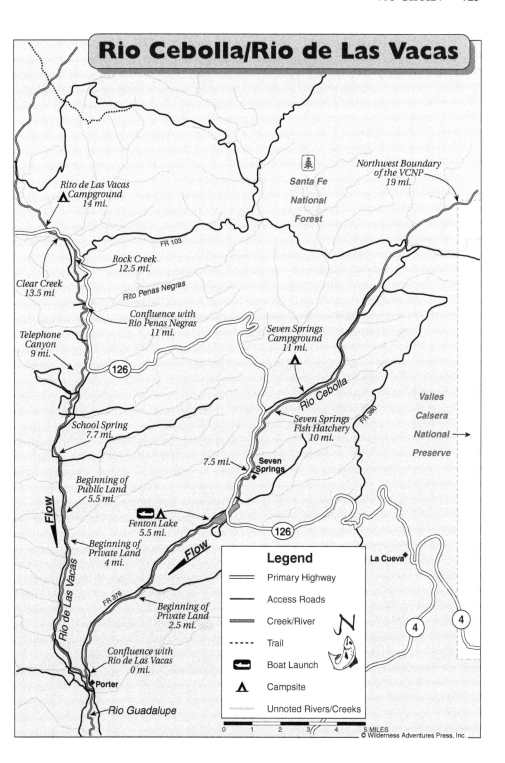

Rio Cebolla/Rio de Las Vacas

Santa Fe National Forest

Northwest Boundary of the VCNP
19 mi.

Rito de Las Vacas Campground
14 mi.

FR 103

Rock Creek
12.5 mi.

Clear Creek
13.5 mi

Rito Penas Negras

Confluence with Rio Penas Negras
11 mi.

Telephone Canyon
9 mi.

126

Seven Springs Campground
11 mi.

Rio Cebolla

Valles Calsera National → Preserve

School Spring
7.7 mi.

Seven Springs Fish Hatchery
10 mi.

FR 380

Beginning of Public Land
5.5 mi.

7.5 mi.

Seven Springs

Flow

Fenton Lake
5.5 mi.

126

La Cueva

Beginning of Private Land
4 mi.

Flow

Rio de Las Vacas

FR 376

Beginning of Private Land
2.5 mi.

Legend

Primary Highway	
Access Roads	
Creek/River	
Trail	
Boat Launch	
Campsite	
Unnoted Rivers/Creeks	

N

4

4

Confluence with Rio de Las Vacas
0 mi.

Porter

Rio Guadalupe

0 1 2 3 4 5 MILES
© Wilderness Adventures Press, Inc.

Adding the new water was a good idea, but the decision to trade or eliminate the old STW made no sense, which is often true of the fisheries management decisions the NMDGF makes each year. Basically, their idea of fisheries management is to build more hatcheries and stock more inferior fish, rather than improve habitat and wild fish stocks, which most modern fisheries programs now try to do. They fight, kick, scratch, and bite every time flyfishers push them to enact special regulations or reduce bag limits, even though their own data shows there aren't enough fish for everyone to keep their limit while maintaining fisheries.

Amazingly, flyfishing clubs, groups, and individuals have still managed to get some great stretches of water designated as Special Trout Water, although it amounts to less than 10 percent of all the quality fisheries in the state. As with most things in New Mexico, we'll be the last state to get on board. I'm grateful that most New Mexico flyfishers are light years ahead of the NMDGF in their management practices and voluntarily release most, or all, fish they catch.

Beginning as several small springs near the northwest rim of the Valles Caldera, the Rio Cebolla flows south through a beautiful, meadow-filled valley for about 6 miles to the Seven Springs Day-Use Area. The entire stretch has been designated a STW. Anglers can use only artificial flies and lures with a single barbless hook, and all trout must be immediately returned to the water.

The Rio Cebolla is just a small meadow creek, but the deep holes and undercut banks shelter amazingly large trout.

The creek is small in this upper section, rarely over 4 feet wide, and tall grass, trees, and willows hang over the bank, making casting difficult at times. Stealth is important here, and the slightest breeze can make hitting the water with your fly quite a challenge. But if you do get it in the water, you'll usually get a strike because the creek is teeming with 6- to 10-inch browns. This is the perfect place for a 7-foot, 2-weight. The fish aren't picky. Hatches are insignificant, and any good attractor, size 14 to 18, will usually work.

The first mile or two above the Seven Springs Hatchery has a good rainbow population, and several beaver ponds provide good holding water for them and some large browns. Be prepared to share the area with other flyfishers and spinfishers on weekends, but during the week it's not so bad—at least not the last time I was there.

To reach the upper Rio Cebolla from La Cueva, go west on NM 126 about 9 miles to Fenton Lake, then continue on about 3½ miles to FR 314 and the Seven Springs Hatchery. FR 314, a decent dirt and gravel road, follows the river to Seven Springs Campground and extends a short distance beyond.

The lower Rio Cebolla has about 4 miles of excellent water. The first mile is situated about a mile below Fenton Lake between two parcels of private land. Access is difficult, but a cross-country hike along the northwest side of the lake and creek, staying out of the private property, will get you there. The other 3 miles continue below the private property. To get there from La Cueva, go west on NM 126 about 3 miles and turn left on FR 376. Go about 6 miles to where FR 376 crosses the Rio Cebolla. The public water extends from the crossing downstream to the confluence with the Rio de Las Vacas, where the Rio Guadalupe begins.

The first mile below the crossing used to be a STW, but general regulations now apply. However, few anglers fish here, and those that do are usually catch-and-release flyfishers. For such a small stream, it has some very good habitat for the large browns that live there. There are numerous bends with deep undercut banks and good overhang from grass and shrubs. Browns up to 18 inches can be found in the deeper bends and drops, while 8- to 14-inch browns show up everywhere else. Don't be surprised if you catch an occasional holdover rainbow.

Like the upper Cebolla, the trout here are opportunistic, and dry-fly fishing can be excellent. The same kind of attractors work, but hoppers and Stimulators are particularly effective. If dries won't work, add a 12-inch dropper with a dark Beadhead Hare's Ear or Pheasant Tail. Fish upstream and keep a low profile, crawling when necessary to prevent spooking fish. In the fall, small dries, nymphs, micro-eggs, and Woolly Buggers can produce some nice browns.

The Rio Cebolla is just a tiny creek, but it offers some of the best dry-fly action in the Jemez region for large trout. To really enjoy it, camp out and fish the upper Cebolla one day and the lower Cebolla the next. There's developed camping at Seven Springs Campground just north of the hatchery and at Fenton Lake. Primitive camping is available along FR 376.

Stream Facts: Rio Cebolla

Season
- May through November.

Special Regulations
- From the Seven Springs Day-Use Area upstream through the headwaters, anglers can use only artificial flies and lures with a single barbless hook, and all trout must be immediately returned to the water, no trout in possession.

Trout
- Wild browns and stocked rainbows 8 to 16 inches, some larger.

River Miles
- Confluence with Rio de Las Vacas—0
- Beginning of private land—2.5
- Fenton Lake—5.5
- Seven Springs—7.5
- Seven Springs Hatchery—10
- Seven Springs Campground—11
- Northwest boundary of the VCNP—19

River Characteristics
- The upper Cebolla is a tiny, meandering meadow stream with undercut banks. The lower Cebolla is larger, with more deep holes and undercut banks.

River Flows
- Winter, summer, and fall: 5 to 10 cfs
- Spring runoff: 10 to 50 cfs

Campgrounds
- Seven Springs, developed with toilets and water.
- Fenton Lake, developed with toilets and water.

Maps
- *New Mexico Atlas & Gazetteer,* page 23; Santa Fe National Forest Map; USGS Quadrangle Maps: Seven Springs, San Miguel Mountain

Agencies and Outfitters
- NMDGF, P.O. Box 25112, Santa Fe, NM 87504-5112

The Jemez Ranger District can provide you with a list of qualified outfitters permitted to operate in the Santa Fe National Forest. Outfitters include:
- High Desert Angler, 460 Cerillos Road, Santa Fe, NM 87501; 505-988-7688, 1-888-988-7688, www.highdesertangler.com
- The Reel Life, Sanbusco Market Center, 500 Montezuma Ave., Santa Fe, NM 87501; 505-995-8114, 1-877-733-5543

Rio de Las Vacas

Fishing on the Rio de Las Vacas and Rito Penas Negras is best right after runoff, from the first part of May through June, when there is good flow. By July the water is shallow and barely moving over exposed rocks, weeds, and woody material, and the trout are so skittish that only the sneakiest and most skilled angler can deliver a cast without spooking every fish in the pool. Even when flows are good, an angler must be patient and approach a pool or run carefully from below, using every possible object to help disguise his presence.

Look carefully into the area you're going to fish, using good polarized sunglasses and a hat to reduce glare and spot the fish you want to cast to. Do not false cast over the fish. False cast with a short line well to the side and then shoot the remaining line on the delivery cast or just roll cast the pre-measured line, aiming so that your fly lands just a foot or two above the target. If you cast too far above, a smaller fish may get to the fly before your targeted fish, thus spooking the larger fish and the entire pool. Then it's off to the next good spot, which are few and far between for the most part.

There are basically two stretches to fish on the Vacas. The lower section runs upstream from its confluence with the Rio Cebolla for a little over 4 miles to the boundary of the Ranchos de Chaparral Girl Scout Camp. The upper Vacas begins at the upper boundary of the Girl Scout camp and extends 8 miles upstream to the headwaters near the Rio de Las Vacas Campground. The Rito Penas Negras adds an additional 6 or 7 miles of decent water, where you're likely to connect with a Rio Grande cutthroat.

The lower Vacas can be reached from Jemez by taking NM 4 north for about 4 miles. Turn left on NM 485 and follow it as it parallels the Rio Guadalupe and then turns into FR 376 at Deer Creek Landing. Continue on this road to the confluence of Rio Cebolla and Rio de Las Vacas. Veer left onto FR 539, which puts you on the Rio de Las Vacas. The best fishing is in the upper mile, just below the Girl Scout camp. Here, you'll find mostly browns and the occasional rainbow from 9 to 12 inches.

Unfortunately, the public can't continue up FR 539 through the Girl Scout camp, so to get to the upper Vacas, which is just 1½ miles upstream from the southern boundary of the camp, you must enter from the north. From Fenton Lake, take NM 126 west for about 11 miles and turn left on FR 20/539, which follows the upper Vacas downstream for 3 miles to the northern boundary of the Girl Scout camp. This stretch combines meadows and canyon, rainbows and browns, and the habitat is better than in the lower Vacas—so is the fishing.

The two miles above NM 126 are private, and the Rito Penas Negras enters the Vacas at the top end of the private stretch. Above the Rito Penas, the Vacas is very skinny and fishing is almost impossible all the way to the Rio de Las Vacas Campground. The Rito Penas Negras, on the other hand, has good flows and some good dry-fly fishing for Rio Grande cutthroats. It's a slow, pastoral stream winding through grassy meadows, and there are plenty of bends with deep holes and undercut banks. The first 3 miles, from the forest boundary upstream, has better flows, more deep holes, and is better suited for flyfishing than the rest of the creek. As with the Vacas, fishing is difficult and the channel is narrow, making accurate casts mandatory.

Hatches on both the Vacas and the Rito are sparse, but hoppers, ants, and moths are plentiful. Use any terrestrial or attractor in sizes 12 to 16. Larger flies will generally result in short takes.

Stream Facts: Rio de Las Vacas

Season
• April through October.

Trout
• Browns, rainbows, and Rio Grande cutthroats 8 to 12 inches, occasional larger trout.

River Miles
• Porter Landing and confluence with Rio Cebolla and beginning of
  Rio Guadalupe—0
• Beginning of private property—4
• Beginning of public property—5.5
• School Spring—7.7
• Telephone Canyon—9
• Confluence with Rito Penas Negras—11
• Rock Creek—12.5
• Clear Creek—13.5
• Rito de Las Vacas Campground—14

River Characteristics
• The upper Vacas and Rito Penas Negras are small, meandering meadow creeks, and the lower Vacas is a shallow meadow stream, but wider with some broken water caused by rocks and boulders.

River Flows
• Winter, summer, and fall: upper Vacas—5 to 10 cfs; lower Vacas—10 to 15 cfs
• Spring runoff: 15 to 100 cfs

Campgrounds
• Clear Creek, developed with toilets and water.
• Rio de las Vacas, developed with toilets and water.

Maps
• *New Mexico Atlas & Gazetteer,* page 23; Santa Fe National Forest Map; USGS Quadrangle Maps: San Miguel Mountain, Rancho del Chaparral

Agencies and Outfitters
- NMDGF, P.O. Box 25112, Santa Fe, NM 87504-5112

The Jemez Ranger District can provide you with a list of qualified outfitters permitted to operate in the Santa Fe National Forest. Outfitters include:
- High Desert Angler, 460 Cerillos Road, Santa Fe, NM 87501; 505-988-7688, 1-888-988-7688, www.highdesertangler.com
- The Reel Life, Sanbusco Market Center, 500 Montezuma Ave., Santa Fe, NM 87501; 505-995-8114, 1-877-733-5543

Rio Guadalupe

The Rio Guadalupe begins at the confluence of the Rio Cebolla and the Rio de Las Vacas. It then flows about 12 miles to its confluence with the Jemez River just 4½ miles north of the village of Jemez. All but the lower 3 miles of the Guadalupe runs through public land. Access from Jemez is via NM 4. Go about 4 miles north and turn left on NM 485 (a paved road), then go about 3 miles to the entrance to the Santa Fe National Forest.

Despite the easy access, the Guadalupe receives only moderate fishing pressure, and wild browns can be found throughout its entire length. The Guadalupe Falls are located about a mile above the private land. Just past the falls, the road goes through a couple of old railroad tunnels and on up the river to Deer Creek Landing, where the terrain narrows to a box canyon.

There are nice browns up to 18 inches throughout the river, but the fishing pressure between the falls and Deer Creek Landing results in less and smaller fish on average. At Deer Creek Landing the road becomes FR 376, a maintained gravel road that weeds out a large portion of the angling public after the first mile or so. The road and river share the canyon for the next 6 miles up to the bridge at Porter and the head of the Guadalupe, where there are some good undeveloped campsites.

It often takes 10 minutes or so of rugged scrambling to get from the road to the river. Park near the side canyons and walk down from there for easier access. There's also easier access in the Special Trout Water section from Porter Landing Bridge downstream for 1.3 miles to Llano Loco Spring. Only artificial flies and lures with a single barbless hook may be used, and all trout must be immediately returned to the water. The NMDGF stocks rainbows near the bridge, and some large holdovers may reach 18 inches or so.

This upper section offers the best fishing on the Guadalupe and spectacular scenery. The channel is narrow and deep, with lots of shade provided by trees and the towering cliffs. Sometimes you'll have no choice but to wade, as the canyon walls drop right to the river's edge. Riffles, pools, holes, and pockets are consistent throughout, providing ample opportunities to catch some nice, plump browns and a few rainbows that drift downstream from Porter Landing.

Trees, brush, and grass grow along the banks, except where rocky cliffs are present, yet casting is not difficult for the seasoned small-stream flyfisher. The river is 20 to 30 feet wide in most places, with good flow and lots of broken water. Long casts are not usually required, except in some of the larger pools. Breathable chest

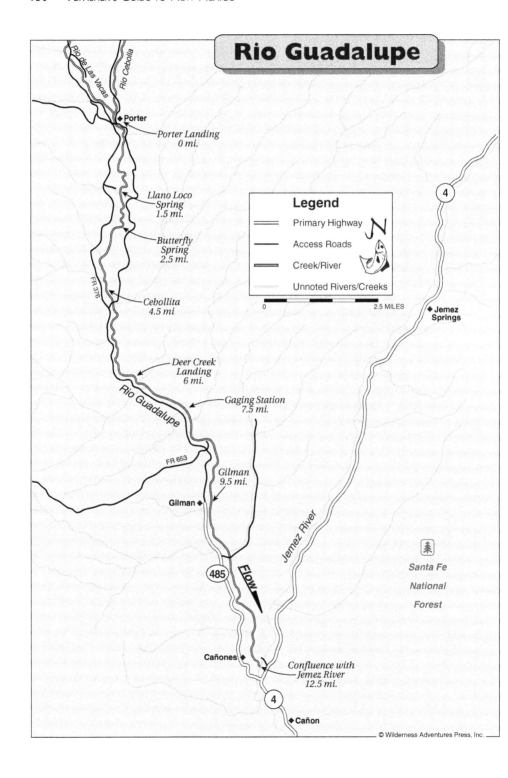

Rio Guadalupe

Rio de Las Vacas

Rio Cebolla

◆ Porter

Porter Landing
0 mi.

4

Llano Loco
Spring
1.5 mi.

Legend

N

═══ Primary Highway

─── Access Roads

═══ Creek/River

Unnoted Rivers/Creeks

Butterfly
Spring
2.5 mi.

0   2.5 MILES

◆ Jemez
Springs

FR 376

Cebollita
4.5 mi

Deer Creek
Landing
6 mi.

Rio Guadalupe

Gaging Station
7.5 mi.

FR 653

Gilman
9.5 mi.

Gilman ◆

Jemez River

485

Flow

Santa Fe

National

Forest

Cañones ◆

Confluence with
Jemez River
12.5 mi.

4

◆ Cañon

© Wilderness Adventures Press, Inc.

or pant waders with felt-soled boots with studs or cleats are best, but hip waders will suffice. More and more these days, I see anglers wet wading during the summer months, a trend that continues to grow with the record hot temperatures we've been experiencing the last few years.

Bugs are plentiful on the Guadalupe, and hatches can be prolific, causing wild browns to feed until they are literally stuffed to the gills. At the end of May 1986, I was fishing in the middle of the upper box during a magnificent stonefly hatch. The bugs were molting on rocks, flying in the air, skittering on the water, having orgies, and laying eggs. Browns were feeding in every likely spot, taking my dead drifted or skittering giant Bird's Stonefly regularly. One even took it in the air as I was skittering the fly.

The feisty 10- to 18-inch browns shredded three or four well-tied stoneflies before the day was over. Many of the plump fish had adult stoneflies coming out of their mouths, yet they still devoured my imitation. I was alone, as I am during most of the best fishing days, and I remember how wonderfully tired I felt as I made my way back to the car under the last glimmer of light. As I fell asleep in my bag that night, all I could think about were colorful browns thrashing my fly. I couldn't wait to wake up and do it again.

In addition to the stoneflies, Pale Morning Duns and Pale Evening Duns hatch from late May through June. They can be imitated using a Hairwing Ginger Dun or Pink Cahill, size 16 to 18. Large Gray Drakes hatch in July, as do Mahogany Duns. They don't usually emerge in the water, so they aren't important until after they hatch and molt into adult spinners, when they return to the river to lay eggs, providing good evening dry-fly fishing. Use a Blue or Ginger Quill, size 12 to 14.

Of course, various caddis hatch from May through September, and there are Blue Dun and Blue-Winged Olive (Baetis) hatches in September and October. For caddis, I like olive Elk Hair Caddis, size 14 to 18, and Goddard Caddis, 12 to 16. For nymphs, try dark and light Hare's Ears, size 12 to 18; olive and green caddis larvae, size 14 to 18; and olive Peeking Caddis, size 14 to 18. Fish the nymphs on a double-nymph rig with a floating indicator, using enough lead to effectively bump the bottom without hanging up too often.

The Rio Guadalupe is a great place to fish and beat most of the crowds because it offers beautiful scenery, good primitive camping, plenty of cool water, great hatches, and a healthy population of brown trout. Throw in the Rio Cebolla and the Rio de Las Vacas, and an angler could fish for days without casting over the same runs twice.

Stream Facts: Rio Guadalupe

Season
- April through November.

Special Regulations
- From Porter Landing Bridge downstream for 1.3 miles to Llano Loco Spring only artificial flies and lures with a single barbless hook may be used, and all trout must be immediately returned to the water.

Trout
- Browns and rainbows averaging 10 to 13 inches, with some to 18 inches.

River Miles
- Porter Landing—0
- Llano Loco Spring—1.5
- Butterfly Spring—2.5
- Cebollita—4.5
- Deer Creek Landing—6
- Gaging station near old railroad tunnels—7.5
- Gilman—9.5
- Confluence with the Jemez River—12.5

River Characteristics
- The Rio Guadalupe is a medium-sized freestone stream. Much of the river flows through a narrow canyon sometimes pinched into a box canyon. There are falls, plunge pools, riffles, deep holes, undercut banks, and boulder-strewn pocket water.

River Flows
- Winter, summer, and fall: 15 to 45 cfs
- Spring runoff: 50 to 200 cfs

Campgrounds
- Lower Jemez, two developed campgrounds with toilets and water.

Maps
- *New Mexico Atlas & Gazetteer,* page 23; Santa Fe National Forest Map; USGS Quadrangle Maps: San Miguel Mountain, Gilman

Agencies and Outfitters
- NMDGF, P.O. Box 25112, Santa Fe, NM 87504-5112

The Jemez Ranger District can provide you with a list of qualified outfitters permitted to operate in the Santa Fe National Forest. Outfitters include:
- High Desert Angler, 460 Cerillos Road, Santa Fe, NM 87501; 505-988-7688,

1-888-988-7688, www.highdesertangler.com
- The Reel Life, Sanbusco Market Center, 500 Montezuma Ave., Santa Fe, NM 87501; 505-995-8114, 1-877-733-5543

The Rio Guadalupe and its headwater tributaries, the Rio Cebolla and Rio de Las Vacas, fish well in every month.

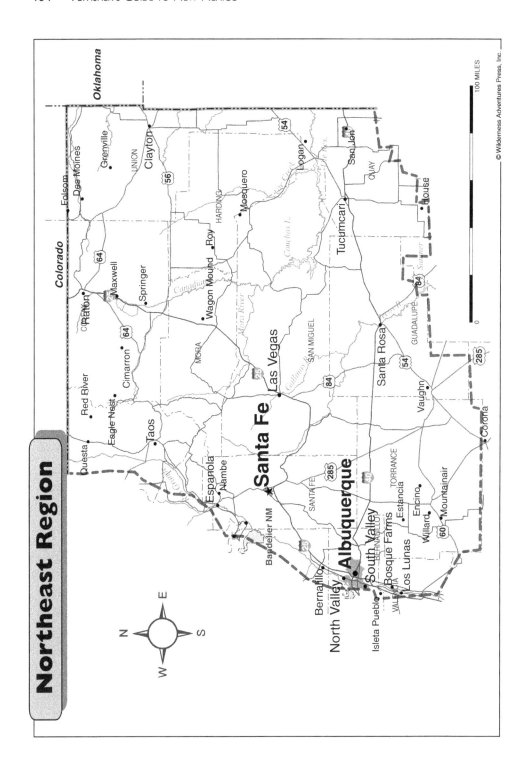

Northeast Region

Northeast Region

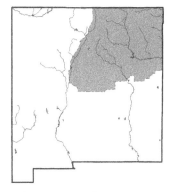

The northeast portion of New Mexico provides as much fishable water as the rest of the state combined. From the top of the Sangre de Cristo Mountains to the bottom of the Rio Grande Gorge, there are hundreds of places to cast a fly. Numerous high-mountain lakes, streams, and creeks in three wilderness areas and over 100 miles of wild rivers that are part of the Wild and Scenic River system provide a wide variety of angling opportunities.

There are millions of acres of public property, and millions more on private ranches and other properties, some of which are open to the public for a fee. There are rainbows, browns, brookies, native Rio Grande cutthroats, northern pike, and smallmouth bass to cast to, and there is great year-round flyfishing.

The climate in the northeast is quite remarkable, as well. The Sangre de Cristos are the tail end of the Rocky Mountains, and because they are so far south, our winters are shorter and milder, resulting in excellent growth rates for trout. You can fish the lower valleys and gorges in winter, yet our summers are mild due to the very high elevation—6,500 to 13,000 feet.

The mainstem Pecos has good fishing and access.

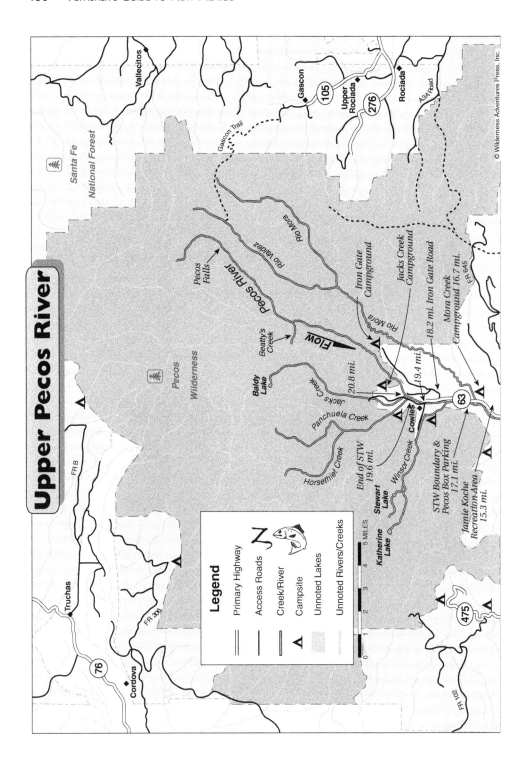

Upper Pecos River

Legend

Primary Highway

Access Roads

Creek/River

Campsite

Unnoted Lakes

Unnoted Rivers/Creeks

N

0 1 2 3 4 5 MILES

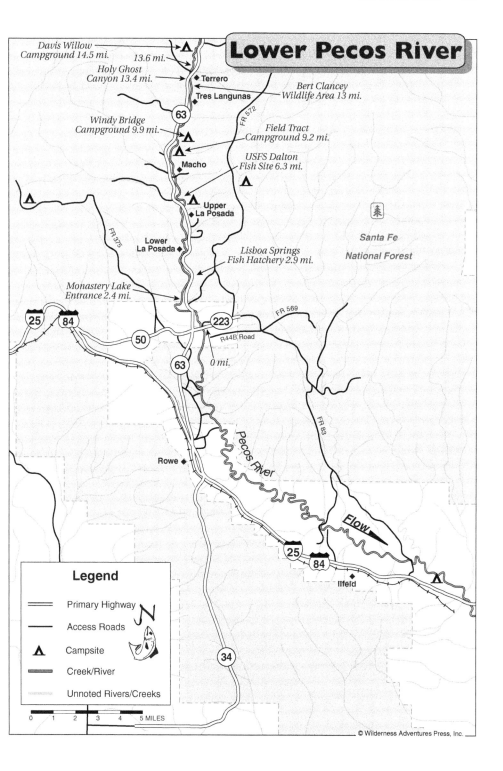

Lower Pecos River

Davis Willow Campground 14.5 mi.

13.6 mi.

Holy Ghost Canyon 13.4 mi.

◆ Terrero

▲ Tres Langunas

Bert Clancey Wildlife Area 13 mi.

FR 572

63

Windy Bridge Campground 9.9 mi.

▲

Field Tract Campground 9.2 mi.

▲

Macho

USFS Dalton Fish Site 6.3 mi.

▲

▲

▲ Upper

◆ La Posada

▲

FR 375

Lower La Posada ◆

Lisboa Springs Fish Hatchery 2.9 mi.

Santa Fe

National Forest

Monastery Lake Entrance 2.4 mi.

25   84

223

50

FR 569

R44B Road

63

0 mi.

FR 83

Rowe ◆

Pecos River

Flow

25

84

Ilfeld ◆

▲

Legend

═══ Primary Highway

─── Access Roads

▲ Campsite

═══ Creek/River

╌╌╌ Unnoted Rivers/Creeks

N

34

0 1 2 3 4 5 MILES

© Wilderness Adventures Press, Inc.

THE PECOS RIVER

The Pecos is the largest and most popular stream originating in the Sangre de Cristo Mountains within New Mexico, especially with flyfishers. I have sentimental reasons for believing this water is special; this is where I learned to dry-fly fish.

My great-grandfather Bengard designed the original hatchery at Lisboa Springs on the banks of the Pecos River, just north of the town of Pecos. He was the first superintendent of hatcheries for the NMDGF, and my grandmother grew up there. Meanwhile, my great-grandfather Beacham opened the first hardware and tackle shop in Santa Fe in 1907, and basically introduced flyfishing to New Mexicans.

His son (my grandfather), Arthur Beacham, met my grandmother and they married and lived at the hatchery. A true flyfishing fanatic, my grandfather taught my father to fish when he was a kid living at the hatchery. Years later, when I was about 14 years old, my family moved to Pecos from Santa Fe and I learned about fishing dry flies on the Pecos River and its many tributaries. Until then, I had only fished with nymphs, wet flies, and streamers.

I fished every chance I had for over four years, and in the summer I pretty much lived in the Santa Fe National Forest, hiking and fishing every lake and stream in the Pecos Wilderness. My parents were friends with Greer Garson, owner of the Forked Lightning Ranch, so I was fortunate enough to fish there a few times, also.

Working a pool on the Pecos near the Dalton fishing site.

As a teenager, I remember my dad complaining that there were ten times as many people fishing as there used to be. Ironically, my great-grandfather, William Beacham, made the same claim in an article he wrote in 1939 for *New Mexico Highway Journal* (now *New Mexico Magazine*). Even more ironic is that I said the same thing when I fished the Pecos one time about 15 years ago. It goes to show that it's all relative to the time in which we live. Each generation thinks the fishing was better and the crowds less when they were younger, and they're probably right. So goes the world. Some call it progress, but I'm not sure what to call it. Nevertheless, the Pecos and its tributaries and headwater lakes still provide excellent flyfishing opportunities in a spectacular setting and, sometimes, solitude.

The Pecos is a diverse fishery, with easy access in the lower reaches where wild brown and stocked rainbows are plentiful. In its middle reaches, narrow and deep canyons make access more difficult and wild browns more plentiful. In its headwaters, the access is by foot only among very high rugged mountain peaks. Snow collects here nine months out of the year, providing an ample volume of clean, clear, cold water for the numerous streams and creeks draining into the valleys. The headwater lakes and streams have wild Rio Grande cutthroats in addition to wild browns and cuttbows.

The Pecos Wilderness and the Headwaters of the Pecos

Situated near the southern end of the beautiful Sangre de Cristo Mountains, the Pecos Wilderness encompasses 223,333 acres of peaks, forests, lakes, streams, and mountain meadows. There is plenty of big game, including cougars, bears, deer, elk, and Rocky Mountain bighorn sheep. And the second and third highest peaks in the state are located here.

Small streams with intriguing names like Horsethief, Panchuela, and Jacks make up the headwaters of the Pecos. The most important headwaters flow is in the Pecos itself—at this point a fairly small but nonetheless distinguished stream. Along with some of the other headwater streams, the Pecos provides habitat to the rare Rio Grande cutthroat, a prized quarry for many anglers.

In their upper reaches, most of the Pecos headwater streams are located within the boundaries of the Pecos Wilderness Area, and therefore may be accessed only on foot or horseback. No wheeled vehicles of any kind are permitted inside the wilderness. Anglers interested in exploring the headwaters of the Pecos are advised to study maps of the wilderness area and to carry a compass. Flyfishers should also be aware that a moratorium currently exists on the issuance of new wilderness outfitting permits. So if you would like to hire a guide for any of the aforementioned streams, it's your responsibility to make sure your guide has the required permit to legally guide you within the Pecos Wilderness.

Within a mile of Cowles, New Mexico, Winsor Creek, Panchuela Creek, Jacks Creek, and the upper Pecos River all come together to form the main stem of the river. Each of the creeks and the river above the wilderness boundary combine to provide many miles of prime small-creek fishing for wild browns, as well as more Rio Grande cutthroats the farther up in the watershed you get.

When fishing in the Pecos Wilderness, make sure you're prepared for any kind of weather, especially early (before mid-June) or late (after mid-September) in the year. I use stocking-foot breathable waders with a light wading boot when camping so I don't have to carry anything heavy and I can stay dry. When I was a kid I just waded wet in Converse tennis shoes, but by the end of the day I'd be cold and soggy. I'd have to spend the night drying everything out next to the campfire. Any lightweight rod 7 to 8 feet long with a short 5X leader (7 to 8 feet) will work. A lone dry fly will usually produce plenty of trout, but in the mornings, when the water is still cold, a beadhead dropper will often work better.

From Cowles, the Pecos River has over 10 miles of good wilderness flyfishing upstream to Pecos Falls and beyond. The first 2 miles above Cowles has a good trail, but above that it gets tough until you get to Beatty's Creek where several Forest Service hiking trails come together. From here up, Rio Grande cutts are more plentiful and willing to take an attractor like a Royal Wulff or Rio Grande Trude. The scenery is also more magnificent the closer you get to Pecos Falls. The best way to access the Pecos Falls area is to hike in from Iron Gate Campground or Jacks Creek Campground (see Mora River below).

Jacks Creek is a small, brushy, tumbling stream with brookies, browns, cutthroats, and some rainbows near the campground. This is a great place to bag a couple of brookies to cook over the evening campfire, but the main fishing is about 5 miles upstream where the creek heads at Pecos Baldy Lake at the base of 12,530-foot Pecos Baldy Peak. An 8-acre glacial lake, it has stocked rainbows and native Rio Grande cutthroats and some cuttbows. As with all the Pecos Wilderness lakes, fishing can be excellent during the warm summer months, although it's also spotty at times. The sheer beauty of the area will leave you delighted no matter how the fishing goes.

Continuing up Trail 251 along Trail Riders Wall for about 5 miles will bring you to perhaps the most stunning place in all of New Mexico—Truchas (Trout) Lakes and Truchas Peaks. There are three lakes, each about 4 acres in size, at the base of three towering peaks around 13,000 feet. Rio Grande cutthroats here average 12 to 16 inches, with larger fish plentiful in some years, depending on how much winterkill there was during the prior winter. These fish like large flies, and black ants or termites, size 14, fished near the banks for cruisers can be deadly. As with all the lakes, freshwater shrimp are also an important food source. Imitate them with an Olive Shrimp, size 16 to 20, and strip the fly near shore and around any deadfall logs and trees.

Panchuela Creek is a little larger than the other creeks, although it's very brushy in most places. But there are some nice beaver ponds, especially near the campground. Bushwhacking will produce plenty of nice fish, but dabbling with just a couple of feet of line and a very short leader (6 feet) works best. From Cowles, the first 1.5 miles are easily accessed, but it's tough going from the wilderness boundary upstream for the next 2 miles. At the confluence of Horsethief Creek it opens up a little, and Horsethief also has a nice meadow where you can fish. It's a tiny creek, but it has a healthy population of small Rio Grande cutthroats.

Winsor Creek is small and brushy too, but has good access and fishing between Cowles Campground and Winsor Campground. Some beaver ponds will grow holdover rainbows and wild browns up to 12 or 13 inches. Continuing up Winsor Creek into the wilderness, there is great fishing for small browns and some cutts. About 2 miles in, it splits and heads up at Stewart Lake and Lake Katherine.

It's about 6 miles from the Winsor Trailhead to Stewart Lake (5 acres) and 8 miles to Lake Katherine (about 11 or 12 acres). Another lake, Spirit Lake (7 acres), at the head of Holy Ghost Creek can be accessed from the same trail. It's about 7 miles from the trailhead. All three lakes have stocked rainbows and wild cutthroats and cuttbows. The standard high-mountain lake patterns all work well, with damselflies, midges, and scuds the most important.

The Mora River is the largest tributary of the Pecos River, and most of it lies within the Pecos Wilderness. One of its tributaries, the Rio Valdez, is an excellent small, brushy creek holding a fairly pure strain of Rio Grande cutts up to 14 inches. It's accessible from the Mora River at the top of Mora Flats via Trail 244 (see the description below). The trail follows the river pretty closely, so you can hop off and fish the more open areas. Standard attractors work well on these ravenous native cutts.

Since starting my guide business in 1982 in Red River, New Mexico, I rarely get a chance to visit, much less fish, the Pecos or the Mora. But the last time I did it was still just as beautiful, and the fishing was actually better than I thought it would be. A friend and associate of mine, Jarrett Sasser, owner of the High Desert Angler, a fly shop and guide service in Santa Fe, knows the Pecos and Mora intimately and guides on them regularly. He describes the Mora River and the mainstem Pecos in the following manner.

Rio Mora

(Contributed by Jarrett Sasser)

The Rio Mora, the largest tributary feeding the Pecos, is a significant stream in its own right and is large enough to provide some great flyfishing opportunities. In fact, the Mora has a special charm for some anglers, who prefer to fish its more intimate waters instead of—or in addition to—trying their skills on the Pecos.

Like the Pecos, the Mora is a classic trout stream. Its headwaters lie generally east and south of the Pecos's origins. It is characterized by a fine mix of deep pools, riffles, runs, and pocket water. Generally smaller than the Pecos, it usually ranges from 8 to 15 feet wide, depending on the structure of the canyon through which it flows. The Mora's banks are forested and often willow-lined. Casting from midstream is usually easier than sticking to the banks.

Access is simple on the Mora. The stream is well marked at the point where it flows under NM 63 and empties into the main Pecos. You'll find a NMDGF campground here too, one of the busiest sites along the entire reach of the Pecos in the summer months. But flyfishers shouldn't be deterred by the campground crowd, which often includes a number of baitfishers. Just hike a mile upstream. You may not be entirely alone, but there's a good chance you'll not feel crowded. Put on a backpack and hike even farther upstream, and you'll likely have the river all to yourself.

Streams like the upper Pecos and Rio Mora are classic trout water. (Jarrett Sasser)

Stocked rainbows may be found in the vicinity of the campground; upstream, the Mora becomes brown trout water. About 2.5 miles above the campground, just above the spot where Bear Creek flows in from the right (as you face upstream), the Mora enters a narrow and difficult canyon that stretches for more than 4 miles. Only the heartiest souls venture into the canyon. Those who can manage the tough going find splendid fishing for wild browns.

Above the canyon, the Mora opens into a wide meadow called Mora Flats. This section of stream provides one of the most beautiful wild campsites in the Sangre de Cristos. The vegetation is lush and thick, and tall trees provide shade and a peaceful streamside setting.

Anglers willing to hike an hour or more from the Iron Gate parking area can reach the Mora Flats, as well as the upper reaches of the Pecos. From its juncture with NM 63, take FR 223 for 4 miles to reach the Iron Gate trailhead. This is a rough, unpaved road, where it pays to have a four-wheel drive; don't attempt it unless dry conditions prevail. Flyfishers who choose to hike into the upper Pecos or Mora from Iron Gate are urged to consult topo maps often, carry a compass, and as always, take lots of drinking water.

To reach the Mora Flats from Iron Gate Campground, locate signs directing you to Trail 249 toward Hamilton Mesa. Follow Trail 249 for about 1.5 miles and then bear right on Trail 250 to Mora Flats. The trails from Iron Gate Campground to Mora Flats run about 4 miles long. Hikers can use maps to locate trails to the upper Pecos.

While trails to the Mora Flats or the upper Pecos are clearly shown on most maps, numerous side trails have been opened by hikers striking out on their own. So it pays to stick with the main trails and to know where you are at all times. And always be prepared for violent summer thunderstorms. Seek shelter off the river during periods of lightning activity, and be alert for the possibility of cold rain, hail, or even brief snow flurries.

The Mora's aquatic life is almost identical to that of the Pecos. Stoneflies start to hatch in May and June, mayflies appear in late June or July, and caddis hatches occur throughout the warmer months.

The Mainstem Pecos River

(Contributed by Jarrett Sasser)

High in the Sangre de Cristo Mountains, above the town of Pecos, emerges a powerful life force known as the Pecos River. The Pecos traces a course down through the canyons of the Sangre de Cristos to the arid lands of southern Texas, where the river eventually merges with the Rio Grande. The river follows a generally southward route for approximately 920 miles. However, it's only the first 25 or so miles that are of principal interest to flyfishers who live in or visit New Mexico. This stretch has many fans in the flyfishing community—and for good reason.

The Pecos River is the very definition of what a classic freestone trout stream is supposed to look and act like. Its waters range from tiny and tight to open and inviting. It offers a broad variety of conditions, from cutbanks and corners to riffles and pocket water. Its waters will challenge flyfishers of every skill level. In fact, many seasoned anglers consider the Pecos one of the great secrets of the Sangre de Cristos.

The river is all the more remarkable because of its close proximity to Santa Fe, one of America's leading tourist destinations. In barely an hour from town, flyfishers can reach almost any point on the Pecos.

Downstream from the Pecos Wilderness Area, several small tributaries contribute more to the flow of the Pecos. By the time the river reaches the town of Pecos, it has an average width of 30 to 35 feet. The cold water rushing in from the creeks keeps the water of the Pecos at relatively cool temperatures. The elevation of the town of Pecos is just shy of 7,000 feet, which also helps keep summer temperatures down. In general, nighttime temperatures are quite cool, while daytime highs in the summer run into the upper 80s. Dress in layers when you visit this area, so you can shed clothes as the day warms up or add layers if thunderstorms develop.

Not many people fish the Pecos during the winter. The river usually freezes over in December and may maintain its icy sheath into early March, since the high canyon walls block the sun for most of the day. Winter fishing is slow and unpredictable.

In warmer seasons, wading the river isn't difficult, but the streambed varies and can be unstable at times. Anglers should always be cautious when crossing or wading, especially in the early spring when the flow volume of the Pecos is swelled by heavy snowmelt in the high mountains. After runoff, it's possible to wet wade, but hip waders or breathable pant or chest waders are usually a better idea because you can stay totally dry if the weather turns nasty.

Unfortunately, cutthroat trout aren't found in the more easily accessible reaches of the Pecos. As mentioned earlier, cutthroats occur naturally in the higher headwater streams. They are unable to maintain a population in the lower stretches of the river due to the degradation of the water quality and competition from introduced rainbow and brown trout. Rainbows are heavily stocked in the Pecos below its confluence with the Mora. Stocked fish generally run about 12 inches, but many of these fish don't survive for long, as baitfishers seem to harvest them almost immediately. The rainbows that are left become selective and are easily spooked. Still, these elusive rainbows can provide some memorable fishing.

The brown trout in the Pecos are wild. They breed naturally in the river, so it isn't necessary or even advisable to stock them. They thrive on their own and show some beautiful color. Their golden hue and scattered orange dots with bluish-white haloes are a sight to see. Simply admiring them for their beauty is one of the rewards of flyfishing here. However, the Pecos does not produce large brown trout. Their average size is around 10 inches; anything larger is usually considered a trophy in these waters. Low nutrients and competition with stocked rainbows limit their growth.

It's not hard to reach the Pecos. Whether coming from Albuquerque or Santa Fe, take I-25 north. About 18 miles north of Santa Fe, take the Glorieta/Pecos exit (299)

Streamside brush makes roll casting necessary in some areas. (Jarrett Sasser)

onto NM 50. Follow the signs to the town of Pecos, about 6 miles from Exit 299. In Pecos, you'll come to an intersection with NM 63. Turn left (north) onto NM 63 and follow it into the canyons of the Sangre de Cristos. The road eventually parallels the river.

To help find camping areas along the river, reset your odometer at the intersection in the town of Pecos. As you head up into the canyon, you will enter the Pecos Ranger District of the Santa Fe National Forest at 4.2 miles. There are numerous private holdings in this area, and access is restricted. Please observe posted signs and respect the rights of property owners.

The Pecos Ranger District is loaded with plenty of well-marked day-use areas and campsites. During the summer and on weekends these areas are heavily used, so be prepared for crowds. Fishing on the public water around these sites can be excellent, especially for stocked rainbows and an occasional wild brown.

At 5.9 miles, the Dalton Day-Use Area is the first public access with picnic tables and parking. Across the road, you'll also find the Dalton Fishing Site, which is simply a parking area with public access to the river. Field Track Campsite is at 8.7 miles, and is primarily a campground. At 9.4 miles, Windy Bridge Picnic Ground is another easily accessible area with a nice stretch of public fishing water. The Bert Clancey Recreation Area is located at 12.3 miles. Just up the road from Bert Clancey, there's a fork in the road; if you turn left you'll find your way into the Terrero Campground, one of the largest camping areas on the Pecos. If you bear right, over the bridge, the road will take you farther north into the canyon.

Just above the bridge, you come to the small community of Terrero and the Terrero General Store, which offers basic supplies and foodstuffs during the summer months. From this point, the road becomes rougher and narrower, but is still paved. You next enter a section of the Pecos called the Terrero Box, which offers splendid views and great fish habitat. (There's another similar area upstream called the Pecos Box, or simply the Upper Box.)

Above the Terrero General Store, the road generally leads higher and away from the river. Getting down the steep canyon banks to the water is difficult, even for anglers used to bushwhacking. A better way to get into the Terrero Box is to walk upstream from the Terrero Campground. It's also possible to walk downstream from the top of the box; park at Jamie Koche Recreation Area (formerly Willow Creek Campground), which is 14.4 miles above the village of Pecos.

Jamie Koche RA is well marked and easily recognized because there has been a good deal of disturbed ground here related to containment from an old mining site. In recent years, Jamie Koche RA has been a restricted-use area because of the project. While the area has been closed to camping, flyfishers can usually find enough space to park before heading downstream into the Terrero Box.

At 13.7 miles above the town of Pecos, you'll come to the junction with FR 646. Follow this road for 5 miles to Davis Willow Campground. Although Davis Willow isn't next to the river, the scenery is outstanding and it feels a little more removed from the summer crowds.

A nice fish from the High Desert Anglers' private water. (Jarrett Sasser)

At 15.7 miles, the Rio Mora empties into the Pecos. There is camping available here, but expect this campground to be the most crowded on the Pecos.

About 18 miles into the canyon you'll pass through the tiny village of Cowles. There is day-use parking here for the river. Two stocked ponds are nearby, one of them reserved for children. The other provides neophyte anglers a place to practice casting and catch a rainbow or two.

If you turn left at Cowles onto Winsor Road, you'll arrive at another camping area. Panchuela Road (FR 305) will take you to the Panchuela trailhead and campground.

All of these areas provide great camping opportunities for anglers who want to spend a few days along the Pecos River. Most of the campgrounds on the upper Pecos are fee areas and well suited for multi-day trips.

The Pecos also has several limited-access areas located on private property that offer superb flyfishing. These properties are managed for larger trout, and guides and shops often lease these stretches. Most sections of private water are stocked with healthy rainbows and have some wild browns. Some have ponds stocked with very large trout, most reaching 20 inches or longer. However, to gain access to these areas you must hire a guide from one of the local guide services.

Some of the nicest stretches of private water on the Pecos are located downstream of the Dalton Campground. As a general rule, the private water is clearly marked, and anglers are urged to respect the rights of property owners. (See the Private Waters section of this book for more details on these areas.)

Although a large stream for this region, the Pecos is still a small river. Short casts and 7½-foot leaders are a good match for the water. The Pecos is mostly pocket water; large boulders and other obstructions create eddies and breaks in the current. The flow of water around these rocks creates some deeper holding lies immediately downstream. The slower water found in eddies or breaks allows trout to maximize food intake. It also makes insects more vulnerable, as they become easier to see and consume. Current seams, one slow and one fast, often hold fish on the inside of the slower side.

The most overlooked areas on the Pecos are close along the riverbanks. As long as the water is around 10 inches deep, there's a strong possibility that trout will hold there. Where the water is relatively shallow and clear, it's important to approach cautiously, fishing upstream to avoid spooking your quarry. Start by making short casts in areas near to you that may hold fish. Going short, before casting farther out, will provide greater opportunities to catch fish.

The browns in the Pecos are extremely difficult to see, so blind fishing is your best tactic. Rainbows, on the other hand, with their bluish-green backs, are easier to spot against the rocks in the river. Sight casting to Pecos rainbows is usually productive.

When fishing small pockets, those about the size of a basketball, drift your fly or flies through at least twice. Fish larger pockets more methodically, dividing them into three areas. Start with the edge closest to you, then work the middle. Finish with the far edge. Fish all of these areas with multiple drifts, but no more than three or four each. As you move from pocket to pocket, watch for other good spots, such as seams or underwater rocks that form structure where trout can hold while they watch for insects to come tumbling by.

There are also numerous pools and deep runs to fish on this river. Start with the water diagonally upstream and across. And remember, where possible, it's better to lengthen your casts than to wade. Wading makes you more visible, produces unnatural wave action, and disturbs the rocks by your feet, creating sounds that make trout cautious and selective. After you have covered the water well, move upstream a few steps and start over again.

One very important technique that will improve your presentation, and thus increase strikes, is hi-sticking. Keep your cast short. The distance between you and the target area will determine your line length. Immediately raise your rod after you cast; your arm should be extended straight out from your body. You are, in a sense, reaching out to the area you're fishing, and your rod becomes an extension of your arm. Try to keep your raised rod tip right over, or just downstream of, the fly, and be ready to set the hook with a gentle downstream tug.

The aquatic insect life of the Pecos River is typical of almost any Rocky Mountain freestone river. You'll find a variety of stoneflies, mayflies, and caddis. Stoneflies are the first to come off, usually starting around late May and lasting through mid-July. Stoneflies hatch from late May to mid-June, with Golden Stoneflies showing up by early summer. Use Sofa Pillows and Stimulators in size 6 to 10. Before the hatch fully commences, heavily weighted stonefly nymph patterns will work. Fishing nymphs directly on the bottom is essential for success. Stonefly nymphs are not great swimmers; they basically crawl along the bottom. If they lose their grip they'll just tumble along the streambed.

Western Red Quills are the most abundant mayfly on the Pecos, hatching from late June through mid-August. Many other mayflies hatch during this timeframe, as well, including PMDs and Speckle-Winged Quills. Mayfly dries you should try are the Little Brown Fly, Dorato Hare's Ear, Blue-Winged Olive, Adams, and Light Cahill in size 14 to 20. Mayfly nymphs worth trying are Hare's Ears, Pheasant Tails, Copper Johns, Prince Nymphs, and HDA Favorites in size 14 to 20.

The caddis hatches last longer than the others. The first hatch starts around mid-June and lasts into late August—maybe into September if the weather stays warm. For caddis dries, pack a good selection of Elk Hair Caddis, Stimulators (royal, yellow, or olive), Seducers, and Peacock Caddis in sizes 10 through 18. Caddis larvae can be very effective, but like stoneflies they must be fished on the bottom. A couple of good patterns are the Rock Worm and Caddis Casin'; both mimic cased caddis, which spend their larval life on the bottom.

As caddisflies hatch, they swim through the water column to the surface to begin their adult cycle. A caddis emerger can work quite well at this time. The Beadhead Hare's Ear and Lafontaine Caddis Pupa are two effective patterns.

The best way to fish these flies is to allow your upstream drift to continue past you, swinging across the current. As the line drags the fly through the water column, it looks like an emerging caddis. Expect sudden strikes.

During the summer months, terrestrials are important, too. Any hopper pattern will work in size 8 to 12. Two flies favored by many guides are Parachute Hoppers and

Yellow Stimulators. And remember, it's never a bad idea to stop at a Santa Fe fly shop and inquire about what's hot at the time of your trip.

Early spring and late fall are the best times to flyfish the Pecos, but the river also fishes well throughout the warmer months. During the prime vacation months—July and August—some sections of public water on the river can be quite crowded. If you don't like crowds, like me, try some of the private water available on the Pecos and other tributaries available through the High Desert Angler in Santa Fe (see Private Waters).

Gearing up for a day on the Pecos near the confluence with the Rio Mora. (Jarrett Sasser)

Stream Facts: Pecos River

Season
- Early April through late November, weather depending. Runoff peaks from early May to early June.

Special Regulations
- The Pecos Box STWs: From ½ mile above the confluence with the Mora River upstream 1 mile to ¼ mile below Cowles Bridge, only artificial flies or lures with single barbless hooks. Two fish 12 inches or larger per angler per day; catch and release is strongly encouraged.
- Catch and release only and artificial flies or lures only on Doctor Creek from ¼ mile above its confluence with Holy Ghost Creek upstream to its headwaters; Jacks Creek from the waterfalls located ¼ mile downstream of the NM 63 crossing upstream to its headwaters; the Pecos River in the Pecos Wilderness above Pecos Falls; and the Rio Valdez in the Pecos Wilderness from ¼ mile below Smith Cabin upstream to its headwaters.

Trout
- Wild browns and stocked rainbows, with some brook trout and cutthroats in upper elevation tributaries.

River Miles
- The intersection of NM 50 and 63—0
- Monastery Lake entrance—2.4
- Lisboa Springs Fish Hatchery—2.9
- USFS Dalton Fish Site—6.3
- Private land, except USNF Field Tract Campground—7.5 to 9.9
- Field Tract Campground—9.2
- USFS Windy Bridge—9.9
- Private land—10.9 to 13
- NMGF Bert Clancey Wildlife Area—13
- Holy Ghost Canyon—13.4
- Terrero General Store—13.6
- Davis Willow Campground—14.5
- Willow Creek Campground—15.3
- End of private land—16.1
- Mora Creek Campground—16.7
- STW boundary and Pecos Box parking—17.1
- Iron Gate Road—18.2
- Cowles Ponds, turnoff for Windsor Creek and Panchuela Creek—19.4
- End of STW—19.6
- Jacks Creek—20.8
- Wilderness parking for upper Pecos River—22.2

River Characteristics
- The Pecos River and its tributaries have classic freestone pool-drop characteristics; some sediment-bottom areas exist, with limestone and granite boulders creating pocket water elsewhere. Most of the pools are carved out of bedrock, some up to 10 feet deep depending on water flows.

River Flows
- Winter mean flows: 20 to 50 cfs
- Summer flows: 100 to 40 cfs
- Fall flows: 30 to 20 cfs
- Spring runoff: The average high water in runoff over the last four years has remained 500 cfs or less. In the last 100 years the river has been over 3,000 cfs just twice. Flows are obviously dependent on snowfall and upper elevation rain year-round.

Campgrounds
- Dalton Canyon, Field Tract, Bert Clancey Wildlife Area, Holy Ghost, Terrero, Davis Willow, Windsor Creek, Jacks Creek.

Maps
- *New Mexico Atlas & Gazetteer,* page 24; Santa Fe National Forest Map; BLM Map: Santa Fe; USGS Quadrangle Maps: Aspen Basin, Cowles, Truchas Peak, Elk Mountain, Pecos Falls, Rosilla Peak

Agencies
- NMDGF, Northeast, 215 York Canyon Road, Raton, NM 87740
- Pecos/Las Vegas Ranger District, Santa Fe N.F., P.O. Box 429, Pecos, NM 87701; 505-757-6121

Outfitters
The Santa Fe N.F. Pecos Ranger District can provide information, including maps and a list of outfitters permitted to operate on public lands. Outfitters include:
- High Desert Angler, 460 Cerrillos Road, Santa Fe, NM 87501; 505-988-7688, 1-888-988-7688, www.highdesertangler.com
- The Reel Life, Sanbusco Market Center, 500 Montezuma Ave., Santa Fe, NM 87501; 505-995-8114, 1-877-733-5543

PECOS RIVER MAJOR HATCHES

Insect	J	F	M	A	M	J	J	A	S	O	N	D	Time	Flies
Caddis				■	■				■				Larva-M Pupa-M/A/E Adult-A/E	Green & olive caddis larva #12–#16; Cased Caddis #12–#18; La Fontaine's Caddis Pupa #12–#18; Lawson's Caddis Emerger #12–#18; olive, tan & gray Elk Hair Caddis #12–#20; olive, gray & peacock Fluttering Caddis #10–#18
Green Drake						■	■						M/A/SF	Olive Hare's Ear #10–#14; Green & Gray Drake Hair-Wing (Wulff style) #10–#14; Green & Gray Paradrake #10–14; Green Drake spinner #12–#14
Red Quill, Ginger, Blue & Mahogany Duns					■	■	■						M/E	Light, dark & olive Hare's Ear Nymph #12–#18; Pheasant Tail Nymph #12–#18; Copper Johns #12–#18; HAD Special #14–#20; light, dark, & pink Adams & Ginger Hair-Wing Duns or Cahills #12–18 or the same in parachutes
Baetis				■	■					■	■		M/A/SF	Dark olive Hare's Ear Nymph #16–#22; Pheasant Tail #16–#22; Van's Rag Fly Nymph dark olive #16–#22; Lawson's BWO Fan-Wing Emerger #16–#22; Olive Parachute #16–#22; Olive Comparadun #16–#22
Salmonfly, Golden Stonefly					■	■	■	■	■				M/A	Black & brown stonefly nymph #6–#14; Golden Stone Nymph #10–#14; Elk Hair Salmon Fly #6–#12; Orange & Gold Stimulators #6–#14

Hatch Time Code: M = Morning; A = Afternoon; E = Evening; D = Dark; SF = Spinner Fall

PECOS RIVER MAJOR HATCHES (cont.)

Insect	J	F	M	A	M	J	J	A	S	O	N	D	Time	Flies
PMDs, PEDs							▮						M/SF	Light, dark & olive Hare's Ear Nymph #12–#18; Pheasant Tail #12–#20; Lawson's Fan-Wing Emerger #14–#22; PMD, PED #12–#20; Hair-Wing or PW Ginger Dun #14–#20, Parachute ginger; light olive #14–#20
Terrestrials					▮				▮				M/A	Para-hoppers tan, yellow #8–#14; Bees #12–14; black & cinnamon ants #14–#18; black & peacock beetles #12–#18

Hatch Time Code: M = Morning; A = Afternoon; E = Evening; D = Dark; SF = Spinner Fall

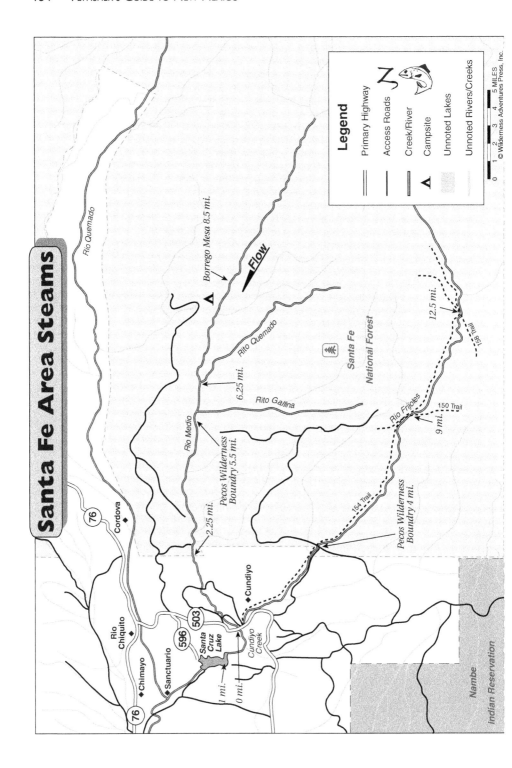

Santa Fe Area Steams

SANTA FE AREA STREAMS

Several small streams or creeks flow out of the Sangre de Cristos within a few miles of Santa Fe, although most require a drive over rough roads and at least some hiking to fish thoroughly. Three of these creeks—Rio del Medio, Rio Frijoles, and Cundiyo Creek—are worth fishing if you live in or are visiting Santa Fe. These streams are part of the same drainage, and all offer good flyfishing with some level of solitude. They can generally be fished year-round, except during runoff from mid-April through late May. Before venturing off to fish one of these great little creeks for the first time, I recommend hiring a good guide or at least consulting a good map.

Rio del Medio

The Rio del Medio is typical of streams flowing from the west side of the Sangre de Cristos. It heads at the base of 12,000- to 13,000-foot peaks, gathering water from melting snow and mountain springs that merge to form a small creek. It then tumbles down through high valleys and tight canyons, picking up more water from small tributaries until it becomes a full-fledged freestone stream about 10 feet wide.

After reaching the valley floor, it gets diverted into irrigation ditches and becomes severely dewatered before merging with the Rio Frijoles, which becomes Cundiyo Creek for the last mile above Santa Cruz Lake. It becomes the Santa Cruz River below the lake, but gets diverted again for irrigation, almost drying up before joining the Rio Grande.

For anglers the best fishing and access starts about 7 miles upstream of Santa Cruz Lake at the Pecos Wilderness boundary.

To get to the Rio del Medio from Santa Fe, go north on US 285 to Nambe and turn right on NM 520/503. Continue about 7 miles to where the routes divide, staying on NM 503 to Cundiyo. Follow NM 503 about 4 miles to Cundiyo, where the Rio Frijoles and Rio del Medio merge to form Cundiyo Creek. Stay on NM 503 for almost 3 miles to FR 306 and turn right, following FR 306 about 6.5 miles to the Borrego Crossing trailhead (Trail 150), the first good access to the Rio del Medio near the wilderness boundary.

It's a little over a mile to the river, and you can go downstream about 2.5 miles before hitting private property or upstream as far as you want. There's less pressure here than 4 miles upstream at Borrego Mesa Campground, but relatively speaking, there's almost no pressure anywhere on the river compared to, say, the Pecos River or its tributaries just over the hill.

Downstream access is difficult because you must bushwhack, but it will get you into some good water in a narrow, rugged canyon with browns and some holdover rainbows that migrate upstream from Santa Cruz Lake and Cundiyo Creek. The banks are very brushy, and wading is often necessary in order to cast in the tight quarters. Hippers with Goodyear soles are an excellent choice because the bottom is not very slick and you'll be hiking on varied alpine terrain when not wading.

The river is swift in some places, but where it slows down or is obstructed by a logjam or boulders there are good holes and pockets that hold 8- to 12-inch trout and a few 15-inchers. A lightweight rod no longer than 8 feet is recommended for the short, tight casts you'll be making. Wade upstream, casting to all likely areas and paying close attention to overhanging banks and deep pockets below logs and boulders.

Hatches are frequent, and at times you may have to match the hatch to fool the wise browns. Hatches seem to be short-lived, though, so be observant. You won't always see the flies on the water, but if you look in the air you'll often notice clouds of flies buzzing above the surface.

Large Golden Stoneflies hatch for a couple of weeks just after runoff in late May, and then caddis and multiple mayfly hatches take over and continue through September. PMDs (June and July) and Green and Gray Drakes (July and August) provide good action from morning through midday. I use a Ginger Wulff, size 16, and a Gray Wulff, size 12 to 14, to imitate these insects, and I like to drop a Beadhead Hare's Ear about 18 inches below the dry fly. I usually catch the majority of the fish on the dropper.

Caddis hatch almost every evening from June through August, with July the peak month. The action can be fast and furious during good afternoon hatches; 8- to 12-inch browns seem to hide behind every boulder and in every riffle or pool. These small browns are scrappers, fighting well in the swift water, and they jump a lot (for brown trout, that is).

In addition to the Rio del Medio, you can fish the Rito Gallina and the Rito Quemado from the Borrego Crossing trail. The Rito Gallina merges with the Rio del Medio where the trail crosses the Rio. It's a thin, brushy creek teeming with small wild browns and is fishable for about 2 miles above the confluence. The Rito Quemado comes in about a half-mile above the Gallina. It's fishable for 2 or 3 miles upstream and has more open areas to fish.

Farther upstream, above Borrego Mesa Campground, the river narrows, passing several springs and tributaries too small to fish. The Rio Medio offers good fishing for about 7 more miles before it gets too small to fish. The farther up you go, the more Rio Grande cutthroats you'll find. These fish are less selective, readily taking attractors and large terrestrials.

To get to Borrego Mesa Campground, go about 3 more miles from Borrego Crossing to FR 435. You'll be on a mesa here, so you'll still have to hike about a half-mile down the trail to the river about 450 feet below. The trail then follows the stream for over 6 miles to its headwaters at the base of Trail Riders Wall, a steep ridge that separates the Pecos and Rio Grande drainages.

There are some open areas with willow-filled meadows, especially in the upper 3 miles where the river meanders more, creating some good undercut banks. There used to be some nice beaver ponds that held larger fish in the upper reaches of the Rio Medio and its tributaries, but each year some get washed out and new ones are built. Just look for standing dead willows and alders and you'll usually find a beaver dam with water backed up above it.

Fish in these beaver ponds can be picky, and you'll sometimes have to go with small midges to fool them. Try a size 18 Griffith's Gnat with a midge pupa, size 18 to 20, on an 18-inch dropper. Cast near a rise and be patient. The cast may spook fish temporarily, but after a few seconds they'll often forget and take one or both of the flies. If they're actively feeding, it's not uncommon to get a double (but remember, two 8-inch browns don't equal one 16-inch brown).

The headwaters flow through the beautiful Pecos Wilderness. Mountain peaks tower above you to the east and the massive Trail Riders Wall extends from Pecos Baldy over 5 miles to Truchas Peak. The Rio Medio is an excellent stream for backpacking and overnight camping.

When I was a teenager, one of my best friends, Terry Beard, and I used to do a six-day backpacking trip from the Borrego Mesa Campground. We'd fish up the Rio Medio to the base of Trail Riders Wall and camp there. The next day we'd hike 5 miles over the Wall to the Truchas Lakes, where we'd camp and fish the lakes before hiking the Wall south to Pecos Baldy Lake. From Pecos Baldy, we'd head to the Pecos River about 4 miles to the east, fishing the Pecos or one of its tributaries on our way south to Cowles, where someone would pick us up. We did this three or four times a year for several years, taking different routes each time so we could fish most of the waters in the region.

The Rio Frijoles

The Rio Frijoles is actually the Rio del Medio's main tributary, and it flows out of the next drainage to the south, merging with the Rio del Medio in Cundiyo to form Cundiyo Creek. You'll find about a mile of good water on Cundiyo Creek between Cundiyo and Santa Cruz Lake, but there's no access to the Rio Frijoles or Rio Medio from Cundiyo. Below the lake, it becomes the Santa Cruz River before its confluence with the Rio Grande in Espanola.

To get to the Rio Frijoles from Santa Fe, go north on US 285 to Nambe and turn right on NM 520/503. Continue about 7 miles to where the routes divide, staying on NM 503 to Cundiyo. Follow NM 503 about 2.5 miles toward Cundiyo. Just past mile-marker 10, turn right on FR 307 (sometimes locals tear down the sign so it may not be there) and go about a mile. Park at the "Road Closed" sign. Hike the closed road for a little over a mile until it drops down to the river and the Santa Fe National Forest boundary. You'll enter the Pecos Wilderness about a quarter-mile upstream. Upstream from the trailhead, there are about 9 or 10 miles of fishable water.

The Rio Frijoles is shorter and drains from lower elevations than the Rio del Medio, so it only carries about half the water volume, although it's still 5 to 10 feet wide. Several small spring creeks in the headwaters add to the water quality of this delightful stream. The first 4 miles or so are a little tough because you're in a tight, brushy canyon, but there are some nice little pools and pockets to dabble in that hold rainbows and browns from 8 to 12 inches, some larger. Fish will key in on a particular hatch at times, but an attractor usually works fine. The hatches are basically the same as for the Rio del Medio, except that the stonefly hatch is not as strong. Ginger and yellow mayflies are abundant, as are olive caddis.

About 4 miles upstream, the creek opens up a bit, providing more casting room. In July and August there are good mayfly and caddis hatches, and a Ginger Dun, size 16, is all I've ever needed to catch fish here. Browns and Rio Grande cutthroats or cuttbows are present in the upper 5 miles, and I once caught a 16-inch cutt in the meadows near Cienega Redonda Spring. It was a pure strain, with a red belly and a brilliant crimson slash under its throat.

A really nice backcountry trip for anglers is to fish the Rio Frijoles up through the headwaters and then take Trail 158 about 3 miles over the mountain to the Rio del Medio. Fish down the Rio del Medio to Borrego Mesa Campground. You should allow at least three days to have enough time to fish, hike, and camp without rushing.

Cundiyo Creek

Cundiyo Creek begins at the confluence of the Rio Frijoles and the Rio del Medio. Park at the bridge on NM 503 in Cundiyo, and take the primitive trail downstream until it peters out near Santa Cruz Lake. From here back to the bridge, there's about a mile of nice water running through a tight, rocky canyon with riffles, pools, holes, and boulder-strewn pocket water. Wading is easy and there's enough room to cast.

There is a healthy population of wild browns and holdover rainbows averaging 8 to 12 inches, with a few to 16 inches. I've caught browns up to 20 inches here in the fall that probably migrated out of Santa Cruz Lake to spawn. Likewise, I've caught nice spawning rainbows sporadically between November and late March.

Unlike the Rio del Medio and Rio Frijoles, which are best during the summer months, Cundiyo Creek fishes best in fall, winter, and spring. Summer fishing can still be good during evening caddis hatches, after the sun leaves the water.

There's a strong Golden Stonefly hatch from late May through mid-June, and nymphing with a beadhead golden stone pattern, size 10 to 14, in the deep holes and pockets can produce some scrappy fish. A Bird's Stonefly with a beadhead dropper will sometimes work, especially after the river drops in June.

Cundiyo Creek receives quite a bit of pressure from local baitfishers, so the trout can be spooky at times. But if you fish here during the week you can still find some solitude. Midday fishing can be tough during the summer months. A good plan is to hit the Rio del Medio or Rio Frijoles during the day, and then stop at Cundiyo Creek on the way home or on the way up in the morning.

During fall Baetis hatches, wild browns are very willing to take a Parachute Olive Dun, size 16 to 20, on the surface. Look for the hatch between 11:00 and 3:00, and start with a dry-dropper combo. When the fish start taking the dry more than the dropper, just remove the latter.

The river can be quite good at times from November through March, particularly on warm days. There are midge hatches and occasional weak caddis or Baetis hatches, but I catch most fish on small nymphs and micro-eggs, size 16 to 20, or Woolly

Buggers fished deep. I've caught spawning rainbows up to 18 inches between January and March, although they are rare.

Between the Rio del Medio, Rio Frijoles, and Cundiyo Creek, an angler can flyfish year-round. The Pecos Wilderness guarantees solitude and a beautiful setting, along with miles of fishable water on the Medio and Frijoles, while Cundiyo Creek offers good fishing 11 months a year—all less than an hour from Santa Fe.

Stream Facts: Santa Fe Area Streams

Season
• Year-round.

Trout
• Wild browns and stocked rainbows from 8 to 12 inches, some bigger; Rio Grande cutts in the headwaters.

River Miles Rio del Medio
• Cundiyo Bridge on NM 503—0
• Santa Fe National Forest boundary—2.25
• Pecos Wilderness boundary—5.5
• Rito Quemado—6.25
• Borrego Mesa—8.5

River Miles Rio Frijoles
• Cundiyo Bridge on NM 503—0
• Pecos Wilderness boundary—4
• Intersection of Trail 154 and 150—9
• Intersection of Trail 154 and 158—12.5

River Miles Cundiyo Creek
• Cundiyo Bridge parking area on NM 503—0
• Santa Cruz Lake—1

River Characteristics
• Rio del Medio and Rio Frijoles are small mountain freestone streams with riffles, pools, shallow riffles, and pockets. Both streams have tight, narrow, brushy canyons in the lower reaches and open meadows with willows and alders in the upper reaches. Cundiyo Creek is a medium-sized freestone stream running through a narrow, rocky canyon with deep holes, riffles, and boulder-strewn pockets.

River Flows Rio del Medio
• Winter, summer, and fall: 20 to 40 cfs
• Spring runoff: 40 to 150 cfs

River Flows Rio Frijoles
- Winter, summer, and fall: 10 to 25 cfs
- Spring runoff: 25 to 100 cfs

River Flows Cundiyo Creek
- Winter, summer, and fall: 20 to 60 cfs
- Spring runoff: 30 to 200 cfs

Campgrounds
- Borrego Mesa Campground on the Rio del Medio, developed campground on a mesa 45 feet above the stream.

Maps
- *New Mexico Atlas & Gazetteer,* page 24; Santa Fe National Forest Map; BLM Map: Santa Fe; USGS Quadrangle Maps: Truchas Peak, Sierra Mosca & Chimayo

Agencies
- Santa Fe National Forest, 1474 Rodeo Road, Santa Fe, NM 87505; 505-438-7840
- NMDGF, P.O. Box 25112, Santa Fe, NM 87504-5112

Outfitters
The Santa Fe National Forest can provide information, including maps and a list of outfitters permitted to operate on public lands. Outfitters include:
- High Desert Angler, 460 Cerrillos Road, Santa Fe, NM 87501; 505-988-7688, 1-888-988-7688, www.highdesertangler.com
- The Reel Life, Sanbusco Market Center, 500 Montezuma Ave., Santa Fe, NM 87501; 505-995-8114, 1-877-733-5543

SANTA FE

Santa Fe is the central hub for anglers and tourists visiting northern New Mexico. For the non-fishers in your group, there's plenty to do—from shopping and gallery hopping the hundreds of custom shops and fine art galleries, studios, and museums to hiking, biking, whitewater rafting, skiing, and snowboarding. They can also visit state and national parks, or one of the eight northern Indian pueblos in the area.

Nestled at 7,000 feet in the foothills of the Rocky Mountains, Santa Fe, the "City Different," is America's oldest capital city and claims a long history and rich cultural heritage. Founded in 1607 by Spanish explorers, it was once claimed by the Pueblo peoples, Spain, Mexico, and the Confederacy. It was finally ceded to the U.S. by Mexico in 1846.

Santa Fe is now known for its contemporary, cosmopolitan sophistication and its ambiance. It's famous for its culture, art, and traditions. Home to America's third largest art market, the city also hosts the Santa Fe Opera, world-class dining, hundreds of quaint shops, and unlimited outdoor activities.

It is an hour's drive north of Albuquerque, the state's largest city and major air gateway. The Albuquerque International Sunport, as the airport is officially known, is serviced by all major U.S. airlines. Flying into Albuquerque and renting a car is by far the most popular way of traveling around New Mexico, but it's not the only way. Train and bus service also provides access to New Mexico on a daily basis. Santa Fe Municipal Airport is serviced by a commuter airlines connection and is open to private aircraft. Shuttle service is available from the Albuquerque airport, Santa Fe airport, and the train station in Lamy, New Mexico, about 20 miles from Santa Fe.

Once in town, getting around is easy. Downtown Santa Fe and the surrounding historic districts are compact and can be reached on foot. For longer trips, there is a local taxi service, a public transportation system, Santa Fe Trails, charter vans, and limousine service. Rental cars can also be picked up in Santa Fe. (See the Northeast Region hub cities for further information.)

I spent most of my childhood years here, until moving 30 mile away to Pecos. My great-grandfather Beacham opened the first hardware and fishing tackle shop in Santa Fe in 1907. An Englishman living in a mostly Hispanic community, he was one of the only flyfishers in the region at that time. Although I never knew him, I felt lucky that my grandfather and father handed down the flyfishing disease to me.

I once got caught ditching school and my dad asked me where the hell I'd been for the last three Thursdays. I confessed to skipping out with a good friend to go fishing. I think he'd rather I'd been drinking than fishing. He told me that one Beacham out of every generation gets the fishing bug, and it looked like I was it. He told me I'd better figure out a way to make money fishing, or I'd never be able to hold down a job. It turned out he was right, and eight years later he visited me in Red River, where I first started my guide and outfitting career. He couldn't believe that anglers actually paid a hundred dollars a day for a flyfishing guide.

I've always been thankful that I got caught ditching school that day in 1974, and that Dad took me fishing every chance he got.

The author holds a plump winter rainbow from the Rio Grande Gorge near Arsenic Springs. (Stephanie Woolley)

THE RIO GRANDE GORGE

Most people think of the Rio Grande as a muddy channel along the Mexican border, but like many great American rivers, the Rio Grande originates high in the Rocky Mountains. Two tremendous mountain ranges, the San Juans and the Sangre de Cristos, are the source of hundreds of crystal-clear creeks, streams, and lakes in northern New Mexico and southern Colorado, all of which are part of the Rio Grande watershed. After gathering these headwaters, the Rio Grande flows through the broad San Luis Valley and enters the Rio Grande Gorge 14 miles north of the New Mexico state line.

Known locally as the Gorge, it was not actually carved by the big river. Rather, the river followed a pre-established and partly filled rift valley. The rift continues to widen today, and ongoing geological activity is evident through heat flow, hot springs, geodesic observations, and some of North America's most recent lava flows.

The Gorge runs parallel to, and slightly west of, the Sangre de Cristo Mountains, splitting northern New Mexico in half. It's over 90 miles long, and four tributaries provide an additional 18 miles of great fishing. The Rio Grande is a challenging river, and anglers should be physically fit before descending into the depths of the mighty Gorge. But it's just the place for anglers who appreciate the finer aspects of flyfishing, such as limitless solitude, magnificent scenery, and a chance to catch large wild trout year-round.

Congress passed the Wild and Scenic Rivers Act in 1968, and the Rio Grande and the lower Red River were the first rivers to be so designated. Although guaranteed to be free flowing and free of pollution, the Rio Grande Gorge and Red River have been marred by mining and farming pollution, and the Rio Grande has dropped below 10 cfs at the Colorado border at least once since the Wild and Scenic designation. Nevertheless, it remains one of the nation's most pristine and important wild trout fisheries.

The "great river" has been under constant change since its beginning, and that evolution continues today. Like many western rivers, the future of the Gorge as a trout fishery remains uncertain because urban and agricultural interests continue to increase their demands for water and climate change continues to threaten trout fisheries in general by raising water temperatures.

Until recently, there was no real scientific data on the number or average size of fish in the Gorge, although anglers who fish the river regularly know that populations are healthy and increasing steadily. In 1993 there were several browns over 8 pounds caught, mostly by baitfishermen. And in February 1994 a 14½-pound cuttbow was caught in the Red River. In 2008, an actual electro shocking survey was done in the Taos Box section of the Gorge that revealed a healthy trout fishery, despite the previous seven-year drought.

Several factors have contributed to the comeback of the Gorge and the lower Red River as fisheries. New water agreements with Colorado, improved farming and irrigation techniques, the elimination of potentially dangerous fertilizers and pesticides, above normal runoff for two decades, mine rehabilitation and closures at several locations, and overall enhancement of the riparian zone and range land within the watershed have all helped the ongoing rehabilitation of the Gorge.

The resurgence has been amazing, with great hatches and spawning runs on both the Red River and the Rio Grande until 2008 when a tremendous flash flood occurred in the upper Red River Canyon. The flood caused the ground at and near the Molybdenum mine to become severely unstable resulting in a gigantic mudslide. It killed virtually everything in the Red River below the slide and significantly impacted the Rio Grande for several miles below the Red River.

Since then, the lower Red River has been struggling to survive and brown and cutbow trout runs have been bleak at best. Stocking of rainbows has helped and there are many small, wild browns present that will eventually replenish this resilient stretch of the Red River. The Rio Grande itself seems to have survived the disaster. It seems as though the fate of the Red River, and to some extent, the lower Rio Grande, is in the hands of the mine and the government. As the mine and the area around it goes, so goes the Red River; let's hope they fix it!

The river's current status proves that when commercial and private users work together with government agencies they can make a difference. Dewatering still remains a major threat, however, and it will require even more effort by everyone involved to avoid a major catastrophe in the future. Huge piles of tailings at the Molycorp Mine, located on the edge of the Red River, have been determined to be unstable, and it's now a question of when, not if, they end up in the Red River and, ultimately, the Rio Grande. Something needs to be done before it's too late for both rivers.

Unfortunately, global warming poses a new threat to the Gorge and all southwestern trout fisheries. In 1997, 2000, 2002, and again in 2003 the middle valley sections of some of the tributaries of the Gorge were drastically dewatered, and some dried up for the first time in recorded history. Where flows remained, the water temperatures soared to a whopping 87 degrees, killing all fish in those sections.

The Rio Grande also reached temperatures above 80 degrees during the drought, and the flow in the spring of 2003 was the lowest ever recorded. Because of these impacts, the northern pike and smallmouth bass population in the Gorge is increasing, and pressure is mounting on government agencies to change its current cold-water designation to a warmwater fishery. From 2005 through 2009, our snow pack in the Rio Grande Basin was considerably above normal and our temperatures around normal resulting in improved fishing throughout the region.

The Gorge is rugged, with rocky and steep terrain, and most access is limited to a few well-developed trails, a dozen or so primitive trails, and just two areas of roadside access. Anglers should be ready to hike in the Gorge, which ranges from 200 to 1,200 feet in depth. A typical trip into the Gorge and back out entails a walk of ½ to 3 miles. Potential hazards include thunderstorms, snowstorms, falling rock, rattlesnakes, dehydration, and uncertain footing.

Hip waders or breathable pant waders with lug soles are ideal for hiking the Gorge, boulder hopping along the riverbanks, and wading the silty river bottom near shore. Breathable chest waders are advisable for aggressive waders, except in the NRA (national recreation area) section, where wading above your knees can be dangerous. Many anglers prefer to wet wade when it's hot.

The Ute Mountain Run is remote, with rugged trails that are few and far between.

Winter can be especially dangerous since snow and ice add to the already difficult terrain. Do not wear felt soles in the Gorge as they are of no use on clay and rock trails, slick, giant boulders in and around the river, ice and snow, which sticks to the felt soles, and steep unstable banks. This lesson was beat into my head on a winter trip into the Gorge in late January 2009.

I was guiding Brandon Mathews and his friend, Bill on a trip to the confluence of the Red River and the Rio Grande. Both anglers were wearing felt soles and it had snowed about an inch or two the night before and many of the boulders were covered with snow and ice. I emphasized to them the dangers, especially having felt soles, and I was instinctively wary from the moment I woke up that morning; almost sensing an impending dangerous situation.

It was a great day, having caught and lost several nice trout before breaking for lunch. They were chomping at the bit to get back to fishing so I checked their rigs and prompted them down the steep, icy trail to the bank of the Red River while I proceeded to pack up after lunch. They were just a few yards away from me for no more than a minute when I heard Brandon yell, "Help! Help!" I knew it wasn't "help, I hooked a fish." It was "help, I'm in danger!"

I dropped everything and scrambled down to where he was and found him soaked from head to toe, sitting on a rock, definitely cold and appearing to go into shock. I said "Okay, you're totally soaked but is there anything else wrong?" He nodded his head and said, "I think I broke my ankle; I heard something snap." I looked around and saw his rod in the water so I picked it up and upon inspection, replied, "Well it wasn't your rod."

I calmed him down and coaxed him to let me help him get up and out of the river and up the hill to the shelter where we had lunch. From here I could get him out of his wet clothes and give him a layer of my dry clothes. Sure enough he had slipped on a big rock and his ankle was broken. And it was 2:00pm in the middle of winter and 1.5 miles straight up to the top, where our cars were parked. Not a good situation to be sure!

After suiting him back up and giving hip several ibuprofen caplets to control the pain and swelling, I tightened his rigid boot around his broken ankle to act as a splint and told him he had a decision to make. Either try to hobble out with some canes and our assistance or wait here with his friend while I get help, in which case he might have to stay down there overnight. It took him one second to say, "I'm walkin' outta' here, I'm not staying down here!" With that I found him a couple of walking sticks and he took off. Meanwhile, Bill was still focused on getting a few more casts in and was already a quarter mile upstream. He looked at me and pointed up to the rim, suggesting that he would meet us at the trail. I thought to myself, "oh my god, that's all I need now is for Bill to fall trying to scramble up the side of the canyon". He didn't, thankfully.

Normally, it takes about 45 minutes to get out but it only took Brandon about an hour and a half and he never complained or groaned, save one time when he had to step up a 3-foot boulder. It turned out he had two spiral fractures on his ankle.

The lessons: Don't wear felt soles and don't try walking on slick, angled rocks near the shore with wet or felt soles!

Each of the river's tributaries adds its own unique qualities to the Gorge. These streams originate high in the Sangre de Cristo Mountains and enhance the water quality of the Rio Grande. Fish regularly migrate between the Rio Grande and the tributaries to spawn, feed, and, in some cases, winter over.

The Gorge and its tributaries represent an immense fishery with varying conditions, and the fish are as temperamental as the river itself. The Rio Grande is a freestone river, and a major rainstorm anywhere in the watershed can make the river murky. Water temperatures drop to 38 degrees in the winter and soar to 70 degrees (sometimes higher) in midsummer. I've seen it go from 40 degrees in the morning to 58 degrees by midafternoon.

All of this can make the Gorge difficult to understand, and for anglers new to the area it can be intimidating. You must meet the Gorge on its own terms and realize that the trout generally feed only when conditions are right. Of course, knowing the optimal times, places, fly patterns, and techniques can greatly increase your chance for success.

During spring, before runoff, and in drought years, the spring Baetis and caddis hatches provide a great opportunity to catch some really big browns, and occasionally fat cuttbows, on dries. During the last drought, the spring fishing was exceptional, the best I've seen since I first fished here in 1964. Various caddis hatches occur throughout summer, and large Golden Stones, Brown Drakes, Pale Morning Duns, and craneflies hatch in June and July. Chubs, minnows, and crayfish are also abundant in the Gorge, providing nourishment for the large browns, 'bows, and northern pike.

A tremendous moth hatch takes place in June and July, providing some great fishing opportunities in the evening and at night. My father and I used to fish at night during these hatches, taking many big browns. After not seeing a rise all day, I'd suddenly hear huge fish thrashing the surface for moths and craneflies.

The Gorge has virtually every type of water, from broad riffles and pools to deep holes and long flats, but the one word that best describes the Gorge is "pockets." The entire Gorge is composed of volcanic basalt, and basalt boulders are strewn throughout the river bottom. This provides maximum cover and holding water, and you never know for sure which pockets are holding fish at a given time.

Except during peak runoff, the Gorge or one of its tributaries is always fishable, making this a true year-round fishery. The best times to fish here are just before and after runoff, early morning and late evening during the summer, all day in the fall, and from about 1:00 p.m. until dark in the winter, except on the lower Red River, where winter fishing is good all day long.

The Gorge also has a significant smallmouth bass population that provides good angling opportunities during the midday heat of summer. Northern pike are present too, especially in Ute Mountain Run and the Lower Box section near Pilar. It's possible to land some very big northerns in winter, spring, summer and fall (see Rio Grande Pike section at the end of this chapter).

From where the Gorge begins in southern Colorado to where it ends near Velarde, New Mexico, the Rio Grande fishery has five distinct sections. From north to south, these are: The Ute Mountain Run, the Wild and Scenic Recreation Area, the Middle Box, the Taos Box, and the Lower Box.

The Ute Mountain Run

The Ute Mountain Run is a remote 40-mile stretch that begins at Lobatos Bridge in southern Colorado and extends downstream to Lee's Crossing in northern New Mexico. This northernmost section of the Gorge is not very wide or deep. The riverbanks are easy to walk along, and they're lined with grass, willows, cedars, and an array of other riparian vegetation.

This stretch can be floated in small rafts or single-man pontoon boats, but be prepared to carry your gear out on a primitive trail at the end of the trip. The put-in is located at Lobatos Bridge, just 14 miles inside Colorado, near Mesita. To get to the bridge from Taos, take NM 522 north about 50 miles to the Colorado border, where the road becomes CO 159, and go another 7 miles to County Road H. Turn left toward Mesita and continue 7 more miles, then turn left on CR 7 and go 1.25 miles to CR G. Turn right, and go 6 miles to Lobatos Bridge. The put-in is on the west side, just below the bridge.

A primitive rim road runs south along the east side of the river all the way to Lee's Crossing, giving the adventurous angler access at about six rugged locations. (It's necessary to scramble over boulders and sometimes do a little free climbing.) An additional three primitive trails located in the lower half of Ute Mountain Run provide better access, and Lee's Crossing, at the bottom of the Ute Mountain Run, is actually a semi-developed trail.

To access the lower half, take NM 522 north from Questa about 9 miles and turn left on Sunshine Valley Road. Follow this dirt road due west for about 8 miles to the east rim road, which you can follow north or south to the various accesses. I hesitate to even call them trails.

The take-outs are unmarked and difficult to find. These are located at about mile 9, mile 14, mile 19, mile 26, mile 35, and mile 40, all off the east rim road. Lee's Crossing, at mile 40, is the main trail used as a take-out by whitewater rafters during spring runoff. Depending on water levels and how much fishing you want to do, you can average between 7 and 10 miles a day. The floating is easy and slow, with numerous long flats; generally Class 1 water with some Class 2. Wading is easier here than in other sections because there is less water, fewer pockets and giant boulders, and more gravel.

The area is a sanctuary for wildlife, including bald and golden eagles, deer, elk, bobcats, geese, ducks, and herons. Big horn sheep and river otters were recently reintroduced and appear to be taking hold. This is the perfect place for anglers who appreciate solitude, beauty, and fishing on one of the wildest and least fished stretches of river in the Lower 48. I consider the entire Gorge my church, but the Ute Mountain Run is my sacred temple. The only trash you see here washes down from the San Luis Valley. It's even rare to see human footprints, and when you catch a hefty trout it has probably never been hooked before. The Ute Mountain Run is truly pristine, the epitome of what "Wild and Scenic River" really means.

The river has a combination of broad riffles and pools, numerous long flats, and some boulder-strewn sections near the bends of the river. The Ute Mountain Run

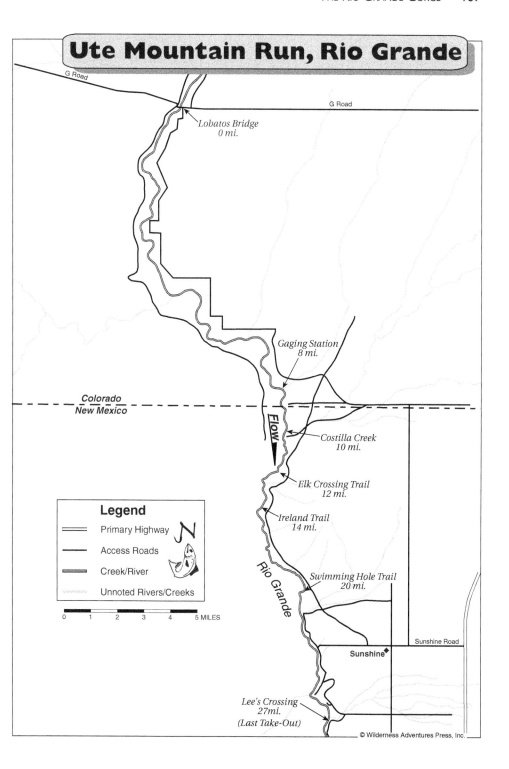

Ute Mountain Run, Rio Grande

G Road

G Road

Lobatos Bridge
0 mi.

Gaging Station
8 mi.

Colorado
New Mexico

Flow

Costilla Creek
10 mi.

Elk Crossing Trail
12 mi.

Ireland Trail
14 mi.

Rio Grande

Swimming Hole Trail
20 mi.

Sunshine Road

Sunshine

Legend

Primary Highway

Access Roads

Creek/River

Unnoted Rivers/Creeks

N

0   1   2   3   4   5 MILES

Lee's Crossing
27mi.
(Last Take-Out)

© Wilderness Adventures Press, Inc.

lacks the water quality, quantity, and temperature found in the interior of the Gorge because much of the water flow during spring and summer is irrigation return flow from farms in southern Colorado.

There are fewer trout per mile in this section, as well, but they are generally larger, averaging 16 to 20 inches, with some browns over 5 pounds. I spotted one brown I estimated at 12 to 15 pounds feeding on giant moths right on the surface. Although the habitat is not suited for large numbers of trout, it's excellent for big trout in small numbers. There is an unlimited supply of crayfish, minnows, chubs, and suckers on which the large browns and cuttbows can feed.

While fishing can be good during spring and summer caddis hatches, the best time to fish the Ute Mountain Run is from September through November when the browns are running. Numerous gravel bars provide good spawning habitat, and some large browns move upstream to spawn here, adding to trout numbers. Unless fish are rising to a hatch, I use large, weighted Soft-Hackle Streamers or big Woolly Buggers. Streamer fishing allows you to cover a tremendous amount of water quickly, and the larger browns tend to lash out at the streamers more readily than small nymphs or dry flies. I can also fish the long stretches of slower water with a large streamer in hopes of catching a rogue big brown giant carp or a toothy northern pike (see Rio Grande pike section at the end of this chapter).

I consider the entire Gorge my church, but the Ute Mountain Run is my sacred temple.

Fall Baetis hatch in abundance at times, and dry-fly fishing can be great, especially on the flats, foam lines, and the tails of riffles. Fish will sometimes move out of the boulder-strewn areas during these hatches to cruise up and down the long flats, gulping insects. When this happens, I match the hatch with a size 16 or 18 Parachute Blue-Winged Olive and sight fish to cruisers. I've experienced this phenomenon only a few times in my life, but each occurrence has a place in my memory as one of the most exciting and fun fishing days of my life. It's one of the things that keeps me coming back to the Ute Mountain Run.

Wild and Scenic River Recreation Area

If you like fishing deep pockets and pools for large trout in an astounding wilderness canyon setting, the Wild and Scenic River National Recreation Area (NRA) is just the place. This is classic Gorge fishing for wild trout at its best.

The area includes 15 miles of the Rio Grande and 4 miles of the lower Red River. Access is good, with several developed trails on both rivers and developed campsites on the rim and at the bottom. Also, there is roadside access to the Red River at the Red River Hatchery north of Taos. (To get to the hatchery, take NM 522 north from Taos about 20 miles, then go west on NM 515 for about 2 miles. Park in the fishermen's parking area and walk downstream to the best water. See the Red River for more details.)

To access the NRA from Taos, take NM 522 north past Questa, go west on NM 378, and then follow the BLM signs to the NRA. There are six good trails, all well marked, and La Junta, Little Arsenic, and Big Arsenic trails interconnect at the bottom. Shelters with tables are available, and there are even a couple of outhouses at the bottom. Floating is not recommended in the NRA due to numerous Class 5 and 6 rapids, which are impassable in the lower flows optimal for fishing. The NRA is dangerous to wade beyond a few feet from the bank because the giant boulders can drop off up to 10 feet directly into fast, deep water. Use breathable hip waders to avoid going in too deep and a good boot with ankle support and "sticky rubber" or "Goodyear" rubber soles for safe walking and wading. The best approach is to boulder hop most of the time, walking in sand (or snow in the winter) where possible. When wading can't be avoided, it's usually only necessary along the edge, to cast to a pocket farther out in the river.

This is perhaps the best section of the Gorge purely from an angler's standpoint. Access is good, water quality and quantity are prime, the scenery is magnificent, and there's a good variety of water types and a healthy trout population. The Red River, once the best wild trout stream in the state, also made an incredible comeback after suffering from years of pollution caused by the Molycorp molybdenum mine between Questa and the town of Red River. The previously mentioned mudslide killed everything in the river and already small wild browns are proliferating. The mine has been selected as a possible Superfund site, and the future of the Red looks good if they address the problem with the tailings piles.

What really makes this section stand out above the rest of the Gorge is spring water. During low flows, much of the water in this section of the Rio Grande comes from the tremendous Rio Grande Aquifer. The spring influence enhances water quality and stabilizes water temperatures, especially in the lower Red River, where even in the dead of winter the water temperature hovers around 48 degrees.

The NRA is fishable year-round, except during runoff. The best fishing is from September through mid-April (when runoff begins) or early morning and late evening during the summer.

Dry-fly fishing can be great during heavy hatches of caddis, Blue-Winged Olives, and midges, but the majority of my time is usually spent fishing wet flies, nymphs, and streamers. During hatches, I like to use an oversized matching dry fly with an appropriate weighted nymph suspended 12 to 24 inches below. Fishing two, or even three, flies at a time has been a standard method on the river since the turn of the last century. Anglers in those days used bamboo rods, gut leaders, and pre-snelled wet flies with loop-to-loop connections, and they caught plenty of fish. They used many of the same flies we still use today, including the Rio Grande King, Coachman, Royal Coachman, Brown Hackle Peacock, Gray Hackle Peacock, and Double Hackle Peacock.

Even when clear, the river has a green tint and runs fast, so the big browns and cuttbows adapt by feeding primarily subsurface. Large basalt boulders create thousands of pockets where fish can hold and feed on nymphs, and occasionally adult insects, drifting by.

I use plenty of weight and a hi-stick nymphing technique when fishing these deep pockets. The closer you get to the pockets, the easier it is to keep excess line off the water, which reduces surface tension and allows the fly to get to the bottom faster. It sometimes takes up to ten casts to get one good drift in the boiling pockets. Don't worry about spooking the fish too much. The trout's vision is severely limited by the distortion from fast-moving water on both sides of the hole.

One of my favorite ways to fish this section is to first spot large fish by climbing up the side of the canyon and looking into the deep pockets. The fish are hard to see until they move, so you must be patient and look for flashes when they feed. During hatches, the trout are easier to spot because they move more consistently and closer to the surface to feed on emergers.

Except during winter midge hatches, I use relatively heavy tippets, generally 3X, even when fishing small nymphs. The water is so fast that you must be able to pressure the fish hard once hooked to prevent it from running downstream through the fast pockets. If the fish gets downstream of your position, it's almost impossible to haul it back up through the fast currents. And maneuvering downstream over enormous boulders can be difficult, dangerous, or simply impossible.

While it's exciting to hook big browns and cuttbows in fast pocket water, landing them is even more rewarding. You're doing well if you can land one fish out of every three hooked. I've had clients hook as many as ten big cuttbows or browns a day on the Red River or Rio Grande and not land a single fish. The lunkers usually break off, pull loose, or straighten hooks when they hit the fast water.

As the water quality in the Red River and Rio Grande has improved, so has the fishing. The number of small fish in the Gorge has increased dramatically in recent years, and since 1993 the Gorge has fished better every year, except during the peak of the drought.

The NMDGF reinstated an old stocking program in the mid-eighties to help offset a lack of spawning habitat. Each year, in conjunction with the BLM and local volunteers, they stock about 200,000 brown trout fry in the Gorge. Using backpacks and jerry jugs, they carry the fry down at various locations. This has dramatically

The Wild and Scenic Recreation Area is in the deepest and most rugged section of the Gorge.

increased the number of browns per mile. Recently, they started stocking Rio Grande cutts in the same manner. I can't wait until they get big enough to start catching. It's been years since I caught a Rio Grande cutthroat in the Gorge.

This is easy work compared to the way they used to stock fish in the 1920s and '30s. My great-grandfather was the Superintendent of Hatcheries at that time, and there weren't any developed trails like we have now. They had to load mules up with old-fashioned milk cans filled with brown trout fingerlings and lead them down the few primitive trails that existed back then. In the early sixties, they stopped raising browns and quit stocking them in the Rio Grande.

The spring-fed section of the Red River extending from the Red River Hatchery downstream about 4 miles to its confluence with the Rio Grande is the main spawning tributary for browns and cuttbows in the Rio Grande. It also provides major winter holding water for big cuttbows and browns because the water stays around 48 degrees all winter long. The Rio Grande averages only about 38 or 39 degrees during the winter. (See the Red River, page 234, for more details on this amazing fishery.)

The NRA is the best section of the Gorge for size and numbers of fish—not to mention the excitement when a 20-plus-inch buck cuttbow slams your caddis pattern and leaps four times in five seconds while ripping downstream over boulders until you can't follow any farther. When it snaps you off you'll be dying for another shot.

Floating is a great way to see and fish the Rio Grande Gorge.

The Middle Box

From the confluence of the Red River downstream for 8 miles to the confluence of Rio Hondo is a section of the Gorge known as the Middle Box. Access to this section is limited to two good trails and one road, the only road that takes you to the bottom of the Gorge in the stretch extending 18 miles south and 65 miles north.

The Cebolla Mesa trail descends from the south rim of the Red River and leads to the confluence of the Red and the Rio Grande. This is one of only two trails into the Gorge where mules are permitted, and it's the only practical put-in for float-fishing from Lee's Crossing to John Dunn Bridge. In contrast to the NRA, the Middle Box has only one Class 3 rapid; the rest of the section is Class l or 2, making it a mild float.

The Middle Box is famous for its many long riffles, especially near Cedar Springs, where an old gold-dredging operation exposed a couple of miles of gravel. The Cedar Springs Trail on the west rim is actually the old miners' road, and it provides good foot access to the area. Big cuttbows seem to congregate here because of the riffles and the influence of the Cedar Springs, which contribute a significant amount of high-quality spring water.

The long riffles also host tremendous populations of caddis larvae and mayfly nymphs. Unfortunately, the caddis hatches peak during the middle of runoff, but there's usually some good fishing to be had at the beginning of the hatch in late April or early May. About one year in seven, a drought occurs that limits runoff and allows the best dry-fly fishing of the year at what would normally be an unfishable time. As runoff subsides, olive and yellow caddis are still hatching, as are numerous species of mayfly. Summer fishing is really only good on cloudy days or during the late evening and early morning when it's cool and the sun is off the water.

The Middle Box is the best section for an extended float-fishing trip because even in low water it's 100-percent passable, unlike other sections. The best times for float-fishing are from mid-April until runoff starts and again from mid-September through November.

I usually allow three days when I float this section of the river. This gives me a day to fish the Red River, then float and fish the Rio Grande for two days. I camp the first night at the Red River confluence and then float to Cedar Springs, where I camp the second night. From there, it's about 4 miles to the take-out at John Dunn Bridge. If time permits, I fish the Rio Hondo for a while.

The Taos Box

From the confluence of the Rio Hondo and the Rio Grande at John Dunn Bridge downstream 18 miles to the confluence with the Rio Pueblo de Taos is a section of the Gorge known as the Taos Box. Famous as the best one-day whitewater float in the Lower 48 states, the Taos Box is a whitewater rafter's dream during high water. With good put-in access at John Dunn Bridge and even better take-out access via NM 570, it would also seem to be the ideal float-fishing stretch. The problem is that the same huge boulders that create good waves during runoff also make it all but impossible to navigate in low water, when fishing is best.

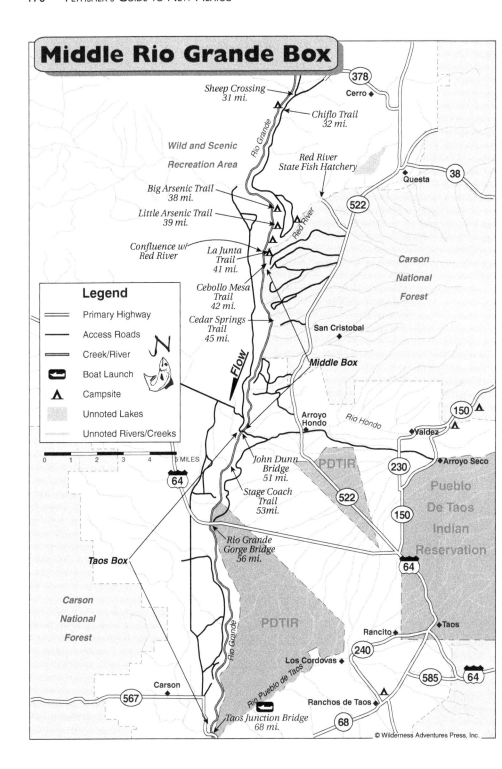

Middle Rio Grande Box

Sheep Crossing
31 mi.

378

Cerro ◆

Chiflo Trail
32 mi.

Rio Grande

Wild and Scenic
Recreation Area

Red River
State Fish Hatchery

◆ Questa

38

Big Arsenic Trail
38 mi.

Little Arsenic Trail
39 mi.

522

Red River

Confluence w/
Red River

La Junta
Trail
41 mi.

Cebollo Mesa
Trail
42 mi.

Carson

National

Forest

Legend

══	Primary Highway
──	Access Roads
══	Creek/River
⬟	Boat Launch
▲	Campsite
▨	Unnoted Lakes
░	Unnoted Rivers/Creeks

Cedar Springs
Trail
45 mi.

San Cristobal ◆

Middle Box

Flow

0 1 2 3 4 5 MILES

64

Arroyo
Hondo ◆

Rio Hondo

150 ▲

◆ Valdez ▲

John Dunn
Bridge
51 mi.

PDTIR

230

◆ Arroyo Seco

Stage Coach
Trail
53mi.

522

150

**Pueblo
De Taos
Indian
Reservation**

Rio Grande
Gorge Bridge
56 mi.

Taos Box

64

Carson

National

Forest

PDTIR

Rancito ◆

◆ Taos

Rio Grande

240

Los Cordovas ◆

Carson ◆

567

Rio Pueblo de Taos

585

64

Ranchos de Taos ◆ ▲

Taos Junction Bridge
68 mi.

68

© Wilderness Adventures Press, Inc.

Other than the roads at the put-in and take-out, there is only one good trail providing access. It's located about 2 miles downstream from John Dunn Bridge at the old stagecoach trail, now marked by the BLM as Manby Springs. Reach the trailhead via Tune Road from US 64 near the Taos Airport. The Taos Box has long been notorious locally for its rugged access, treacherous fast water, and lunker browns. The river warms a little as it winds its way south from the spring-influenced sections upstream, resulting in more browns and fewer rainbows. There are long riffles and pools, as well as deep holes and an endless array of pockets. Big browns can be found in all types of water, but the pockets produce the most action.

Northern pike up to 25 pounds have been caught in the Taos Box, and their populations are healthy. Look for them in long, deep pools and deep holes. A small rainbow or brown trout streamer works well. I use a stiff 9-foot, 7-weight rod with a sink-tip line and about 5 feet of 25-pound-test hard mason monofilament for a leader. Many anglers prefer steel leaders, but I find that the fly behaves more naturally with hard mason. I tie on a weighted streamer to get down deep unless the pike are lying in the shallows. And I like an active retrieve with a definite pause between strips (see Rio Grande Pike section at the end of this chapter).

Prolific caddis hatches occur here from mid-April through July, but fishing is best just before and after runoff. These are also the best times to float-fish the river because there is enough water present, yet the river is clear enough to fish. The best way to float is in a single-man pontoon boat designed for extreme whitewater or a small whitewater raft. You must have tons of experience before attempting this excursion.

I have two rods set up when floating: one with a streamer to pick the numerous pockets as I drift, the other with an Elk Hair Caddis and weighted Double Hackle Peacock suspended under it to fish the riffles and banks, especially when caddis are fluttering on the water. I get out and wade the good runs before floating through. Even when fishing with small dries, I use 4X tippet in order to land the heavy browns in fast water. I like a 9-foot rod for 6-weight line so I can work the pockets easily even when it's windy.

Once the Taos Box gets too low to float, the best wading is between Manby Warm Springs and John Dunn Bridge on the east side. Some big browns have been caught in here in the last few years since the water quality has improved.

The Taos Box is an 18-mile stretch that begins here at John Dunn Bridge and ends at Taos Junction Bridge. There are only one or two primitive trails into this area.

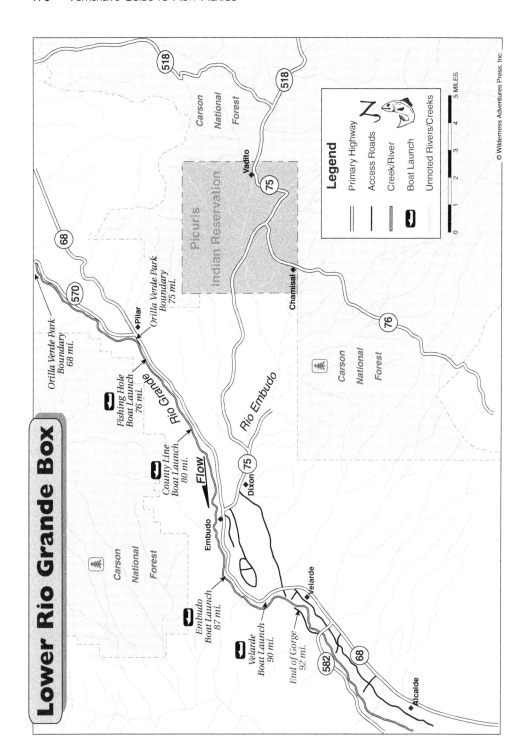

Lower Rio Grande Box

The Lower Box

From the confluence of the Rio Grande and the Rio Pueblo de Taos (Taos Junction Bridge) downstream 15 miles to the confluence with the Rio Embudo, then 9 more miles down to the town of Velarde, is a stretch of the Gorge known as the Lower Box.

NM 570 parallels this southernmost stretch of the Gorge for the first 5 miles through the Orilla Verde Recreation Area. NM 68 (the main road from Taos to Santa Fe) then follows the river for 10 miles to the confluence with the Rio Embudo, continuing to parallel the water for 9 more miles to Velarde at the end of the Gorge.

The Lower Box is one of my favorite sections of the Rio Grande, even though it doesn't offer the best fishing. It's easy to get to, has great hatches, and is easily floated. And it's where my father taught me to fish. We used to stop and fish near Pilar on our way home from fishing a mountain stream or creek during the middle of the day. We'd arrive just as the sun was leaving the water, which allowed us a couple of hours of good fishing. Often we'd camp in the old state park (now Orilla Verde Recreation Area) and night fish a broad riffle or deep hole, then fish again in the morning before the sun hit the water. During fall months, we'd fish all day.

One of my grandfather's favorite holes (and mine) is located about a half-mile above Pilar along NM 68. He was fishing here one day in early May 1966 with his son, Roy, using a double hook set-up. The river was already rising and murky from melting snowpack, so large wet flies were their choice. They caught several browns and rainbows before taking a lunch break and drinking a beer or two.

After smoking an unfiltered Camel, he approached the river and cast into the head of a riffle. As the flies drifted into the deep part of the riffle, the line tightened and he felt a couple of taps. He lifted his rod tip and felt the aggressive wriggling of trout on the other end. He fought the fish, a rainbow and a brown, to the bank before looking around in a daze and finally collapsing and falling to the ground. My uncle Roy carried him to the car and drove him to the clinic in Embudo. It was determined that he died of a stroke, which may have been brought on by a mild heart attack he suffered the week before. He died too young, but he died doing what he loved most. And he was successful to the end. His ashes were scattered in the mighty river close to where he caught his last double.

The section within the recreation area is fairly remote and very scenic. The water is gentle here, with several easily waded riffles and pools, long flats, and a few pockets. Because of its proximity to Taos and Santa Fe, the easy access, and the fact that it's a developed recreational area, it gets more fishing pressure than the rest of the Gorge combined. Nevertheless, it offers some good fishing.

The recreation area is the ideal floating section, with roadside access and nice wide runs to float and fish. Float-fishing before runoff, during the spring Baetis and caddis hatches, can be world class. The put-in is at Taos Junction Bridge, and there are numerous take-outs along NM 570 and NM 68. The river isn't suited for drift boats, however, because there aren't any boat ramps. Small rafts or pontoon boats are a better choice; they're easy to carry and they bounce off rocks without damage.

The caddis hatch is extremely prolific. It starts in the Lower Box and quickly progresses upstream as the days lengthen. The hatch has become famous in recent years. It typically kicks off around April 15 or when the willows begin to bud out and lasts about a month, until the next species starts hatching. Unfortunately, except during drought years, spring runoff starts in early May, putting an end to the great dry-fly fishing.

The beginning of the hatch is best. Later on, the trout are gorged to the point that they won't come to the surface anymore. The hatch is so thick some years that rafts of caddis can be seen floating down the foam lines, and you can't walk along the boulders without stepping on insects. When they're that thick the best fishing is early in the day before the hatch builds up and again just before dark, during what my father used to call "the frenzy," when it seems that every fish in the river starts thrashing the surface.

It was during one of these frenzies that I first learned about skittering caddis. The technique incorporates a downstream drift coupled with an upstream mend strong enough to actually move the fly up a foot or two; let it drift a few feet, then repeat the mend. Each time you mend, your fly imitates a caddis laying eggs, which is irresistible to a feeding trout. I've had browns actually come out of the water and take the fly in the air during the middle of a mend. Sometimes, after fishing upstream through a riffle without results, I turn around and skitter a caddis over the same water and catch fish that wouldn't take the earlier dead drifts.

As with much of the Gorge, the fishing is temperamental and most anglers don't do well here. The average trout is smaller too, but there are still some big fish. Rainbows are stocked frequently, and the holdovers that don't get caught by bait- and spinfishermen become hefty fish. Now they stock pure Rio Grande cutthroats on a regular basis too. Hopefully, it will soon be possible to catch trophy-sized cutts in the Rio Grande just like my father, grandfather and great grandfather in the 1910s to 1950s.

The Rio Grande, and the Lower Box in particular, are famous for an aquatic insect that is just now gaining fame elsewhere. It's called a cranefly larva, and it's extremely abundant in the Gorge and its tributaries. It looks like a grub worm and lives in the rocks, where it feeds on organic material like the weeds and moss growing on boulders.

The Double Hackle Peacock is the most popular fly in northern New Mexico, but most anglers don't know it imitates the cranefly larva. It can be fished deep like a nymph, although most locals fish it using the traditional wet-fly method—throwing two or three flies (on droppers) straight out or a little downstream and letting them swing downstream through the current. The fish take the flies on the swing or at the end of the drift. I used to watch my father and grandfather use this technique to land doubles and occasional triples during cranefly, caddis, or White Miller hatches near dark in the recreation area.

Good dry-fly fishing sometimes occurs during the middle of winter, when midges hatch every afternoon. The fish feed freely on the abundant flies in the flats once the sun leaves the water. On cloudy days, prior to a southern storm, the fishing can be good all day. A Griffith's Gnat or a black and gray Mating Midge, size 16, works well when the trout are feeding on top. The best technique for fooling the selective feeders is to position yourself upstream of the sippers and use a downstream slack-line cast to place the fly no more than 2 or 3 feet above the fish. If you don't get a strike as the fly drifts over the fish, skate it to the side (away from the sippers) before pulling some slack in and picking up to cast again. False cast away from the risers to avoid spooking them with water spray.

If the water temperature drops below 39 degrees or the air temperature drops below zero for more than a couple of days it can put the fish down, sometimes indefinitely. In 1990, 1993, and again in 2000, it got so cold for one week that the midge fishing shut down for the rest of the winter. In most years, however, it's very consistent, although the trout caught rarely exceed 12 inches.

The next 10 miles of the Gorge run through a series of fast pockets, deep holes, and finally some long riffles and pools amid cottonwoods and apple orchards. There are big fish throughout the entire stretch, despite the fact that a major highway parallels the river. This run is not developed like the recreation area, and access from the road is generally rugged and steep. Most anglers don't know how to attack the endless array of pockets here, so there's less pressure and more holding water, which translates into more big fish.

The spring caddis hatch provides excellent dry-fly opportunities, although an incredible Blue-Winged Olive hatch, which precedes the caddis by a week or two,

The Lower Box has over 25 miles of good roadside access to the Rio Grande.

sometimes masks it. The action can be fast and furious, and in recent years it hasn't been uncommon to have some 30- to 50-fish days using a dry-dropper combo.

If you're an experienced floater this is a fun stretch to tackle in a single-man pontoon boat, especially during the caddis hatch. But there are many Class 3, and some Class 4, rapids and endless boulder gardens, especially in low water. The put-in is at the Quartzite parking area near Pilar. The take-out is at the County Line parking lot.

From the County Line parking lot downstream 10 miles to the town of Velarde, there is a nice stretch of water with decent roadside access. The upper 7 miles are mostly private, but the lower 3 are all public. This is a good stretch to float, as it's mostly Class 1 and 2 water with lots of long riffles and pools. The put-in is at the County Line parking lot and take-outs are scattered from Embudo Station to Velarde.

RIO GRANDE PIKE (ESOX LUCIUS)

By Ed Adams

The Rio Grande in northern New Mexico and southern Colorado offers a unique angling experience that is just coming into vogue. Folklore has it that in the late 1950s, a private lake in southern Colorado stocked with northern pike was breeched and the contents flowed into the Rio Grande. Over the ensuing six decades, they have flourished and spread throughout the river from Del Norte to Santa Fe. In the process they have bumped the trout down a notch in the hierarchy of predators in the Rio Grande drainage.

There is a very healthy pike population throughout the above mentioned area, but I suspect that fears of a devastating impact on the trout in the river are for the most part unfounded. Pike are the ultimate predators and feed on almost anything that moves. They are opportunistic and while they won't turn down a trout offering, they prefer slower, less agile fare. Carp, chubs, suckers and crawdads are abundant and a lot easier to ambush.

We have seen fish up to 50 inches and 20 pounds in the Rio Grande. This fall, my daughter, Rita and her friend JP, spotted a 7-pound carp, or rather what was left of it, floating downstream. The aft section of the fish had been violently severed, an obvious victim of Esox Lucius, a.k.a. northern pike. With a mouth full of very sharp teeth, these toothy monsters should be handled with care; a pair of long handled pliers and gloves should be part of your gear.

Pike tackle is a bit stouter than that used for trout. A 7 or 8 weight rod with a floating or sink-tip line is advisable. Some fishermen use a wire "shock tippet" but I find these difficult to cast and really not necessary. Pike teeth are more like needles than razors and cases of a pike severing the 20-pound tippet I use are few and far between. A far bigger issue is frayed tippet and checking your terminal tackle after each encounter is a good idea.

My recipe for a pike leader is about 2 feet of 20-pound mono blood-knotted to a 4-foot section of 40-pound mono (here I use a slightly tinted mono) and finally

another 2-foot section of 20-pound mono to which I tie the fly with some sort of loop knot (Duncan or Uni). Flies are not as critical as with trout but must be big and flashy. I prefer a visible fly that I can pick up earlier in the retrieve (the tinted 40-pound mono lets me know the fly will soon come into view) as pike often like to follow its prey before striking. It's not uncommon for a pike to follow and turn off a fly a couple of times before finally taking it. Varying your retrieve is as complicated as this type of fishing gets. The real key is finding the "pike water".

One of the reasons trout and pike can coexist is that they don't like the same type of water. Trout like moving, oxygenated water that brings food to their table. Pike prefer slow or stillwater where they can lurk with little movement and wait, much like a mugger. In my experience where you find one pike there are bound to be more so don't be in hurry to move on after catching one or two. Look for calm or stillwater adjacent to the current with a silty bottom. If you can find structure in this type of water, so much the better. Pike love to ambush prey from the shelter of large rocks, logjams, and beaver dams.

Even in the best trout sections of the Rio there are some inviting pike lies that most trout anglers routinely pass up. During the spawn (February and March) large females are often seen in very shallow water accompanied by one or more smaller males. They don't spook easily and will return to their lie in a short period of time. They are not as into feeding during this period but may strike out of curiosity or aggression. Post spawn is the best of the spring pike season, when mating is over and hunger sets in. Good pike action can be found up until the high water starts.

My favorite time to hunt pike is in the fall before winter makes wading and hiking less of an option. Fishing can be good from mid-October through November or until the first heavy snow and frigid temps close a lot of pike spots for the winter.

Access to the pike fishing on the Rio Grande is the same as for the trout fishing but two of the best areas are in the Orilla Verde Recreation Area south of Taos and the Ute Mt. Run near the Colorado border. The former has good roadside access and the latter is accessed via rugged, primitive roads and a handful of steep, unmarked trails.

Stream Facts: Rio Grande Gorge

Season
- Fishing is open all year. Remember, the weather can do anything here, so prepare for the worst and hope for the best. Always carry a minimum of 2 quarts of water in the summer and at least a quart during winter.

Special Regulations
- The Rio Grande from the Colorado border downstream to the Taos Junction Bridge on NM 570 just north of Pilar is designated Special Trout Water. The daily bag and possession limit is three fish. No tackle restrictions.
- From Taos Junction Bridge on NM 570 downstream to the town of Velarde, general regulations apply. The daily bag and possession limit is five fish except that only two may be cutthroat (any trout with a red slash under its jaw is considered a cutthroat).
- The Red River from a quarter-mile below the Red River Hatchery to the confluence with the Rio Grande is designated as Special Trout Water. The daily bag and possession limit is three trout. No tackle restrictions.

Trout
- Abundant brown trout averaging 12 to 15 inches, with many larger (up to 10 pounds or more). Rainbows and cuttbows aren't as prolific, but good populations exist from Lee's Crossing to Rio Hondo and on the lower Red River. Cuttbows average 16 to 20 inches, some to 24 inches or more. Good populations of stocker rainbows are present from Taos Junction Bridge to Velarde; average size 12 inches.

River Miles
- Lobatos Bridge in Colorado—0
- Gaging station at the Colorado border—8
- Costilla Creek Trail (primitive, unmarked, undeveloped)—10
- Elk Crossing Trail (primitive, unmarked, undeveloped)—12
- Ireland Trail (primitive, unmarked, undeveloped)—14
- Swimming Hole Trail (primitive, unmarked, undeveloped; good for take-out)—20
- Lee's Crossing Trail (marked, semi-developed, rugged, about ¾ mile; good for take-out)—27
- Sheep Crossing Campground and Trail (developed NRA trail, ¾ mile)—31
- Chiflo Campground and Trail (developed NRA trail, ¾ mile)—32
- Big Arsenic Springs Campground and Trail (developed, about 1 mile)—38
- Little Arsenic Springs Campground and Trail (developed, about 1 mile)—39
- La Junta Campground and Trail (developed, with group facilities and a good trail 1.25 miles long leading to the confluence of the Rio Grande and the Red River)—41
- Cebolla Mesa Trail (developed USFS campground and trail about 1.5 miles long; one of the only trails where pack animals are permitted; put-in for Middle Box)—42
- Garapata Trail (primitive, unmarked, undeveloped, rugged, about 1.75 miles)—45

- Cedar Springs (Miners') Trail, West Rim (primitive trail, about 1 mile)—45
- John Dunn Bridge (take-out for Middle Box; put-in for Taos Box; rough dirt road access)—51
- Manby Springs (Stagecoach) Trail (primitive trail, about 1 mile)—53
- Rio Grande Gorge Bridge (no trail)—56
- Taos Junction Bridge (put-in for Lower Box; take-out for Taos Box; access via NM 570)—68
- Orilla Verde NRA northern boundary (roadside access for 7 miles through the NRA; several campgrounds, including two group shelters call BLM Taos Resource Area for reservations)—68
- Orilla Verde NRA southern boundary—75
- Fishing Hole (put-in and take-out; roadside fishing access between Fishing Hole and County Line)—76
- County Line (put-in and take-out)—80
- Embudo Station (put-in and take-out; good roadside access between Embudo Station and Velarde)—87
- Velarde (put-in and take-out and the end of the Gorge)—90

River Characteristics
- A mostly inaccessible freestone river with over 90 miles of rugged canyon. Water types range from broad riffles and pools to boulder-strewn pockets, deep holes, and long flats. Except for roadside access areas, you should be physically fit to hike in and out of the Gorge.

Cautions
- The Rio Grande Gorge presents many dangers including unstable ground, primitive trails, large boulders, fast, deep whitewater, flash floods, falling rock, lightning and inclement weather at any time of year. Do not use felt soles in any remote hike-in areas of the Gorge or when snow or ice are on the ground and rocks. Only people with whitewater experience should float the Gorge. Always let someone know where you are going and when you will be back and take at least one or two quarts of water per person per day.

River Flows
- Winter: ranges between 100 and 300 cfs at the Colorado border to between 250 and 600 cfs at Embudo Station.
- Spring runoff: ranges between 300 and 5,000 cfs.
- Summer: ranges between 50 and 500 cfs at the Colorado border and between 250 and 700 cfs at Embudo Station.
- Fall: ranges between 50 and 300 cfs at the Colorado border and 200 to 600 cfs at Embudo Station.

Maps
- *New Mexico Atlas & Gazetteer,* page 16; Carson National Forest Map; BLM Taos Resource Area Map; USGS Quadrangle Maps: Ute Mountain, Sunshine, Guadalupe Mountain, Arroyo Hondo, Los Cordovas, Taos SW, Embudo

Agencies
- BLM Taos Resource Area, 224 Cruz Alta Road, Taos, NM 87571
- USFS Carson National Forest, Questa Ranger District, Questa
- NMDGF, Raton

Outfitters
The BLM Taos Resource Area can provide information, including maps and a list of outfitters permitted to operate in the Gorge. Outfitters include:
- The Solitary Angler, 204B North Pueblo Road, Taos, NM 87529; 1-866-502-1700, www.thesolitaryangler.com
- Ed Adams Flyfishing, P.O. Box 428, Questa, NM 87556; 505-586-1512
- Taylor Streit Fly Fishing Service, P.O. Box 2759, Taos, NM 87571; 505-751-1312
- High Desert Angler, 460 Cerrillos Road, Santa Fe, NM 87501; 505-988-7688, 1-888-988-7688, www.highdesertangler.com

Stripping large, ugly streamers is the best way to cover the water quickly and connect with the enormous trout in the Ute Mountain Run.

RIO GRANDE GORGE MAJOR HATCHES

Insect	J	F	M	A	M	J	J	A	S	O	N	D	Time	Flies
Midges		■										■	M/E	Red & olive midge larva #16–#20; olive, gray, black and zebra midge pupa #18–#24; Disco Midge #18–#24; Mating Midge #14–#20; Griffith's Gnat #16–#22; Snowfly #16–#26
Caddis			■	■	■	■	■	■	■				M/A/E	Green & olive caddis larva #12–#16; Double Hackle Peacock #12–#16; Van's Rag Pupa or LaFontaine's Pupa #10–#18; green or olive Green Weenie #12–#18; olive, tan & gray Elk Hair Caddis #12–#20;
Craneflies					■	■	■	■	■				M/A/E	Cranefly larva peacock, gray or dark olive #6–#16; Taylor Streit's Poundmeister #6–#14;
Green, Gray Drake						■	■	■					M/A/SF	Olive Hare's Ear #10–#14; Van's Rag Fly #10–#14; Green & Gray Drake Hair-Wing (Wulff style) #10–#14; Green & Gray Paradrake #10–14; Green Drake spinner #12–#14
Ginger, Yellow, Blue & Mahogany Duns					■	■	■	■	■				M/E	Hare's Ear Nymph #10–#18; Pheasant Tail Nymph #12–#18; light, dark, pink & ginger Hair-Wing Duns #12–18; Ginger, Red & Blue Quills; Royal Wulff, Rio Grande King Hair-Wing or Rio Grande Trude #12–#18; H&L Variant #12–#18

Hatch Time Code: M = Morning; A = Afternoon; E = Evening; D = Dark; SF = Spinner Fall

RIO GRANDE GORGE MAJOR HATCHES (cont.)

Insect	J	F	M	A	M	J	J	A	S	O	N	D	Time	Flies
Baetis				█					█	█	█		M/A/SF	Dark olive Hare's Ear Nymph #16–#22; Pheasant Tail #16–#22; Van's Rag Fly Nymph dark olive #16–#22; Lawson's BWO Fan-Wing Emerger #16–#22; Olive Parachute #16–#22; Olive Comparadun #16–#22
Large and Medium Golden Stonefly					█	█	█						M/A	Black & brown stonefly nymph #6–#10; Golden Stone Nymph #10–#14; Orange & Gold Stimulators #6–#14; Terminator #12–#16
PMDs, PEDs					█	█	█	█					M/SF	Light Hare's Ear Nymph #12–#18; Pheasant Tail #12–#20; Van's Rag Fly Nymph light olive #14–#20; Lawson's Fan-Wing Emerger #14–#22; PMD, PED #14–#20
Terrestrials							█	█	█				M/A	Para-hoppers tan, yellow #8–#14; Bees #12–#14; Elk Hair Moths #8–#14

Hatch Time Code: M = Morning; A = Afternoon; E = Evening; D = Dark; SF = Spinner Fall

RIO COSTILLA WATERSHED

The Rio Costilla on Valle Vidal

Originating as several tiny creeks high in the Sangre de Cristo Mountains of Colorado, the headwaters of the Rio Costilla gather in New Mexico on Vermejo Park, a huge private ranch currently owned by Ted Turner. (See page 349 in Private Waters for details on Vermejo Park.) After several miles, it flows into Costilla Reservoir. It then becomes a small tailwater flowing from the bottom of the reservoir, leaving Vermejo Park and entering the Carson National Forest about a half-mile below the dam.

For the first 6 miles below the dam, the Costilla runs through a National Forest Management Unit known as the Valle Vidal, and it's closed to fishing from January 1 to June 30 each year to protect spawning Rio Grande cutthroats and calving elk. Once open, Special Trout Water regulations apply—artificial flies and lures only with a single barbless hook and catch and release only.

Reminiscent of the small streams in Yellowstone National Park, the Rio Costilla winds through beautiful alpine meadows filled with wildflowers. The scenery is astounding, and the fish and wildlife are abundant and carefully managed. It's not uncommon to see deer, elk, bear, turkey, and other wildlife while fishing. Once part of Vermejo Park, the 100,000-acre Valle Vidal Unit was donated to the public by the previous owners in settlement for taxes due in 1982.

The river is about 20 feet wide in most places and has many long riffles, deep undercut banks, and gravel bars with shelves that drop into deep holes. Most of the river within the Valle Vidal is wide open, with the exception of the occasional alder, making it a great stream for novice casters.

The Rio Costilla's expansive high alpine meadows, spectacular views, abundance of wildlife, and native cutthroats will all remind you of Yellowstone National Park.

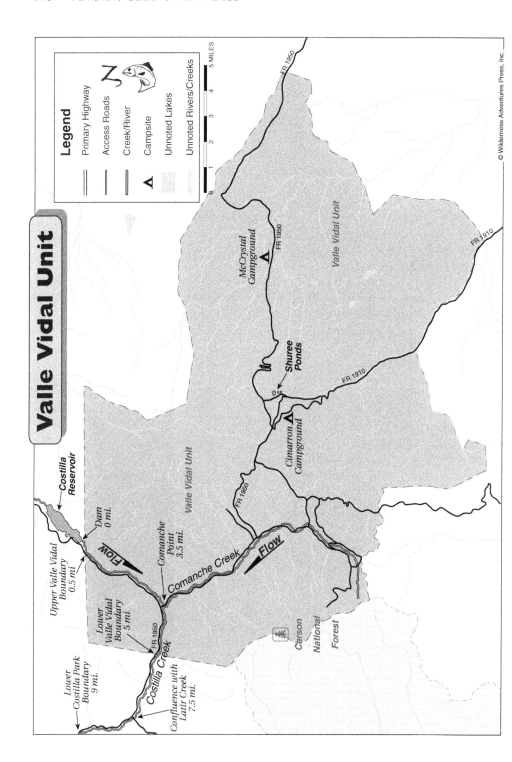

Valle Vidal Unit

Legend

Primary Highway
Access Roads
Creek/River
▲ Campsite
Unnoted Lakes
Unnoted Rivers/Creeks

0 1 2 3 4 5 MILES

© Wilderness Adventures Press, Inc.

FR 1950

McCrystal Campground

FR 1950

Shuree Ponds

FR 1910

Valle Vidal Unit

FR 1910

Cimarron Campground

FR 1950

Valle Vidal Unit

Costilla Reservoir

Dam 0 mi.

Flow

Upper Valle Vidal Boundary 0.5 mi.

Comanche Point 3.5 mi.

Comanche Creek

Flow

Lower Valle Vidal Boundary 5 mi.

FR 1950

Costilla Creek

Carson National Forest

Lower Costilla Park Boundary 9 mi.

Confluence with Latir Creek 7.5 mi.

The majority of the trout are native Rio Grande cutthroats or cuttbows that average 8 to 12 inches, with some up to 18 inches. Rainbows, browns, and brookies show up occasionally, and they all take dry flies readily. The actual numbers vary year to year, but there are between 2,000 and 5,000 catchable-sized trout per mile in the first 4 miles below the dam. That's a lot of fish for a river that averages 40 to 50 cfs during the release period for irrigation by local farmers and ranchers, which runs from May through September. After the irrigation season ends, flows get shut off at the dam until May. It's amazing the fish even survive under such water management, much less flourish.

The trout school up in deep holes and wait for winter to end and the state to open the gates. And when they do open, the water is going full bore so downstream users can flood their fields for the first spring watering. Until 2007, flows from the bottom of Costilla Reservoir were high during the week in the irrigation season, between 70 and 100 cfs from 5:00 p.m. Sunday until 9:00 a.m. Friday, at which time they would reduce the flows to around 25 to 30 cfs for weekend anglers. Now they moderate the flow between 50 and 75 cfs continually until the end of the irrigation season.

As with cutthroats everywhere, these fish like attractor patterns such as Royal Humpies and Trudes, although they sometimes become selective if there's a hatch, or during periods of high angling pressure like around the Fourth of July or Labor Day weekend.

The Rio Costilla is a rich tailwater, but it also has a steep grade and strong currents, which means it has a wide variety of large, swift-water aquatic insects. Giant Golden Stones, various caddis, large brown sedges, and Gray, Olive, and Brown Drakes, PMDs, and Blue Duns start hatching in June and continue through mid-August. Ginger Duns and PEDs hatch from July through mid-September, and the evening spinner fall can bring some larger trout to the surface. Hoppers and a variety of ants are plentiful along the tall grassy banks from July through September, and yellow pine moths frequently find themselves trapped in the fast currents and back eddies.

I use a light 3- or 4-weight here, no more than 8 feet long, with a 7½-foot, 5X leader. If they're taking dries I use a single dry fly and match the hatch, but if they aren't tearing it up I add a weighted nymph slightly smaller than the dry fly about 18 inches down. If something takes the submerged nymph it will tug on the indicator fly, revealing a strike.

Often, the addition of a weighted nymph on the dropper will slow the drift of the dry fly just enough to make it seem more vulnerable to fish, resulting in more strikes on the dry fly than if it were fished alone. I've tested this theory by taking the nymph off. I stopped getting strikes on the dry fly, so I added a dropper and just put small split shot on instead of a nymph. I immediately started getting strikes again. The dry-dropper technique works especially well during higher flows over 70 cfs.

I keep my line short and get as close as I can to the fish when the water is high in order to keep most of my line off of the water, which ensures a good drift in the tight eddies, seams, and pockets the trout are holding in. They won't hold in the faster main current very often, so pay more attention to the few calm areas. And don't overlook smaller side channels and flooded backwaters. It's possible to pluck some nice fish out of these spots.

Fishing the shelf holes, fast riffles, and deep seams using a hi-stick nymphing technique can be very effective when you can't get fish on the surface. I start with two full layers of twist-on lead about an inch long to get the fly down in the fast currents, and then I adjust the amount of lead up or down depending on whether I'm bumping the bottom or not. I continue to adjust the lead as I fish different spots.

During low flows, the technique is completely different. I try to match the hatch exactly when there is one, otherwise I use whatever I know has been hatching or working recently. I fish directly upstream and make my casts as long as possible while still avoiding drag in the system, continually mending and throwing in slack. If I don't get any action I add a dropper with a matching nymph, sometimes with a bead to keep it down. I rarely nymph fish in low flows because the cutts will usually come to the surface for my dry fly or take the suspended dropper.

Hardly anyone fished the Rio Costilla the first few years that the Valle Vidal was open, but now it has become the premier dry-fly stream in the state from July through September, especially on weekends. But it's still possible to find solitude during the week.

Stalking a Rio Grande cutthrout in the lower meadows on the Rio Costilla in the Valle Vidal.

Comanche Creek

The Valle Vidal also includes three small creeks but only Comanche Creek is worth a look. It's a small tributary of Rio Costilla that enters the river about 4 miles below the dam. There are 4 miles of roadside access upstream from the confluence, and a parking area where the road leaves the river provides walk-in access to another 3 miles.

Comanche Creek is a miniature version of Rio Costilla, and I do mean miniature. A small leap will get you across it in most places, but don't let that deceive you. The creek is chock full of native Rio Grande cutts from 6 to 12 inches, with a few larger fish. The banks are severely undercut, providing excellent cover for trout.

Stealth is key when fishing Comanche Creek, and long, accurate, delicate casts are sometimes required to get a strike in the narrow pools. At other times, just a dabble over the edge of a grassy bank will work. The first time I fished Comanche I was astonished at the number and size of the cutthroats in this tiny creek. I landed over 50 fish in just a few hours, and a dozen were over 12 inches, including one 16-inch whopper. Pressure and drought have since impacted the creek, especially where the road runs near the creek.

New Mexico Trout, a local club, has been working with the Carson National Forest over the last few years to restore and improve conditions during low flows, especially in drought conditions. Because of its diminutive size, the creek is highly susceptible to drought cycles; consequently, the trout populations are cyclical, as well.

If the fish aren't spooked, just about any caddis or parachute dry fly between size 14 and 18 will bring fish to the surface. I prefer a fly called a Terminator, which was designed and named by Eddie Adams of Eddie Adams Flyfishing, an excellent local angler and guide. It's similar to an Elk Hair Caddis, with a golden body, ginger butt, and palmered grizzly hackle. It effectively imitates everything from small Golden Stones to caddis and pine moths.

Shuree Ponds

There are three man-made ponds in the Valle Vidal, located about 8 miles from the confluence of Comanche Creek and Rio Costilla. One of them is reserved for kids under 12 years of age, and they are all heavily stocked with large rainbows. They are regulated as Special Trout Waters: artificial flies and lures only with single barbless hooks. The daily bag and possession limit is two trout over 15 inches.

Many of the stockers hold over for several years, and they get very large. In fact, Ron Williams, of Taos, New Mexico, caught a 14-pound rainbow on an olive Woolly Bugger here, and fish up to 5 pounds aren't uncommon. The upper pond is large enough to float tube, but it can also be fished from shore. All three ponds have plenty of weed beds that provide abundant sources of food ranging from scuds, snails, and minnows to damselflies, dragonflies, midges, and large olive sedges.

The sedges hatch during July and August, and when they come off the big rainbows can't let one go by. The giant bugs skitter along the surface in a circular path for long periods, making all kinds of disturbance until they can fly away—if they don't get gobbled up first. After observing this the first time, I developed a technique that involves casting a size 6 or 8 olive Elk Hair Sedge near a skittering natural. I then mend the line so that it lies on the water in a semi-circle. As I strip the line, the fly follows its circular path, thus imitating the motion the natural makes. The strike is vicious and unmistakable as a hefty rainbow slams the fly and surges toward the weeds, leaping out of the water and ripping your line into the backing before turning and finally giving in.

Cimarron Campground, a good Forest Service fee-area developed campground, is located less than a mile from Shuree Ponds. Primitive camping is also available in the Rio Costilla Park.

Rio Costilla Park

The Rio Costilla leaves the Valle Vidal about 6 miles below the dam, entering the Rio Costilla Park for the next 6.5 miles. It then runs through a series of small private ranches, where it gets diverted into so many irrigation ditches in Colorado and New Mexico that it eventually dries up before reaching the mighty Rio Grande Gorge.

The Rio Costilla Park encompasses over 80,000 acres, of which 10,000 are open to recreation. It's owned by the Rio Costilla Cooperative Livestock Association (RCCLA), a 182-member association made up mostly of landowners in the lower Rio Costilla Valley. They use it for grazing cattle in the summer, as well as for hunting, fishing, camping, and wood gathering. The RCCLA property includes over 6 miles of the Rio Costilla, 2.5 miles of Latir Creek, nine glacier lakes known as the Latir Lakes, and Little Blue Lake. The six miles of Rio Costilla are leased by the NMDGF and it is open to the public for fishing year round.

From the Valle Vidal boundary downstream about 3 miles to its confluence with Latir Creek, the Rio Costilla is much like the Valle Vidal section of the river, except that it's much wider, has more shallow riffles, and less undercut banks due to long-term overgrazing. Nevertheless, there are some good deep holes, especially at the bends, and the fish are larger than in the Valle Vidal. There are fewer pure cutthroats, though, and the NMDGF stocks rainbows here that can hold over and get quite large. It's managed as Special Trout Water: artificial flies and lures only with a single barbless hook and catch and release only.

Large and small Golden Stoneflies, caddis, and Western Drakes hatch in June and July, and Ginger Duns, caddis, and Yellow Sallies hatch in August and September. Of course, hoppers, ants, and pine moths are also abundant. The Terminator is my favorite fly for this area, but Stimulators, olive Elk Hair Caddis and Goddard Caddis also work well, especially with a nymph dropper. During Ginger Dun hatches, I use a parachute or thorax-style poly-wing dun.

Below Latir Creek, the Rio Costilla runs through a canyon with sheer granite walls for 3 miles. Some larger fish inhabit this section, including holdover stocker rainbows up to 20 inches. General regulations apply, so expect to see some bait- and spinfishers, especially on the weekends. But the water still fishes pretty well because

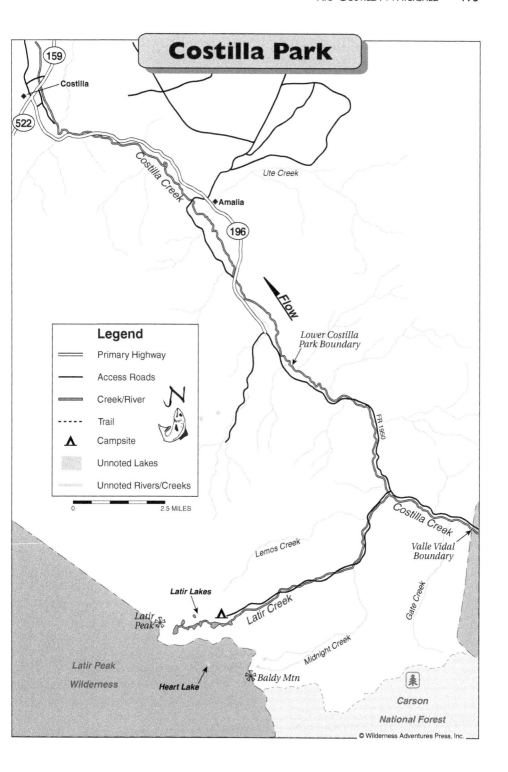

Costilla Park

159

Costilla

522

Costilla Creek

Ute Creek

◆Amalia

196

Flow

Lower Costilla
Park Boundary

Legend

—— Primary Highway

—— Access Roads

—— Creek/River

- - - Trail

Λ Campsite

Unnoted Lakes

Unnoted Rivers/Creeks

N

0   2.5 MILES

FR 1950

Costilla Creek

Lemos Creek

Valle Vidal
Boundary

Gate Creek

Latir Lakes

Latir
Peak ✳

Λ

Latir Creek

Midnight Creek

Latir Peak
Wilderness

Heart Lake

✳ Baldy Mtn

🌲

Carson

National Forest

© Wilderness Adventures Press, Inc.

those anglers generally don't cover the water as thoroughly as flyfishers.

The casting is more challenging in the canyon, as alders, firs, spruce, and shrubs line the rocky banks. Many deep holes and boulder-strewn pockets hold nice trout, though. Dry-dropper rigs work well here, as do standard nymphing techniques. I like to use a size 12 Golden Stimulator or size 8 Parachute Hopper with a size 14 dark Hare's Ear or olive caddis larva for a dropper. Stripping a Woolly Bugger through the deep holes and pockets will also turn a few fish. I prefer a size 8 or 10 Woolly Bugger in black or black with brown hackle and a large gold bead head. During high flows, I add enough weight to the leader to ensure that I get the Bugger deep enough in the fast currents, pockets, and deep pools.

Latir Creek

From its confluence with the Rio Costilla upstream for about 2 miles, Latir Creek provides an opportunity to catch some pure Rio Grande cutthroats in classic freestone water. Above this point, it splits into two smaller creeks, Latir and Midnight. Both have an abundance of small cutthroats, but you'll be dabbling just a foot of line and your leader most of the time since the creeks are no more than a couple of feet wide and lined with brush and trees. The Latir Lakes are located at the head of Latir Creek.

There are some great primitive campsites on lower Latir Creek, which are available for a modest fee (paid at the RCCLA entrance gate located at the confluence of Rio Costilla and Latir Creek).

Latir Lakes

The Latir Lakes are a string of nine natural glacier lakes connected by Latir Creek. It's about 6 miles from the RCCLA entrance gate to the third lake and the end of the rocky, rutted four-wheel-drive road. The lakes are numbered 1 through 9, starting from the bottom. All but #1 and #2 are large enough to float tube, and the lakes are only about a quarter-mile or so apart so access is fairly easy. Lakes #3 through #9 are between 2 and 10 surface acres, with #3 and #9 the largest. The lakes have fewer nutrients as you move up toward tree line at Lake #9, which lies in a rugged, barren bowl at the base of Latir Peak.

Permits can be obtained at the pay station at the Latir Creek and Rio Costilla confluence or at the main office located in the town of Costilla. The phone number is 1-800-Rio-Park. The current fees are: $20.00 per vehicle per day, with an additional $7.00 per angler per day. No tackle restrictions and a daily bag and possession limit of four trout over 12 inches. No motorized boats allowed.

Horses are allowed in the park, but it's best to leave the truck and trailer where the road starts up the mountain near the confluence of Latir and Midnight Creeks, because the road is rough from there on. There are good primitive campsites at the lakes, and the trail between the lakes is pretty beaten up from over 200 years of use by hunters and anglers. Some huge Rio Grande cutts have been caught here over the years, including the state record, caught in #9 on an Olive Scud in 1982, when the lakes were in their prime. The giant cutt was a 24-inch slab weighing over 10 pounds, and it was typical of the pigs with fins that cruised these lakes and spawned in the creek before a mysterious decline occurred in the size and number of fish during the mid-eighties.

Studies showed that the top six lakes were almost totally void of fish, but a definitive cause was never found. One professor I talked to when I was up there guiding a client theorized that a series of events combined for the demise, but that the final blow was after a rough winter in '84. We had a lot of snow early that year, followed by a cold mid-winter, heavy late snow, and a warm, wet spring. He thought that one of two things might have happened. The first possibility was that the early snow froze into a sheet of ice on the steep mountains surrounding the lakes. Then the late, heavy snow avalanched into the lakes, killing most of the fish. His second theory was that there was a build up of weeds in the lakes, which died under the deep ice and snow, and the fish were overcome by noxious gas as the weeds rapidly decomposed.

It remains a mystery, but the top six lakes were closed for a few years to be restocked and restored. Unfortunately, the RCCLA didn't have a source for Rio Grande cutthroats so they've been stocking Snake River cutthroats and rainbows. Now there's a mix of rainbows, cutthroats, and cuttbows.

Rainbows are still being stocked in the Latir Lakes, but future plans are to kill everything and start fresh with a Rio Grande cutthroat stocking program. Once established, stricter regulations will go into effect in order to protect the wild, naturally reproducing, native Rio Grande cutthroat population within the Latir Lakes and the

For a nominal fee, Rio Costilla Park provides fishing access to the Latir Lakes, nine natural glacial lakes at the base of several 12,000-foot peaks.

entire Latir drainage. Until then, there's some very big trout cruising the lakes.

The lakes are usually closed until late June to allow the cutthroats to spawn undisturbed. If you're planning a trip early in the year, be sure to call the RCCLA to check when they're opening. The lakes are situated between 11,000 and 12,000 feet, and it can snow any month of the year. The nights can be cold, so bring plenty of layers and a good sleeping bag if you're camping.

All the lakes have weeds and the usual high-country aquatic insect assortment. Scuds are particularly abundant, and the evening midge hatches can be excellent. Terrestrials include ants, termites, budworms, pine moths, beetles, and some hoppers. Of course, there are also minnows and large swimming damsel and dragonfly nymphs.

Unless there is surface activity, I usually start with a triple scud rig, with two Olive Scuds followed by an Orange Scud, all size 14 or 16. I use a full-sink or sink-tip line with a 9-foot, 5X leader due to the crystal-clear water, and I add a little bit of lead about a foot above the top fly. I usually fish the scuds fairly close to shore and near logs and other structure, stripping 2 feet at a time while wriggling the rod tip, followed by a short pause. Many strikes come at the very end of the retrieve.

I always carry two rods, even when float-tubing. One is rigged with nymphs, scuds, or streamers, and the other with a dry fly or dry-dropper combo for casting to risers and shallow cruisers. This saves valuable time otherwise lost to changing rigs and lines, and it ensures that you are ready for any situation, including a broken rod. The best dry-fly fishing is usually during evening midge hatches, but be on the lookout for bank cruisers taking terrestrials at any time of day. The inlets and outlets are great places to strip or drift nymphs.

On my first trip to the Latir Lakes, I was fishing the inlet to #3, where I could see giant cutts feeding on something just under the surface. I drifted a small Orange Scud into them and had hook-ups on the first five casts. But every one wrapped me around a dead tree root and snapped me off, despite the fact that I dropped back to 2X tippet.

I finally landed one, a beautiful 8-pounder, and a quick sampling of his throat revealed not Orange Scuds but bright-orange caddis pupae. I didn't have any of those patterns with me, but the scuds seemed to be doing fine. I eventually landed about five more fish between 18 and 22 inches and broke off several others. I've never duplicated that day, but I've had some spectacular fishing over the years and plan on having many more in the future.

The scenery around the lakes is nothing short of spectacular, and wildlife is abundant. This includes black bears, so don't leave food out if you're camping. For hikers, the Latir Wilderness boundary is less than a half-mile from #7 via Trail 115 to Heart Lake. There are no significant fisheries within the wilderness area, but it's beautiful high country with an excellent trail system and few visitors. Wilderness permits can be purchased at the Questa Ranger District office.

Access to Valle Vidal and Rio Costilla Park

To get to the Valle Vidal and Rio Costilla Park from Taos, take NM 522 north about 48 miles to the village of Costilla, then go east on NM 196. Follow the signs for about 13 miles to the entrance of Rio Costilla Park, where the road becomes FR 1950. From there, it's a little over 3 miles to the pay station and entrance to Latir Lakes.

Following FR 1950 for another 3 miles will bring you to the entrance of Valle Vidal. The road follows the Rio Costilla for about 1.5 miles to Comanche Point and then continues up Comanche Creek for another 4 miles before leaving the creek and heading 6 more miles to Shuree Ponds and Cimarron Campground. From Comanche Point, you can also continue up the Rio Costilla toward Costilla Reservoir another 3.5 miles via FR 1900.

Rio Costilla Park and the Valle Vidal and Latir Wilderness Area offer visitors over 200,000 acres of magnificent country without huge crowds. The entire Rio Costilla watershed is the best-managed fishery in the state, and the combination of high-mountain lakes, ponds, streams (one tailwater), primitive and developed camping, and good access makes it the best, most flyfisher-friendly location in New Mexico. I wish the state managed all the major streams in the same manner.

Stream Facts: Valle Vidal and Rio Costilla Park

Season
- Rio Costilla in the Valle Vidal and the rest of Valle Vidal—open July 1 to December 31; daylight hours only.
- Rio Costilla in Costilla Park from the upper Valle Vidal boundary downstream about 7 miles to the lower Rio Costilla Park boundary—open year-round.
- Latir Lakes—late June through September.

Special Regulations
- Rio Costilla in the Valle Vidal and Rio Costilla in Costilla Park from the upper Valle Vidal boundary downstream about 3 miles to the confluence with Latir Creek—artificial flies and lures only with a single barbless hook, catch-and-release only.
- Rio Costilla from its confluence with Latir Creek downstream 2.5 miles to the lower Costilla Park boundary—general regulations apply; daily bag and possession limit five trout of which only two can be cutthroat (any trout with a red slash under their jaw).
- Shuree Ponds—artificial flies and lures only with a single barbless hook; daily bag and possession limit of two trout at least 15 inches or longer; the lower pond is reserved for kids under 12 year of age.
- Latir Lakes—no tackle restrictions (check with the RCCLA for updated regulations); daily bag and possession limit of four trout over 12 inches.

Trout
- Rio Grande cutthroat, cuttbows, rainbows, brookies in the Rio Costilla, and cutthroats and cuttbows in all other streams. Stocker rainbows in Shuree Ponds.

Campgrounds
- Cimarron Campground Questa Ranger District, 9,300 feet; 14-day length of stay limit; pay campground open May to October; 36 campsites for tents and trailers; tables, fireplace, toilets; drinking water available; some sites with horse facilities. Directions: From NM 522 in Costilla, travel east on NM 196 past Amalia to the intersection of FR 1950. Travel on 1950 (a gravel road) east to the Unit boundary. Follow FR 1950 to the junction with FR 1900 and turn right to cross Costilla Creek. Continue on FR 1950 10 miles to the junction with FR 1910. Climb 1 mile up the hill to the campground.
- McCrystal Creek CampgroundQuesta Ranger District, 8,100 ft. elevation; 14-day length of stay; pay campground open May to October; 60 campsites for tents and trailers; tables, fireplace, toilets; 6 campsites for horse campers;Water from creek not recommended for drinking.Directions: From the town of Cimarron, drive 5 miles northeast on US 64 to Cerrososo Canyon. Follow this canyon approximately 21 miles to the Valle Vidal Unit boundary. Signs mark the route. From the boundary, travel 7 miles on FR 1950. These graveled roads are not maintained during the rainy season and may be passable only with a four-wheel-drive vehicle.
- Primitive camping available at Costilla Park.

River Miles
- Costilla Dam—0
- Upper Valle Vidal boundary—0.5
- Comanche Point—3.5
- Lower Valle Vidal/upper Costilla Park boundary—5
- Confluence of Rio Costilla and Latir Creek—7.5
- Lower Costilla Park boundary—9

River Flows (Rio Costilla in the Valle Vidal)
- During storage (late fall through April): 5 cfs
- During release (late April through mid-October): between 40 and 120 cfs for farmers to irrigate.

Maps
- *New Mexico Atlas & Gazetteer,* page 16; Carson National Forest Map; BLM Taos Resource Area Map; USGS Quadrangle Maps: The Wall, Ash Mountain, Comanche Point, Latir Peak

Agencies
- USFS Carson National Forest, Questa Ranger District, P.O. Box 110 Questa, NM 87556
- NMDGF, P.O. Box 25112, Santa Fe, NM 87504-5112

Outfitters

The Carson National Forest can provide information, including maps and a list of outfitters permitted to operate in the Valle Vidal. Outfitters include:

- The Solitary Angler, 204B North Pueblo Road, Taos, NM 87529; 1-866-502-1700, www.thesolitaryangler.com
- Ed Adams Flyfishing, P.O. Box 428, Questa, NM 87556; 505-586-1512
- Doc Thompson's High Country Anglers, P.O. Box 52, Ute Park, NM 87749; 505-376-9220
- Taylor Streit Fly Fishing Service, P.O. Box 2759, Taos, NM 87571; 505-751-1312
- High Desert Angler, 460 Cerrillos Road, Santa Fe, NM 87501; 505-988-7688, 1-888-988-7688, www.highdesertangler.com
- The Rio Costilla Park can issue permits to fish and camp in the park, including at Latir Lakes. They can be reached at: Rio Costilla Park, P.O. Box 111, Costilla, NM 87524; 1-800-RIO-PARK, www.riocostillapark.com

VALLE VIDAL/RIO COSTILLA MAJOR HATCHES

Insect	J	F	M	A	M	J	J	A	S	O	N	D	Time	Flies
Midges										■	■		M/E	Red & olive midge larva #16–#20; olive, gray, black and zebra midge pupa #18–#24; Mating Midge #14–#20; black & gray Midge Clusters #10–#16; Griffith's Gnat #16–#22; Snowfly #16–#26
Caddis									■				M/A/E	Green & olive caddis larva #12–#16; Double Hackle Peacock #12–#16; Van's Rag Pupa or LaFontaine's Pupa #10–#18; green or dark olive Green Weenie #12–#18; olive, tan & gray Elk Hair Caddis #12–#20; olive, gray & peacock Fluttering Caddis #10–#18
Craneflies									■				M/A/E	Cranefly larva peacock, gray or dark olive #6–#16; Taylor Streit's Poundmeister #6–#14; Double Hackle Peacock #6–#16; Foam Body Cranefly #6–#16
Green, Gray Drake									■				M/A/SF	Olive Hare's Ear #10–#14; Van's Rag Fly #10–#14; Green & Gray Drake Hair-Wing (Wulff style) #10–#14; Green & Gray Paradrake #10–14; Green Drake spinner #12–#14
Ginger, Blue & Mahogany Duns							■		■				M/E/SF	Light, dark & olive Hare's Ear Nymph #10–#18; Pheasant Tail Nymph #12–#18; light, dark, pink & ginger Hair-Wing Duns or Cahills #12–#18 or the same in parachutes; Ginger, Red & Blue Quills; Royal Wulff, Rio Grande King Hair-Wing or Rio Grande Trude #12–#18; H&L Variant #12–#18

Hatch Time Code: M = Morning; A = Afternoon; E = Evening; D = Dark; SF = Spinner Fall

VALLE VIDAL/RIO COSTILLA MAJOR HATCHES (cont.)

Insect	J	F	M	A	M	J	J	A	S	O	N	D	Time	Flies
Baetis				■						■			M/A/SF	Dark olive Hare's Ear Nymph #16–#22; Pheasant Tail #16–#22; Van's Rag Fly Nymph #16–#22; Lawson's BWO Fan-Wing Emerger #16–#22; Olive Parachute #16–#22; Olive Comparadun #16–#22
Salmonfly, Large and Medium Golden Stonefly							■						M/A	Black & brown stonefly nymph #4–#10; Golden Stone Nymph #10–#14; Elk Hair Salmonfly #4–#8; Orange & Gold Stimulators #4–#14; Terminator #12–#16
PMDs, PEDs					■	■	■						M/SF	Light Hare's Ear Nymph #12–#18; Pheasant Tail #12–#20; Van's Rag Fly Nymph light olive #14–#20; Lawson's Fan-Wing Emerger #14–#22; PMD, PED #14–#20
Terrestrials						■	■	■	■	■	■		M/A	Para-hoppers tan, yellow #8–#14; Bees #12–14; Elk Hair Pine Moths #8–#14; beetles & ants #12–#18

Hatch Time Code: M = Morning; A = Afternoon; E = Evening; D = Dark; SF = Spinner Fall

LATIR LAKES MAJOR HATCHES

Insect	J	F	M	A	M	J	J	A	S	O	N	D	Time	Flies
Blue Damselfly							▮	▮					M/E	Olive Marabou Damsel #8–#14; Extended Body Parachute Blue Damsel #8–#14
Midges							▮	▮					M/E	Red & olive midge larva #16–# 20; olive, gray, black and zebra midge pupa #18–#24; Pheasant Tail #16–#22; Disco Midge #18–#24; Mating Midge #14–#20; black & gray Midge Clusters #10–#16; Griffith's Gnat #16–#22; Snowfly #16–#26
Scuds							▮	▮					M/E	Olive & light orange scuds #14–#20
Callibaetis							▮	▮					M/A/SF	Dark Olive Hare's Ear Nymph #14–#18; Para Adams #14–#18; Blue Quill #14–#18; Speckled-wing Dun #14–#18; Callibaetis Spinner #16–#20
Caddis							▮	▮					M/E	Olive & orange Elk Hair Sedge #8–#14; dark olive micro-caddis #18–#22
Minnows							▮	▮					M/E	Soft-Hackle Streamers or Woolly Buggers in assorted colors #4–#14
Roe (Trout Eggs)							▮						M/E	Orange, gold, chartreuse, peach micro-eggs #16–#18
Terrestrials							▮	▮					M/E	Ants, termites, true flies, beetles, bees #12–#18

Hatch Time Code: M = Morning; A = Afternoon; E = Evening; D = Dark; SF = Spinner Fall

FLYFISHING THE ENCHANTED CIRCLE

The Enchanted Circle contains many surprises, not the least of which is the diversity of the landscape. This 86-mile trip through the southern Rocky Mountains will dispel any thoughts you may have of New Mexico being strictly a desert state. The circle is anchored by Wheeler Peak, which at 13,161 feet is the highest point in New Mexico. Taos is the area hub, but you can start your journey from several communities along the way—Questa, Red River, Eagle Nest, or Angel Fire.

Starting from Taos, take US 64 east for about 18 miles before going over Palo Flechado Pass and dropping down into Angel Fire, one of the fastest growing towns in New Mexico. Continue on US 64 a few miles past the turnoff to Angel Fire, where you'll see Wheeler Peak on your left and Eagle Nest Lake on your right.

Eagle Nest Lake

Eagle Nest Lake and the village of Eagle Nest lie just a few miles beyond the turnoff to Angel Fire. Shopping or staying in the nearby village is like stepping back into the Old West—with modern conveniences, of course.

Constructed for irrigation in 1918 by ranchers Charles and Frank Springer, 2,200-acre Eagle Nest Lake offers anglers excellent opportunities to catch rainbow trout and kokanee salmon. The lake is very popular among trollers and shorebound baitfishers, but flyfishers are uncommon here.

Years ago, before the NMDGF leased the lake, fishing was fabulous for trophy-sized rainbows. Since they've taken over, the fishery has declined significantly in terms of average fish size. High bag limits and no tackle restrictions, combined with dramatically increased pressure and too many chubs, suckers, and perch, have led to its current status.

The state bought the lake, and it became a state park in 2005, leading to more pressure but more stocking of rainbows and browns and, hopefully, better regulations eventually. The state stocks kokanee salmon in Eagle Nest, and they do feed on flies until mature.

Due to high winds on the lake, it's not very friendly for flyfishers, but it does still offer some excellent opportunities when calmer conditions prevail. The wind rarely blows from sunrise through midmorning, and evening midge hatches bring some nice trout and salmon to the surface after the afternoon breezes die down.

Float tubes are great if you stick close to shore, which is fine since the best surface activity is usually near shore where there are more weed beds and more hatching midges and feeding fish. A boat is better for getting around the lake—and getting off the water when the wind begins to howl. And I mean howl. Thirty- to 40-mph winds are common, and I've seen it get up to 70 mph at times. Don't wait too long to head in when the wind picks up or you may have to deal with 3- to 5-foot whitecaps, which can cause problems for smaller boats.

The best time to flyfish Eagle Nest for big fish is from just after the ice breaks up through May, when fish cruise close to shore looking for minnows, chubs, and

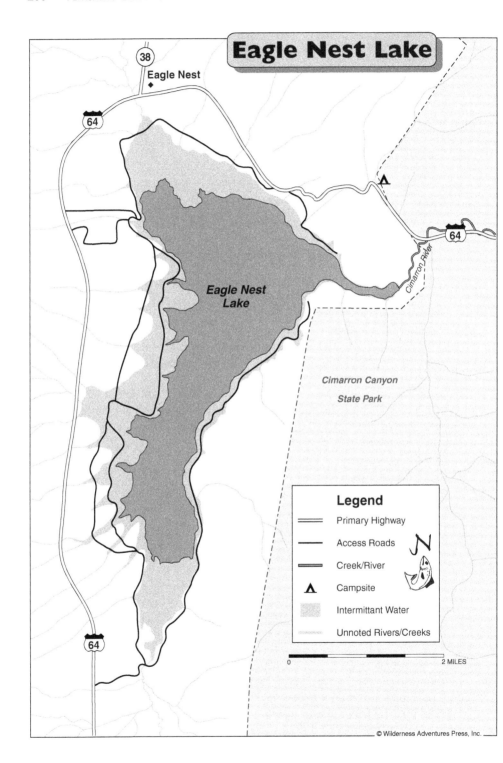

Eagle Nest Lake

Eagle Nest

Eagle Nest
Lake

Cimarron River

Cimarron Canyon
State Park

Legend

Primary Highway

Access Roads

Creek/River

Campsite

Intermittant Water

Unnoted Rivers/Creeks

0   2 MILES

© Wilderness Adventures Press, Inc.

crayfish. Various streamers work well at this time, and my favorite is a black and white Soft-Hackle Streamer or a black and brown Woolly Bugger, both in 2X long, size 4 to 8.

To catch the bigger fish, watch for shallow cruisers near the weed beds and shoreline. Look for the V-shaped wakes as fish attack chub and sucker minnows, then throw the streamer in their path and start stripping, with a slight pause between strips. Incorporate a wriggle of the rod tip as you strip. When you get a strike, just lift and tighten up, don't set real hard or you could break off.

Rainbows and cuttbows also run up the tributaries to spawn at this time providing some great stream fishing above the inlets. A micro egg is the most productive fly when going after these spawners. The problem is that the suckers are spawning at the same time and you end up snagging five suckers for every trout. When this happens I switch to streamers, which will only catch the trout but maybe not as many.

As summer approaches in June, damselfly nymphs and midge larvae become more significant. An olive marabou damsel, size 10 to 14, will usually do the trick. To imitate the midge, try an olive or red midge larva, size 16 to 22. Look for fish rising to midges in the morning and late evening from June through September. Try a Griffith's Gnat, black Midge Cluster, or Mating Midge, and cast close to the rise. Sometimes suspending a midge larva or pupa under the Midge Cluster will produce more action, especially if fish are feeding just under the surface.

On calm days through August, there are vigorous hatches of Callibaetis, which are the most fun hatch because the trout sip them lazily. Imitate them with a Speckle-Wing Dun, Blue Dun, Adams Irresistible, Parachute Adams, or Callibaetis Spinner, size 16 to 20.

Fall is usually very windy, but on quiet evenings through October the midge fishing can be quite good. Kokanee salmon also become very active by late October, and if caught before they turn pink on the outside, they can be excellent eating. Use streamers in fairly bright colors like yellow, orange, and red with Krystal Flash, size 4 to 10. Look for salmon near inlets and outlets and around shallow gravel.

Various access points can be found on the north and west sides of the lake, and the new marina is located on the west side. Eagle Nest Marina & Mountain View Cabins has boat rentals, tackle, hunting/fishing licenses, and guided trips available; call them at 575-377-6941.

Contact the Eagle Nest Chamber of Commerce at 1-800-494-9117 or www.eaglenest.org for more information.

Lake Facts: Eagle Nest Lake

Season
- Ice-out (mid-April) through October.

Trout
- Rainbows, Snake River cutthroat (rare), some browns and kokanee salmon in the 2,200-acre lake.

Campgrounds
- RV parks in Eagle Nest.
- Tolby Campground on US 64 just below Eagle Nest Dam in the Colin Neblett State Wildlife Area on the Cimarron River.

Maps
- *New Mexico Atlas & Gazetteer,* pages 16 and 17; Carson National Forest Map; BLM Map: Wheeler Peak; USGS Quadrangle Maps: Eagle Nest

Agencies
- NMDGF, P.O. Box 25112, Santa Fe, NM 87504-5112

Outfitters
- The Solitary Angler, 204B North Pueblo Road, Taos, NM 87529; 1-866-502-1700, www.thesolitaryangler.com
- Ed Adams Flyfishing, P.O. Box 428, Questa, NM 87556; 505-586-1512
- Doc Thompson's High Country Anglers, P.O. Box 52, Ute Park, NM 87749; 505-376-9220
- Taylor Streit Fly Fishing Service, PO Box 2759, Taos, NM 87571; 575-751-1312

The author's father with a nice Cimarron brown caught during an evening caddis hatch.

EAGLE NEST LAKE MAJOR HATCHES

Insect	J	F	M	A	M	J	J	A	S	O	N	D	Time	Flies
Blue Damselfly				▓	▓	▓	▓	▓	▓	▓			M/E	Olive Marabou Damsel #8–#14; Extended Body Parachute Blue Damsel #8–#14
Midges				▓	▓					▓	▓		M/E	Red & olive midge larva #16–#20; olive, gray, black and zebra midge pupa #18–#24; Pheasant Tail #16–#22; Disco Midge #18–#24; Mating Midge #14–#20; black & gray Midge Clusters #10–#16; Griffith's Gnat #16–#22; Snowfly #16–#26
Scuds				▓	▓	▓	▓	▓	▓	▓			M/E	Olive & light orange scuds #14–#20
Callibaetis					▓	▓	▓	▓	▓				M/A/SF	Dark Olive Hare's Ear Nymph #14–#18; Para Adams #14–#18; Blue Quill #14–#18; Speckled-wing Dun #14–#18; Callibaetis Spinner #16–#20
Caddis						▓	▓	▓					M/E	Olive & Orange Elk Hair Sedge #8–#14; Dark Olive Micro-caddis #18–#22
Minnows				▓	▓	▓	▓	▓	▓	▓	▓		M/E	Soft-Hackle Streamers or Woolly Buggers in assorted colors #4–#14
Roe (Trout Eggs)					▓					▓			M/E	Orange, gold, chartreuse, peach micro-eggs #16–#18
Terrestrials							▓	▓	▓				M/E	Ants, termites, true flies, beetles, bees #12–#18; Dave's Hoppers

Hatch Time Code: M = Morning; A = Afternoon; E = Evening; D = Dark; SF = Spinner Fall

Cimarron River

The Cimarron River is a splendid tailwater spewing out from the bottom of Eagle Nest Dam, located where the panoramic Moreno Valley meets the Cimarron Canyon. It winds through the tight, brushy canyon for about 7 miles before opening up into Ute Park, and finally continuing through 8 miles of the Philmont Boy Scout Ranch.

Most streams in northern New Mexico flow into the Rio Grande and, eventually, the Gulf of Mexico. The Cimarron, however, flows east into the Canadian and Arkansas Rivers, which dump their flow into the mighty Mississippi. It wasn't always this way, evidenced by the fact that the Cimarron watershed has Rio Grande cutthroats. The cutthroats migrated into the river before the last ice age, when the Cimarron flowed into the Rio Grande.

It's difficult to find cutthroats now, but the Cimarron is a very rich tailwater loaded with 10- to 14-inch browns, with a decent population of fish running 12 to 18 inches. Unfortunately, the NMDGF heavily stocks the river with inferior 9-inch rainbows. The Cimarron once was, and still could be, one of the best wild brown trout streams in the West, but a combination of mismanagement by the state, increased fishing pressure and harvesting of fish, decreased winter flows, and drought have all plagued the marvelous little stream.

Nevertheless, the river remains New Mexico's premier brown trout fishery, boasting a whopping 3,000-plus trout per mile (less than half of its population in 1982). There is hope that water-flow problems in winter can be remedied now that the state owns Eagle Nest Lake, as they have limited water rights when there is excess water in the reservoir. This won't help during periods of drought, but it could be beneficial when there is average or better snowpack.

As far as management goes, NMDGF officials aren't very aggressive in implementing special regulations and usually oppose recommendations that restrict methods and reduce bag limits. But there is a Special Trout Water section on the Cimarron, located just below Tolby Creek Campground. I recommended the new regulation in 1988 at a proclamation meeting where the state takes recommendations from the public, but back then nobody used to show up except for me and another local outfitter, Taylor Streit.

That was the first time we were able to get any type of meaningful regulations passed, but we still didn't get what we asked for. Instead of the recommended 4.5 miles of water, artificial flies and lures only, and a daily bag limit of one trout over 18 inches, they gave us 1.4 miles of water and a daily bag limit of two trout over 12 inches. This, of course, targeted the larger fish for harvest, mainly brood trout that keep the populations healthy and diverse. They're also the most fun to catch and release.

They began stocking the STW with 9-inch rainbows, which just enticed illegal baitfishermen into the supposed wild trout water. We were finally able to convince them to stop stocking the STW in 1994. After presenting them with over 1,600 signatures requesting an extension to 3 miles and a change in the bag limit, they amended the regulations to one trout over 16 inches in 2000. But they wouldn't extend the distance, despite the fact that this is one of the most popular and productive flyfishing streams

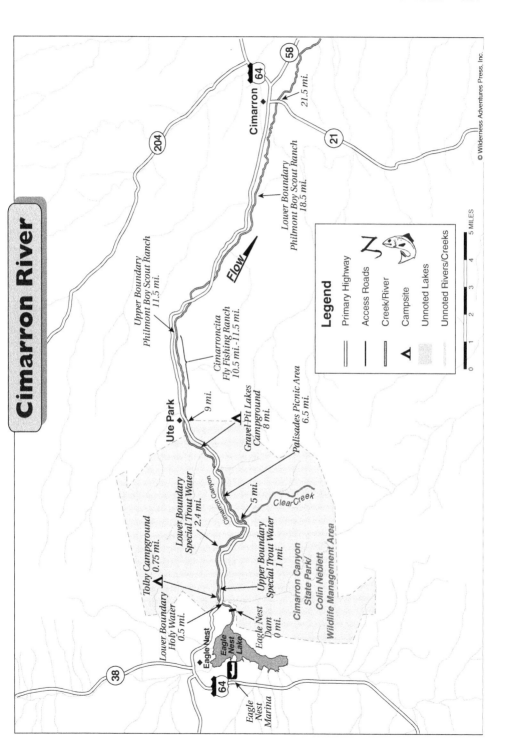

Cimarron River

Cimarron

Upper Boundary
Philmont Boy Scout Ranch
11.5 mi.

Lower Boundary
Philmont Boy Scout Ranch
18.5 mi.

21.5 mi.

Flow

Ute Park

9 mi.

Cimarroncita
Fly Fishing Ranch
10.5 mi.–11.5 mi.

Gravel Pit Lakes
Campground
8 mi.

Palisades Picnic Area
6.5 mi.

Cimarron Canyon

Clear Creek

5 mi.

Lower Boundary
Special Trout Water
2.4 mi.

Upper Boundary
Special Trout Water
1 mi.

Cimarron Canyon
State Park/
Colin Neblett
Wildlife Management Area

Tolby Campground
0.75 mi.

Lower Boundary
Holy Water
0.5 mi.

Eagle Nest
Dam
0 mi.

Eagle Nest

Eagle
Nest
Lake

Eagle
Nest
Marina

Legend

‖	Primary Highway	
	Access Roads	
	Creek/River	
▲	Campsite	
	Unnoted Lakes	
	Unnoted Rivers/Creeks	

N

0 1 2 3 4 5 MILES

© Wilderness Adventures Press, Inc.

in the state. Eventually, if sportsmen are persistent, we may convince them to extend the Special Trout Water to 3 or 4 miles.

The Cimarron is a medium-sized stream by New Mexico standards, about 20 feet wide in most places, except in the beaver ponds, which can be quite large. It averages about 35 cfs when they're releasing water for downstream farmers. This starts in late April or early May and lasts into mid-October or later.

Hip waders with felt or lug soles are sufficient, and wading is easy except when flows exceed 50 cfs. The river bottom is mostly medium-sized rock down to gravel, although deep holes and beaver ponds are usually filled with silt and should be approached with caution. My father broke his ankle in 2001 when wading a silty backwater on a stretch of private water called the Holy Water. He hooked a hefty brown while standing in a couple of inches of silt, and when he tried to move toward the bank to land the fish he lost his balance and fell. One foot stuck in the silt, snapping his ankle as he went down. After getting his foot loose, he crawled through the water to the bank and landed the 16-inch trout, his last brown for six months.

Let's look at the river section by section. The Holy Water is private and includes the first half-mile of the Cimarron below Eagle Nest Dam. It's owned by the C. S. Cattle Company, the former owners of Eagle Nest Lake. The C. S. Ranch is one of the largest working ranches in America, and it has been in the same family for at least four generations. (For information on fishing the Holy Water on the Cimarron, see page 368 in Private Waters.)

The Cimarron River enters the Colin Neblett Wildlife Area below the Holy Water, where Tolby Creek joins it just before the US 64 crossing. Tolby Campground is located just below the bridge in the cottonwoods next to the river; it's a nice campground with good bathrooms. The Special Trout Water starts less than 100 yards below the campground. Camping in the wildlife area is restricted to two developed campgrounds, Tolby and Gravel Pit Lakes. The latter is located about 6 miles downstream, near the end of the wildlife area.

US 64 parallels the Cimarron, crossing it several times, and there are plenty of pullouts for anglers to park in. The Cimarron Canyon is beautiful, with an abundance of wildlife easy to spot at dusk and dawn when animals come down to the bottom of the canyon to water, browse on the lush vegetation, and in some cases, bed down for the night in the tall grass. The canyon is heavily forested with scrub oak, cottonwood, fir, spruce, and pine trees, and the riverbanks are choked with overhanging brush. The river exhibits a unique combination of riffles, pools, pockets, deep holes, undercut and overhanging banks, logjams, and beaver ponds, all of which provide excellent cover, holding water, and spawning habitat for the trout. Aquatic insects thrive in all the weed beds and around submerged logs and bushes, boulders and gravel bars.

Below the wildlife area, the Cimarron runs through the small community of Ute Park and then into a ranch called Cimarroncita. This delightful mile-long stretch of private water is the most open part of the river, and it has a good combination of riffles, pools, holes, and undercut banks at the many bends in the river. It's managed by Doc Thompson, a professional flyfishing outfitter, guide, and owner of High Country

Anglers; a guide is required to fish this water. Doc limits the pressure to a maximum of four anglers per day. (To fish the Cimarroncita, contact Doc Thompson at P.O. Box 52, Ute Park, NM 87749; 505-376-9220 or www.flyfishnewmexico.com.)

Below Cimarroncita, the Cimarron continues running on private property, this time through the Philmont Boy Scout Ranch for 7 miles and then across a series of private ranches before joining the Canadian River.

Casting on the Cimarron is difficult at best, and a short, light rod—about 7½ to 8 feet long and 3- or 4-weight—is required to keep your line out of the brush. I recommend using a double-taper floating line and a 7½-foot, 5X tapered leader. Wade slowly upstream, staying close to the bank and using the bushes for cover, so you can get as close as possible to the fish without spooking them. Keep your line short. If you need more distance try to shoot more line on your delivery cast, avoiding the brush, rather than false casting more line.

To effectively fish this river, an angler must know how to cast forehand and backhand, roll cast, flip cast, bow cast, swing cast, and steeple cast, mend line smoothly, and control slack. If you don't already have these skills you will after a few days on the Cimarron. It's an intermediate to advanced stream, but still a great place for beginners to learn on because of the number of different techniques used and the number of opportunities to succeed.

The Cimarron's fish are very hatch-oriented, and pressure in recent years has made the wild browns very selective, adding to the difficulties of angling on this challenging stream. The good news is that there are multiple hatches, and you can usually match the size, shape, and color of one insect or another. After matching the hatch, drift is all-important; any drag in the system will result in missed opportunities. But don't worry, there are plenty of opportunities.

The Cimarron River is one of the finest dry-fly streams in the state, boasting great hatches and a healthy population of wild browns.

Hatches are prolific and season-long, with something usually happening on top. If not, nymphs fished deep can yield some nice fish. Early in the year, before they turn the river up, scuds are a primary food source in the first couple of miles below the dam. The fish tend to school up in the holes and beaver ponds during low flows, so stealth is important. Using very little weight and a small strike indicator, approach the bottom of a pool slowly and cast to the head of it, letting the scud drift through. Strikes can be subtle, so set the hook on anything that moves the indicator. If fish are spooking because of your indicator, take it off and reduce the lead, then watch for fish flashing at or near your fly or look for the white of their mouths as they take the scud before you set the hook.

Look for fish rising to midges in the beaver ponds. If they are, match the natural with a size 20 to 22 Snow Fly or Griffith's Gnat. Wade along the edge and carefully position yourself just above the rise so you can cast out and slightly downstream, landing the fly no more than a foot or two above the rise. And make sure you have some excess slack in the line so that it can drift drag-free into the trout's feeding lane.

When they first turn the river up in late April or early May, the water is full of scuds flushed out of the bottom of the reservoir and from the first few miles of river bottom. The trout really turn on when this happens, sometimes feeding with reckless abandon on the helpless scuds. With the higher, turbid flows, an angler can get closer to the fish without spooking them, resulting in less snagging in the bushes and more hook-ups on trout. You may want to add more weight and a larger indicator or use a hi-stick nymphing technique. I usually use a double-nymph rig with an Orange

The water flowing through the Colin Neblett Wildlife Area has some big browns.

Scud on top and a Pheasant Tail on the bottom. An untrained eye may not be able to actually spot fish, but working the main riffles, seams, and undercut banks can produce some hefty bottom feeders.

By early May, Blue-Winged Olives (Baetis) start coming off from about 11:00 to 3:00 daily, and they hatch better on cloudy days. Look for risers in the slower pools and beaver ponds and match the insects with a BWO Dun or Olive Parachute, size 18 to 20. If fish aren't taking the dry, try a dropper 12 to 18 inches long with a Beadhead Pheasant Tail, size 16 to 18. Try the faster, deeper riffles and holes when using the dropper. If you still don't have success, try nymphing with a double-nymph rig, using a size 18 Pheasant Tail and any medium-sized nymph.

Late May brings the large and famous Golden Stonefly and Salmonfly hatches, sometimes in large volume. These typically start down near the town of Cimarron on the private Philmont Boy Scout Ranch and progress upstream, ending at the top of the Colin Neblett Wildlife Area near the dam in late July. My favorite imitations are orange and golden Bird's Stoneflies, Terminators, and Stimulators, size 8 to 16. Fish these as dries or use a sparsely hackled version with a floss body and fish it wet, just under the surface, early in the day or when they won't take anything on top.

My first experience with this hatch was on June 9, 1979, at the grand opening of Eagle Nest Lake, which had recently been leased by the state. When my oldest brother Bill and I arrived at the lake there were over 200 cars trying to get in at two accesses, and it was a mess. My uncle, Al Hobday, was the NMDGF news and public relations person and was there to record opening day events, so we stopped to chat with him for a minute.

An avid angler, he told us that if he could fish that day he'd get the hell out of there and go down to the lower Cimarron where the willow flies (what we used to call stoneflies because they hang out and mate on the willows) were hatching and catch wild browns rather than deal with this zoo. He pulled a couple of snelled Sofa Pillows from his old leather fly book and directed us to Philmont Boy Scout Ranch, which was public water at the time.

When we got out of the car, the large orange willow flies were flying all around us. A quick shake of a willow branch revealed the bumper crop that was coming off that year. The river was slightly murky, but a glance into the hole we parked near revealed a rise or two. With shaky hands, I quickly attached the snelled fly with an old-fashioned loop-to-loop connection and ran down to the pool.

My first cast fell short of the rise, but another trout took the irresistible imitation. I quickly landed the fat 12-inch brown, and while removing the hook, I noticed that the fish was so full of orange stoneflies that they were coming out of its mouth. The fish was literally stuffed to the gills. We ended up catching and releasing over 50 browns each, mostly between 8 and 13 inches, with a few up to 16. Bill even caught one 18-inch hen that weighed over 3 pounds. After that day, the Cimarron became my favorite dry-fly stream in the state, and I usually had it to myself until about 1983, when other anglers began discovering this hidden jewel.

Also hatching in June and July are PMDs and Gray and Olive Drakes. Ginger, Mahogany, and Blue Duns hatch in July and August. Match the hatches with the appropriate size, shape, and color of parachutes, Wulffs, or traditional patterns like light, dark, or pink Cahills and Hendricksons. Use Blue, Ginger, and Mahogany Duns or quill patterns to imitate spinners. Of course, more exact imitations such as Comparaduns, Lawson's No Hackles, thorax duns, poly-wing spinners, and emergers also work well at times. My favorite mayfly patterns are a thorax-style or Wulff-style Ginger Dun, size 14 to 18, and a good old standby, the Adams Irresistible, size 12 to 18.

From late May through July, the peak dry-fly season, it's not uncommon for a good angler to catch fish all day long, switching flies occasionally as different hatches occur. During the evening frenzy, when spinners from the day's hatches are littering the water's surface and multiple caddis species are hatching, the river appears to be boiling, as every fish in the river starts rising to the smorgasbord of insects.

The action is fast and furious, and as the light gets lower at dusk it becomes harder to see the fly, so I adopted what I call the three-second rule. After casting in the general vicinity of a rise, I count to three and set the hook. My brother Robert and I had the experience of a lifetime in 1984 while fishing the head of a giant beaver pond just below Tolby Campground during an evening frenzy. Every brown in the beaver pond was stacked in the riffle that feeds it, and we caught dozens of fat browns up to 18 inches, most of them after dark using the three-second rule. Some of the largest were caught using a downstream skitter.

The daytime hatches in August are sparse, except when it clouds up in the afternoons just before a rain shower and in the evening after the sun leaves the water. Evening hatches of midges will also bring sippers to the surface in the beaver ponds. Use 6X tippet and a size 20 Griffith's Gnat or midge pupae and make a downstream slack-line cast so the fly drifts over the fish before the line or leader. When you get a strike, hesitate just a split second then set the hook gently by just raising the rod tip.

Terrestrials are also important in August and September, especially when there aren't any hatches. Ants, beetles, hoppers, woolly worms, and bud worms are abundant, and because there's so much overhanging brush, they frequently end up in the water. Browns seeking shade from the midday sun are willing customers for such groceries. Some of the biggest browns my clients and I catch are on terrestrials, mainly ants, close to the banks under overhanging brush in the middle of the day.

Some stretches of the Cimarron have so much vegetation that you're almost under a canopy, and the only way to cast is by creeping very close to the target and using a roll or bow cast. When you hook a fish, the real challenge is keeping it from wrapping you around a limb or root and breaking off or getting loose. The best method is to fight the fish on a short line, stripping it in rather than using the reel. And don't let it have any line if possible; instead, bend your rod more to wear it down quickly. In the more open areas, wade upstream close to the bank and try casting the fly above the overhanging brush or tree branches, letting it drift under the branches instead of trying to cast under them.

Baetis start hatching by mid-September, continuing through October. A Parachute Olive, size 18, is my favorite pattern for this hatch because of its low profile, which imitates the freshly emerged insects trying to break free of the surface film. They can be the hardest flies to mimic because they tend to hatch in slower currents, making it easier for fish to inspect your pattern and causing undetectable micro-drag to line, leader, and fly.

The only fly that is more difficult to imitate is a midge in low water. When downstream farmers stop calling for water around the end of September, they start reducing the outflow from Eagle Nest Lake. And trout love to feed on midges in low water, particularly in the beaver ponds. A Griffith's Gnat or Snow Fly works well for the selective sippers; try a midge pupa in the surface film. If you're a good fish spotter and the light is right, you can sometimes see the browns stacked like cordwood just under the surface as they feed on emerging pupae. If they aren't rising or feeding on emergers try a red midge larva, size 20, with a tiny bit of weight.

The enormous brown trout population begins spawning at the end of October, continuing through November. It's unbelievable that they can reproduce and survive in such low flows (between 5 and 15 cfs), much less thrive. Blue-Winged Olives will hatch on overcast days, bringing some fish to the surface, while others will take a Pheasant Tail or micro-egg along the bottom.

When nymphing in such low water, I usually don't use an indicator unless I'm fishing the deeper beaver ponds. A trained eye can usually spot many fish in the low water, making it easy to sight fish and select the larger browns and egg-sucking rainbows. If the river drops below 15 cfs I usually quit fishing because the fish are stressed enough without being harassed by anglers. By mid-November, they often shut the river off almost completely (between 1 and 7 cfs) for the winter, putting an end to fishing until spring.

Before the dam was repaired in the early nineties, it leaked about 6 cfs, which was just enough, combined with the outflow, to keep incubating brown trout eggs, fish, and aquatic insects from dying over the winter. Within two years of repairing the leaks and reducing the winter flow, there was a reduction in aquatic insects and trout reproduction, population, and average size. Despite all this, the Cimarron remains a great brown trout stream for flyfishers. I can only imagine what it would be like if we could get a minimum winter flow of 15 to 20 cfs. It may happen some day now that the state owns Eagle Nest Lake. Of course, passing an instream flow bill in New Mexico would also help tremendously.

To get to the Cimarron River from Taos, take US 64 west and travel about 30 miles to the town of Eagle Nest and continue for about a mile to where US 64 drops down into Cimarron Canyon just below Eagle Nest Dam. As soon as you drop down into the bottom you'll cross the river as it leaves the Holy Water and enters the Colin Neblett Wildlife Area. The campgrounds are self-pay, administered by the State Parks and Recreation Division.

From Red River, take NM 38 south over Bobcat Pass about 18 miles to the intersection with US 64 in Eagle Nest. Turn left on US 64 and follow the above directions from there. From Cimarron, drive west on US 64 about 15 miles just past Ute Park to the eastern entrance to Colin Neblett Wildlife Area. Over 7 miles of public water are available in the wildlife area.

If you're in northeast New Mexico, don't pass up a chance to fish this splendid stream. One of my clients, the former attorney general for the state of Texas, fished his way from New Mexico to Alaska after he retired. He wrote me after the trip that he'd fished many of the most popular streams in the country, but his best memory was the day he fished the Cimarron with me and caught and released over 50 browns. I've had many testimonials such as this over the years. Try this gem yourself, and you'll see why.

Stream Facts: Cimarron River

Season
- Fishing is permitted year-round, but low flows prevent fishing from the end of October through March.

Special Regulations
- From the east end of Tolby Campground downstream 1.4 miles to the next bridge as posted, use only artificial flies and lures with a single barbless hook. Daily bag and possession limit is one trout over 16 inches.

Trout
- Abundant wild brown trout averaging 10 to 14 inches, some to 20 inches or more. Stocked and wild rainbow trout from 9 to 12 inches, some hold over and grow to 18 inches or so.

River Miles
- Eagle Nest Dam—0
- Lower boundary of the Holy Water (private) and upper boundary of the Colin Neblett Wildlife Area—0.5
- Tolby Campground—0.75
- Upper boundary of the Special Trout Water—1
- Lower boundary of the Special Trout Water—2.4
- Clear Creek—5
- Palisades Picnic Area—6.5
- Gravel Pit Lakes campground—8
- Lower boundary of the Colin Neblett Wildlife Area and the village of Ute Park—9
- Cimarroncita Fly Fishing Ranch—10.5
- Upper boundary of Philmont Boy Scout Ranch—11.5
- Lower boundary of Philmont Boy Scout Ranch—18.5
- Village of Cimarron—21.5

River Characteristics
- The river is about 20 feet wide in most places, except in the beaver ponds, which can be quite large. It averages about 35 cfs when they're releasing water for downstream farmers, starting in late April or early May and lasting into around mid-October. Good variety of water types and hatches.

River Flows
- Late spring through fall: 30 to 90 cfs at Eagle Nest Dam; 15 to 60 cfs near village of Cimarron
- Winter and early spring: 0.5 to 7 cfs at Eagle Nest Dam; 5 to 15 cfs near village of Cimarron

Campgrounds
- Tolby Campground has tables, bathrooms with running water, self-pay station.
- Gravel Pit Lakes Campground has tables, bathrooms with running water, self-pay station.

Maps
- *New Mexico Atlas & Gazetteer,* page 17; Carson National Forest Map; BLM Taos Resource Area Map; USGS Quadrangle Map: Eagle Nest, Touch-Me-Not, Ute Park, Cimarron

Agencies
- NMDGF, P.O. Box 25112, Santa Fe, NM 87504-5112

Outfitters
- The Solitary Angler, 204B North Pueblo Road, Taos, NM 87529; 1-866-502-1700, www.thesolitaryangler.com
- Doc Thompson's High Country Anglers, P.O. Box 52, Ute Park, NM 87749; 505-376-9220
- Ed Adams Flyfishing, P.O. Box 428, Questa, NM 87556; 505-586-1512
- Taylor Streit Fly Fishing Service, P.O. Box 2759, Taos, NM 87571; 575-751-1312

A nice-looking brown just before the release.

CIMARRON RIVER MAJOR HATCHES

Insect	J	F	M	A	M	J	J	A	S	O	N	D	Time	Flies
Midges				█	█	█	█	█	█	█			M/E	Red & olive midge larva #16-#20; olive, gray, black and zebra midge pupa #18-#24; Mating Midge #14-#20; black & gray Midge Clusters #10-#16; Griffith's Gnat #16-#22; Snowfly #16-#26
Caddis					█	█	█	█	█				M/A/E	Green & olive caddis larva #12-#16; Double Hackle Peacock #12-#16; Van's Rag Pupa or LaFontaine's Pupa #10-#18; green or dark olive Green Weenie #12-#18; olive, tan & gray Elk Hair Caddis #12-#20; olive, gray & peacock Fluttering Caddis #10-#18
Craneflies						█	█						M/A/E	Cranefly larva peacock, gray or dark olive #6-#16; Taylor Streit's Poundmeister #6-#14; Double Hackle Peacock #6-#16; Foam Body Cranefly #6-#16
Green, Gray Drake							█						M/A/SF	Olive Hare's Ear #10-#14; Van's Rag Fly #10-#14; Green & Gray Drake Hair-Wing (Wulff style) #10-#14; Green & Gray Paradrake #10-14; Green Drake spinner #12-#14
Ginger, Gray, Blue & Mahogany Duns									█				M/E/SF	Light, dark & olive Hare's Ear Nymph#10-#18; Pheasant Tail Nymph #12-#18; light, dark, pink & ginger Hair-Wing Duns or Cahills #12-#18 or the same in parachutes; Ginger, Red & Blue Quills #12-#18

Hatch Time Code: M = Morning; A = Afternoon; E = Evening; D = Dark; SF = Spinner Fall

CIMARRON RIVER MAJOR HATCHES (cont.)

Insect	J	F	M	A	M	J	J	A	S	O	N	D	Time	Flies
Baetis				▮	▮					▮	▮		M/A/SF	Dark olive Hare's Ear Nymph #16–#22; Pheasant Tail #16–#22; Van's Rag Fly Nymph #16–#22; Lawson's BWO Fan-Wing Emerger #16–#22; Olive Parachute #16–#22; Olive Comparadun #16–#22
Salmonfly, Golden Stonefly, Yellow Sally					▮	▮		▮					M/A	Black & brown stonefly nymph #4–#10; Golden Stone Nymph #10–#14; Elk Hair Salmonfly #4–#8; Orange & Gold Stimulators #4–#14; Terminator #12–#16
PMDs, PEDs				▮	▮				▮				M/SF	Light Hare's Ear Nymph #12–#18; Pheasant Tail #12–#20; Van's Rag Fly Nymph light olive #14–#20; Lawson's Fan-Wing Emerger #14–#22; PMD, PED #14–#20
Terrestrials						▮	▮	▮	▮	▮			M/A	Para-hoppers tan, yellow #8–#14; Bees #12–14; Elk Hair Pine Moths #8–#14; beetles & ants #12–#18

Hatch Time Code: M = Morning; A = Afternoon; E = Evening; D = Dark; SF = Spinner Fall

THE RED RIVER

Headwater Lakes: Lost, Horseshoe, and Middle Fork Lakes

The headwaters of the Red River begin high in the Wheeler Peak Wilderness Area of the Carson National Forest. The headwater creeks—West Fork, Middle Fork, East Fork, and Sawmill Creek—are small and difficult to fish except in a few areas where beaver ponds and open meadows are present. The beaver ponds are loaded with brookies, while the undercut banks of the meadow sections hold mainly Rio Grande cutthroats. In the beaver ponds and in a few deep holes, there's a chance to get a holdover cuttbow up to 18 inches.

Other than two lakes, Lost Lake and Horseshoe Lake, the headwaters within the wilderness area are insignificant. Both lakes are glacial and medium-sized, with magnificent views in all directions. Less than a mile apart, the lakes offer excellent flyfishing for native Rio Grande cutthroats that average 15 to 18 inches. Perhaps the most beautiful of all cutthroats, Rio Grandes are brilliantly colored, with golden sides, large brown dots, and bright red bellies. They grow fat and fight better than most cutthroats of equal size. This is perhaps due to our southern latitude, which results in a longer growing season and a broader food base, even in the highest lakes and streams.

Both lakes are situated at tree line, around 11,500 feet, so there's plenty of room to cast from shore. The water is gin-clear, and the fish tend to cruise close to shore where the habitat is best, feeding on the abundant supply of scuds, midges, terrestrials, snails, minnows, and eggs. I've found that sight fishing is the best approach. I strip out enough line to cast 30 or 40 feet and loop it in my left hand. Then I watch for a cruiser to come by. I lead it by at least 30 feet because the water is so clear that the fish will spook if you don't.

If they cruise within 10 feet of your fly, they'll see it, and if you're using 6X or smaller tippet, they'll probably hit it. After watching a few fish, you can figure out where the cruising lane is and then target your casts accordingly.

The fish here aren't usually picky, although they do like certain flies better than others, especially if there is a hatch. Midges hatch daily and flying termites and ants hatch sporadically from mid-July through September. If you're there during a termite hatch be ready for some of the most fun dry-fly fishing you've ever seen, as 16- to 20-inch Rio Grande cutts cruise within 15 feet of the bank to gulp the large black bugs. It's an incredible visual experience, and the anticipation is overwhelming as you watch the cutthroats approach your fly.

Less than a mile from the wilderness boundary, at the head of Middle Fork Creek, there's another glacier lake situated just a little lower in elevation than Horseshoe and Lost Lakes. Accessible by four-wheel drive, ATV, horseback, or foot travel only, Middle Fork Lake is a great stillwater for float-tubers. Over 70 percent of the shoreline is forested, and the banks are too steep to cast from effectively.

Like most glacier lakes in the region, Middle Fork Lake is crystal clear. It provides excellent opportunities for sight fishing, particularly when fish are cruising close to shore. Food sources are the same as in Horseshoe and Lost Lakes, except that there are more terrestrials here due to the increased vegetation at the lower altitude. Cicadas, beetles, ants, and even hoppers are present during the summer months.

Middle Fork receives more pressure than Horseshoe and Lost because of its accessibility, so the fish tend to be leader shy. The lake has been stocked with rainbows and Snake River cutthroats, so there aren't any pure Rio Grande cutthroats left, but the resulting hybrid cuttbows are very hardy fish.

Once, back when I first started guiding, I was watching fish cruise around a log pile to feed on something subsurface. I was fishing the inlet from shore, stripping a small Olive Scud because they are a major food source, but I just kept getting refusals. I tried different flies, smaller tippets, and different stripping techniques, all to no avail. Finally, I caught a 16-inch cuttbow on my original Olive Scud, and a quick pumping of the throat revealed nothing but Olive and Orange Scuds just like the imitations I was using.

I put down my rod and walked out on one of the largest logs and just watched the trout feed for about 10 minutes. What I observed were scuds traveling in and out of the logs, but I also noticed that they were swimming in single-file groups, much the way ants often crawl. I immediately added two droppers about 12 inches apart, for a total of three scuds. I cast out to where the trout were feeding near the logs and barely

The author float-tubing Middle Fork Lake. (Cathie Hughs)

started stripping when two trout raced over. After 10 minutes I landed the double cuttbows, a pair of 17-inchers. I proceeded to catch several more fish, including one of about 22 inches, my largest ever in Middle Fork Lake. Since then, I've used this technique successfully many times in other lakes where freshwater shrimp are present.

To access Middle Fork, Horseshoe, and Lost Lakes and the headwaters of the Red River, follow NM 578 south from the town of Red River to the end of the pavement where the four creeks converge. To get to the Middle Fork, West Fork, and Middle Fork Lake, turn right on FR 58 just before the pavement ends and follow the creek about 2 miles to where the road leaves the creek and turns into FR 487 (four-wheel drive required). The 2.5-mile-long road is steep and rough and there are 23 switchbacks so tight that the driver must go up every other switchback in reverse. The alternative is to use an ATV, motorcycle, horse, or your feet to get to the lake or hire a flyfishing guide or jeep-tour guide to take you. Both are available in Red River (see the Northeast Region hub cities).

To access East Fork, Sawmill Creek, and Horseshoe and Lost Lakes, turn right at the end of the pavement on FR 58A and follow it for a couple of miles to Ditch Cabin. From there you can fish Sawmill or East Fork or take the Lost Lake Trail on foot or horseback. The trail is well marked and developed, although the terrain is steep and rugged. It's about 6 miles to Lost Lake and about 7 miles to Horseshoe Lake, and a wilderness permit is required. These can be obtained at the Questa Ranger District headquarters in Questa. Camping is available at both lakes.

Beaver ponds in the headwaters of the Red River provide excellent habitat for brook and rainbow trout.

MIDDLE FORK, LOST & HORSESHOE LAKES MAJOR HATCHES

Insect	J	F	M	A	M	J	J	A	S	O	N	D	Time	Flies
Blue Damselfly						■	■						M/E	Olive Marabou Damsel #8–#14; Extended Body Parachute Blue Damsel #8–#14
Midges				■	■	■			■	■			M/E	Red & olive midge larva #16–#20; olive, gray, black and zebra midge pupa #18–24; Pheasant Tail #16–#22; Disco Midge #18–#24; Mating Midge #14–#20; black & gray Midge Clusters #10–#16; Griffith's Gnat #16–#22; Snowfly #16–#26
Scuds									■	■			M/E	Olive & light orange scuds #14–#20
Snails					■	■	■						M/E	Peacock Double Hackle on 1X short hook (fat body) #12–#18
Callibaetis								■	■				M/A/SF	Dark olive Hare's Ear Nymph #14–#18; Para Adams #14–#18; Blue Quill #14–#18; Speckled-wing Dun #14–#18; Callibaetis Spinner #16–#20
Caddis						■	■	■	■				M/E	Olive & orange Elk Hair Sedge #8–#14; dark black micro-caddis #18–#22
Minnows								■	■				M/E	Soft-Hackle Streamers or Woolly Buggers in assorted colors #4–#14
Roe (Trout Eggs)								■					M/E	Orange, gold, chartreuse, peach micro-eggs #16–#18
Terrestrials								■	■				M/E	Ants, termites, true flies, beetles, bees, Elk Hair Pine Moths #12–#18

Hatch Time Code: M = Morning; A = Afternoon; E = Evening; D = Dark; SF = Spinner Fall

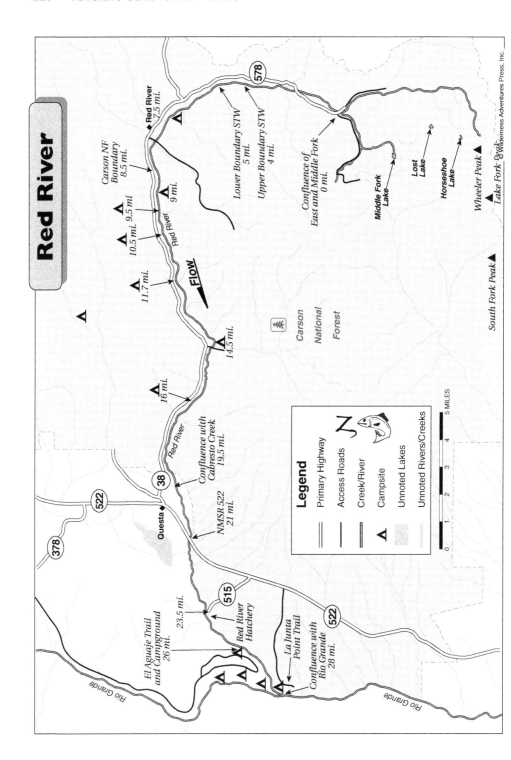

Red River

Carson NF Boundary 8.5 mi.

Red River 7.5 mi.

Red River 9 mi.

9.5 mi.

10.5 mi.

11.7 mi.

Lower Boundary STW 5 mi.

Upper Boundary STW 4 mi.

Confluence of East and Middle Fork 0 mi.

FLOW

14.5 mi.

16 mi.

Red River

Confluence with Cabresto Creek 19.5 mi.

38

522

378

Questa

NMSR 522 21 mi.

Carson National Forest

Middle Fork Lake

Lost Lake

Horseshoe Lake

Wheeler Peak▲

South Fork Peak▲

Lake Fork Peak▲

Lake Fork

Legend

Primary Highway

Access Roads

Creek/River

▲ Campsite

Unnoted Lakes

Unnoted Rivers/Creeks

0 1 2 3 4 5 MILES

5 MILES

515

Red River Hatchery

La Junta Point Trail

Confluence with Rio Grande 28 mi.

522

El Aguaje Trail and Campground 26 mi.

23.5 mi.

Rio Grande

Rio Grande

©Wilderness Adventures Press, Inc.

Upper Red River

From the end of the pavement on FR 58A downstream for about 4 miles the Red River is private, but most of the landowners will let you fish as long as you stay close to the river. Always obtain permission first. The upper 2 miles of this private stretch include several beaver ponds, interspersed with nice riffles, pools, and undercut banks. Because it's private, there's not much pressure and most of the fish are wild. However, the NMDGF stocks rainbows throughout the river, and the Red River Chamber of Commerce also stocks rainbows—some very big—and a fraction of them migrate into the private waters.

The wild browns, cuttbows, and brookies average about 8 to 12 inches, and they are usually opportunistic, except during a good hatch when you may have to match the hatch. A standard dry-dropper with an Elk Hair Caddis on top and a beadhead nymph on the bottom will usually do the trick. A 7- to 8-foot, 2- to 5-weight rod is best since the river is only 15 to 25 feet wide. Like most streams in New Mexico, it would be considered a creek in the northern Rockies. Wade upstream, casting short, except in the beaver ponds where a longer cast may be necessary. Hip boots are sufficient.

The river reenters the national forest, and for the next 4 miles it runs through a tight, narrow canyon with fast water interrupted by frequent boulders and logjams that create good pockets and pools. In part of this section, anglers are restricted to artificial flies and lures only with a single barbless hook; the daily bag limit is two trout over 16 inches. There are some big stockers in this section, and after they've been in the river a while they act much like wild trout.

There are some good hatches starting right after runoff, usually around early to mid-June. Caddis, Ginger Duns, and Brown Stoneflies are the most significant hatches. When no fish are rising, use a large attractor or hopper-dropper with a light or dark Hare's Ear, size 12 to 16, on the bottom. In August, large ant patterns also work well.

After it leaves the canyon, the river runs through the tourist/ski town of Red River. This 2-mile stretch isn't exactly a flyfisher's dream, but it does have some decent fishing. Once nothing more than a ditch running through town, the river has improved over the last few years, and now there are some good holes and runs that didn't previously exist. The Chamber of Commerce and the town of Red River heavily stock this stretch, and there are a lot of put-and-take bait- and spinfishers. But if you're staying in Red River you might try it some evening.

The town is a great place for a family vacation, with an Old West atmosphere and plenty of motels, condos, cabins, lodges, inns, and bed and breakfasts, as well as good restaurants and great entertainment at night. The ski area is modest, but the Taos Ski Valley is less than an hour away.

Middle Red River

From the town of Red River, the river flows through another rocky canyon for about 8 miles to the town of Questa. Most of this section runs through national forest with roadside access, but only the upper 4 miles from the town of Red River downstream to the Molycorp Mine are very good. From there to just below the town of Questa is basically a dead zone for fish and aquatic insects. However, it had been on a path to recovery until a massive mudslide occurred in 2008 that wiped out the entire Red River again. There are six developed campgrounds in the canyon that provide plenty of room for campers and RVs.

One bright spot in this otherwise tarnished stretch is a small tributary called Cabresto Creek and it's mother, Cabresto Lake. The dam is being rebuilt now in 2010 so it should be around for a long time. The lake covers about 15 acres and holds rainbows, cuttbows, Rio Grande cutts, and a healthy population of brookies. Access is rough, and a high-clearance vehicle is required, preferably four-wheel drive. There are good primitive campsites at the lake, but firewood is scarce so bring your own. It's a good lake for float tubes and small pontoon boats. There are weed beds near the inlet and the southwest shore, and the east side has many dead trees, downed logs, and snags that provide good cover for trout and aquatic insects.

The inlet is especially good for brookies and some nice cutthroats in late spring and brookies up to 16 inches in the fall. The lake is full of large lake midges, so a size 16 to 20 Zebra Midge or Pheasant Tail Midge Pupa dropped off a size 16 to 18

Big browns, like this one caught by Jack Heaton, migrate up from the Rio Grande to spawn in the fall.

Griffith's Gnat can be deadly during evening hatches. If there's no action at the inlet, try stripping small nymphs or Woolly Buggers around the logs on the east shore. Or try stripping a damselfly nymph over the weed beds during the day.

Cabresto Creek is small, less than 10 feet wide, but if you like dabbling with short leaders it can be very productive for 8- to 12-inch rainbows, brookies, and the occasional cutthroat. There is good roadside access and primitive camping can be found nearby. This type of creek is great for kids, as they can learn about sneaking up on fish and spotting them while getting lots of action.

Access to Cabresto Creek and the lake is via NM 38 out of Questa (toward Red River). After a quarter-mile, turn left on the road marked Cabresto Lake. After weaving through a community, the road becomes FR 134. Follow the gravel road about 3 miles to the Cabresto Lake turnoff on the left, FR 134A. Follow this for 2 miles to Cabresto Lake. Four-wheel-drive and high-clearance vehicles recommended. Primitive camping is available.

To fish Cabresto Creek, follow FR134 past the turnoff to Cabresto Lake and look for pullouts over the next few miles.

The Lower Red River

The lower Red River, once the best wild trout stream in the state, is making an incredible comeback after suffering from years of pollution caused by the Molycorp molybdenum mine between Questa and the town of Red River.

From just below Questa, near the hatchery, the Red River transforms into an entirely different kind of river. From its headwaters to the town of Questa, it's just another small freestone stream coming out of the Sangre de Cristo Mountains. But below Questa it leaves the mountains and descends rapidly into a crack, or box, canyon in the Rio Grande Rift, known as the Lower Red River Box. As the Red plunges through this magnificent box canyon for the next 5 miles on its journey to the Rio Grande Gorge, it gathers three times its normal flow from area springs, giving it a spring creek–like quality. The Rio Grande Aquifer supplies the rich water for the river and for the largest hatchery in the state, the Red River Hatchery.

Nutrients from the hatchery add to the richness of the river downstream, and the springs help dilute tainted runoff from the Moly Mine upstream. Fortunately, the mine has been closed much of the time since about 1992 and it has been selected as a possible Superfund site. Recently, the mine announced it will be developing one of the largest solar arrays in the country. It may improve their image but it will not solve the ongoing problem of seepage from the mine or the tremendous tailings piles that threaten the entire drainage including the Rio Grande.

The fishing in the Red River seems to go hand in hand with how much run-off and seepage from the mine gets in the river. As the water quality in the Red River has improved, so has the fishing and vise versa as we are seeing now after the mudslide.

The lifeblood of the Rio Grande Gorge, the spring-fed section of the Red River extending from the hatchery downstream about 4 miles to the confluence with the Rio Grande is the main spawning tributary for browns and cuttbows in the bigger river. It also provides major winter holding water for big cuttbows and browns since the water stays about 48 degrees all winter long.

Due to the warmer water temperatures, the Red River is the premier natural winter fishery in northern New Mexico. Sight fishing can be great for large cuttbows in the winter and browns in the fall. The weather is generally mild, with air temperatures ranging from 40 to 70 degrees. On a good day, a decent angler might land 20-plus fish, of which half might be between 16 and 24 inches or more. The number and size of fish have been down considerably since the mudslide in 2008 but it still is fun to fish and I am seeing signs of a rapid recovery. During fall 2009, I saw a few large browns and during the winter, I caught far more big cuttbows than the previous year.

The main food sources in the Red River are Baetis, caddis, midges, and Dark Brown Stoneflies. The hatches have improved with the water quality, giving rise to some good dry-fly fishing the last few years. The best surface action is during the early spring Baetis and caddis hatches before runoff, during late June stonefly and caddis hatches, and again during Baetis hatches in October and November. Closer to the hatchery, midges bring wild browns and stocked rainbows to the surface all winter long.

I fish the Red much the same way I do the Rio Grande Gorge in the NRA, fishing upstream and making short casts into the pockets, while keeping most of the line off the water to minimize drag. I use an 8-foot rod for 4- or 5-weight line because of the brush that lines the banks. If there's a hatch, I use the appropriate dry-dropper rig. Otherwise, I use a double-nymph rig with about a 12-inch dropper and enough weight to bump along the bottom of fast pockets, riffles, and seams.

Big browns run up the Red River in November and stack in certain areas. It's best to leave these fish alone; besides, they aren't really interested in flies once they're spawning. Using a big streamer in late October and early November—at the beginning of the run—can produce some good browns, especially when they're resting in deep pockets and holes.

I spend much of my fishing time on the Red in the winter months. In fact, the winter is when I do most of my fishing, since I'm usually too busy guiding during the rest of the year. I can be at the confluence of the Rio Grande and Red River in less than an hour, and that's including the 1.4-mile hike from top to bottom. As the crow flies, it's less than 5 miles from my house.

The river runs east to west, so the north bank is in the sun all day long. And we are usually under a high-pressure weather pattern during the winter months, which means we have very little wind. The sun beats down on the black basalt boulders, and they collect and hold the heat. Add in a consistent water temperature of 48 degrees, a healthy supply of caddis, midges, and mayflies, and large wintering cuttbows and resident browns, and you have a recipe for some awesome winter fishing.

There are daily midge hatches, and on nice days Blue-Winged Olives hatch from 1:00 to 3:00 p.m. Occasionally, caddis hatch in late afternoon. Egg patterns also work well at times, as do small streamers. The best winter dry-fly fishing is close to the hatchery, where access is easy, but the fish are mostly resident browns and rainbows from 8 to 14 inches.

To get to the hatchery, take NM 522 north from Taos about 20 miles, then go west on NM 515 for another 2 miles. Park in the fishermen's parking area and walk downstream to the good water.

There are two well-developed trails located in the Rio Grande Wild and Scenic National Recreation Area below the hatchery. To reach them, take NM 522 north from Questa about 3 miles, go west on NM 378, and then follow the BLM signs to the NRA. Continue to La Junta Point Campground and Trail, the confluence of the Red and Rio Grande. Follow signs to the trailhead. To get to the other trail at El Aguaje Campground, stay on NM 378 for about a mile past the La Junta turnoff. Follow the signs to the trailhead. A self-pay parking fee is required at all NRA parking areas.

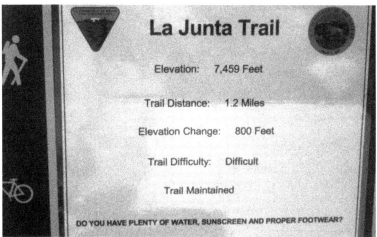

The La Junta Point Trail leads to the confluence of the Red River and Rio Grande. This area offers perhaps the best year-round flyfishing in the entire Gorge.

The confluence of the Red River and the Rio Grande from the rim at La Junta Point.

Stream Facts: The Red River

Season
- Headwaters, glacier lakes, and Cabresto Lake and Creek: year-round, but best fishing is from mid-June through September.
- Lower Red River below the Red River Hatchery: year-round except during runoff.

Special Regulations
- Upper Red River from the confluence of Goose Creek upstream 1 mile as posted: Artificial flies and lures only with a single barbless hook. Daily bag and possession limit two trout at least 12 inches long.
- Lower Red River from 0.25 mile below the hatchery as posted downstream to the confluence with the Rio Grande (about 3.5 miles): No tackle restrictions. Daily bag and possession limit is three trout any size except that only two may be cutthroat (any trout with a red slash under the jaw).

Trout
- Rio Grande cutthroat, cuttbows, rainbows, brookies.

River Miles
- The confluence of the east and middle forks on NM 578—0
- Upper boundary of Special Trout Water and the entrance to Carson N.F. and upper Red River canyon—4
- Lower boundary of STW and the confluence of Goose Creek—5
- Red River Village limits—7.5
- Carson N.F. boundary—8.5
- June Bug Campground—9
- Fawn Lakes Campground—9.5
- Elephant Rock Campground—10.5
- La Bobita Campground—11.7
- Molycorp molybdenum mine—12 to 17
- Columbine Creek and Campground—14.5
- Goathill Campground—16
- Cabresto Creek—19.5
- NM 522—21
- Red River Hatchery—23.5
- Upper boundary STW and BLM land—24.5
- El Aguaje Trailhead and Campground—26
- Confluence of Red River and Rio Grande and La Junta Trailhead and Campground—28

River Characteristics
- Upper Red River: A medium-sized freestone stream with beaver ponds, meadows, and undercut banks in the headwaters, and a combination of riffles, pools, and pocket water running through a brushy, narrow canyon from above the town of Red River to the Red River Hatchery.
- Lower Red River: Year-round fishery. A freestone river with spring influence that runs through a narrow basalt box canyon. Similar to Rio Grande, but much smaller, with numerous boulder-strewn pockets and deep holes. Important spawning grounds for cuttbows and browns migrating from the Rio Grande Gorge. Excellent fall and winter fishery.

River Flows Upper and Middle Red River
- Winter, summer, and fall: 10 to 35 cfs
- Spring runoff: 35 to 200 cfs

River Flows Lower Red River
- Winter, summer, and fall: 35 to 50 cfs
- Spring runoff: 50 to 250 cfs

Campgrounds
- Elephant Rock Campground, 2.8 miles west of Red River on NM 38; pay campground open May to October; 10 campsites for trailers and 12 campsites for tents or trailers; tables, fireplaces, toilets; drinking water available; parking for backcountry visitors
- Fawn Lakes Campground, 3.2 miles west of Red River on NM 38; pay campground open May to October; 22 tent or trailer campsites; tables, fireplaces, toilets; drinking water available; water from river not recommended for drinking
- Goat Hill Campground, 3.5 miles east of Questa on State Highway 38; pay campground open May to October; 6 campsites for tents or trailers; tables, fireplaces, toilets; water from river not recommended for drinking
- June Bug Campground, 2.2 miles west of Red River on NM 38; pay campground open May to October; 7 campsites for trailers, 13 campsites for tents or trailers; tables, fireplaces, toilets; drinking water available; parking for backcountry visitors
- Columbine Campground, 5.1 miles east of Questa on NM 38; pay campground open May to October; 7 campsites for trailers, 20 campsites for tents or trailers; tables, fireplaces, toilets; drinking water available; parking for backcountry visitors
- Cebolla Mesa Campground, NM 522 4.9 miles south from Questa to FR 9, then west 3.4 miles to campground; 14-day length of stay limit; no fee; no garbage pick-up; pack it in/pack it out; 5 campsites for tents and trailers; tables, fireplace, toilets; no water available

Maps
- *New Mexico Atlas & Gazetteer,* page 16; BLM Taos Resource Area Map; USGS Quadrangle Maps: Wheeler Peak, Red River, Questa, Guadalupe Mountain

Agencies
- BLM Taos Resource Area, 224 Cruz Alta Rd, Taos, New Mexico 87571
- Carson National Forest, Questa Ranger District, P.O. Box 110 Questa, NM, 87556
- NMDGF, Raton

Outfitters
The Carson National Forest and the BLM Taos Resource Area can provide information, including maps and a list of outfitters permitted to operate in the Gorge. Outfitters include:
- The Solitary Angler, 204B North Pueblo Road, Taos, NM 87529; 1-866-502-1700, www.thesolitaryangler.com
- Ed Adams Flyfishing, P.O. Box 428, Questa, NM 87556; 575-586-1512
- Taylor Streit Fly Fishing Service, P.O. Box 2759, Taos, NM 87571; 575-751-1312

Angler Andrew Brooks carefully plays a big Red River cuttbow in March.

Rio Hondo

The Upper Rio Hondo

The Rio Hondo is a small freestone stream from its headwaters to where it leaves the Sangre de Cristo Mountains and picks up water from several springs draining out of the Taos Plateau. It then descends into a basalt gorge for 3 miles, adding more springs before joining the Rio Grande at John Dunn Bridge.

From its beginning at Taos Ski Valley, it runs 10 miles through a tight canyon in the Carson National Forest, which it shares with NM 150. There is good roadside access here and four developed campgrounds. Several tiny creeks with names like Gavilan, Itallianos, Manzanitas, and Yerba increase the upper Hondo's flow, which averages about 20 to 30 cfs except during runoff, when it can rage.

Typical of most of the westslope streams in the Sangre de Cristo Mountains, the upper Hondo is small and brushy with a nice combination of riffles, pools, pockets, and beaver ponds. Wild browns, cutthroats, a few brookies, and, of course, stocker rainbows average 8 to 12 inches, some larger. A 7½- to 8-foot, 2- to 4-weight rod is ideal for the short casts you'll be making.

Despite its small size, the upper Hondo is one of the best dry-fly streams in the Taos area, and some very good hatches provide surface action most of the day, all season long. PMDs start hatching as soon as runoff subsides, usually in early June, offering good morning action. By mid-June, Golden Stoneflies start hatching, bringing every fish in the river to the surface during the day. Afternoon and evening caddis hatches occur from July through mid-September, and Ginger Duns, Blue Duns, and Yellow Sallies hatch from August through September. Midges and Blue-Winged Olives hatch in September and October and are significant food sources for fish in the beaver ponds.

I use a short leader here, no more than 7½ feet tapering to 5X, with a nymph dropper if fish aren't feeding on top. The usual flies all work well here: Terminators and Stimulators, size 10 to 16; olive and brown Elk Hair Caddis, size 14 to 18; Parachute Gingers, Parachute Adams, Parachute Olives, all size 14 to 18; and Griffith's Gnats, size 16 to 20. For nymphs, try light and dark Hare's Ears, Pheasant Tails, and olive caddis pupae, size 12 to 18; Golden Stones, size 8 to 16; red midge larvae, size 16 to 20; and in November, golden micro-eggs, size 16 to 18.

The stream is small, brushy, and crystal clear, so the best method is to creep upstream, keeping a low profile to avoid spooking fish. Make short casts and keep slack to a minimum to ensure a good drift and prevent snagging bushes and trees. Cover the water thoroughly, but keep moving because the trout spook easily in such small water. I change flies as the day progresses, matching the hatches unless they're actively taking the fly I have on, and even then I'll sometimes change just to see what they won't hit. Of course, I always go back to what they seem to want.

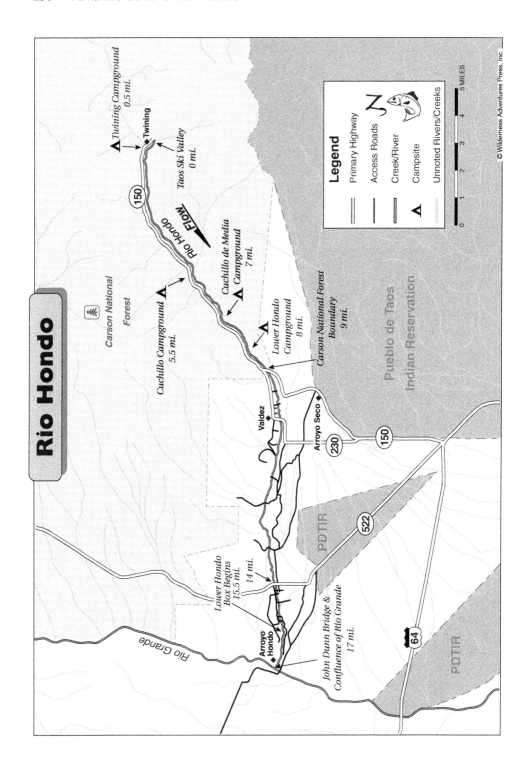

Rio Hondo

Twining Campground
0.5 mi.

Twining

Taos Ski Valley
0 mi.

150

Rio Hondo FLOW

Carson National
Forest

Cuchillo de Media
Campground
7 mi.

Cuchillo Campground
5.5 mi.

Lower Hondo
Campground
8 mi.

Carson National Forest
Boundary
9 mi.

Valdez

Arroyo Seco

230

150

Pueblo de Taos
Indian Reservation

PDTIR

522

Lower Hondo
Box Begins
15.5 mi.

14 mi.

Rio Grande

Arroyo
Hondo

John Dunn Bridge &
Confluence of Rio Grande
17 mi.

64

PDTIR

Legend

Primary Highway

Access Roads

Creek/River

Campsite

Unnoted Rivers/Creeks

0 1 2 3 4 5 MILES

© Wilderness Adventures Press, Inc.

The upper Hondo is convenient for anglers staying in Taos, and if you get tired of catching small trout it's just a few miles to the lower Hondo and its confluence with the Rio Grande, where some larger trout live. The confluence provides the only roadside access to the mighty Rio Grande Gorge for a distance of over 80 miles.

To get to the upper Hondo from Taos, take US 64 west for 4 miles to the Taos Ski Valley Road (NM 150). Turn east, and drive about 8 miles to the Carson National Forest entrance.

The Lower Rio Hondo

Because its water is cooler and clearer than the Rio Grande, the lower Rio Hondo offers good dry-fly fishing all summer long. Caddis hatch through July, mayflies during the evenings through August, and fall Baetis consistently through November.

The Rio Hondo is the smallest tributary of the Gorge, but it produces nice trout (8 to 14 inches). Migratory browns move in and out of the Rio Grande, especially during the spawn in late fall.

The last 2½ miles of the Rio Hondo are reminiscent of the Gorge, as the Hondo runs through a basalt gorge lined with cedar, juniper, and piñon trees. Several springs enter the Rio Hondo in this section, keeping the river just warm enough to fish during the winter.

The Hondo has some deep pools, but fast pocket water predominates. And there are some big pockets holding larger fish. Except during winter, I match the hatch and use an appropriate dry fly. If I don't get much action I add a dropper and suspend a weighted nymph about 12 inches down. In winter, I use small nymphs, micro-eggs, and small Woolly Buggers.

A road parallels the Hondo all the way downstream to its confluence with the Rio Grande at John Dunn Bridge. The road isn't numbered, but you can find it by taking NM 522 north from Taos 8 miles to the town of Arroyo Rondo. Turn left as soon as you cross the Rio Hondo and follow the road and the stream to the confluence with the Rio Grande.

Stream Facts: Rio Hondo

Season
• Fishing is open year-round.

Special Regulations
• Daily bag and possession limit for cutthroats is two fish.

Trout
• Upper Hondo: brown, cutthroat, brook, and rainbow trout; Lower Hondo: brown, cuttbow, and rainbow trout.

River Miles

- Taos Ski Valley—0
- Twining Campground—0.5
- Cuchillo Campground—5.5
- Cuchillo de Medio Campground—7
- Lower Hondo Campground—8
- Carson National Forest boundary—9
- NM 522—14
- Beginning of Lower Hondo Canyon (look for a dirt road intersecting the main road on your left at the top of the hill and a pullout on the right to a primitive trail leading to the bottom of the canyon, about ¼ mile)—15.5
- John Dunn Bridge—17

River Characteristics

- The upper Rio Hondo is a small, brushy freestone stream with about 9 miles of public access. The middle Hondo runs through private farms and ranches, and the lower Hondo runs through a basalt box canyon for 1.5 miles before joining the Rio Grande at John Dunn Bridge. It's a fast, medium-sized stream with boulder-strewn pockets reminiscent of the Rio Grande Gorge.

River Flows

- Winter, summer, and fall: 15 to 35 cfs
- Spring runoff: 35 to 200 cfs

Campgrounds

- Twining Campground, 19.7 miles north of Taos on NM 150; no fees; open May to October; no garbage pick-up, pack it in/pack it out; 4 campsites for trailers; tables, grills, toilets; water from stream not recommended for drinking
- Cuchilla del Medio Campground, 13.0 miles north of Taos on NM 230; no fees; open May to October; no garbage pick-up, pack it in/pack it out; 3 campsites for trailers; tables, toilets; water from stream not recommended for drinking
- Lower Hondo Campground, 12.1 miles north of Taos on NM 230; no fees; open May to October; no garbage pick-up, pack it in/pack it out; 4 campsites for trailers; tables, toilets; water from stream not recommended for drinking

Maps

- *New Mexico Atlas & Gazetteer,* page 16; Carson National Forest Map; BLM Taos Resource Area Map; USGS Quadrangle Map: Wheeler Peak, Arroyo Seco, Arroyo Hondo

Agencies

- BLM Taos Resource Area, 224 Cruz Alta Road, Taos, NM 87571
- Carson National Forest, Questa Ranger District, P.O. Box 110, Questa, NM 87556
- NMDGF, P.O. Box 25112, Santa Fe, NM 87504-5112

Outfitters

The BLM Taos Resource Area and the Carson N.F. Questa Ranger District can provide information, including maps and a list of outfitters permitted to operate on public lands. Outfitters include:

- The Solitary Angler, 204B North Pueblo Road, Taos, NM 87529; 1-866-502-1700, www.thesolitaryangler.com
- Ed Adams Flyfishing, P.O. Box 428, Questa, NM 87556; 575-586-1512
- Taylor Streit Fly Fishing Service, P.O. Box 2759, Taos, NM 87571; 575-751-1312

The author with an upper Rio Hondo brown. (Cathie Hughs)

TAOS

Taos is the best place for visiting anglers to set up a base. I located my guiding business, The Solitary Angler, here for good reason. There's a tremendous amount of flyfishing opportunities close by and the town is excellent for locals and tourists alike. It's fast becoming a popular destination for angling families too, because there is plenty for non-fishers to do in the area.

The history of Taos is quite remarkable and it goes way back. In fact, the Taos Pueblo is one of the longest continually lived in communities in the country, going back a thousand years or more. The Spanish Conquistadors settled in Taos in 1540, and the mountain men began to show up in the 1800s to trap and hunt the abundant game at that time.

While some folks consider Taosenos loony radicals because of the communes of the sixties, some prominent, intelligent, active members of the community have promoted and developed innovative ideas, facilities, energy systems, agricultural techniques, and even entire communities that integrate sustainable use as the dominate theme of their operations. Taos is a community of visionaries from different cultures that believe clean air, water, and environment, combined with sustainable use and a mind, body, spirit connection, is the direction we should go as a planet.

Above all else, though, Taos is an art community. It is rich in history and culture, which is evident everywhere you look, from the Taos Pueblo to the Saint Francis de Assisi's Church to the irrigated valleys and pastures. The local shops and art galleries are perhaps the driving force of the tourist economy. Hundreds of artists make Taos their home, and for a town this size there are more artists, galleries, studios, art schools, and seminars than anywhere in the country, including Santa Fe.

There are many quaint restaurants, bars, nightclubs, coffee shops, and pubs where talented entertainers perform. Musical events take place throughout the year, from the Jazz Festival to the big event of the year, the Taos Solar Fest, which is held during the last weekend in June each year to promote solar energy of all types.

Whitewater rafting in the Rio Grande Gorge is one of the most popular activities in Taos. The Taos Box has more whitewater than any one-day float trip in the Lower 48, and it's an exhilarating adventure in a magnificent box canyon. Check with the BLM in Taos for a list of outfitters.

For anglers that come here to ski, Taos is becoming more popular because of the great winter flyfishing available on the Rio Grande, Red River, and Culebra Creek (see Private Waters). Sometimes the lower reaches of the Taos area streams can also be quite good in winter.

RIO PUEBLO DE TAOS AND LITTLE RIO GRANDE

The Little Rio Grande is actually the combination of three smaller streams: the Rio Pueblo de Taos, the Rio Don Fernando de Taos (Taos Creek), and the Rio Grande del Rancho. These streams drain an immense region on the west slope of the Sangre de Cristo Mountains near Taos. From the north end of the Taos Pueblo south to the top of US Hill on NM 518, every creek and spring drains into the Little Rio Grande, locally called the Rio Pueblo or Los Cordovas Riffles.

Unfortunately, local farmers, the town of Taos, and the Taos Pueblo combine to suck most of the streams dry before they reach the Little Rio Grande, and as the area grows and develops, the competition for surface water only increases. Since New Mexico is the only state west of the Mississippi that doesn't have an instream flow bill to protect free-flowing waters from drying up, the Little Rio Grande's future may be in jeopardy.

For the first time in known history, the midsections of all three streams dried up and all fish died during the droughts of 1998, 2000, and 2002. Fortunately, the river doesn't ever dry up in the headwaters above the diversions, and the lower Rio Pueblo continues to flow due to springs that drain from the Taos Plateau.

The abundant wild brown trout population depends on the entire watershed from the Rio Grande to the headwaters for spawning, rearing juveniles, and growing large browns, so losing the midsection to development would affect the entire fishery. This is just one example of what could become commonplace in much of the West during the next century if current growth rates continue and more pressure is put on water systems, especially if predictions by an overwhelming number of scientists about global warming are true.

Despite these ongoing and potential problems, there's currently some great fishing to explore within minutes of Taos, the center of the best flyfishing in the state. The headwaters of the Rio Pueblo de Taos are all on Taos Pueblo land and closed to the public. After leaving the Pueblo, it runs through private property until its union with the Rio Grande del Rancho, where the Little Rio Grande Box begins. Most of the flow comes from the Rio Pueblo de Taos, and the rest from the Rio Grande del Rancho. Taos Creek is fully diverted before it reaches the confluence with the Little Rio Grande at the bottom end of the Taos Valley.

US 64 parallels upper Taos Creek west of Taos and there are about 5 miles of public access; the rest is private. The first 3-mile stretch begins a few miles east of the Taos Plaza on US 64, just as you leave the valley and enter Taos Canyon (a sign marks the entrance to Carson National Forest). Next, there is about a half-mile of private water and then another 2 miles of pubic access. The area is convenient for campers and RVers, with five developed campgrounds and one picnic ground.

The creek is only about 5 to 8 feet across, but the habitat is perfect for trout and difficult for anglers. It's a medium-grade stream, with lots of twists and turns, and alders, willows, pines, cedars, firs, and other brush cover the entire riparian zone. There are beaver ponds, lots of pools with overhanging brush, and undercut banks for the healthy, under-fished brown trout to hide under. These browns are abundant too, with an 8- to 12-inch fish everywhere you expect one.

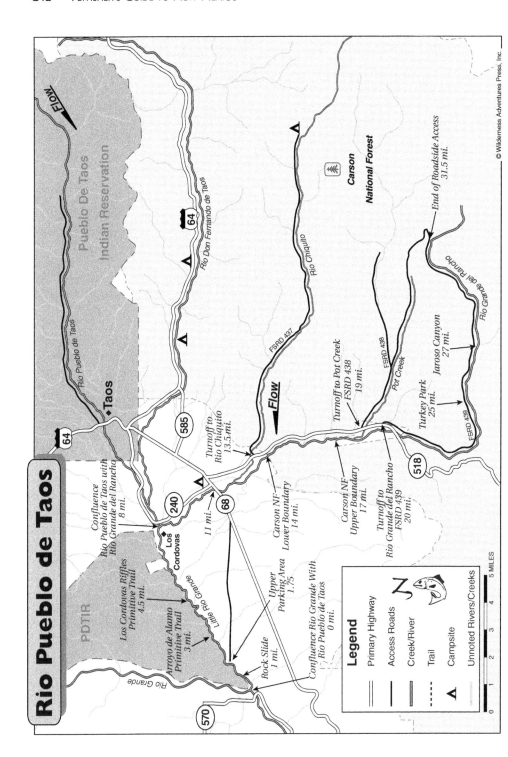

Rio Pueblo de Taos

Legend

Primary Highway
Access Roads
Creek/River
Trail
Campsite
Unnoted Rivers/Creeks

0 1 2 3 4 5 MILES

© Wilderness Adventures Press, Inc.

Pueblo De Taos
Indian Reservation

FLOW

Rio Pueblo de Taos

Taos

64

Rio Don Fernando de Taos

64

Carson
National Forest

FSRD 437

Flow

Rio Chiquito

End of Roadside Access
31.5 mi.

Rio Grande del Rancho

Jaroso Canyon
27 mi.

FSRD 438

Pot Creek

Turnoff to Pot Creek
FSRD 438
19 mi.

Turkey Park
25 mi.

FSRD 439

518

Turnoff to
Rio Grande del Rancho
FSRD 439
20 mi.

Carson NF
Upper Boundary
17 mi.

Carson NF
Lower Boundary
14 mi.

Turnoff to
Rio Chiquito
13.5 mi.

585

240

68

11 mi.

Confluence
Rio Pueblo de Taos with
Rio Grande del Rancho
8 mi.

Los
Cordovas

Little Rio Grande

Los Cordovas Riffles
Primitive Trail
4.5 mi.

Arroyo de Alamo
Primitive Trail
3 mi.

PDTIR

Rio Grande

Upper
Parking Area
1.75

Rock Slide
1 mi.

Confluence Rio Grande With
Rio Pueblo de Taos
0 mi.

570

The problem is getting your fly to the spot. It's like casting in a bus—there's just no room. Crawling on your hands and knees through the bushes and dabbling your fly over the edge is the best technique. Bow casts under bushes and roll casts when possible are all that you'll need.

I remember the first time my father brought me to Taos Creek. I was about eight years old and we had been fishing the Rio Grande on a hot, sunny day in July to no avail. This was before catch and release, and at that time very few anglers fished the small creeks. They were so overpopulated with small browns that the NMDGF imposed high bag limits. At that time, the daily bag limit was 16 and the possession limit 32. Not wanting to go home without supper, he hauled us over to Taos Creek to "round out" as he called it.

Upon arrival, he shortened my leader and handed me the old cane rod and said, "Don't let any line out and don't let anything but the fly hit the water or you'll be in the bushes, and I don't want to have to come get you out." Having learned to fish on tiny, brushy creeks I went right down to the creek and poked my rod through a hole in the bushes and dropped my oversized Rio Grande King on the surface. A 12-inch brown immediately slammed it, and I plucked him out of the water and onto the bank. I quickly killed the fish and stuffed it through the hole on the top of my wicker creel. We proceeded to "limit out" on 10- to 14-inch browns and had more fish than we knew what to do with, which of course is why we must catch and release today. It never ceases to amaze me how greedy we humans are. We always have to learn things the hard way.

There are actually hatches on the creek, although the fish aren't picky, but if there is a hatch I try to match it. Otherwise, a Terminator, Stimulator, caddis, or any attractor (size 12 to 16) will do.

The Rio Grande del Rancho has over 35 miles of access in its drainage, including two small tributaries, the Rio Chiquito and Pot Creek. All three creeks are small, brushy, steep, and contain riffles, pools, pocket water, beaver ponds, and meadows with undercut banks. Rio Chiquito has over 10 miles of roadside access and 3 miles of hike-in access. Pot Creek has 4 miles of roadside access and 8 miles of hike-in access at the end of the road. Rio Grande del Rancho has 11 miles of roadside access and the most flow.

The creeks are no longer overpopulated with browns, and the ridiculous general regulations that exist in New Mexico (allowing 5 fish a day) don't help much. If everyone that fished the creeks kept a limit there wouldn't be a single fish left. Thanks to difficult fishing conditions and the self-restraint of catch-and-release anglers, there's still a lot of fish—some larger than they used to be. Native Rio Grande cutthroats are also coming back in the upper reaches, where the Forest Service and NMDGF have initiated a restoration program.

The standard small-creek patterns work well, including, of course, Rio Grande Kings, Royal Wulffs, Stimulators, and H&L Variants. Hoppers are plentiful, particularly in the meadow sections, and a Joe's Hopper or Parachute Hopper, size 10 to 14, usually does the job. Try a dropper with a Beadhead Prince or Pheasant Tail if they won't come to the surface.

To access the Rio Grande del Rancho and its tributaries from the Taos Plaza, go 4 miles south on NM 68 to Ranchos de Taos and continue east on NM 518 for a little over 2 miles to the entrance of Carson National Forest, which is marked with a sign. Just before the entrance, take FR 437 to access Rio Chiquito.

The lower reaches of Rio Grande del Rancho are paralleled by NM 518 from the forest entrance upstream for about 6 miles. The lower 3.5 miles are public, while the upper 2.5 are private. At the top of the private property, take FR 439 to access the headwaters of the Rio Grande del Rancho for 11 miles. To access Pot Creek, take FR 438 from NM 518 just before the FR 439 turnoff.

The Little Rio Grande Box begins where the Rio Grande del Rancho and the Rio Pueblo de Taos join 5 miles west of Taos. Resembling the Rio Grande Gorge in many ways, this 7-mile canyon is known locally as simply the Rio Pueblo. In the first 5 miles above its confluence with the Rio Grande, the Rio Pueblo is classic pocket water. Every few feet there's another pocket with the potential for a fish. Some of the boulders are huge, creating deep pockets and holes that can hold big browns.

Like the Rio Grande, the Rio Pueblo has an abundance of chubs, minnows, and crayfish for the browns to feed on once they grow to 12 inches or so. Resident browns up to 9 pounds have been caught in the Rio Pueblo, and I have caught several browns (and lost many more) over 20 inches. Like the Rio Grande, the Rio Pueblo does not fish well during the day in the summer. Late-evening caddis hatches and Ginger Dun spinner falls bring some big fish to the surface, though. Try a Peacock Caddis or a Goddard Caddis, size 14 to 18, or a Ginger Dun, size 14 to 18.

The Rio Pueblo de Taos (Little Rio Grande) offers year-round flyfishing within 20 miles of downtown Taos.

My favorite overall fly is a black and brown Woolly Bugger with Krystal Flash and chain-bead eyes. I call it a Pickpocket because I use it to pick my way through the endless array of boulder-strewn pockets. The Rio Pueblo really defines pocket water.

In the upper 2 miles of the Rio Pueblo, the river's character changes dramatically. Much like the Ute Mountain Run on the Rio Grande, this upper section runs through a series of long riffles, pools, and flats known as Los Cordovas Riffles. The usual hatches of caddis in the spring and summer and the tremendous hatches of fall Baetis bring big browns to the surface.

NM 570 used to parallel the Rio Pueblo and 5 miles of the Rio Grande between Taos and Pilar, but a landslide of basalt boulders closed the section of road that went from the top of the rim to the bottom. There are three or four unmarked primitive trails on the section above the obstruction, and there is roadside access to the confluence at the bottom end of NM 570 from Pilar. To get there, head south from Taos on NM 68 for about 17 miles to the village of Pilar and turn right on NM 570. Follow the Rio Grande upstream 6 miles to the confluence with the Rio Pueblo and park near the barricade. It's foot travel only from there, and you must stay on the southeast bank at all times because the other side is Taos Pueblo land.

The Rio Pueblo watershed offers a great variety of flyfishing opportunities on a year-round basis. The headwaters are an excellent place to explore and cool off in the middle of summer, when you can count on good dry-fly action and an afternoon shower almost every day. The lower Rio Pueblo Box is rugged, rocky, and wild—a miniature version of the Rio Grande itself—and it's great for the more adventurous angler who wants a chance at some nice browns. It can easily be combined with fishing the Rio Grande, as well.

You can have all of this fishing less than 20 miles from downtown Taos, an amazing art-oriented town with one of the finest ski areas in the country. Anglers are now discovering that they can combine some good flyfishing with skiing in northern New Mexico because our winter climate is mild compared to the rest of the Rocky Mountains.

Stream Facts: Rio Pueblo and Little Rio Grande

Season
- Fishing season is year-round, but only the lower Rio Pueblo Box is actually fishable in the winter.

Special Regulations
- The daily bag and possession limit for cutthroat trout is two fish (any trout with a slash under its jaw is considered a cutthroat).

Trout
- The headwaters have brown, cutthroat, cuttbow, brook, and rainbow trout that average 8 to 12 inches, some larger. The lower Rio Pueblo Box contains almost all browns that average 10 to 14 inches, with a few to 18 inches or more. An occasional straggler rainbow or cuttbow drifts in from upstream.

River Miles (from the confluence with the Rio Grande to the headwaters)
- The confluence of the Rio Grande and the Rio Pueblo Box just above Taos Junction Bridge on NM 570—0
- Lower barricade parking area at the end of NM 570—0.5
- Rockslide—1
- Upper barricade parking at the end of NM 570—1.75
- Arroyo del Alamo primitive trail (unmarked)—3
- Los Cordovas Riffles primitive trail (unmarked)—4.5
- Confluence of Rio Pueblo de Taos and Rio Grande del Rancho near Los Cordovas—8
- NM 68 crosses Rio Grande del Rancho—11
- Turn off to Rio Chiquito, FR 437—13.5
- Carson National Forest lower boundary—14
- Carson National Forest upper boundary—17
- Turn off to Pot Creek on FR 438—19
- Turn off to upper Rio Grande del Rancho on FR 439 and Carson National Forest boundary—20
- Turkey Park—25
- Jaroso Canyon—27
- End of roadside access—31.5

River Characteristics
- The headwaters of the Little Rio Grande consist of several small streams. The Rio Pueblo de Taos, which has the most flow, runs through the Taos Pueblo, and is private. The Rio Don Fernando de Taos (Taos Creek) is small, brushy, and difficult to fish, but it's under-fished, has good access, and many developed campgrounds. The Rio Grande del Rancho has over 35 miles of access in its drainage, including two small tributaries, the Rio Chiquito and Pot Creek. All three creeks are small, about 10 to 15 feet wide, brushy, steep, and exhibit a wide array of water types.
- The first 4 miles of the lower Rio Pueblo Box are shallow, with numerous broad riffles and pools, long flats, and some deep holes. The canyon gets deeper and the grade steeper in the last 4 miles before it joins the Rio Grande. Boulders create a complex series of pockets, some big enough to hide a Volkswagen. Extremely wild and beautiful, but with difficult access.

River Flows Headwater Streams
- Winter, summer, and fall: between 5 and 10 cfs
- Spring runoff: between15 and 120 cfs

River Flows Lower Rio Pueblo Box
- Winter, summer, and fall: between 15 and 35 cfs
- Spring runoff: between 40 and 250 cfs, average 200 cfs

Campgrounds
- Capulin Campground, 7 miles east of Taos along US 64; pay campground open May to October; 11 family unit, toilets, and drinking water; adjacent to Rio Fernando
- La Sombra Campground, 8 miles east of Taos along US 64; pay campground open May to October; 13 family units, toilets, drinking water; adjacent to Rio Fernando
- Comales Campground, 8 miles east of Taos along US 64; pay campground open May to October; 10 parking spaces, no grills or tables or drinking water; adjacent to Rio Pueblo

Maps
- *New Mexico Atlas & Gazetteer,* page 16; Carson National Forest Map; BLM Taos Resource Area Map; USGS Quadrangle Map: Taos

Agencies
- Carson National Forest, Questa Ranger District, P.O. Box 110, Questa, NM 87556
- NMDGF, P.O. Box 25112, Santa Fe, NM 87504-5112

Outfitters
The Carson N.F. Questa Ranger district can provide information, including maps and a list of outfitters permitted to operate on public lands. Outfitters include:
- The Solitary Angler, 204B North Pueblo Road, Taos, NM 87529; 1-866-502-1700, www.thesolitaryangler.com
- Ed Adams Flyfishing, P.O. Box 428, Questa, NM 87556; 575-586-1512
- Taylor Streit Fly Fishing Service, P.O. Box 2759, Taos, NM 87571; 575-751-1312

RED RIVER, RIO HONDO, TAOS AREA STREAMS MAJOR HATCHES

Insect	J	F	M	A	M	J	J	A	S	O	N	D	Time	Flies
Caddis									▮				M/A/E	Green & olive caddis larva #12–#16; Double Hackle Peacock #12–#16; Van's Rag Pupa or LaFontaine's Pupa #10–#18; green or dark olive Green Weenie #12–#18; olive, tan & gray Elk Hair Caddis #12–#20; olive, gray & peacock Fluttering Caddis #10–#18
Craneflies									▮				M/A/E	Cranefly larva peacock, gray or dark olive #6–#16; Taylor Streit's Poundmeister #6–#14; Double Hackle Peacock #6–#16; Foam Body Crane Fly #6–#16
Green, Gray Drake (Sparse Hatches)						▮		▮					M/A/SF	Olive Hare's Ear #10–#14; Van's Rag Fly #10–#14; Green & Gray Drake Hair-Wing (Wulff style) #10–#14; Green & Gray Paradrake #10–14; Green Drake spinner #12–#14
Ginger, Gray, Blue & Mahogany Duns									▮				M/E/SF	Light, dark & olive Hare's Ear Nymph #10–#18; Pheasant Tail Nymph #12–#18; light, dark, pink & ginger PW or Hair-Wing Duns or Cahills #12–#18 or the same in parachutes; Ginger, Red & Blue Quills #12–#18
Baetis				▮							▮		M/A/SF	Dark olive Hare's Ear Nymph #16–#22; Pheasant Tail #16–#22; Van's Rag Fly Nymph #16–#22; Olive Parachute #16–#22; Olive Comparadun #16–#22

Hatch Time Code: M = Morning; A = Afternoon; E = Evening; D = Dark; SF = Spinner Fall

RED RIVER, RIO HONDO, TAOS AREA STREAMS (cont.)

Insect	J	F	M	A	M	J	J	A	S	O	N	D	Time	Flies
Salmonfly, Golden Stonefly						▓	▓						M/A	Black & brown stonefly nymph #4–#10; Golden Stone Nymph #10–#14; Elk Hair Salmonfly #4–#8; Orange & Gold Stimulators #4–#14; Terminator #12–#16
Brown Stonefly				▓	▓	▓	▓						A	Dark Hare's Ear #10–#16; brown Elk Hair Caddis & Gold Stimulators #10–#16; Charlie's Little Brown Killer #12–#16
PMDs, PEDs					▓	▓	▓	▓	▓				M/SF	Light Hare's Ear Nymph #12–#18; Pheasant Tail #12–#20; Van's Rag Fly Nymph light olive #14 –#20; Hair-Wing, PW or Para Ginger or Light Olive Dun #14–#20
Terrestrials										▓	▓		M/A	Para-hoppers tan, yellow #8–#14; red w/ black underwing Desert Hopper #6–#14 Bees #12–#14; Elk Hair Pine Moths #8–#14; beetles & ants #12–#18
Minnows			▓	▓	▓	▓	▓	▓	▓	▓	▓	▓	M/E	Assorted colors of Soft-Hackle Streamers, Woolly Buggers, and Muddlers #2–#12 (long shank)

Hatch Time Code: M = Morning; A = Afternoon; E = Evening; D = Dark; SF = Spinner Fall

RIO EMBUDO

The Rio Embudo is the southernmost tributary of the Rio Grande Gorge, and the biggest. It drains an area that includes some of the highest country in the state, with more average snowpack than other watersheds of the Gorge. It's composed of three small streams: the Rio Pueblo (not to be confused with the Rio Pueblo de Taos or the Rio Pueblo Box), the Rio Santa Barbara, and La Junta Creek, as well as dozens of tiny, insignificant creeks. Most of the headwaters are in the Carson National Forest, and the Rio Santa Barbara's headwaters are located in the northern end of the spectacular Pecos Wilderness. The lower Rio Embudo flows through a 6-mile-long unique box canyon, locally known as the Dixon Box, and then through 7 miles of private farmland before uniting with the Rio Grande Gorge near Embudo.

To access the headwaters from Taos, take NM 518 south over US Hill and down to the intersection with NM 75, known as the Rock Wall. Heading east on NM 75 will take you to the Rio Pueblo and La Junta Creek, while a drive west will take you to the Rio Santa Barbara and the Dixon Box. The Rio Pueblo, named after the Picuris (pronounced Peek-yu-reese) Pueblo, is private from the Rock Wall upstream for about 1.5 miles, where it enters the Carson National Forest. NM 518 parallels the river, crossing it several times as it runs through the national forest off and on for the next 12 miles.

There are three developed roadside campsites and a few areas for primitive camping. From the forest boundary upstream for 7 miles, the Rio Pueblo runs through a tight, narrow, medium-grade canyon lined with brush and forest. The river is about 20 to 30 feet wide, and wading is fair on the river bottom. Currents are strong, though, and there are some deep holes with areas that drop several feet in one step, so caution is advised.

About one measly mile of water, from the bridge at mile marker 55 just below Comales Campground to the Canon Tio Mesa trailhead, is designated Special Trout Water. Regulations allow the use of artificial flies and lures only with a single barbless hook, and the daily bag and possession limit is two trout over 12 inches.

The river has a healthy "wild" brown trout population, along with a few native Rio Grande cutthroats and cuttbows. The NMDGF stocks rainbows, and some of these hold over and become larger. The average fish is 8 to 12 inches, but some make it to 16 inches before getting caught or dying of natural causes. The largest one I ever caught here was an 18-inch brown during an evening Ginger Dun spinner fall.

The hatches are frequent from mid-June through September, and they cover the entire spectrum. Midday hatches of Blue-Winged Olives (spring Baetis) start in June, followed by midmorning hatches of PMDs in late June. Golden Stones, Salmonflies, and Gray Drakes start in late June and last through July. Blue Duns and Ginger Duns start in late July and last into late August, while evening caddis and midge hatches occur off and on from June through September. Bud worms, pine moths, beetles, and cicadas are significant in some years, especially during a drought, and ants, termites, and hoppers are always present from June through September.

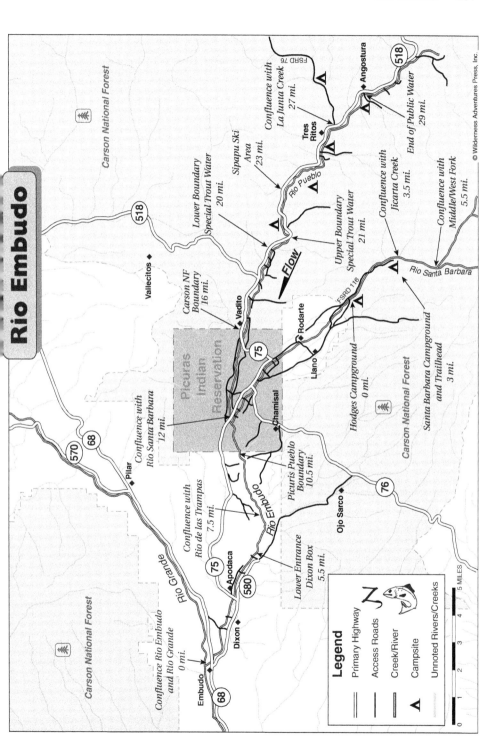

Rio Embudo

Carson National Forest

Carson National Forest

FSRD 76

Angostura

518

Confluence with
La Junta Creek
27 mi.

Tres
Ritos

End of Public Water
29 mi.

Sipapu Ski
Area
23 mi.

Confluence with
Jicarita Creek
3.5 mi.

Confluence with
Middle/West Fork
5.5 mi.

Rio Pueblo

Lower Boundary
Special Trout Water
20 mi.

518

Upper Boundary
Special Trout Water
21 mi.

Flow

Vallecitos

Carson NF
Boundary
16 mi.

Rio Santa Barbara

Vadito

FSRD 116

Rodarte

Santa Barbara Campground
and Trailhead
3 mi.

Picuris
Indian
Reservation

75

Hodges Campground
0 mi.

Llano

Carson National Forest

Confluence with
Rio Santa Barbara
12 mi.

Chamisal

570

68

Pilar

Picuris Pueblo
Boundary
10.5 mi.

76

Ojo Sarco

Confluence with
Rio de las Trampas
7.5 mi.

Rio Grande

Rio Embudo

75

Apodaca

580

Lower Entrance
Dixon Box
5.5 mi.

Carson National Forest

Confluence Rio Embudo
and Rio Grande
0 mi.

Dixon

Embudo

68

Legend

N

— Primary Highway
— Access Roads
▲ Creek/River
▲ Campsite
    Unnoted Rivers/Creeks

0 1 2 3 4 5 MILES

Dry-dropper rigs work well, particularly during a hatch, while nymph rigs perform better during non-hatch periods. My favorite imitations include various Stimulators, Terminators, Bird's Golden Stones, Gray Wulffs, Ginger Duns, Adams Irresistibles, Olive, Adams, and Ginger Parachutes, olive Elk Hair Caddis, Cicadas, and Parachute Hoppers. For nymphs, I like light and dark Hare's Ears, Pheasant Tails, and Golden Stones (all beadhead and standard).

I always wade upstream to avoid spooking fish and to cast to all possible holding spots. At midday, I concentrate most of my casts close to the bank unless I'm nymph fishing, in which case I hit the deep seams, pools, and riffles. I keep moving, covering the water thoroughly, and I try to match whatever is hatching with a high-floating imitation. I usually add a dropper about 15 inches long with a beadhead nymph unless most of my strikes are on the surface near the bank, in which case I remove the dropper and fish with a single dry fly to avoid snagging the bank and overhanging brush.

The browns like to stay close to the banks in the shade, while the rainbows prefer the faster riffles and deep holes. During evening hatches, they all move to the heads of pools, runs, and riffles to compete for food.

Pressure has increased on the Rio Pueblo in recent years, especially from baitfishers who keep fish. Unfortunately, this pressure has translated into a decrease in the size and number of fish and a marked increase in litter—mainly bait boxes, hook packages, and beer cans. The Special Trout Water helps the situation a little, but it needs to be expanded to protect the fishery from further degradation.

The river splits near the town of Tres Ritos. The highway continues to follow the Rio Pueblo upstream, eventually onto private land, and La Junta Creek enters the Rio Pueblo from the north. It's accessed via FR 76 just past Tres Ritos. A maintained dirt road follows the creek for 5 miles, at which point the water is too small to fish. There are two nice campgrounds here, and primitive camping is allowed throughout the area.

The creek is full of small browns and cutthroats, which are more abundant the higher you go, but there are a few surprisingly larger fish as well, especially early in the year when the flows are robust. Because it comes from a smaller, lower, south-facing watershed, La Junta Creek runs off sooner in the spring than the Rio Pueblo, making it a good early-season fishery. The fish are opportunistic and hatches insignificant, so any medium-sized fly that floats well will usually work. There are nice little pools and a few beaver ponds, but also quite a bit of brush.

A short, light rod like my 7½-foot, 2-weight is great for casting to and fighting the small trout, which average 8 to 12 inches, and some larger. I teach kids to fish here because they don't have to cast far and the fish are usually accommodating.

The upper Rio Embudo—also known as the Rio del Pueblo—offers excellent dry-fly fishing from June through September.

Rio Santa Barbara

From the Rock Wall downstream 2.5 miles, the Rio Pueblo is private before it runs through the Picuris Pueblo for 5.5 miles and then enters BLM land at the top end of the Dixon Box, where it's joined by the Rio Santa Barbara. The river in the Picuris Pueblo is closed to the public.

The Rio Santa Barbara is a beautiful, crystal-clear, freestone stream that begins high in the southern end of the Pecos Wilderness on the north slopes of some of the highest peaks in the state; an average runoff can last until late June and in heavy snowpack years it can last into July. This makes it a great summer fishery (when other streams are too warm during the midday hours). The best fishing doesn't usually start until around noon, after the water warms up a little bit and flies start hatching. By mid-September the river starts cooling off, and the fishing is usually finished sometime around the end of the month.

To get the Rio Santa Barbara from the Rock Wall, go west on NM 75 about 5 miles to the village of Penasco and the intersection with NM 73. Turn left on NM 73 and go about 1.5 miles to FR 116 (on the left), marked by a sign to the Pecos Wilderness and Santa Barbara Campground. Follow FR 116 about 4.5 miles to the Carson National Forest boundary. From the boundary upstream, there are approximately 3 miles of roadside access to the Rio Santa Barbara and two developed campgrounds: Hodges Campground at the boundary and Santa Barbara Campground at the end of the road. This stretch is brushy and best accessed at the bridges and campgrounds. Just stay in the water, fishing upstream and making short casts.

The Rio Santa Barbara is famous for its remote and pristine condition, magnificent views, variety of wildlife, and abundance of wild Rio Grande cutthroats. There are also browns throughout the watershed, and rainbows are stocked near the bridges and campgrounds. As with most streams in the Sangre de Cristos, the cutthroats are more abundant the higher you go.

There are sporadic hatches of stoneflies, PMDs, Western Drakes, and caddis, but the cutts are opportunistic, eating whatever they can grab in the fast currents. Attractors such as Terminators, Stimulators, Royal Wulffs, Humpies, and hoppers work well, and a dropper with a Beadhead Prince or Flashback Pheasant Tail Nymph will usually work when the dries don't.

Trail 24 will take you into the Pecos Wilderness, where the Rio Santa Barbara splits into three branches—the West, Middle, and East Forks. Trails follow each fork, offering over 10 miles of wilderness flyfishing for the adventurous angler looking for solitude, scenery, and native trout. The creeks have beaver ponds, meadows, and brushy canyon sections, and the native cutts average 8 to 12 inches, some up to 16 inches in the beaver ponds. My personal best is a cutthroat I caught in a beaver pond on the West Fork that I had to stretch to make 18 inches.

The West Fork has a gentler flow and more open meadows and beaver ponds than the other forks. General regulations apply throughout the Rio Santa Barbara, but as always, catch and release is recommended.

This entire area is great for backpacking, and there are plenty of good campsites. The scenery is some of the best in New Mexico, with several high peaks towering above, including the 13,000-plus-foot Truchas Peaks. Several other small creeks nearby provide endless opportunities for the flyfisher, and the headwaters of the splendid Pecos River are just a short hike over the Truchas Peaks. A permit is required to enter the Pecos Wilderness; it can be obtained at the Camino Real Ranger Station in Penasco.

Dixon Box

The Rio Santa Barbara joins the Rio Pueblo at the top end of the Dixon Box on the Picuris Pueblo, where it becomes the Rio Embudo. From there it flows through the Picuris Pueblo for another 1.5 miles before entering BLM land.

The Dixon Box is a sheer canyon about 7 miles long, named after the nearby town of Dixon, and it's distinctly different from other tributaries of the Rio Grande Gorge. The canyon is composed of granite, sandstone, and other rock types instead of basalt. The Rio Embudo comes from very high north-facing peaks, plunging quickly into a mountain valley before running directly into the Dixon Box. The flow is better and colder than other tributaries, so summer fishing is more productive and hatches are prolific at times. The habitat is subalpine, with occasional Ponderosa pines, Douglas firs, and alders along the rocky bank.

When I was a kid my father used to tell me about the mysterious Dixon Box and about the many nice browns he used to catch back when you could drive down to the river at the old Hardy Mine, which has long since closed. He told me about the deep, crystal-clear pools and pockets that held 16- to 20-inch browns and the willow flies (actually stoneflies) that were so thick the fish would gorge on them until stuffed to the gills.

For some reason he never took me to the Dixon Box, so when I turned 17 and bought my first vehicle, a 1969 Toyota Land Cruiser station wagon with running boards and fender wells, I set out to explore the place. I got out my topographical map and drove up and down every primitive road and walked up and down every rugged trail I could find. I fished every foot of the Dixon Box in four days, and I never saw a soul.

As usual, the first day was the best. There were stoneflies and Ginger Duns hatching all day, followed by a great caddis hatch at dusk. I caught and released over 50 browns that day between 12 and 18 inches, all on dry flies. My greed almost caught up with me, though, as I didn't have a flashlight and took a wrong side canyon while hiking out in the dark. Just about the time I was ready to build a fire and wait until morning, I bumped into my car.

I realized why my father hadn't shared this glorious place with me. He never liked steep, rugged, cross-country hikes the way I do. He was fortunate to grow up at a time when you could drive right up to where you wanted to fish without other anglers competing for space. Now, you have to work to find such places.

The Dixon Box is a remote stretch of the Embudo that offers great flyfishing for wild browns up to 18 inches.

Since that early trip I've been fortunate to visit the Dixon Box a few times a year. Although I've never duplicated that first day, I still have some great days and always a good time. That's the magic of flyfishing; it's the pursuit of that which is tempting, elusive, and ever changing, yet attainable, providing endless satisfaction.

Because of its remote, rugged, unmarked access—and the wading required—the Dixon Box doesn't receive a lot of pressure. Still, some locals know it well and many harvest fish, so the fishery isn't quite as good as it once was. There are plenty of "wild" browns from 8 to 13 inches, but far less over 13 inches than there used to be, although there's still a chance to catch fish up to 18 inches. There is also a chance to catch the occasional cutthroat or stocker rainbow that drifts down from the Rio Pueblo or Rio Santa Barbara.

The Embudo picks up flow from two small creeks, Chamisal and Las Trampas, which also help keep the river cool on hot summer days. The river is 15 to 30 feet wide, with a combination of riffles, pools, deep holes, and pockets. Many deep undercuts against the cliffs hold large browns. The river bottom includes well-worn bedrock 4 to 6 inches in diameter, smaller rock, pebbles, gravel, and silt at the end of pools and in back eddies.

I prefer breathable, stocking-foot hip waders and wading boots with rubber, whirling disease–proof soles because they're easy to hike in and they're good on almost any wet surface. The canyon is so tight that you must cross from time to time to avoid granite walls that come right to the water's edge.

The Dixon Box is a sheer canyon about 7 miles long.

It's often possible to enjoy some good flyfishing before runoff, which usually starts in May. Try nymph fishing or stripping streamers. Caddis, PMDs, and Golden Stones hatch through mid-July, but the river is normally high from runoff until mid-June. July and August bring late-evening caddis and assorted mayfly hatches, including some Gray Drakes and Ginger Duns. The fast water also provides good habitat for powerful clinger mayflies, such as *Epeorus*. Blue-Winged Olives hatch from September through October, providing good dry-fly opportunities.

My favorite imitations include the usual assortment of Terminators and Stimulators, size 6 to 14; olive and brown Elk Hair Caddis and Goddard Caddis, size 12 to 16; Ginger, Gray, and Olive Wulffs or Parachutes, size 12 to 18; light and dark Hare's Ears and Pheasant Tails (beadhead and regular), size 12 to 18; Golden Stone Nymphs (beadhead and regular), size 8 to 16; and assorted Woolly Buggers (beadhead and regular), size 6 to 14.

I prefer an 8½- to 9-foot, 4- or 5-weight with a 9-foot, 5X leader. I usually go with a dry-dropper rig or a double-nymph rig with enough twist-on lead to get to the bottom of the fast pockets, riffles, and pools. I wade and fish upstream to avoid spooking the trout, which face upstream in the clear, cold water as they wait for food to come downstream. Even during hatches they aren't very selective because they must decide instantly whether or not to take your fly in the rapid current. I usually select an imitation slightly larger than the natural to make sure they see it.

Access into the Dixon Box is difficult at best. Inquire at local shops in Santa Fe or Taos for guides and directions or spend a couple of days with a map and a good four-wheel drive just investigating different roads and trails. There are no signs along the maze of dead-end roads on the rim, and only a few lead to actual trails.

From Penasco, take NM 75 west about 4.5 miles and start looking for dirt roads on your left for the next 3 miles. To access the Dixon Box from Santa Fe or Taos, take NM 75 east from NM 68, go 3 miles through Dixon, and then turn on the unmarked, paved road just before crossing the Rio Embudo. It's paved for a couple of miles before it turns into an all-weather dirt road. Drive about 1.9 miles past the pavement and look for a primitive dirt track that veers left and starts up the mesa. Take the dirt track until you come to an arroyo. Park just before it or, if you are a daring driver, keep going to the top of the mesa and park. Follow the path that leads to a slot in the canyon wall (actually a side canyon) and continue down the rugged trail to the Rio Embudo.

An angler could spend a whole week fishing the Rio Embudo and its tributaries, working a different type of water each day. From the icy cold waters of the Rio Santa Barbara to the depths of the Dixon Box, from dabbling flies for pan-sized cutts and browns in La Junta Creek to nymphing the swift riffles of the Rio Pueblo, there is something to suit any angler.

Stream Facts: Rio Embudo—Rio Pueblo, Rio Santa Barbara, and Dixon Box

Season
- Fishing is open year-round, but the Rio Santa Barbara is only fishable from June through September and the Rio Pueblo is fishable just before runoff in April and then just after runoff (mid-June) through October. La Junta Creek runs off earlier and is usually fishable in late May. The Dixon Box fishes well in April until runoff starts and then after runoff through November. It's fishable during the winter in mild years.

Special Regulations
- Headwaters: The daily bag and possession limit on cutthroats is two fish. (Any trout with a red slash under its jaw is considered a cutthroat.)

Trout
- Rio Pueblo, La Junta Creek, Rio Santa Barbara: Brown, cutthroat, cuttbow, and rainbow trout averaging 8 to 12 inches, some to 18 inches.
- Dixon Box: Brown trout and occasional rainbow and cutthroat trout averaging 12 to 15 inches, some to 20 inches.

River Miles Rio Embudo (from the Rio Grande confluence upstream to headwaters)
- Confluence of the Rio Grande and Rio Embudo—0
- Lower entrance to the Dixon Box—5.5
- Confluence with Rio de las Trampas—7.5
- Confluence with Chamizal Creek and the entrance to Picuris Pueblo—10.5
- Confluence with Rio Santa Barbara on Picuris Pueblo and bridge on NM 75—12
- Entrance to Carson National Forest on NM 75 and east boundary of the Picuris Pueblo—16
- Lower boundary of Special Trout Water at the bridge near mile marker 55—20
- Upper boundary of Special Trout Water at the Cañon Tio Mesa trailhead—21
- Sipapu Ski Area—23
- La Junta Creek confluence and FR 76—27

River Miles Rio Santa Barbara
- Hodges Campground just inside Carson N.F. on FR 116—0
- Santa Barbara Campground and trailhead—3
- Jicarita Creek confluence, hike-in access only—3.5
- Middle Fork/West Fork confluence, hike-in access only—5.5

River Characteristics
- Rio Pueblo: Medium-sized freestone stream running through a tight, brushy, alpine canyon with good roadside access and several miles of public water. Mostly fast water with pockets, pool drops, holes, riffles; beaver ponds in the upper reaches.

- Rio Santa Barbara: Small, fast freestone stream. Brushy in the lower reaches and a little more open in the upper reaches, where there are meadows and willows.
  - Dixon Box - Narrow box canyon with hike-in access via rugged, steep, unmarked trails. Fast pocket water with deep plunge pools, deep holes and riffles. Good hatches of stoneflies, caddis, and mayflies.

River Flows Rio Pueblo
- Winter, summer, and fall: between 15 and 45 cfs
- Spring runoff: between 60 and 300 cfs

River Flows Dixon Box
- Winter, summer, and fall: between 50 and 70 cfs
- Spring runoff: between 80 and 400 cfs

Campgrounds
- Camino Real Ranger District, 11 miles east of Penasco along NM 518; pay campground open May to October; 44 family units, toilets, no drinking water; adjacent to Rio Pueblo
- La Junta Campground, 4 miles northeast of Tres Ritos along FR 76, off NM 518; pay campground open May to October; 9 family units, toilets, no drinking water; adjacent to Rito la Presa
- Hodges Campground, 10 miles southeast of Penasco along FR 116, off NM 73; pay campground open May to October; dispersed sites for camping or picnicking, toilets, no drinking water; adjacent to Rio Santa Barbara
- Santa Barbara Campground, 12 miles southeast of Penasco along FR 116, off NM 73; pay campground open May to October; 22 family units, toilets, drinking water; adjacent to Rio Santa Barbara; trailhead into the Pecos Wilderness

Maps
- *New Mexico Atlas & Gazetteer,* page 16; Carson National Forest Map; BLM Taos Resource Area Map; USGS Quadrangle Maps: Tres Ritos, Penasco, Trampas

Agencies
- BLM Taos Resource Area, 224 Cruz Alta Road, Taos, NM 87571
- USFS Carson National Forest, Questa Ranger District, P.O. Box 110, Questa, NM 87556
- NMDGF, P.O. Box 25112, Santa Fe, NM 87504-5112

Outfitters
The BLM, Taos Resource Area and the Carson N.F. Questa Ranger District can provide information, including maps and a list of outfitters permitted to operate on public lands. Outfitters include:
- The Solitary Angler, 204B North Pueblo Road, Taos, NM 87571; 1-866-502-1700, www.thesolitaryangler.com
- Tailwater Gallery & Flyshop, 204B Paseo del Pueblo Norte, Taos, NM 87571; 575-758-5653
- Ed Adams Flyfishing, P.O. Box 428, Questa, NM 87556; 575-586-1512
- Taylor Streit Fly Fishing Service, 308 Paseo del Pueblo Sur, Taos, NM 87571; 575-751-1312

Southwest Region

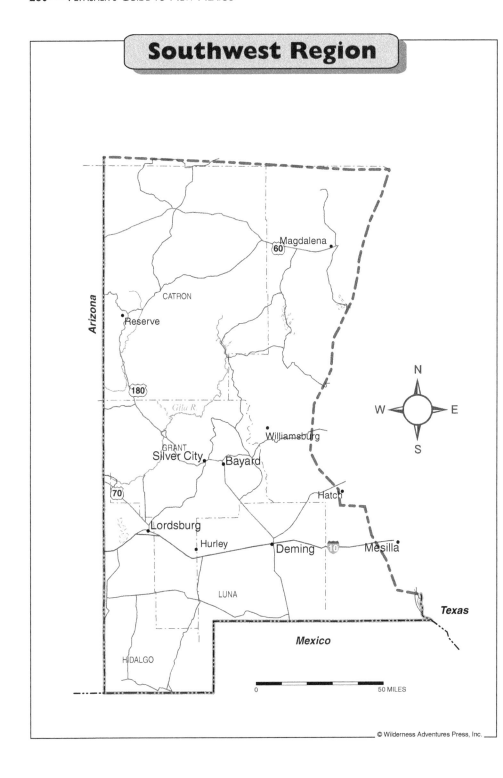

Southwest Region

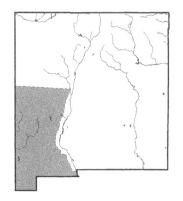

When I first started researching this book I thought it would be an easy job. After all, I'd fished over 90 percent of the waters in northern New Mexico, and the waters of southern New Mexico would be easy to check out since most were within the Gila National Forest. Having never cast a line in this area, I was very excited that I was finally going to fish the oldest wilderness area in the country.

My father had told me about the place when I was a boy, and several close angling buddies and guides had told me how wonderful the fishing was and how remote the wilderness was. "It's like stepping back in time," said Mark Cowan.

"I've never seen another angler while fishing there, Van, it's just your kind of place," said Greg King. "And you can fish for a week, catching fish all day long using the same fly until it's shredded."

So in June of 2003 I convinced my friend Kelly to join me for a fact-finding trip to the Gila. From Taos, it takes a full day to get to Silver City, the main tourist town in the Gila region. Once I left I-25 the traffic was almost nonexistent. I felt like I was on a remote road in southwest Wyoming, It was desolate.

As we approached Kingston, the gigantic, black thunderheads that I'd been watching build for the last two hours were releasing their energy and water. The radio announced a flash-flood alert for the Kingston area, saying over an inch of rain had fallen in less than a half hour. By the time we got to Kingston there were over 4 inches of hail on the road and every little wash was running full of chocolate water. Just my luck! The one time I come to the Gila and there's more rain than they've had all year in this seventh year of a serious drought. As it turns out, only the Mimbres and the East Fork were muddied up, but that was the least of my problems.

I had four days of fishing ahead of me, or so I thought. The next morning we got up and headed for the Forest Service ranger station to get the maps we would need to check out the region. By the time we left it was 10:00 a.m., so we headed toward the confluence of the East, Middle, and West Forks of the Gila. I figured this would be a good place to start.

As we entered the Gila National Forest, the road got narrower and very serpentine, slowing us down. And the views at every bend were unbelievably expansive, revealing endless miles of desolate wilderness, which we had to stop to admire. By the time we got to the confluence of the forks it was past 2:00 p.m. The East Fork was muddy, but the main stem and the other two forks were clear. I pulled over at the Heart Bar Riparian Area, one of the few places to fish without hiking. I figured I could at least get some photos of the river, and based on information from friends, I assumed I could catch at least a couple of stockers since I was next to the road, where stocking is easy.

I had to walk about a quarter-mile to get away from the swimmers and bathers trying to cool off. As I reached down to check the water temperature with my hand I thought, "My God, I don't know how a bass could live in this bath water, much less a trout." After confirming a temperature of 86 degrees with my thermometer, I knew I wouldn't be catching trout. I tied on a Woolly Bugger and began fishing the beautiful, surprisingly clear pools, hoping to tie into a bronze bass.

I fished five pools without a strike, although I did spook a couple of large fish, but I couldn't tell what species. Based on the amount of water that was flowing, less than 30 cfs, I wondered how much there would be in the headwaters and how far up I would have to go to find water cool enough to hold trout.

We packed up and headed for the Middle Fork trailhead. By the time we got there it was already near 4:00 p.m., so we headed upstream and, as suspected, the flow was minimal. I could see that the lush riparian zone, which used to be under water, was becoming narrower due to drought. After a few hundred yards we came upon a beaver pond, which backed up enough water to form a deep pool.

I saw bass darting into the tall grass growing along the edge of the pond. I unhooked my Woolly Bugger, pulled 3 or 4 feet of line off my reel, and flipped the fly into the narrow, open slot between the grassy banks. Five or six bass raced out from their hiding places to compete for the prize. Immediately, I had a smallmouth on, and the fight was impressive for a fish no longer than 10 inches.

I caught about ten bass in that pond, the largest 13 inches, and I thought I was on my way to an afternoon of fish after fish. I continued fishing upstream for another half-mile, but only found one more spot that was deep enough to hold a fish—and I spooked him. The water was clear, and I could see frogs, crayfish, and minnows everywhere, but no bass and no trout. The water temperature was still high, about 84 degrees, and I knew I would have to head farther upstream than I had time for in order to find trout.

I hadn't brought a backpack, and it would require at least two days of hiking to get 20 or more miles upstream where the trout might be. As we were getting ready to turn around, Kelly said she found something interesting. I walked upstream a couple of hundred yards to find her lying in a steaming-hot pool on the side of the creek. She'd found a hot spring, and there wasn't much to do except join her. We enjoyed the soak for about an hour before a storm passed over and the lightning got too close for comfort. We jumped out and headed for the vehicle, but we got drenched to the bone. We decided to head back to Silver City to ask some questions.

I'd heard stories of the years of drought and forest fires that were causing problems, dumping tons of ash into some rivers. And some small streams were drying up completely. It was even getting bad in northern New Mexico and the rest of the Rockies, so I knew it was going to be tough in the Gila, but this was dismal.

In talking to locals in Silver City I found that it was much worse than I thought. The drought had resulted in very low flows and warmer than normal water temperatures, and the trout's range had been moved far up into smaller areas in the headwaters. Meanwhile, the smallmouth bass were expanding their range. Much of the headwaters so critical to the survival of the endangered Gila trout were closed to fishing until they could be downgraded to a threatened species.

Until the drought let up, the Gila wasn't a great place to go for trout, but flyfishing opportunities still existed for other species, particularly smallmouth bass.

Mostly what I learned on my initial trip was that I would need far more time than I could find to accurately research and describe this immense wilderness fishery. Indeed, it could take years of nonstop research to get the kind of accurate information I'd need. In talking to people "in the know," one man's name kept coming up time after time, "Dutch" Salmon. I had read his recent article on the Gila in *New Mexico Magazine* (June 2003), which made me anxious to fish the Gila.

Dutch was the man to talk to they all said. "He's fished all the streams around here with a fly rod, and he can catch anything from a carp or catfish to smallies and brightly colored Gila trout, and he knows where to go to get any species or all species."

So I decided to give him a call. Sure enough, he knew his stuff and was quick to volunteer to help. He's contributed a delightful, informative guide to the Gila country, something I couldn't have written in a million years—something no one could have written so well.

After you read this, you're going to want to visit the Gila someday. And when you do, make sure to allow enough time to really enjoy this massive region. A day or two isn't enough; five days to two weeks is necessary to really get a feel for this wilderness that Aldo Leopold so enjoyed he was moved to fight until the headwaters of the Gila were declared the first wilderness area in the country in 1924.

The mainstem Gila River. (Jan Haley)

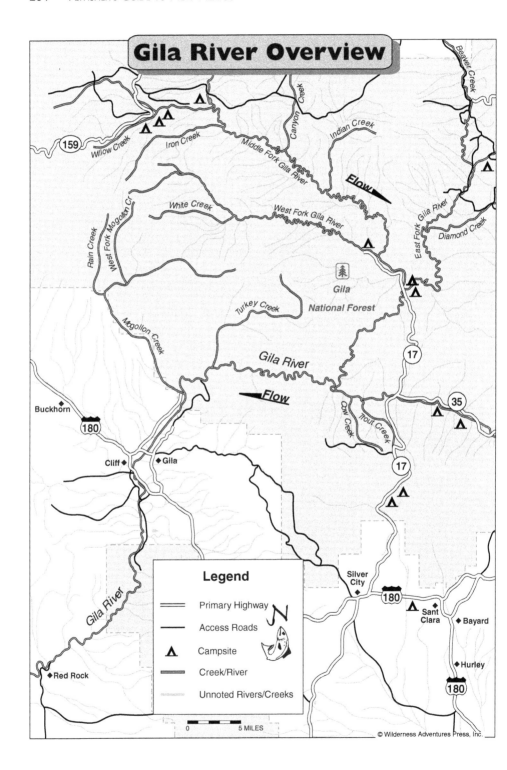

THE GILA COUNTRY

(Contributed by Dutch Salmon)

The 3.3 million–acre Gila National Forest contains virtually all of the available trout waters in the southwest quadrant of New Mexico. This is the only place in the state where you may find good numbers of smallmouth bass living in a trout stream. These fish offer all the best qualities of flyfishing for wild trout, only they fight harder.

There is very little private land to contend with, you don't have to pay, and you rarely need permission. There are also a very limited number of vehicular access points to reach the fish; this is good or bad depending on your point of view. Most of the waters are within the Gila or Aldo Leopold Wilderness Areas, some 800,000 acres in all, the first of our nation's roadless areas so protected and by far the largest wilderness expanse remaining in the Southwest.

The whole thing appears almost an anomaly—a huge, mountainous uplift, filled with piñon, oak, pine, and impossible canyons, in the middle of the desert. The Gila is where the Rocky Mountains meet the Sierra Madre. Thus, this forest is not as verdant as the Carson or Santa Fe National Forests. The rivers are really streams; the streams are creeks; and many of the creeks you can step across. But even the creeks have fish, and if you're willing to walk or ride a horse you can find them.

Flyfishing itself is something of an anomaly in the region. Although the sport has caught on here, as elsewhere, in recent years, most of the local anglers are still quite happy with bait or lures. And most non-local anglers have never heard of the place. The Gila National Forest is hardly a destination flyfishing locale. The streams are 200 miles or better from any large city, and while none of them are inaccessible, almost none of them are readily accessible, due to remoteness, rugged terrain, and a lack of roads and vehicular access.

The principal towns that a visiting flyfisher would use as a staging area are Silver City in the south (pop. about 10,000), Glenwood in the middle (pop. about 300), and Reserve in the north (pop. about 500). You can find gas, food, and lodging at these and a few other towns, but don't come here expecting to get outfitted for flyfishing. There are no fly or trout shops, per se. There is a Wal-Mart in Silver City and a general-interest outdoor store (Rough Country Outdoors) that will have the basics. In the smaller towns, the general store may or may not have what you need for flyfishing.

There are virtually no flyfishing guides, either, although there are a number of fine outfitters who will take you fishing. Many specialize in horse and mule pack trips, but day trips can also be arranged. The list of permitted guides and outfitters can be had from Gila Forest Headquarters in Silver City (505-388-8201). The Gila Forest offices will also have the maps you need to explore and fish the Gila.

The drought years of the new millennium that stressed and depleted gamefish populations in the Gila drainage through 2004, abruptly ended in the winter and spring of 2005 with a heavy snow-pack (129 inches deep at the Whitewater Baldy snowtel marker) and a subsequent blow-out flood that surpassed 20,000 cfs at the Cliff/Gila gauge. From a low point in the summer of 2005 when fishing could only be described as "poor", gamefish populations have slowly but steadily increased throughout the drainage and all perennial flows are brim-full and flush with promise as the fishing season kicks off in the spring of 2010. Sometimes dubbed "the only warm-water trout fishery in America", the Gila drainage, as it descends, is more precisely a peculiar and rapid transition from a cold-water trout fishery to a mid-elevation bass fishery to a warm-water catfish/carp fishery with some interesting overlaps hardly found elsewhere. For example, this may be the only place in North America where you can catch a wild trout and a flathead catfish out of the same pool (I've done this). Aside from the improvement in habitat and general angling, the big change in the Gila fishery is the 2007 downlisting of the region's native Gila trout from Federally Endangered to Federally Threatened. As a result, you and I may now fish – on a limited basis – for Gila trout!

A close reading of the current New Mexico Fishing Proclamation is essential to keep within the rules. In sum, counting the upper West Fork of the Gila, which is expected to have Gila trout by the fall of 2010, the species is now considered recovered in approximately 100 miles of stream reach. Fishing – some of it strictly catch and release – is only allowed in a few of the renovated streams, however, including portions of Black Canyon Creek. Mogollon Creek, and Iron Creek. Surplus Gila stock have also been added to the mix in Gilita Creek, Willow Creek, The Forks area (where the West, Middle, and East Forks join), and Sapillo Creek, places where they may share habitat with browns, rainbows, and sometimes bass. I've caught them in Black Canyon and the Forks and would offer this quick critique of the Gila trout: the bronze-yellow sheen is distinctive and flashes in the water; a dry fly is largely a waste of time but they hammer a well-presented drifting nymph; the fight is deep, frenetic and lasting.

Most of the Gila's gamefish are non-native, introduced species (smallmouth and largemouth bass, brown and rainbow trout, carp, channel and flathead catfish), albeit they are now self-sustaining and naturally reproducing in these waters. Aside from the Gila trout, two other native fish, marginal perhaps as game fish, should be mentioned as they have some size and you will from time to time find them taking your fly.

The roundtail chub – called headwaters chub from the Forks upstream – may reach 18 inches and will hit your fly as readily as any trout. The fight is spirited . . . .for about 20 seconds. Then the fish flags and comes readily to hand; he seemingly knows he's on the State Endangered list and must be released. The Sonora sucker, regardless of his less than attractive mouth (shaped like the end of a garden hose) is for me a more interesting fish. A 20-incher is not unusual; my son, Bud, caught a 26-inch Sonora sucker summer of 2009. And despite the scavenging mouth this powerful native will chase down a deep, slow-drifting nymph, curl your rod, run your line and fight you all the way to the bank. He's not protected but he's bony so, like the chub, you let him go.

Tools of the Trade

An angler with a 5-weight rod, matching floating line, and a handful of standard dry and wet flies—Adams, Parachute Adams, Elk Hair Caddis, Prince Nymph, some

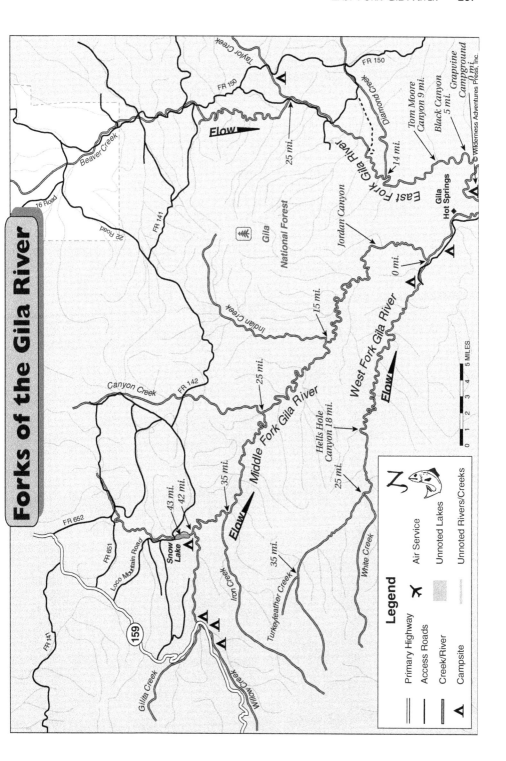

Forks of the Gila River

Flow

25 mi.

Taylor Creek

FR 150

FR 150

Diamond Creek

FR 150

Tom Moore Canyon 9 mi.

Black Canyon 5 mi.

Grapvine Campground 0 mi.

© Wilderness Adventures Press, Inc.

Beaver Creek

East Fork Gila River

14 mi.

Gila Hot Springs

16 Road

22 Road

FR 141

Gila

National Forest

Jordan Canyon

0 mi.

15 mi.

West Fork Gila River

Flow

Indian Creek

25 mi.

Canyon Creek

FR 142

Middle Fork Gila River

Hells Hole Canyon 18 mi.

25 mi.

5 MILES

0   1   2   3   4

35 mi.

43 mi.

42 mi.

FR 652

Snow Lake

Flow

Iron Creek

35 mi.

Turkeyfeather Creek

White Creek

FR 651

Loco Mountain Road

159

Gilita Creek

Willow Creek

FR 141

Legend

Air Service

Unnoted Lakes

Unnoted Rivers/Creeks

Primary Highway

Access Roads

Creek/River

Campsite

N

beadhead nymphs, Woolly Buggers, Pistol Petes, a couple of popping bugs—is well outfitted for the Gila Forest streams. The fish aren't that selective, as the Gila's most famed flyfisher, Rex Johnson, taught me years ago.

For kicks, I once fished a whole morning with a Royal Coachman, a beautiful fly considered obsolete by many, and caught a bunch of bass until I lost the fly to a good fish and a worn knot. I'd wager a Silver Doctor or Parmachene Belle would do as well. Because many of the streams are small and close-quartered, and many of the trout small as well, a 7-foot, 2-weight rod would be handy, making the small fish fight "bigger." On the other hand, in some streams you may tie into a carp or catfish, either by accident or on purpose; this could mean a 10-pound-plus fish. After spending more than an hour with a couple of carp last summer I'm now in the market for a 7-weight rod.

I seldom wear hip boots or waders in the Gila Forest. I wade wet and change into dry socks and boots back at the truck or at camp. It's usually warm enough to do that comfortably, and most Gila fishing involves a lot of hiking. Big boots wear you down.

Steve Siegfried with a nice bronze bass. (Jan Haley)

EAST FORK OF THE GILA RIVER AND TRIBUTARIES

The East Fork of the Gila River, about 25 miles in length, drains out of the remote Black Range, much of it within the Aldo Leopold Wilderness area, where in the 1920s and '30s houndmen like Ben Lilly and Dub Evans, and trappers like Albert Pickens, killed some of the last grizzlies and wolves in New Mexico. Base flow is about 30 cfs. Low flows will be less than half that, while a recent high flow inundated a supposedly safe and venerable ranch cemetery, routed out several of its inhabitants, and carried the coffins miles downstream. As with any stream exploration in this canyon country, watch yourself!

The East Fork runs a bit

warmer on average than the Middle or West Forks of the Gila, so smallmouth bass predominate and a few stream-oriented largemouth bass show up as well. They are found from the lower confluence, where the East Fork runs into the main Gila at Grapevine Campground, to the headwaters of Beaver Creek more than 30 miles upstream. Rainbows and rainbow/Gila trout hybrids are found in lesser or greater numbers, depending on the year, from the Beaver Creek confluence on down to Grapevine. A few browns show up from time to time in this same section, probably entries from Black Canyon. Don't be surprised if a bullish channel catfish or carp takes a drifting nymph bounced off the bottom. Like much of the fishing waters of the mainstem Gila, the East Fork can resemble a coldwater trout fishery one day and a warmwater mixed bag the next.

Generally, you fish the pools, with the better ones sporting lovely green water, excellent clarity, and 3 to 5 feet of depth. The deep, fast-water chutes that run into these pools are also good holding areas for trout and bass. Between the pools are reaches of riffle habitat that get longer and more boring as you hike upstream from Black Canyon. Here, you are wasting your time. But there are enough pools to keep you going—usually every few hundred yards—keeping in mind there may be a 3-pound bronze bass at the next one.

I have taken several 18-inch bass from the Gila watershed but the largest, a 21-inch smallmouth, came from the East Fork in the summer of 2009. Whether trout or bass, you will hook a lot of fish under a foot long and cover a lot of miles, but the lunkers are there.

What works on the East Fork? It's only a slight exaggeration to say that what works on the East Fork also works on the other two forks and the main Gila—whatever you throw at them. It would take more of an entomologist than I am to explain it, but the Gila and its tributaries seldom see the kind of concentrated hatches that cause fish to rise in numbers to a particular food.

Sift the shallows with a net and the mayfly nymphs, stonefly nymphs, dragonfly nymphs, caddis nymphs, Dobsonfly nymphs (hellgrammites), water beetles, etc., are there, often in impressive numbers. The nymphs must certainly hatch, but they do so discreetly, on their own time, and seldom all at once. In the deeper flows (the three forks and the main Gila), beadhead nymphs, Woolly Buggers (often with a split shot on the line to get them down), Pistol Petes, and streamers both subtle and outlandish all work when the fish are in the mood, and they'll usually outfish any dry fly.

That doesn't mean the fish are easy. Bass or trout, catfish or carp, these are wilderness creatures, most of them wild—born in the stream—and unwise to any of the artificials we may cast their way. Most of them aren't fussy about what you present, but they are very fussy about the way you present it; i.e., they are easily spooked. A sloppy cast is death (to the angler). And remember: if you can see him, he can probably see you. And if he sees you, he will be very difficult to catch.

A rarity in the area, there are private, posted parcels to deal with above the Grapevine Campground that require the angler to make a lengthy hike to come in above the last property at Lyons Lodge. The Military Trail, an old cavalry wagon road, goes off NM 15 just past Copperas Vista. It's not a bad hike in, but the 1,000-foot-plus hike out is a bugger. It's also possible to scramble around the private lands by making a bushwhack trail on the south side of the river. Up-to-date information on access to the lower East Fork can be found at the Gila Visitor's Center at the dead-end of NM 15.

The middle section of the East Fork is best accessed off FR 150, a rough but passable road that runs between the Mimbres Valley and Beaverhead. Turn west onto FR 225, then take a right fork on FR 18 to the river. The upper section is accessed where FR 150 crosses Taylor Creek. Hike down the creek about 3 miles to the river. From there, you can go down the East Fork or up Beaver Creek. Good clearance and four-wheel drive are recommended for vehicles in this section.

Once down along the East Fork, you will find little or nothing in the way of a hiking trail, no campgrounds (though you can camp anywhere), trail markers, or trash—an indication of how little use this long stretch of water receives. I've camped there for days and never seen a soul. Take a pal for safety, and make sure you're in shape.

Beaver Creek and Taylor Creek

I read various flyfishing rags, and in all of them the fishers are a-flutter over spring creek fishing, where cold flows from underground form trout waters in improbable places that sport trout of improbable size. Beaver Creek is a spring creek, but its seminal flow fresh from the ground more closely resembles a hot spring; you think, do I fish this or take my clothes off and climb in?

It's too warm for trout, but the bronze bass love it. As the creek gradually cools over the 6 miles downstream to the East Fork, aquatic plant growth lines the banks and the food base must be phenomenal, as the often outsized bass flourish in the slim flow—1 to 2 pounds and occasionally much more. Pick the creek up at the confluence with Taylor Creek and the East Fork and head upstream. You will likely have the place to yourself.

Taylor Creek is also a spring creek, but overgrazing and the artificial Wall Lake, which has silted in, have compromised its qualities. You may find some small bass and trout in the creek between the lake and the East Fork.

Black Canyon

About 20 miles north of the Mimbres Valley, up FR 150, the rough road crosses Black Canyon. Some 20 miles long, the upper portion of Black Canyon (east of the road crossing) is currently being "renovated" for the native and endangered Gila trout. Fishing is now allowed here for Gila trout, catch and release, artificials only, single barbless hook. No limit on any browns you might catch in this section however.

There is a primitive campground at the road crossing, a good staging area for a trip below (west) of the bridge, where fishing is still permitted as of this writing. This is another of those streams with no trail and little or no sign of human visitation. There are 10 or 12 miles between here and the East Fork, and in time the stream boxes up. Here you need to be part angler, part rock climber. Rainbows, and browns up to 20 inches, find the deeper pools and take on some size in this stretch.

You can also visit Black Canyon from below, hiking upstream from where it meets the East Fork; the fish in the very lower reaches can be more easily reached from this west end. To fish the whole reach, hitting all the pools, is as much an expedition as an outing.

Las Animas Creek

Las Animas Creek doesn't run to the East Fork, but I include it here as the last of the Black Range streams currently offering fishing. This is possibly my favorite flyfishing location ever, although its future is in doubt.

Animas Creek drains east out of the Black Range and holds fish over some 10 or 12 miles, less during drought years. At one time, eons ago, it ran as a steady flow to the Rio Grande and its original game fish was the Rio Grande cutthroat, easily the southernmost locale of this subspecies. Over time the stream became isolated from the river and its trout isolated as well, so by the time European settlers came in and found these surprising fish they were probably best described as a race of cutthroat all their own.

Ash runoff from forest fires hit these fish hard in the 1950s, and the NMDGF stocked a new population of cutthroat trout, of uncertain subspecies, to replace them. They mixed with any of the originals that may have survived the fires. Regardless of heredity, the trout in the stream today are wild fish, about 90-percent cutthroat in the upper headwaters, known as Holden Prong. Recent rainbow releases from a private pond have corrupted the strain to some extent, especially in the lower reaches. The solution advocated by some anglers, myself included, is to electro-shock the entire stream, throw out any fish that show rainbow characteristics, then let the wild cutthroats that remain repopulate the stream.

NMDGF and the USFWS, however, will not willingly tolerate any fish less than 100-percent pure by genetic analysis. They propose to poison the entire stream, kill all the fish, and replace the wild natives with Rio Grande cutthroats from a hatchery.

Whichever fish win out, Animas Creek will always be a marvelous place to fish. Just a few miles as the crow flies from the Chihuahuan desert, it's an icy, spring-fed flow amid aspen, spruce, and fir—a Canadian-looking canyon not far from Mexico. Typically, the fish are spooky but dumb; dry flies work well, nymphs work as well or better. Frankly, a piece of tinfoil would catch them so long as you don't spook them. Lots of 7- to 10-inch trout are present, but I've taken them better than a foot. Whatever their pedigree, these Animas Creek cutthroats are the most colorful trout I have ever seen in life, print, or film, with an unreal magenta-red stripe from the gill covers and throat to the tail that looks like it's painted on.

It's a mean hike to reach the fish, though. The best route is to pick up Forest Trail 129 at Railroad Campground, then take FT 128 up to the Black Range Crest, then down Holden Prong to the fish on FT 114. It's about 8 miles (5 hours of hiking), mostly uphill, so this is not a day trip.

Last fall, I packed in on foot, spent a few days here, and caught some beauties. Poisoning and renovation could begin at any time; when (or if) it occurs, expect the stream to be closed to fishing for one to three years.

Bass love structure, so always work the water above and below rocks. (Jan Haley)

MIDDLE FORK OF THE GILA RIVER AND TRIBUTARIES

The Middle Fork of the Gila is some 40 miles long, all of it accessible by foot or horseback only. It sports rainbow and brown trout throughout and bronze bass in the lower reaches. Base flow is about 25 cfs, with flood flows (wherein the water gets too murky to flyfish) or low flows not uncommon. These are mostly wild fish, though stockers from Snow Lake do get down in the river at times.

The first few miles below Snow Lake offer generally poor habitat, but as you get closer to the confluence of Iron Creek things rapidly improve. From Iron Creek on down, there is some wonderful canyon country with dandy deep pools here and there where trout of size have been taken, including browns up to 20 inches. General agreement is that the Middle Fork is not the stream it was in times past, with fires, ash runoff, poor grazing management, and overfishing in spots being variously named as culprits. There are still some fine opportunities, however, and the possibility for improvement.

The ash runoff from the fires can kill fish all right, but in the long run fire will improve the watershed and, in time, the fishing. There is evidence the Forest Service is slowly getting a handle on better grazing management in the watershed uplands. As for overfishing, the typical fisher on the Middle Fork in the past used bait or lures. Even if he used flies, there was a strong ethic among many local anglers to keep as many as the law allowed, or more if you could get away with it. That ethic is slowly changing toward catch and release, or at least a selective harvest.

Do as I have done: Take a weeklong hike down the Middle Fork with a pack on your back and a rod in your hand. This is wilderness fishing like nowhere else in the Southwest. You are a long way from a road and will see few other anglers. You'll have time to put whatever ails you behind, and take on the pace of the stream.

Browns predominate higher up, rainbows in the middle reaches, and bass farther down. If it's summer, you may find the fish sluggish in the heat of the day. Early morning is good, though. Come evening, you can make your camp early near some good pools and whitewater chutes. Unlimber your first quartering-upstream cast as soon as you see shade on the water. You may even find a hatch worth imitating. If not, you will catch fish anyway, with an Adams or a black ant or a Prince Nymph, or most anything once they start feeding.

There is no higher calling among anglers than to catch the wildest trout in the wildest place. And a "native" brown or rainbow from the heart of the Middle Fork is certainly in the running for the moniker, "wildest fish." As elsewhere in the Gila, the Middle Fork doesn't offer you the biggest fish in the Southwest, or the most. But they may well be the best because they come from the best place.

Day trips on the Middle Fork are a stretch. You could drive to Snow Lake and drop off into the river, but the first few miles are poor fishing. Other trails in to the upper portions of the Middle Fork are longer; by the time you make the river you've got just a few hours before you have to head back out.

But there is one Middle Fork section where a day hike is truly inviting. Park at the Gila Visitor's Center (where NM 15 dead ends some 40 miles north of Silver City) and head up the Middle Fork on foot, just above where it runs into the West Fork. Go early, during the long days of summer, and you can cover quite a bit of river in a day. Forget hip boots or waders; too clumsy, and you want to cover some ground. Wade wet. As you slosh upstream and climb banks you will get a considerable workout. You won't notice it till the next day, though, as you will be intent on scouting pools and runs, sneaking up on individual fish, and trying to fool them. I fish this reach often each year. I usually catch a trout or two, and a dozen bass or more, sometimes a lot more. The trick is to catch a bigger one amid all the "fiddlers," but more on that later.

Willow Creek

Here's a stream you can fish from the road—at least in the lower portion—as the Bursum Road runs right along Willow Creek for several miles until the creek runs into Gilita Creek to form a principal headwater of the Middle Fork. The rainbows in here are mostly stockers, but fish during the week and this heavily used area can still offer some nice fishing.

Hike up the headwaters of Willow Creek, toward its source at Bead Spring on Willow Mountain at over 10,000 feet, and you will find wild browns and Gila hybrids. They're not big and you will be "dapping" little pools, but there should be plenty of fish. It is in such tiny, clear streams of the Gila that the dry fly begins to offer some advantage to the angler. The pools may be so small and clear that the fish will often spook at any fly that hits the water. But the dry fly—with fine tippet—obviously will spook them less.

Even if they spook, you may well catch them. Time and again I have watched fish here run from even a small fly, then turn in curiosity to see what it was. They will often make a run at it. If they're hesitant, jig the nymph or skate the floater—turn your imitation into a momentary attractant—and you'll have a fish on. I realize this is not the classic approach, but the idea is to fool them, feel their wildness on the end of the line, then let them go.

Gilita Creek

Gilita Creek may be seen as an extension of Willow Creek, flowing for about 6 miles to its confluence with the Middle Fork. You pick it up from the Bursum Road, but then it leaves the road to enter wilderness. As it is downstream from campgrounds, roads, and formerly heavy grazing, it doesn't live up to its potential as a classy trout stream. But it seems to be getting better and, as noted earlier, here and in Willow Creek, Gila trout have been stocked amidst the predominant browns. No limit here on the browns and up to two Gila trout may also be kept.

Iron Creek

Here is a small stream in the heart of the wilderness that does largely live up to its potential, featuring wild trout almost entirely. Browns predominate, rainbows and rainbow/Gila hybrids show up, and in the upper reaches above a man-made barrier, there is a population of Gila trout. We may now fish for these Gila trout and up to two a day may be kept. FT 151 comes off the Bursum Road and a 4- or 5-mile hike will get you to Iron Creek.

Fishing downstream from here is best. It's brushy and there are blowdowns, but the fish, once again, are susceptible to a variety of flies. They're also very wary. A small fly and fine tippet are less likely to spook them, but the best idea is to fish slowly, looking up ahead to see the good water before the fish see you, then find a way to get your fly in there with a light landing. If you do, something colorful will hit it.

WEST FORK GILA RIVER AND TRIBUTARIES

Some years ago I would have used this section to describe possibly the best trout fishing in the Gila Forest, but times change.

The ash runoff from recent forest fires has hammered the West Fork. In the fall of '03, NMDGF poisoned the upper West Fork (from a high falls a few hundred yards below the White Creek confluence upstream) as part of the Gila trout recovery program. This treatment included a half-dozen confluence streams in that section. They recovered only about a dozen trout—browns and Gila/rainbow hybrids—in some 20 miles of stream. The ash runoff had already done a massive kill in those waters.

The plan is to stock these headwaters with Gila trout, with fishing there possibly re-opening within three years if the fish are delisted. Below the natural barrier—the high falls referred to above—fishing remains open, but it's unclear how well the fish have survived the recent fires in the lower West Fork. While some of the best waters are above the barrier, some excellent fishing has traditionally been found below as well, with browns and rainbows well over a foot long found in the better pools. In all, we are talking about some 35 miles of stream, plus numerous tributaries like White Creek, Cub Creek, Langstroth Canyon, and others.

The fish will recover from the fires. Gila trout will be stocked above the barrier. And the surviving browns and rainbows will reproduce and come back below the barrier. Also, some bronze bass have migrated into the lower portion of the West Fork, down toward the Cliff Dwellings, and they will come back, too.

There is a lot of stream to fish here, with the middle portion of the West Fork—the reaches immediately above and below the White Creek confluence—being as remote a section as remains in the Southwest. Here you are not one, but two days of hiking from the nearest road. In steep canyons, waterfalls drop into clear pools more than a dozen feet deep. Historically, according to NMDGF records, Gila trout exceeding 20 inches lived here, even into the 1930s. A 22-inch Gila trout was recorded from this section, giving credence to this species as a serious game fish. One can only hope that the superb trout fishing that once existed here will return, with the bonus that some of the fish will again be Gila trout.

Access to the lower end of the West Fork is at the Gila Cliff Dwellings. This section offers the poorest fishing, but habitat gets better the farther upstream you go. To access the headwaters, take FT 151 off Bursum Road, hike to Iron Creek, and then stay on 151 over Turkey Feather Pass to Turkey Feather Creek, which soon makes a confluence with the West Fork coming off Mogollon Baldy.

The Middle Fork is only accessible by foot or horseback. (Jan Haley)

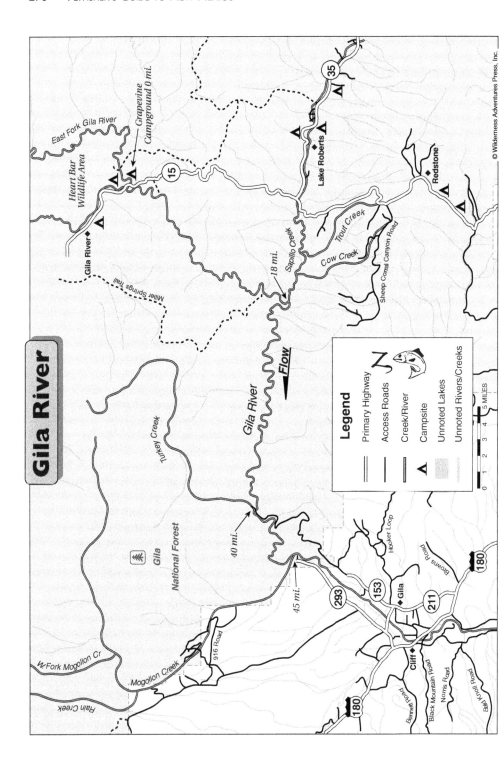

Gila River

© Wilderness Adventures Press, Inc.

MAINSTEM GILA RIVER AND TRIBUTARIES

The Middle and West Forks of the Gila River converge near the Gila Visitor's Center. Just below is the Heart Bar Wildlife Area, which has some good trout and bass habitat worth fishing before the river flows down through some private parcels. Within 5 miles, the East Fork joins in and the main stem of the Gila is born, descending once again into wilderness. From here down, it's close to 40 miles to the next road head near the Turkey Creek confluence, and another 5 miles to where the river finally emerges from the canyon at Mogollon Creek.

Flows through the wilderness will vary from, say, 25 cfs during a June drought, to several hundred cfs during a good spring runoff in March and April, to several thousand cfs during flood stage. Given a good snowpack up high, you can canoe or raft this section in the spring, fishing along the way.

Other than the snowpack runoff season and the occasional flash flood, the Gila from Grapevine Campground to Mogollon Creek can be fished on foot. With the exception of late fall or early spring, I seldom bother with waders or hip boots. This is warm-weather fishing, and most of the time it actually feels good to get wet. Descend into the heart of this canyon and you will find a very special kind of American bass fishing.

No, I don't mean the most bass, or the biggest bass. But consider that you will be in pursuit of the "gamest fish that swims," born and raised in the stream, in the nation's first wilderness area. There is nowhere else you can do all of the above in the same place. Near the road heads at Grapevine, Turkey Creek, and Mogollon Creek, you may see another fisherman (you may see me), but hike just a mile or two from the road and most days you will have the stream to yourself.

Here is one portion of the Gila where I can say that fish habitat is improving. Better grazing management has allowed a whole new growth of cottonwoods, willows, sycamores, and various weeds and grasses to come in along the banks. The river still twists and turns, but now it's narrower, the chutes and pools deeper, the water cooler.

Since the water warms as it descends in elevation, you are more likely to catch trout in the upper half, above Sapillo Creek. These will be rainbows, but only rarely a brown. Bass are found throughout. The trick to catching the trout is to recognize that this is a marginal water temperature for them. They will often lie at the foot of a whitewater chute, just where it descends into the pool—that's where the water is coolest and most oxygenated. The bass will most likely be in the pool itself.

All the usual flies work, but the difference on the main Gila is that you now have room to actually "cast" a fly. On the tiny streams of the Gila I find myself dapping most of the time. I sometimes find room for a back cast on the East, Middle, and West Forks, but a simple roll cast works better much of the time. But down on the main Gila you can often stand back and really throw one out there—just like you see in the movies!

Also, I've had some luck catching bass on surface flies in the evening here— various poppers, gurglers, etc. I don't claim these floaters necessarily work better than, say, a Woolly Bugger, but it's a nice change of pace to see a fish make a splash when it hits the fly. And it will be something new to any bass jaded by the usual hellgrammite imitation.

As for fishing the "usuals," I generally make a cast quartering upstream, then stand ready as the drift comes down with the fly underwater and often out of sight. I'm watching the line, and I want just a bit of slack (so the drift is natural), but not too much (so I'll see the line check when the fish takes the fly). When it hesitates, I tighten up on the fish. Some anglers like a strike indicator for this sort of fishing, but I prefer the old-fashioned way.

For all of that, I'd guess I catch half my Gila River bass after the drift is finished. The current takes the fly into a drag at the end of the drift, changing a drifting Woolly Bugger or Pistol Pete into a fast lure, and a bass that may have been reluctant on the drift is enticed into striking. And if that doesn't work, I strip in with speed and purpose, adding the occasional jigging motion.

Often, the major frustration one faces deep in the Gila Wilderness is trying to catch a bass over a foot long, as the "fiddlers" are so numerous. On one 4-day pack trip down the river Stephen O'Day and I caught 40 to 50 bass apiece. Only a handful passed that magic 12-inch mark, and the biggest was 14 inches. It doesn't take long to get tired of 9-inch fish when you know there are bigger bass in the pools. It's impossible to reach them on many days, but here are some methods that may help.

The most obvious thing to do is try a bigger fly. Use a #6 Woolly Bugger instead of a #8 or #10. Use a crawfish imitation that is as big as a real crawfish—some of the ones in the Gila are scary to pick up. Use a split shot to get your fly on the bottom quickly. My theory is that the big ones often lay low during the day. Your chances are better if your fly is literally bumping the bottom of the pool. Finally, fish early in the morning, in the evening, or even at dark. Like big brown trout, lunker stream bass may be too wary to come hunting except at low light. And keep fishing—the big ones are in there.

There are also good numbers of channel and flathead catfish in this section of the Gila. And carp. These fish are worthy of mention.

I sometimes catch a catfish while flyfishing the Gila, but I can't claim I know how to do it on purpose. I bump a fly along the bottom and now and again I catch a cat instead of a bass. But here's the thing. We've all been taught to let our wild trout, or bass, go. Catch and release is practically a religion now, yet most of us still like to eat fresh fish. I let most of my fish go, although I'll keep one or two now and again. Still, I confess that I sometimes feel funny knocking a prime bronze bass or trout on the head and frying him up. But I don't feel funny about eating a catfish. So here's what you do.

Just before dark take your fine mesh net, turn over some rocks in fast water, and gather up a few hellgrammites. The Gila has some the size of your little finger. Change to 10-pound tippet, add a split shot, hook the hellgrammite through the collar with a #6 hook, and roll cast that nasty thing out into a backwash pool. Hooked through the collar, they stay on just as if you were casting an artificial fly. A 2-foot channel cat is a real possibility. So is a flathead over 30 inches long. They all fight like bull terriers, especially on a fly rod. Let the trophies go, but keep a couple of 20-inchers for breakfast. There's nothing better than wilderness catfish. Think of it as flyfishing with real flies.

As for carp, flyfishers everywhere are discovering they can be caught on purpose with artificial flies. I'm just getting the hang of it myself, but the knock on carp—that they are a "dirty" fish—just won't hold up when they are taken from a wilderness stream like the Gila. Here, they are just as "clean" as the trout or bass they share the stream with.

The Gila is often clear enough that you can sight fish to these bruisers. Watch them from a distance in the pool, and you'll learn to tell when they're bumping the bottom, feeding. That is when you want to put a nymph in front of one; often well in front so he doesn't spook. When he sees it, give the fly a little action. When he puts his nose on it, tighten up and hang on. I caught a 30-incher last year on a 5-weight rod and 4-pound tippet, and it took me an hour and a half to get him in.

Below the Mogollon Creek confluence, the mainstem Gila leaves canyon country for a time and enters private lands. There are still some bass in here, but fewer of the holding pools that they favor. After 20 miles or so—past the town of Cliff and Bill Evans Lake—the Gila reenters national forest and another stretch of canyon country. The heart of this 15-mile stretch is known as the Gila Middle Box.

There are some bass here, though not as many as up above. The water is warmer and catfish are more and more dominant. Take US 180 west from Silver City about 25 miles to the sign marking the turnoff to Bill Evans Lake. This road follows the river. Don't turn off to the lake; instead, go straight another 5 miles to the cul-de-sac at the Gila River Bird Sanctuary. It's a two-wheel drive road. Park here and start hiking downstream.

Large colorful streamers work well on the Gila River. (Jan Haley)

The river begins as a lovely, lush riparian area and gradually narrows into a rock canyon. The farther you go, the narrower it gets. The last 5 miles, within the Box, the canyon walls are so narrow there is no place to walk. You have to hop over rocks, wade, or swim pools, and in places you can reach out and touch both walls with your outstretched arms. Never go down in here during high water, though, or when heavy rains are expected. It's just too dangerous.

The deepest pools on the river are within the Box. I know of a 44-pound flathead catfish taken from this stretch (my own best fish was 34 inches with weight unknown because I let him go). It stands to reason that the biggest carp and biggest bass would be here, too. Not many bass are taken in this awesome canyon, but that may be because anglers drawn to the area are catfish oriented. That has been my pattern of fishing here, as well. Still, I've taken bass on flies in the bird area just above. I believe

This nice smallmouth bass from the mainstem Gila River fell to Dutch Salmon's hellgrammite imitation. (Jan Haley)

the biggest bass in the river could be holed up in the Box. The 15-mile stretch from the bird area to where the Box emerges from the canyon above the community of Red Rock bears further exploration by the flyfisher.

Sapillo Creek

This creek runs into the main Gila about halfway between Grapevine Campground and Mogollon Creek. It originates about a dozen miles upstream from cold springs that are now covered by Lake Roberts. The runoff from Lake Roberts flows for several miles through the Lake Roberts community, then enters wilderness below NM 15. This is the usual access point. The next 7 or 8 miles of stream can offer some nice fishing.

These are rainbows here, and no doubt some are stockers from Lake Roberts. But wild trout are also present in the canyon, and while many are under a foot long, some will surprise you with their size and beauty. The purple/gray par marks they sometimes sport will make you think they carry some Gila trout blood and currently, some large, older Gila trout brood fish are being stocked in Sapillo Creek and a 20-incher is a real possibility.

After the first mile or so, there is no trail down Sapillo Creek. Below the confluence with tiny Trout Creek, the stream boxes up. There is no shoreline anymore and the usual procedure is to fish a pool, then wade or swim through it to fish the next one. You will also climb over and around some boulders whose size will take your breath away. Needless to say, you don't want to be down in this canyon during a flash flood.

On a recent trip down here I caught seven of the prettiest trout I've ever seen, and on the way out I stood for a long moment with a rare Sonoran mountain king snake between my legs, a constrictor that rivals the coral snake in bright coloration. Fishing the Gila country is always an adventure.

Trout Creek

The lower portion of tiny Trout Creek, from its confluence with Sapillo Creek upstream for 3 to 4 miles, offers good to poor fishing—depending on the year and the flow—for brown and rainbow trout. It will take you most of the morning to hike down Sapillo Creek to the confluence, and of course there is no trail up Trout Creek, so you have to bushwhack. But pack in and take your time and you can catch wild trout where few others have fished before. On a good year, some fish will be more than a foot long. Few fish can live in this stream during drought conditions, though, so you'd best leave this canyon alone for a while.

Cow Creek

Cow Creek runs into Sapillo Creek a couple of miles below Trout Creek, but there is no access at the confluence. The smaller creek squirts a stream of water into the larger creek from a high wall; you can admire it, but unless you're a rock climber you can't reach it from the canyon floor. What you can do is take FR 282 (the Sheep Corral Road) off NM 15 to FT 233, then bushwhack down into the headwaters of Cow Creek.

It has a more reliable flow and more water than Trout Creek, and in most years a large number of wild rainbow (or rainbow/Gila) trout. Even during the current drought, a surprising number of fish are surviving in the better holes. There are some remarkable falls down in the canyon, dropping into some lovely pools full of fish. Many of the pools are bathtub-sized and deeper than they are wide, and you'll find trout over a foot long in some of them. If you are stealthy, one of the large fish may beat all the little ones to the strike.

Turkey Creek

This is a substantial stream by Gila standards, and it holds fish for a dozen miles or more. To reach it, take NM 293 from the town of Gila. This turns into FR 155, which goes over a mountain. It'll take you nearly an hour to go a dozen miles or so to the trailhead at the Gila River. The road is rough but passable in a two-wheel-drive pickup, except during bad rains. You then hike up the Gila River about 1.5 miles to where Turkey Creek meets the river.

I was up there last summer, thinking I'd fish Turkey Creek, but ash runoff from recent fires had turned the creek into gray sludge. I fished the river instead. Below where the gray water came in I could catch nothing, but I did well on bass and catfish in the clearer water above.

The fires certainly killed fish in Turkey Creek. Wild trout are survivors, though, and the stream will come back. Don't be put off if the mouth of Turkey Creek is dry; there is flowing water not far up. In normal years you will find both bass and rainbows in the first 5 miles or so, below a major hot springs about 6 miles up. You won't find many anglers on Turkey Creek, but you will see plenty of bathers at the hot springs.

The creek is much cooler above the hot springs. Bass disappear and trout become more numerous. These must be hybrids because they sport a variety of colors, depending on where along the stream you catch them. I suppose they are predominantly rainbows, but they must carry some Gila trout blood to exhibit the array of colors they do. These days, hybrids are castigated all over the West, victims of perceived "impurities." I'm all for saving natives, but these hybrids are native too, in the sense that they are born and raised in the stream. In any event, you will find that the Turkey Creek trout, and their relatives in several tributaries along the way, are wild, beautiful fish.

Mogollon Creek

Mogollon Creek runs into the Gila River about 5 miles below the Turkey Creek confluence. It is generally dry at its mouth, but above the confluence with Rain Creek it becomes a trout stream, potentially one of the best in the Gila Forest. This stream is now open July 1 to October 31 for Gila trout, catch and release, artificials only. A good flow and deep pools mean the potential is here for 15 to 20 inch native Gila trout, if they take hold as predicted. The browns and rainbows that previously inhabited the stream occasionally reached that size.

To access Mogollon Creek, take FR 754 to the trailhead for FT 153. Roughly three or four hours of hiking will take you up and over Seventy Four Mountain and down into the Mogollon Creek Canyon.

A hook-up on the mainstem Gila River. (Jan Haley)

West Fork of Mogollon Creek

This is another tough hike to wild water where you can catch small trout all day, and occasionally surprise yourself with a "lunker" of 12 to 15 inches. The West Fork runs 10 miles or so to join Mogollon Creek at a favored pool called Bud's Hole. There are other wonderful holes along those 10 miles, many of the best accessible to only the most fit and ambitious angler willing to descend long, steep banks to individual pools.

Fish one pool and it's a hard climb up and then down to get to the next one. Not all the holes are that tough, of course, but the tough ones are the ones that may be a dozen feet deep and hold the largest trout. These are rainbows or rainbow/Gila hybrids.

To find the West Fork of Mogollon Creek, take FR 147 to FT 189. Hike down to Rain Creek; stay on the trail and cross a saddle over to the West Fork. Or you may just want to try Rain Creek first.

Rain Creek

Rain Creek is a lesser version of the adjacent West Fork. It's a few miles shorter and has a less reliable flow, but in places it sports similar deep pools below scenic falls. In good years, it has provided me with some wonderful fishing for 6- to 12-inch rainbow/Gila hybrids. But recent years have not been good. In fact, ash runoff and drought several years running caused a Gila Forest ranger to opine recently in the local papers that the Rain Creek trout had all been killed off. I was there last summer and much of the stream was indeed dry. Still, I found and caught (and released) a few trout in some remnant pools well upstream; these fish are survivors.

They can't survive poison, however. Rain Creek is scheduled for "renovation" by NMDGF for the reintroduction of Gila trout, and possibly the West Fork, as well. As with the cutthroats in Animas Creek, one can rightfully question whether the hatchery-raised Gila trout proposed for renovation will survive the harsh conditions of Rain Creek as well as the wild but non-native hybrids that have evolved there over recent decades. That's why some of us have suggested that the agencies should "swamp" these streams with Gila trout, rather than poison their wild inhabitants, then let the best trout populate the stream over time. It's an interesting point of debate in current fish management. Regardless, anglers will need to check the Fish Proclamation year by year to keep within the law.

SAN FRANCISCO RIVER AND TRIBUTARIES

The San Francisco River starts in Arizona, near the town of Alpine, as the overflow from small, artificial Luna Lake. Another source of water comes off Escudilla Mountain via Stone Creek. The Frisco then runs for some 100 miles in New Mexico, mostly in remote country but also intersecting the towns of Luna, Reserve, and Glenwood, before crossing back into Arizona and finally meeting the Gila River below the town of Clifton. It is currently a very iffy stream from the flyfisher's point of view.

In the better years, before the drought began in 1998, some good, if spotty, fishing for rainbows could be had in the canyon reaches of the Frisco between the Arizona state line and the town of Luna. It's a lot spottier now with the drought. The same goes for the used-to-be-good stretch below the town of Luna, from where Centerfire Creek comes in on down for several miles and into the 3-mile-long Frisco Box. I had a recent report from there that the trout fishing was now poor and the stream mostly sported an oversupply of crawfish. The spring of 2010 held the best runoff in many years and the promise that the Frisco's depleted fishery might eventually be recovered and restored.

These are the reaches of the Frisco that traditionally support trout fishing, and will again when the drought ends. The surviving fish will respond to the good conditions, and stockers coming down from Luna Lake will augment the population. In good water, some stockers survive and reproduce, and the offspring, born and raised in the stream, may fairly be called wild trout.

The canyon reaches above the town of Luna, and the Frisco Box below Centerfire Creek, are marvelously scenic in times of plenty, with pools harboring 12- to 16-inch rainbows amid many smaller ones and few fishermen.

US 180 between Alpine and Luna crosses the river in two places, and these are access points to fishing. FR 61 out of Luna crosses the Trout Creek (not to be confused with the Trout Creek near the Gila River) tributary. In good years, there is fishing for rainbows above the bridge, and sometimes below in this version of Trout Creek.

In a few more miles, FR 61 leads to FR 210. This road goes to Centerfire Creek and then meets the Frisco downstream from Luna. With normal flows, fishing is good for several miles from here on down into the Box, where it gets better. We shall all pray for rain, then try these spots again to see how much they've revived.

Below the Box, the Frisco gradually widens, slows, weakens, and gets warm. Excepting the occasional bullhead or sucker, it offers little to the angler until it reaches the town of Glenwood, where Whitewater Creek helps it. At this point, elevation is down near 4,500 feet, and the Frisco is no longer a trout stream. Still, the remote, pristine canyon below Glenwood that runs some 50 miles to the town of Clifton, Arizona, is worthy of mention.

Base flow on the Frisco below the Whitewater Creek confluence averages 20 to 50 cfs. It's a lovely stream beneath towering walls and has a wonderful riparian growth of cottonwood, sycamore, hackberry, oak, and willow. It has all the qualities of a pristine trout stream with the exception of the water temperature; this is a subtropical life zone. Gila monsters, coatimundi, and javelina are all found here, along with bear,

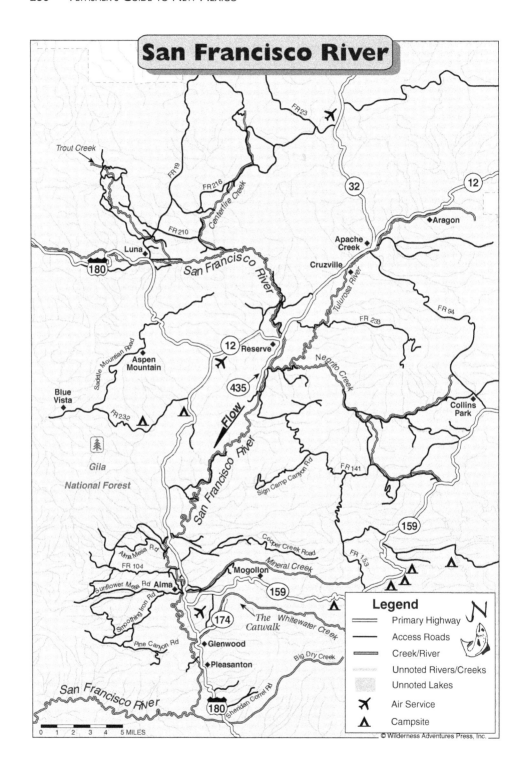

San Francisco River

Trout Creek

FR 23

FR 19

FR 216

Centerfire Creek

32

12

Aragon

FR 210

Luna

San Francisco River

Apache Creek

Cruzville

Tularosa River

FR 94

180

FR 233

Saddle Mountain Road

Aspen Mountain

12 Reserve

Negrito Creek

Blue Vista

FR 232

435

Flow

San Francisco River

Collins Park

Gila

National Forest

Sign Camp Canyon Rd

FR 141

159

Alma Mesa Rd

Cooper Creek Road

FR 153

FR 104

Mineral Creek

Sunflower Mesa Rd Alma

Mogollon

159

Smoothing Iron Rd

174

The Whitewater Creek

Catwalk

Pine Canyon Rd

Glenwood

Pleasanton

Big Dry Creek

San Francisco River

180

Sheridan Correl Rd

0 1 2 3 4 5 MILES

Legend

———	Primary Highway
———	Access Roads
═══	Creek/River
	Unnoted Rivers/Creeks
	Unnoted Lakes
✈	Air Service
⛰	Campsite

© Wilderness Adventures Press, Inc.

mountain lion, turkey, deer, and bighorn sheep on the canyon ledges. If it weren't too warm for trout, the flyfisher would be in business.

The bronze bass may be sneaking in here, however. NMDGF surveys have turned up a few, and local anglers have reported to me that they occasionally catch one. But I've yet to catch a bass in my fishing expeditions to this remote area. I have caught big flathead and channel catfish, however, and one of the flatheads had a keeper bronze bass in his stomach. Others had consumed bluegills, another flyfishing possibility. If the bass do take hold in this 50-mile stretch, bass fishing would rival the Gila, for the water, scenery, and pools are every bit as good.

Meanwhile, catfish and carp are there in numbers. A careful angler, using a split shot for weight and bumping a large hellgrammite imitation or streamer slowly along the bottom, could have the fight of his life if a cat over 2 feet long takes his fly. Fishing for catfish is best in morning or evening when shade is on the water. They feel more secure then and feed more readily, yet they can still see the fly. I've caught them that way along the Frisco, flyfishing with a Pistol Pete, though I confess I sometimes cheat and use a real fly (i.e., a live hellgrammite).

Sight fishing for hefty carp is a real possibility, too. It's the perfect scenario for the peculiar elements necessary to flyfish for carp—the water is usually clear, the fish numerous, and for the most part the carp stick to their home pool. Sneak up and put your fly in a good place on the bottom of one of those pools and a cruising carp is likely to come across it.

A beadhead nymph, size 8 to 12, is ideal. The bead puts the nymph on the bottom without any added weight, and the gold bead seems to attract fish. When a cruising carp approaches, jig or "crab" the nymph along the bottom. You'll soon find out that carp are indeed sight feeders. Like bonefish, they will go nose down and tail up to take the fly. Though they are big fish, there's no need to rear back on the rod; just tighten up on the line and let the bow of the rod set the hook. Compared to trout, a carp is much harder to fool, and by size alone is tougher to land.

About 6 miles south of Glenwood, off US 180, is a turnoff to the trailhead to the Frisco Canyon. It's about a half-mile to the parking area and a 45-minute hike to the river. From their downstream there is no road access for more than 30 miles. The first 20 miles or so are in New Mexico. You'll know you are about to cross into Arizona when you see a high power line overhead. This is often considered the finest, most biologically diverse, and most remote riparian area remaining in the Southwest. If only it weren't too warm for trout…

Tularosa Creek and Negrito Creek

A few miles south of Reserve along NM 435, Tularosa Creek feeds into the San Francisco River. The Tularosa, in turn, is fed by Negrito Creek a few miles upstream. Both are potentially good trout waters that have been much modified (negatively) by various human incursions, mostly grazing and logging. The lower several miles of both streams are worth a look, and in good years they have produced sizeable rainbows, especially the box canyon in the lower section of Negrito Creek (not far above its meeting with the Tularosa).

Whitewater Creek

This is probably the best trout stream in the Gila Forest on a consistent basis. It's long—about 15 miles—and drops several thousand feet over that distance, giving it plenty of white water and oxygen and the pools, drops, and swift chutes that trout love. Unlike the Frisco proper, which it meets at Glenwood, its water temperatures are always cold. In so many Gila streams and rivers, trout must share their range with a plethora of suckers, chub, bass, catfish, carp, or whatever else can live in the fertile but not-quite-cold water. But Whitewater Creek is a true trout stream in a spectacular canyon. In places its flow is more than 3,000 feet below the surrounding peaks.

The usual access point is the famed Catwalk, a Gila Forest hiking and picnic area a few miles from Glenwood. Get there early if you want to fish or the better pools will be taken over by bathers. One morning I got there late, only to find my favorite pool below a waterfall taken up by what looked to be an enormous extended family splashing in the water. I hiked on down the canyon and found a measure of peace behind a huge boulder. I could still hear the screams of children, but could no longer see the non-fishermen of this world.

A small but deep pool bent around another boulder, and I was tempted to lean over the rock and look downstream, which surely would have spooked any fish therein. Instead, I bent a short, blind roll cast around the rock. I have perhaps overemphasized how Gila Forest trout are both furtive and non-selective, yet here it was again—having no idea I was there, the best trout in the pool hammered the nondescript nymph as soon as it hit the water. He was all over the pool, jumping and jumping and jumping. It turned out to be one of the few Whitewater trout I've caught that reached a foot long. And let me tell you about the colors.

He had a red throat slash, which makes no sense as cutthroats are not supposed to inhabit the stream. But there it was. The blood-red rainbow stripe did not resemble the lateral color generally present on rainbows or cutthroats. It was so bright it looked artificial. He had a yellowish/orange belly, and dark purple/gray par marks intersected the lateral colors—all reminiscent of a Gila trout. The dark green back looked pure rainbow. Lord knows what he was by genetic markers, but he was a trout, and gorgeous, and he sure didn't come from a hatchery. It was a pleasure to let him go.

Above the Catwalk, both bathers and anglers thin out, but not the fish. Indeed, the small ones (under 10 inches) are so numerous that it's hard to catch the few larger ones that invariably inhabit the bigger pools. The whole 15 miles is in wilderness, but a good trail (FT 207) parallels the stream, although at times it climbs well above the water.

To access the upper portion of Whitewater Creek, FT 179 is recommended. The trailhead is a few miles east of the village of Mogollon off NM 159. This is not a day hike, as it will take the average hiker three or four hours going in and the same coming out. It's steep—uphill or down—all the way.

Of course, if it were easy to reach everyone would be in there. When Stephen O'Day and I backpacked in there in the fall a couple of years ago we had the place to ourselves. The stream was maybe 5 cfs, at best, but the pools were deeper than they looked due to the clarity of the water. We could watch trout move around while we sat on a rock and drank coffee in the evening at camp.

The last day we found the pool you always dream of on a trout trip, below a 20-foot waterfall and seemingly inaccessible from where we stood looking down from an adjacent cliff. So we cast from above, 30 feet of roll cast going down, down, and every time a nymph drifted beneath the falls a trout struck. The better ones were nearly a foot, and after they wore down we had to crank them 20 feet up in the air to turn them loose. Of course, a lot of them could flip the barbless hooks once we got them in the air, but the others were rare wilderness jewels that we admired and then sent on a long dive back home.

The South Fork of Whitewater Creek meets the main stem about 3 miles above the Catwalk, and a decent trail follows it. This is a slim flow, but as with Whitewater Creek proper, the good pools you come upon will fool you with their depth and numbers of fish. A few miles up you hike through a narrow slot called the Devil's Elbow, and above there, oddly, you will find brook trout mixed with the rainbows.

The only brook trout in the forest, their presence tells you how cold the water is up there, though it's only a few miles as the crow flies from cactus and mesquite. Long dead biologists no doubt put them there and now some living biologists with federal and state agencies would like to get rid of them, lacking any regard for non-native fish. My own view is that the Gila trout recovery is a positive endeavor that can be accomplished within an overall goal of fish diversity. That is, we can add (restore) the Gila trout to the mix, and give it exclusivity in some streams, without eliminating all the non-native salmonids from the drainage. But then I'm just a stumbling flyfisher.

Mineral Creek

Mineral Creek could be described as a lesser version of Whitewater Creek: not quite as long, a little less water, lots of trout, but perhaps a bit smaller in average size. It runs parallel to Whitewater Creek on the other side of NM 159, but nearly impassable uplifts separate the two.

A local rancher told me recently that in the old days Mineral Creek not uncommonly flowed all the way to the San Francisco River, or at least to the town of Alma, but today you drive along miles of dry wash (FR 701) and sometimes hike miles of FT 201 before you meet the first section of perennial stream. He blamed the overgrowth of piñon, juniper, and pine, which has sapped the normal precipitation in the uplands. Maybe so. Still, Mineral Creek has a decent trail along its entire length, offering a dozen miles or so of remote canyon filled with small, wild, mostly-rainbow trout. The upper portion of Mineral Creek can be reached via FT 202 off NM 159.

Big Dry Creek

Big Dry Creek probably has the best brown trout fishing in the Gila Forest. The creek is usually dry in its lower reaches, but up high it's a slim but fine permanent flow with trout up to 12 to 15 inches long.

The best access is from FR 146 off US 180, about 6 miles south of Glenwood. After a 5-mile drive you dead end at the wilderness boundary. Another 5 miles of hiking on FT 181 and 225 gets you to the creek. It's a lovely arrival, and welcome after a long, hot descent, with the cabin of Skunk Johnson, one of the last of the Gila mountain men, extant near a grove of fruit trees that still bear nature's bounty in the good years.

From this locale, you can find fish for some 2 to 3 miles downstream and more than double that upstream. Things get tricky upstream, though, as the canyon gradually narrows and huge boulders block your path. But each scenic pool, virtually lost in the narrow canyon, becomes memorable. Of course, brown trout are notoriously challenging, but these are less so. Their very wildness, and the remoteness of their location, means these fish see few artificials. The stealthy angler will do well with a variety of wet or dry patterns.

At the upper end of Big Dry Creek is a 30-foot natural barrier that marks the end of legal fishing. The waters above are reserved for the reintroduced Gila trout. The waters below may one day be reserved for Gila trout too, though many a local angler hopes this brown trout fishery—among the few remaining in the Gila Forest—survives.

MIMBRES RIVER

The Mimbres is more of a small to medium-sized stream (2 to 10 cfs, on average) than a river. It heads up in the Black Range and flows west and south through wilderness and then the populated Mimbres Valley before dying in the desert sands north of Deming. It is ephemeral in the valley due to irrigation schedules, but when it has water it has rainbow trout. This is private land with numerous owners over a 20-mile stretch, and you'll need permission to fish.

There is about 10 miles of fishable water up in the forest where the stream is perennial. It can be quite good. Traditionally, rainbows were the game, and that is what I've caught there. More recently on several trips to the Mimbres, I've found the brown trout about as numerous as the rainbows, if somewhat harder to catch. Not even the Game & Fish Department can tell you how they got in there.

The traditional trail access to the Mimbres River was near Cooney Campground. This is now discouraged because of complications with a private parcel. Stop at the Mimbres Ranger Station, a few miles north of the town of Mimbres, to get directions for the new trail. Once at the river you can fish upstream for many miles, usually in perfect solitude, as the habitat goes from pine to spruce, fir, and aspen—a taste of the far north not far from Mexico.

SNOW LAKE

Snow Lake, a 72-acre impoundment along Snow Creek, offers a lovely setting at 7,400 feet, with big evergreens and expansive montane grasslands in view from anywhere on the shoreline. There is a nice campground here and a gravel road coming in from Reserve (FR 141) that even a passenger car can manage during good weather.

The lake is stocked with rainbows, although even in this high country they have trouble surviving the warm summers. Still, one hears of trout well over a foot at times.

As with the other Gila Forest lakes, no gas motors are allowed, but you can troll the lake with an electric motor and this seems the most popular form of "flyfishing." Of course, float tubes and canoes are fine, too.

Because it's mostly open around the lake, you can also cast from the bank with some success. Woolly Buggers are a standard here, along with Pistol Petes and Peacock Nymphs. Anything large and gaudy will work when trolling. As elsewhere, crowds thin out after Labor Day, and fall is also the time to hear elk bugle—there are some fine herds in this part of the forest.

Like any impoundment, Snow Lake has, over time, taken on problems related to siltation and water quality. Overall, the fishery is in a slow but inevitable decline and, though no date has been set, silt removal and construction of catchments are in the near future for this lake.

LAKE ROBERTS

This is a 70-acre impoundment referred to earlier in the discussion of Sapillo Creek. It lies about 25 miles north of Silver City, along NM 15 (20 miles) and then NM 35 (5 miles). Boats and floats tubes are allowed, but no gas motors.

Lake Roberts was dredged in the late 1990s after nearly filling in with silt, and as is often the case, the stocked rainbows have done well in the restored depth and fertile new vegetation. It's still a put-and-take fishery, but the stockers show good size and growth before warm summer water temperatures send them to the bottom—or float them to the top.

Where you can find room for a back cast, you can catch fish off the bank with a long throw and, preferably, a sinking line. Often, there is no room for such a cast, so I prefer to put a canoe on the water. Trolling a fly with an electric motor is the most popular approach here, and Woolly Buggers, damsel nymphs, Pistol Petes, and almost any gaudy streamer will work when fish are in the mood. I've caught trout just by drifting the fly behind the canoe in a slight breeze.

The lake takes on weeds and moss as the summer wears on, particularly at the east end, which forces the fishermen, if not the fish, into the open areas. Channel catfish are also stocked in the lake, and unlike the trout, they can survive the warm summers and even achieve some natural reproduction. But flyfishing for catfish is much more plausible in the Gila River, where fish can be located easily, than in any lake.

A few years ago, somebody apparently achieved an outlaw introduction of largemouth bass into Lake Roberts. Wildlife professionals were not happy but the culprits achieved their goal; a new gamefish in the lake that, unlike the trout, reproduces and is self-sustaining. Flyfishers can hardly complain; I include popping bugs in my trip list to Lake Roberts now.

QUEMADO LAKE

This is a high-elevation impoundment (7,600 feet) and the largest in the forest at 131 surface acres. Traditionally, this lake has also produced the biggest trout in the region, a claim that little by little was eroded by weeds and, of all things, goldfish.

The weed growth was getting worse year by year, but it has been held in check somewhat by the release of sterile grass carp, which are weed eaters and grow huge. You might even catch one. The goldfish presumably got in the lake by accident, via baitfishers, but they bred like rabbits and virtually took over the lake. Millions of them literally turned the surface gold. Recently, NMDGF stocked sterile tiger musky fingerlings in the lake to relieve the trout of the goldfish menace, hoping that they will prefer goldfish to trout. Meanwhile, anglers can catch tiger muskies as well as trout. The muskies should show remarkable growth. With muskies, rainbows, grass carp, and goldfish all in the same water, a trip to the lake should be most interesting.

Quemado Lake lies 14 miles south of the town of Quemado on NM 32, then 4 miles east on NM 103. There is a store at the lake, and campgrounds and trailer hookups.

BEAR CANYON LAKE

This little 22-acre lake has also been restored recently through silt dredging. It is stocked with rainbows, bluegills, largemouth bass and channel catfish, and its fishing should be prime in the first few years after restoration.

BILL EVANS LAKE

This is my favorite of the Gila region lakes, although I generally prefer streams and rivers. Bill Evans Lake is an off-stream reservoir, formed by Gila River water pumped out of the main stem of the river, over a divide, and into a side canyon. Thus, it avoids the siltation that eventually plagues all in-stream reservoirs, and the water usually shows good clarity.

Though only about 60 surface acres, this lake is up to 90 feet deep in places. Incredibly, the current state-record largemouth bass came out of this pond-sized impoundment, a 15-pound, 13-ounce bruiser. There are also channel catfish over 20 pounds, and I've caught carp from the lake more than 30 inches long. Add in the bluegills and crappie, and this lake is worth a visit.

Flyfishers seeking bass should fish a big streamer, Woolly Bugger, or Pistol Pete on a sinking line, and head to the deeper west side. Or, more to my liking, you can opt for surface poppers, gurglers, and the like to fish the shallow, weedy east side during the flat calm of evening or even at night. For the rainbows, which are stocked in winter, most of the local anglers troll flies. You can also stalk the bank at the shallow east end looking for feeding carp.

Bill Evans Lake is owned by New Mexico Game & Fish with some of its water used for local mining operations by Freeport/McMoran Inc.

Much of the lake is open enough for fly casting from the bank. To get there, take NM 180 for 26 miles west of Silver City, turn left on FR 809, and go about 3 miles to the sign for the lake. It's up over the hill, less than a mile from the Gila River.

Drought can make flyfishing very tough, especially in southwest New Mexico where we're lucky to have any water in the first place. It takes determination and energy to get to some of those secret places.

STEALING A DAY IN THE WILD

By M. H. "Dutch" Salmon

L ately, I find myself watching the thermometer. Every day for months it has risen above what the weatherman says is normal for this time of year. Or so it seems. Meanwhile, the soil in my garden, the dry creek in front of the house, and that same weatherman all tell me we're in a drought.

It's all rather depressing, if you're not careful. And making it worse is my business, which has been good, which is bad, because it's hard to get away during the week. Thus afflicted, a wise man will hark to the Red Gods and try to steal a day in the wild.

I chose Memorial Day. It was a national holiday, so I had the official OK not to work, but how do you beat the crowds? It is said that Memorial Day is the busiest day of the year. Here in New Mexico, anyplace close to water is jammed with car campers, swimmers, anglers, and picnickers. It seems most of them have powerboats or ATVs, and all of them are desperate for fun. It's all rather depressing, if you're not careful. But I know a little stream...

There are several roosters at my place, and I was up when the first one crowed. I'd loaded my gear in the truck the day before so it was still black night when I headed out. Gray dawn was just approaching when I left the truck in an unobtrusive spot at roadside, shouldered my pack, and eased into the canyon. I had a license, and didn't plan to kill anything anyway, but I moved like a poacher.

If there was going to be a crowd, at least I'd beaten them to the spot. I made a few miles downstream before I stopped to rig up. A nondescript black nymph looked good, and I tied it on.

Fishing small streams is not easy; that is, if you count success as catching something. The trout are wild, and while they aren't generally that fussy about what you put over them, the pools are so small and clear that it's a task to sneak up on them. I fished perhaps a mile of the creek and couldn't raise a strike. The only fish I saw were suckers, and with the water even lower than usual I began to wonder if perhaps the drought had done the trout in. Either that, or I'd lost my touch.

A big slash pile up ahead had made a pool 10 yards long. The water was dark, meaning deep, especially at the downstream end right in front of the slash. If there were trout in the stream, they'd surely be here. I came into the upstream end on my hands and knees and stayed down as I made a cast to the deeper end. False casting may impress other anglers, and it looks pretty on film, but it can spook wild trout in a small stream. So I just lay some slack line out upstream on the water and rolled a cast downstream to the deep end of the pool. The nymph hardly had time to sink before a fish whacked it.

He wasn't big, but when he jumped he threw the fly. I was perhaps too tight on the line and when it came sailing back in front of my face it landed upstream in perfect position for another cast. So I rolled it down there while the ripples from the jump still lingered on the water. The fly sank then drifted. I jigged it and came up tight to a fish.

This was a bigger trout, and like the first one he cleared the water. Then he jumped twice more—big jumps—the kind rainbows are famous for. I brought him to hand, nice colors, about 11 inches, a dandy from a small stream.

By noon I had landed a couple more. I found some shade and broke out lunch. I reveled in the fact that I not only hadn't seen anyone all day, but since the first mile of my hike in I hadn't seen a footprint, a beer can, or a bottle cap. Even the trail along the creek had long since disappeared. I could not help but recall that a few nights earlier I had seen our president, George W. Bush, on TV. He was addressing a large crowd in a parking lot at one of our busiest national parks. The President said that we could all count on his administration to protect such areas, what he called "America's silent places."

That's a nice line, but I'm sure he didn't write it himself. And if he thinks that national park is a silent place he's never visited small streams in the Gila National Forest.

Below, the canyon narrowed to a mere slot in the rocks. There was no bank to walk on, and when I finished casting to a pool I was forced to wade through it to get downstream, emerging wet to the waist. I caught the best trout of the day here, which was, alas, still not quite 12 inches long. But every one was a leaper.

I could see more pools, perhaps the best ones, ahead. But it had clouded over and, of all things, it was raining. It was just a sprinkle in the canyon, but it could be a deluge upstream, and you don't want to be in a canyon with sheer walls when the water starts to rise. Even on a straight hike I was hours from the truck, so I headed out.

Surely, I thought, I will meet some Memorial Day revelers on the way out. But the only life I noted was two snakes—a rattler that I offered plenty of room and what had to be a Sonoran mountain king snake. Why would Mother Nature put such colors on a serpent? I noted the pattern and wrote it down—yellow/black/red/black—an Arizona species that may be extending its range into the Gila Forest.

On the drive home I stopped for a brew, for a cold beer tastes extra good in a drought. It was Happy Hour and the place was filling up with Memorial Day traffic. The waitress noted my clothes and remarked that it looked like I'd fallen in the lake. This is where you wish you could think to say something abstract and profound, like, "I stole a day in the wild." But of course you never do.

"No," I said, "it was only a stream."

Southeast Region

Most of southeast New Mexico lies in a vast dry region of high desert and grassland. Virtually all the water important to flyfishers flows out of the only significant mountain range in the region. The Sacramento Mountains, mostly within the Lincoln National Forest and the Mescalero Apache Indian Reservation, have a variety of streams and lakes that hold trout, but some of the best waters are on private property.

Streams and lakes in this region are on the edge of a harsh temperate zone where drought and heat are a constant threat. The trout have adapted to the extreme conditions, and they are very resilient survivors. When there is plenty of water the flyfishing can be phenomenal, with a wide variety of opportunities. When there is a drought, it's hard to find much moving water.

But even under drought conditions there are places to fish because most of the streams are spring-fed, and the trout know where to go in order to survive. Often, after a heavy rain or wet period, the streams swell and trout spread out into areas that just a few days earlier were barren. As the waters recede, so do the trout, until they're concentrated in areas where there is enough spring flow.

Due to the mild climate in the southeast, there is good year-round fishing available. In fact, the best fishing is usually in fall, winter, and spring, with summer being too hot except early in the morning and late in the evening. Great hatches of midges, mayflies, and even stoneflies can be found in the middle of January, and I've seen hoppers in this region in December. Whenever you fish here you'll find it fascinating, as I did, to catch nice, wild trout in clear, cold water on the edge of the desert far from the famous flyfishing hotspots.

RIO RUIDOSO

(Contributed by Winston Cox and Charles Dixon, with Additions by Van Beacham)

Anglers visiting the Sacramento Mountains of south-central New Mexico will find several flyfishing opportunities in the Ruidoso area, the Lincoln National Forest, and the Mescalero Apache Indian Reservation. These are small fisheries by normal standards of trout water, but miles of clear streams and several lakes offer a shot at naturally reproducing brook, brown, and rainbow trout.

The primary stream fishery is the Rio Ruidoso, which heads with three main forks on the eastern slopes of 11,973-foot Sierra Blanca Mountain. The North, Middle, and South Forks join to create the Rio Ruidoso on the Mescalero Apache Indian

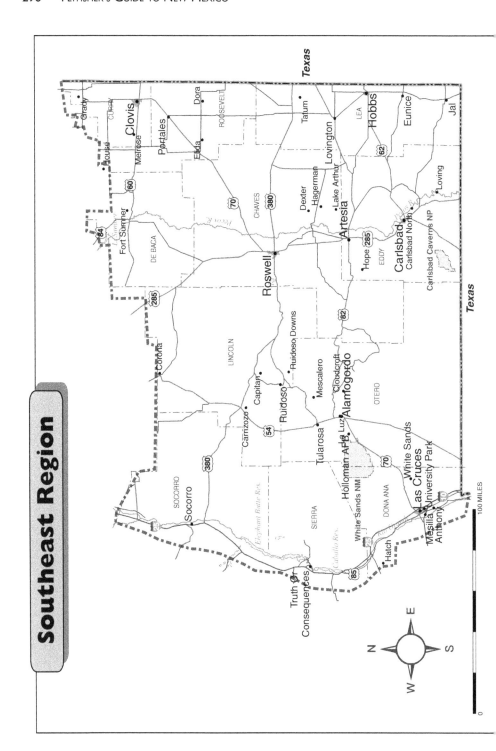

Southeast Region

Reservation a few miles west of downtown Ruidoso, in an area known as the Upper Canyon. From there, it flows east through the central business district of Ruidoso, and eventually through the Hondo Valley to its confluence with the Rio Bonito, where the Rio Hondo is formed.

The Upper Ruidoso can be described as the water within the boundaries of the Reservation, beginning 3 miles west of downtown Ruidoso. To get there from Ruidoso, go west on Sudderth Drive to the Upper Canyon and continue for a couple of miles to the gate. Just beyond the gate is a building where you can obtain camping and fishing permits. Reservation waters are generally open from April 1 to October 5.

The three forks contain large populations of brook, brown, and rainbow trout. The headwater streams are small and the banks extremely brushy, making them ideal for 7-foot rods. The forks of the Rio Ruidoso fish well throughout the summer, and the largest water flow is usually in March and April. The best months for hatches and flyfishing are May and June, when there's still enough water and the temperatures are still cool enough. September and October can also be very good, after things cool off in normal years.

Each fork is similar in size and character, except that the North Fork has about 4 miles of fishable water, while the Middle and South Forks have only about 2 miles of fishable water each. Reservation officials may occasionally close the upper stretches of the North Fork.

Each of these forks experienced extreme high waters after a heavy monsoon rain in the high country in 2008 and two years later these waters are returning to a good fishery. In summer months, the river is stocked with rainbows from the Reservation's trout hatchery.

Although there are hatches of small stoneflies, caddis, and mayflies, the trout in the upper Ruidoso are usually opportunists. Fly patterns recommended by locals include the standard Beadhead Pheasant Tails, Beadhead Prince Nymphs, and Copper Johns in size 14 to 18. Good dry patterns are Parachute Adams and Elk Hair Caddis, again in size 14 to 18. Grasshopper and ant patterns can also work well in midsummer.

From its confluence with the North Fork the river runs through the Upper Canyon for about 1½ miles, and this is the best stretch of water on the Reservation. There's usually good flow, shade provided by the canyon walls, several plunge pools below boulders, pockets, and some deep holes. There's also a healthy population of small browns, some to 14 inches, and stocked rainbows.

After leaving the Reservation, the river continues east to downtown Ruidoso and the Chamber of Commerce on Sudderth Drive, Ruidoso's main drag. This 5-mile section is open to fishing 12 months a year and parking and river accesses are available at several locations, including Eagle Drive, the Chamber of Commerce, and Gavalan Canyon.

As previously mentioned, the river experienced a very high flow in 2008 due to monsoon rains and changed many of the characteristics of the river from the Reservation boundary through town. Over time, the stream is adjusting to a new streambed in many locations and is expected to return to a good fishery over time and with care.

Rio Ruidoso & Rio Bonito

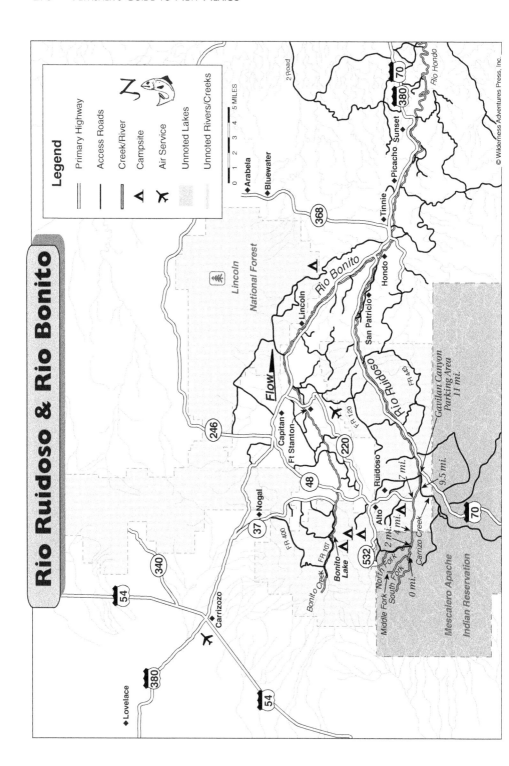

The Ruidoso River Association (RRA) contributes to the wellness of the river and has been in existence since 1966. It is involved in the continual improvement of the quality of the water and is dedicated to the future of this coldwater fishery. The Association organizes public awareness programs and sponsors an annual "river cleanup" that attracts hundreds of volunteers. The RRA has also been awarded, and has subsequently expended as of early 2010, over $850,000 in grant monies received from the New Mexico Environment Department for rehabilitation projects along the Rio Ruidoso designed to improve the fishery. The projects, according to Dick Wisner of the RRA, include such diverse activities as rebuilding ski runs at the Ski Apache Resort, designing a pump back system to return leaking water for a vital reservoir, rebuilding the river channel through a popular park, and many more.

This portion of the river has less gradient than the forks on the Reservation, resulting in more quiet water and slower bends. There are several nice riffles, pools, and undercut banks at the bends. Large rock formations also provide pools that are favorite holding spots for all three trout species.

The same flies work here as on the forks, but there is a significant Golden Stonefly hatch in May and June. Match them with a Gold Stimulator, size 10 to 16, or go subsurface with a Copper John in the same size range. Of course, caddis and various mayflies are present, too, and sometimes it's important to match them. Elk Hair Caddis and various mayfly patterns normally work well from April through October, but during drought conditions fishing can be iffy after June. Amazingly, the browns seem to survive droughts. After a good summer or fall thunderstorm, the water rises and begins to clear and fishing can be fantastic.

Wading is fairly easy, and although there are plenty of willows, brush, and other

The Rio Ruidoso is a medium-sized stream that offers good year-round flyfishing right in downtown Ruidoso.

obstacles along the banks, the river is still fairly open compared to the forks upstream. Hip boots are sufficient when it's cool, otherwise wet wading is recommended.

The lower section begins at the Chamber of Commerce, where Carrizo Creek joins the river. Carrizo Creek flows northeast from the Reservation, and despite its small size, it offers about 2 miles of good fishing for 8- to 10-inch wild browns. Permission to fish this section must be obtained from homeowners along the Carrizo.

East from the Chamber, or downstream, there are approximately 2 miles of the Rio Ruidoso to fish. The increased water flow from Carrizo creates more pools and flat stretches east to Friedenbloom Drive, which is recognized as the end of public fishing waters. While the Rio Ruidoso continues east through the Ruidoso Downs Racetrack and parallels US 70 for several miles, all property along the river is private and permission must be obtained from individual property owners. The lower Ruidoso contains all three trout species, and rainbows are stocked by the NMDGF. A good fish in the lower Rio Ruidoso is 12 to 14 inches, although an occasional brown or rainbow over 20 inches is caught.

From the Reservation boundary downstream to Friedenbloom Drive you can keep only three fish of any length. Flyfishing and catch and release are highly encouraged on this limited, delicate fishery.

While a variety of fly patterns are successful on the Rio Ruidoso, the most popular are Beadhead Pheasant Tails and Princes in size 14 to 18, as well as the Green Rock Worm, a local fly that represents caddis larva. Popular dries include Blue-Winged Olives, Parachute Adams, and Renegades, as well as Elk Hair Caddis, size 14 to 20.

Fish the Rio Ruidoso as you would any small stream, casting upstream, moving slowly, using brush to conceal yourself, and keeping casts as short as possible. Dries work well at times, but if fish won't come up try putting on a dropper with a beadhead nymph.

Stream Facts: Rio Ruidoso

Season
- Headwaters of the three forks on the Mescalero Apache Indian Reservation are open April 1 to October 5, according to Reservation officials, and a tribal fishing permit is required.
- Rio Ruidoso from the Reservation boundary east through the village of Ruidoso is open for fishing 12 months a year.

Special Regulations
- Rio Ruidoso from the Reservation boundary east through the village of Ruidoso: The only restriction is a three-fish-per-day limit.

Trout
- Rainbow, brown, and brook trout that average 8 to 12 inches, some bigger.

River Miles
- Confluence of the South and Middle Forks—0
- Confluence with the North Fork—2

- Mescalero Apache Reservation boundary—4
- NM 48—7
- Carrizo Creek—9.5
- Gavilan Canyon parking area—11
- End of public water—12

River Characteristics
- The upper Ruidoso on the Reservation is small fast water, especially in the higher elevations, and most streambanks are thick with brush. The middle Ruidoso, from the Reservation east for 5 miles, runs through housing and commercial development and slows down, offering pools and slow deep bends. The lower Ruidoso consists of 2 miles of water with a larger flow, below where Carrizo Creek joins the river at the Chamber of Commerce. This stretch is semi-brushy along the banks and offers opportunities for some normal casts. This area contains large numbers of rainbows.

River Flows
- Winter, summer, and fall: about 2 to 5 cfs, but can change dramatically
- Spring runoff: about 5 to 10 cfs, but much higher in a good snow year

Campgrounds
- Although there are no campgrounds on the Rio Ruidoso itself, you'll find several in the nearby Lincoln National Forest. They include:
- Cedar Creek Campground on CR 88
- Oak Grove Campground on NM 532
- Skyline and Monjeau Campgrounds on CR 117
- Westlake and South Fork Campgrounds on CR 107 near Bonito Lake

Maps
- *New Mexico Atlas & Gazetteer,* page 40; Lincoln National Forest Map; BLM Map: Ruidoso; USGS Quadrangle Maps: Sierra Blanca Peak, Ruidoso, Ruidoso Downs, Ft. Stanton, Angus, Nogal Peak

Agencies
- Lincoln National Forest Supervisors Office, 1101 New York Ave., Alamogordo, NM 88310-6992; 505-434-7200, www.fs.fed.us/r3/Lincoln
- Smokey Bear Ranger district, 901 Mechem Dr., Ruidoso, NM 88345; 505-257-4095
- NMDGF, P.O. Box 25112, Santa Fe, NM 87504-5112

Outfitters
The Lincoln National Forest office can provide information, including maps and a list of outfitters permitted to operate on public lands.

Rio Bonito

Anglers who enjoy hiking in the high country have an excellent opportunity for small brook and rainbow trout from 6 to 10 inches in two canyons on the east side of Sierra Blanca in the Lincoln National Forest. There is also the added bonus of seeing deer, elk, bear, and other wild critters.

The two forks of the Rio Bonito, the South Fork and the Bonito, hold naturally reproducing brook and rainbow trout year-round. Each one has about 4 miles of fishable water in normal years, but during drought you may have to go to the upper 2 miles on Bonito Creek.

While the small streams flow in winter and spring, in dry years active stream flows no longer occur. These high country trout are tough and a good deal of fun to catch and release. Both forks are rated as moderate for hiking and challenging for fishing. A short, light rod with matching light line is ideal. Most casts are less than 10 feet due to the heavy brush, large rocks, and tight conditions.

The South Fork is reached by parking at the Lincoln National Forest South Fork Campground on the west side of Bonito Lake. To reach Bonito Lake from Ruidoso, take NM 48 north about 9 miles and turn left on NM 37. Then turn west on FR 107 and go 3 miles to the lake. The road parallels Rio Bonito from NM 48 to Bonito Lake. The final mile of the Rio Bonito beginning at the US Forest Service boundary and continuing to Bonito Lake is public water but has a tendency to dry up in late summer. When the flow remains healthy throughout the spring, NMGF may stock this section. The Rio Bonito below Bonito Lake is not a reliable fishery.

After leaving the Forest Service parking area on the banks of the South Fork, anglers can follow the main trail more than 5 miles up the South Fork. Some sections may be dry, but you'll find more water the higher you climb. Don't bother with waders, just wear comfortable hiking boots for the trail.

Trout in these waters prefer small flies ranging from size 16 to 20. Beadheads work well when waters are flowing, but they aren't necessary in the still pools. Pheasant Tails and Hare's Ears are favorites, as are small Parachute Adams, Elk Hair Caddis, and Renegades.

I (Winston Cox) still frequently fish this stretch, but I actually made my first fishing trip to the South Fork in May 1941, a month after I was born. My father was an enthusiastic camper and trout fisherman, and old photos taken at South Fork show the group beside the 1940 family Chevy with the mattress from home tied on top for travel. Mother said she was not about to camp out by sleeping on the ground, so the mattress had to go to Bonito Lake.

In this same area of the Lincoln National Forest you can try the main fork of the Rio Bonito. Access it by taking FR 107 west of Bonito Lake to the trailhead for Trail 36 at the end of the road, a distance of about 4 miles. Most of the valley leading to the trailhead is open for camping. Normally, this stretch would also offer good flyfishing for small rainbows and brookies, but during drought it almost dries up.

Anglers simply hike up Trail 36 until fishing water is located. It's about 5 miles to the headwaters of this fork of Bonito, and depending on how much water there is, you'll find between 2 to 5 miles of fishable water. The creek is only about 2 feet wide, and it's very brushy in most places. Water conditions generally mirror those on the South Fork, and recommendations for catching the small trout include light tackle, small flies, and delicate presentations.

The best months for both forks are May and June and again in October. Maps of the area can be obtained from the Smokey Bear Ranger Station at 729 Mechem Drive in Ruidoso or other Lincoln National Forest offices.

GRINDSTONE LAKE

This public stillwater is a water-supply reservoir for Ruidoso, located about a mile from downtown. This lake has about 35 surface acres and receives most of its water by a diversion from the Rio Ruidoso. It can be reached off Sudderth Drive by taking Carrizo Canyon Road and then Grindstone Canyon Road.

The lake is stocked with rainbows and also contains a good population of large browns. As with most lakes, the best dry-fly action occurs in late evening. It is open to fishing year-round, but the prime flyfishing months are April through November. Float tubes and canoes are allowed on the lake and permits are available at the Ruidoso Parks and Recreation Department at 801 Resort Road near the lake.

Evening flyfishing can be good in the shallow water at the upper end of the lake. Tube anglers generally prefer to strip large streamers on sinking lines before switching to dry flies in late afternoon.

There are hatches of midges, Callibaetis, and damselflies. Recommended flies in sizes 14 to 20 include the Parachute Adams, Mosquito, Elk Hair Caddis, Renegade, and Parachute Blue Damsel, along with Marabou Damsel Nymphs, size 8 to 14. Chocolate foam emergers and red midge larvae can be good, and the same goes for Pheasant Tails, Prince Nymphs, and Coppers Johns. Large Woolly Buggers and Bunny Leeches in black or brown can also be effective in early evening.

Nice, fat rainbows in Grindstone average about 10 to 15 inches, with occasional holdovers up to 18 inches. Browns between 5 and 7 pounds have been caught here on occasion, although they are rare.

BONITO LAKE

This 60-acre impoundment is also a water storage facility for several communities, and float devices are not allowed. The fishing season for this lake is April 1 through November 30. From Ruidoso, take NM 48 north, then NM 37 west 2 miles before turning west on FR 107 for about 5 miles. Bonito Lake is the most heavily fished water in the area and is regularly stocked with rainbow trout during the summer months. There's also a decent brook trout population and a few wild browns, which somehow manage to get quite large.

As with Grindstone, late evening offers the best flyfishing, and midge hatches occur daily throughout late summer and early fall. Steep banks surround most of the lake, which makes casting a challenge, but the west end offers gradually sloping banks that allow easier back casts. Most hatches occur in the area where Bonito Creek enters the lake. Recommended flies are the same as for Grindstone, including gray and black midges in size 20.

RIO TULAROSA

This small river heads in the southwest corner of the Mescalero Apache Indian Reservation, flowing through the town of Mescalero before exiting the Reservation near the village of Bent. It then parallels US 70 to Tularosa. After it crosses the highway, it runs for about 5 miles through a mix of state and federal land. Below this stretch the water is too warm for trout in the summertime. Brown and rainbow trout average 8 to 12 inches in the public water.

The creek is small and open, meandering through a flat-bottomed canyon with lots of willows that provide cover and shade. There are plenty of shallow riffles, pools, and some good undercut banks near the bends. Elk Hair Caddis, parachutes, Hare's Ears, and Pheasant Tails work well, and hoppers will sometimes produce during summer and fall.

RIO PENASCO

This stream is formed by several small tributaries on the eastern slopes of the Sacramento Mountains east of Cloudcroft. The Penasco flows through Mayhill on US 82, and fishing usually begins just east of Mayhill. The Penasco is spring fed east of Mayhill, and the permanent water flow has contributed to a tremendous trout fishery for several miles downstream on private ranches that offer trout-fishing memberships. Some also offer day-fishing opportunities. Rainbows and browns are found on this stretch of river. (See page 400 in Private Waters for a map and details on this excellent spring creek.)

SACRAMENTO RIVER AND AGUA CHIQUITA CREEK

These small streams lie south of Cloudcroft in the Lincoln National Forest. In the recent past they held large numbers of brook trout and provided excellent fishing. Due to ongoing extreme drought conditions, they are now dry for part of the year and are unable to support a viable trout population so the NMGF has stopped stocking trout indefinitely.

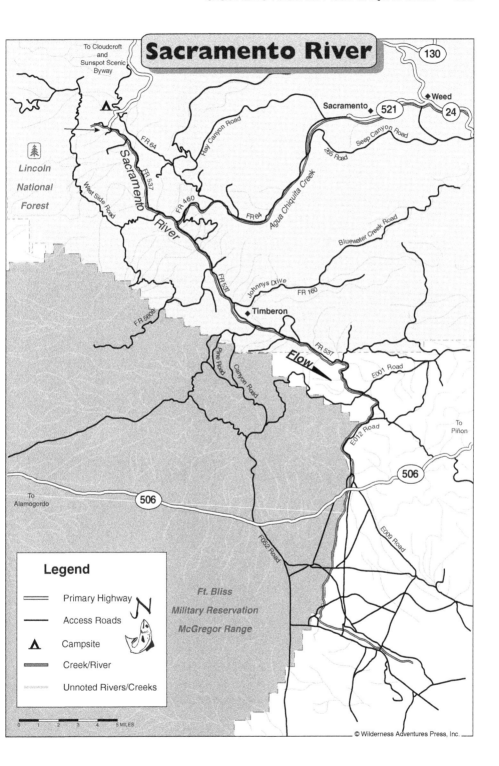

To Cloudcroft
and
Sunspot Scenic
Byway

Sacramento River

130

Sacramento ◆ 521 ◆ Weed

24

FR 64

Hay Canyon Road

Seep Canyon Road

🌲

Lincoln

285 Road

National

Forest

FR 64

West Side Road

FR 537

Agua Chiquita Creek

FR 460

Sacramento River

Bluewater Creek Road

FR 537

Johnnys Drive

FR 160

FR 5608

Timberon

FR 537

Flow

E001 Road

Pine Road

Canyon Road

E012 Road

To
Piñon

506

To
Alamogordo

506

E009 Road

F052 Road

Legend

═══ Primary Highway

N

── Access Roads

▲ Campsite

═══ Creek/River

Unnoted Rivers/Creeks

Ft. Bliss
Military Reservation
McGregor Range

0 1 2 3 4 5 MILES

© Wilderness Adventures Press, Inc.

MESCALERO APACHE INDIAN RESERVATION

The Mescalero Apache Reservation is located in southern New Mexico near the city of Ruidoso. The Mescalero Apache are very ambitious in their economic endeavors. The tribe owns a wood-products business, a world-class resort, a ski area, and a livestock enterprise. Mescalero lands also offer exciting opportunities for outdoor adventurers, from fishing at two of the tribal lakes to big game hunting.

In addition to the Rio Ruidoso discussed earlier, several other waters are available for trout fishing during the spring and summer: Eagle Lakes on the Ski Apache Road about 9 miles northwest of Ruidoso; Mescalero Lake, 3 miles south of Ruidoso on Carrizo Canyon Road; and Silver Lake, 25 miles south of Ruidoso on NM 244.

Mescalero Lake

Located at the Inn of the Mountain Gods Resort, this beautiful 90-acre lake is stocked with cutthroat and rainbow trout. From Ruidoso, take Carizzo Canyon Road to the Inn of the Mountain Gods. Daily fishing permits may be purchased at the boat rental. Boat rentals are available, and docks are open from April through September. Fishing hours are from sunrise to sunset.

Trout in Mescalero Lake can get quite large, over 20 inches and this is a great brown trout fishery. Strip damsel nymphs or Woolly Buggers near the weed beds, especially at the inlet where Carrizo Creek comes in. Look for rises near sunset, when midges usually hatch.

Eagle Lakes

These lakes are located about 3.5 miles off NM 48 up Ski Run Road. More like ponds, they are stocked with rainbow trout every week, mainly for use by put-and-take baitfishers. Wading and floating devices are not allowed. Nevertheless, the flyfishing is pretty good and you can find places to cast from shore. Daily fishing permits must be purchased at the lake area entrance office. Call 505-336-4668 for information.

Silver Lake

This 5- or 6-acre lake is located about 25 miles south of Ruidoso. Take US 70 south and then turn left on NM 244. Follow it through Elk Canyon until it intersects with Apache Road 2. Turn left onto Apache Road 2, and Silver Lake is on your right. There are plenty of stocked rainbows from 8 to 12 inches (some larger) in the lake, but it gets a ton of pressure from local baitfishers so don't expect an ideal setting for flyfishing. Try a Mating Midge or a gray Midge Cluster in the evenings.

For more information on Reservation fishing and camping, call the Reservation offices at 575-464-4427 in Mescalero. All waters are open April 1 to October 5, according to a Reservation spokesperson.

Private Ponds

Seeping Springs Trout Lake

This is a rich spring trout pond located just 4 miles east of Ruidoso Downs racetrack. A fishing license is not required. It's open March through September for family-oriented camping and fishing. Call 575-378-4216 for information.

Ranch Sosegado Trout Pond

This private trout pond is set in a lovely location with the surrounding mountains forming the backdrop. It's open every weekend and on weekdays by appointment. Call 575-671-4580 for information. The pond is located 24 miles west or Ruidoso just off US 70 in Bent. This is a great place for families, and a fishing license is not required.

Elephant Butte Lake

When I set out to get information on massive Elephant Butte Lake in the south-central part of the state I found that nobody wanted to talk about it. Apparently, anglers in the know were trying to protect it from being recognized as a great warmwater fishery for flyfishers. Then one of them finally told me that it was because they were afraid there wouldn't be a lake there by the time the book came out due to the current drought. How could this be true? The largest lake in the state, with the largest game fish in the state, was drying up? Well, as it turns out, it probably won't dry up, but it is very low and we're still dry, although things are slowly improving.

The Butte's water is heavily relied upon by downstream users along the Rio Grande, and the dam was built to provide water for them during drought conditions. Hopefully, it won't actually go dry. As of this writing the snowpack in the Rio Grande Basin is over 100 percent so maybe there's some relief in sight.

Just when I was thinking I was going to have to try to write about this lake on my own, I ran into a good friend and associate, Bob Widgren of Los Pinos Rods in Albuquerque. We were shooting the bull at the New Mexico Trout's Annual Conclave, and I asked him if he knew anyone that might be able to help me. He quickly informed me that he knew a little bit about the lake. Of course, he was being his usual modest self, as is evident from the following contribution.

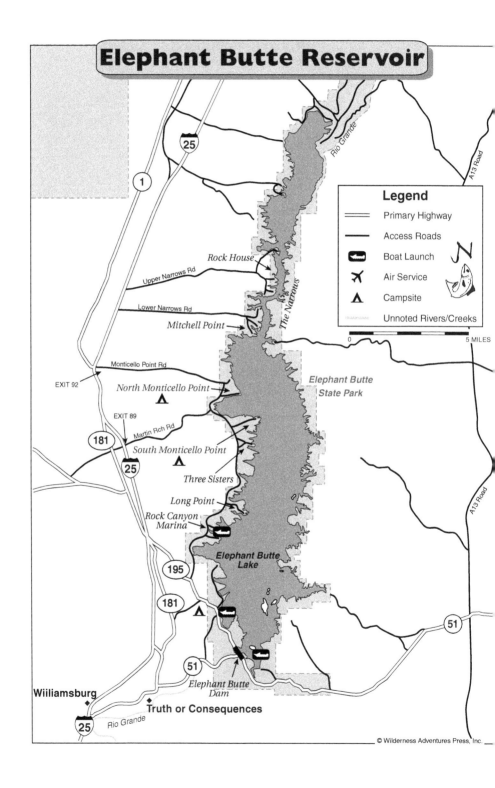

Elephant Butte Reservoir

Legend

═══	Primary Highway
───	Access Roads
🚤	Boat Launch
✈	Air Service
▲	Campsite
	Unnoted Rivers/Creeks

0   5 MILES

Rio Grande

A13 Road

25

1

Rock House

Upper Narrows Rd

The Narrows

Lower Narrows Rd

Mitchell Point

Monticello Point Rd

EXIT 92

North Monticello Point
▲

Elephant Butte
State Park

EXIT 89

181

Martin Rch Rd

25

South Monticello Point
▲

Three Sisters

Long Point

Rock Canyon
Marina
🚤

Elephant Butte
Lake

195

8

181

▲
🚤

A13 Road

51

51

Elephant Butte
Dam

Wiiliamsburg

Truth or Consequences

25   Rio Grande

© Wilderness Adventures Press, Inc.

Fishing Elephant Butte Lake

(Contributed by Bob Widgren)

If you want to catch big fish in New Mexico, and I mean *big* fish, go south from Albuquerque about 150 miles to the largest body of water in the state, Elephant Butte Lake. Considered to be one of the top ten bass lakes in the country, here you'll have the opportunity to fish for white and black bass, largemouth bass, walleye, crappie, catfish, and even the odd rainbow trout. But for the flyrodder, one of the main draws is striped bass. Stripers range from a few pounds to a whopping 50-plus pounds. The record for striped bass in Elephant Butte Lake is over 54 pounds. Largemouth bass have been taken over 11 pounds, and if catfish are your thing the flatheads can reach 70 pounds or more.

The dam, which was named after the large rock island that resembles an elephant's head and torso, holds back the Rio Grande and was completed in 1916 to control the downstream flooding and to provide water for farming in the lower Rio Grande Valley. The lake is over 40 miles long and is actually two lakes connected by the Rio Grande river channel, called the Narrows. The lake elevation is normally around 4,400 feet, but with the recent drought conditions in New Mexico the lake has fallen over 100 feet, although it has actually started to rise again as of this writing. There are over 200 miles of shoreline, and when full, the lake can hold over 2 million acre-feet of water. Three hydroelectric generators were added in the late 1930s to provide over 30 megawatts of electrical power.

The water temperature usually runs between 72 and 80 degrees from May through September. In the spring, around March, the water temperature hovers in the 60-degree range, and fish near the surface can provide some very exciting takes. Using topwater poppers with a floating fly line, the bass angler can do very well in the upper lake for largemouth bass. And while white bass are just about everywhere in the spring, one of my favorite spots is the Narrows. Also, try McRae Canyon on the eastern side of the lake, almost from Marina del Sur. McRae Canyon is one of the most popular spots on the lake. It's a mix of shallows, drop-offs, and islands.

The upper lake is a little more susceptible to temperature changes than the lower lake, which varies less, and at a slower rate. The upper lake is not as deep as the lower, and it actually traps a lot of sediment. This is good for the lower lake, in that the water remains clearer throughout the year.

Most of the good fishing spots on Elephant Butte are reached by boats equipped with the latest in fish-finding sonar technology. This is a huge lake and finding the baitfish is imperative. If they aren't leaping out of the lake trying to avoid being eaten, you'll have to find them electronically. Threadfin shad are the main diet of the bass, and patterns with darker tops and pearl or Mylar bodies will serve you well.

The typical setup for bass is a 9-foot rod, 8- to 10-weight with multiple heads. When the bass are on the surface a floating line is your best choice, but most of the time you will have to go deep to hunt up the big stripers. A 10-weight with a 300- to 500-grain sinking head is a must. Casting a 10-weight with a 500-grain, 24-foot

Flyfishers have their best chance at stripers here in the spring before the fish head to deeper water.

sinking-tip all day can be tiring, but when you hook up to one of these big boys you'll soon forget all the hang-ups, the broken leaders, and lost flies.

The first time you tie into a large striper you'll think you just snagged the fastest tree stump in the whole lake. Then the line will rip through the guides, and you'll have to put your back into it to stay in the fight. The fish will try to wrap you around the nearest underwater hazard, but you must quickly get the upper hand in order to keep the fish's head up. You'll be amazed at the size and strength of these fish. Not to diminish the largemouth, the whites and blacks, or even the smallies, but the stripers are at the top of the food chain here. They hit your fly hard, with a slashing strike that will sometimes leave you looking at the shredded end of your leader.

There was a hold on stocking stripers (as they do not spawn in Elephant Butte Lake) for several years, but now NMDGF officials are planning to stock 50,000 fingerlings in the summer of 2004.

The top spots for stripers in April are the Narrows, Ash Canyon, McRae Canyon, and the Dirt Dam area. As the temperature rises, the fishing gets slower until fall arrives, and September is considered the best overall month for fishing for everything. The stripers are still hanging around the Kettle Top area at this time. As the season gets further into the fall, the fish start heading for the deeper water, down to 20 or 30 feet. When the dead of winter arrives the fish are on the bottom at almost 50 to 60 feet, all but out of reach of the flyrodder. Sometimes, a warm sunny day will bring a few bass to the shallows, but winter usually means that there are several months to wait for the striper action to pick up again.

Lake Facts: Elephant Butte Lake

Lake Volume
- Since 2004, the lake has risen to almost 40 percent of capacity.

Marinas
- Marina del Sur, Rock Canyon Marina, and Dam Site Marina.

Camping
- Tent and RV sites (some of the areas require reservations), picnic tables, restrooms, showers, and handicapped access. The park has numerous camping and picnicking areas, with more than 200 developed campsites and 100 electrical hook-ups for RVs and trailers. There are day-use and overnight camping fees.
- See Truth or Consequences in the Southwest Region hub cities for more options

Maps
- *New Mexico Atlas and Gazetteer,* pages 38 and 46; BLM map: Elephant Butte; USGS Quadrangle maps: Truth or Consequences, Elephant Butte

Agencies
- NMDGF, P.O. Box 25112, Santa Fe, NM 87504-5112
- Elephant Butte Lake State Park, P.O. Box 13, Elephant Butte, NM 87935; Park Manager Ray Kirkpatrick, 575-744-5923

Elephant Butte Reservoir is famous for its large striped bass.

TIGER MUSKIES IN NEW MEXICO

(Contributed By Bob Widgren)

Muskie madness is one way to describe flyfishing for tiger muskies. Either you will go mad from casting 10,000 times or you will totally lose control when one of these prehistoric monsters grabs your fly. Flyfishing for tiger muskies is very risky in that you will have to be determined that you want very much to land one of these dynamic fish on the fly and then survive the release of the fish with all your fingers.

This game fish is not for the faint of heart as you will cast 9,999 times and just when you think there isn't any fish around at all they will jerk your fly rod out of your hands or shred the fly completely off, but will definitely wake you up. This is one of the most common errors when fishing for this top predator - the fish will lull you to sleep, and just when your eyes are getting heavy and your back is tired ... bam!

Hooking a muskie is like trying to break your rod in half. Don't be timid and try a dainty little trout hook set; jam the fly into the fish's mouth as hard and as deep as you can. Their mouths are hard and tough and setting the hook can be difficult. The typical tiger muskie has about 3,000 teeth and they all point the wrong way, so landing one of these dinosaurs can be like wrestling with an alligator. I have found that using a large fish cradle landing net is a must and two anglers, one with a jaw spreader and net and the other with the fish is the safest way to land and release the fish. The cradle net is a four-foot-long, two-handled net that the fish is slipped into and is restricted from slashing back and forth, not only perhaps injuring the angler but also the fish. The jaw spreader is inserted between the top and bottom jaw and the spring tension of the spreader keeps the fish from clamping down on your pliers or your hand. Be careful with these fish as there have been some injuries to anglers who forgot to respect the tiger muskie. After you have successfully removed the fly, hold the fish at a 45-degree angle with one hand carefully inserted at the jaw/gill point and have your buddy take the trophy photo. Do not hold the fish at the jaw only as it may damage the jaw.

As of 2010, anglers are allowed to keep one fish over 40 inches; up until this year, both Bluewater Lake and Quemado Lake were no-kill lakes for tiger muskies. As a side note; because these lakes had good populations of rainbow trout, some trout have survived and we have caught and released several rainbows in the 22- to 24-inch class. Another reason I don't use too large of fly - sometimes a trout saves the day.

Tiger muskies are a hybrid between a male pike and a female muskie. The hybrid has distinct tiger bars on a light background, similar to the barred coloration pattern of some muskie. Its fins and tail lobes are rounded like a northern pike's but colored like a muskie's. The cheekscale and mandible-pore patterns are intermediate between a northern pike's and muskie's. The tiger muskie grows slightly faster than either pure-strain parent - in the first several years of life and they can exceed 30 pounds. Some tiger muskie occur naturally, though most hybrids are produced in hatcheries. They are useful in stocking because they grow quickly and endure high temperatures better than either parent, and are easier to raise in a hatchery than pure-strain muskie. The hybrid tiger muskie is sterile and they were introduced in 2003 in Bluewater Lake and Quemado Lake to control the infestation of goldfish and other trash fish. They were planted as fingerlings and as of 2010, some have grown up to 44 inches long and 25 pounds (although the majority of the fish I've caught on the fly have been in the three-foot class). You will not have any problem distinguishing the tiger muskie from other fish as there are no pike or standard muskies in the lakes.

The typical fly gear is an 8 to 10 weight rod with either a floating line or an intermediate sinking line. I prefer the intermediate line that pushes the leader and fly beneath the surface. The flies are usually not gigantic and therefore not too difficult to cast. Some anglers prefer the 8- to 10-inch flies but I have done very well with the smaller 3- to 4-inch flies. Fly selections for tiger muskies are typically on the larger size such as a Mad Pup in tan or white 1/0; Rainy's Green Attractor 2/0; Rainy's Bronze/Tan Tandem 3/0 and, one of my favorites, Rainbow Trout 1/0.

Leaders are typically 9-foot, 0x to 2x depending on your fly choice and I like to use a 40-pound bite tippet about 8 to 12 inches long. It is not necessary to use wire for the bite tippet but that's up to each angler. The tiger muskie's teeth are not as sharp as a pike but a bit more smooth and rounded (but still sharp). Don't let that fool you, I've had 40-pound tippet and flies bitten completely off and even wire doesn't hold up to some of the ferocious strikes.

April, May, September and October are the best times for taking the tigers on the fly (when the water temperature reaches between 50 and 60 degrees). I think the best temperature for tiger muskies near the top is around 58 degrees. During the hot summers, the fish go deep and sulk until the water temperature begins to cool and they start feeding near the surface again and are fattening up for the winter. We have been able to take them on and near the surface in shallow water that is less than 5 feet. Fishing either from a boat or from the shore is productive as the fish are usually looking for a meal near the shore where the baitfish hang out. If you are fishing from a boat, the majority of your casts should be towards the shore. I recommend a more angled cast instead of the straight out in front of you cast. The angled cast covers more of the water they like and gives the muskies a better look at your fly. Whether in a boat or from shore, target the rocky points and the edges of the small coves as these fish are ambush type feeders. Cover all of the water within your casting range but concentrate on the points and just inside the coves.

Being able to cast a large rod is paramount and if you are not used to the larger rods and larger flies, practice before you go or invest in a casting lesson with big rods. I have seen a lot of anglers have trouble casting large rods with large flies particularly in the wind, although tiger muskies tend to like the calmer days - when there is a lot of wind, they can be tough to find. Weather of course is as unpredictable as fishing, but the calmer the forecast the better your chances. When the wind is up I will concentrate deep in the coves and try to find the least amount of wind. The fish have just as hard a time seeing in choppy water as we do. If the chop is moderate, try using a faster sinking tip or full sinking line. I've had some success on windy days using a 350 grain full sinking 10 weight but that also means a lot of heavy casting. And the chances of getting snagged and losing some flies are high. When using heavy gear, use a more open cast or even a swing-around Belgian cast. Don't try to keep a tight loop with large junky gear as you will foul more often than not. If you are in a boat with your fishing buddy, make sure you both get it right so someone doesn't get hooked.

Tiger muskies will eat just about any food available but they tend to prefer the softer suckers, goldfish and even trout over the more spiny backed fish. Tiger muskies do something that is a mystery and other muskellunges don't do; they will swim about with their heads out of the water as if they are surveying the water and will do this for up to 50 yards. Quite strange and nobody knows why, but I think they are looking for float tubers and other easy prey. Float tubing for tiger muskies is not recommended and not because you can't hook one but what are you going to do with it when you do. Landing a tiger in a tube is not something I would recommend.

The tiger muskies were brought into New Mexico by Game & Fish for controlling the suckers and goldfish infestations, but now has become a viable sought-after game fish. There were reports of large goldfish schools that actually changed the color of the lake in some areas when viewed from above. Thanks to this predator fish, the goldfish is now somewhat rare as I have only seen a few in the lakes (but the ones who have survived are large by typical goldfish standards). We have seen goldfish in the 16- to 18-inch class!

This is a relatively new phenomenon and now many flyfishers are excited about catching one of the toughest fish in North America. Tiger muskies and standard muskies have been in the Midwest and the Great Lakes area forever. The two New Mexico lakes are the southern-most habitat. Members of a local muskie club have been working on a stocking program and have planted structures throughout the lakes to give the baitfish some cover.

If you have fished for pike with a fly rod before you are already prepared to go after tiger muskies. If you haven't fished for toothy critters before, do yourself a favor and try it sometime. Be prepared to spend some time fishing for tiger muskies and be prepared to pay your dues but in the end you will be rewarded with one of the most spectacular and toughest fish in New Mexico.

Bluewater Lake

About 20 miles southwest of Grants, this 2,350-acre impoundment is one of New Mexico's most popular lakes and state parks. Bluewater Lake and Bluewater Creek are stocked with rainbow trout, cutthroat trout and catfish. Some trout caught in Bluewater have weighed 9 pounds. Access to good fishing areas are easily reached by car. The park is also a popular spot for ice fishing in the winter months. Bluewater State Park areas can be reached from I-40 at Exit 63 (Prewitt) to get to the main park, and at Exit 53 (Thoreau) to visit the west side. The state park has two paved ramps at the Prewitt side and one at the Thoreau side. No marinas.

Quemado Lake

The 800-acre Quemado Lake Recreation Area is located approximately 20 miles south of Quemado. On I-40 west of Albuquerque, take exit 89 before Grants on NM117 south then take NM36 south to Quemado. From Quemado take NM32 south then turn left on Forest Rd 13 to Quemado Lake. The recreation area includes the 131-acre manmade trout lake with two ADA fishing piers, two boat ramps, seven developed campgrounds and one primitive campground.

Private Waters

In the last 20 years flyfishing has become so popular that it's hard to find a place to fish many streams and lakes without having to share water with other anglers. Historically, flyfishing has been about the union of angler and nature in its purest form. Solitude is an important element in achieving that connection. When the water you're fishing has already been disturbed that week, day, or hour by another angler it can lessen the power of the experience.

Small streams and creeks are even more vulnerable to pressure than large rivers, and catch-and-release flyfishing has created a whole new phenomenon in recent years—educated fish.

The trout in streams or mountain lakes that get fished even once or twice a season exhibit new behavior. And if the same stretch of water gets fished more than once or twice a week you'll see a dramatic decline in the catch rate, even though the trout population remains the same. Simply put, the more pressure there is, the more difficult it is to catch fish.

Unfortunately, most of my clients today expect to see other anglers and fully accept it, while I still get upset if I see another angler or hear a car pull up near where I'm fishing. When I was growing up we never fished a stretch of water that might have been fished that day. Today, on some streams in America, you are lucky to find a pool or riffle that isn't currently being fished, much less a stretch of water that hasn't been pounded that day.

Fly shops, guides, outfitters, writers, and word of mouth have seemingly exposed every good stream and lake in the country. Flyfishing has become an industry, and as with any industry, the desire to make money outweighs the ability to protect the resource. Sometimes those of us who make money through flyfishing have to walk a fine line between preserving our business and protecting the sport and habitat.

I realized early on that the quality of fishing I was promoting to get business was declining as a result of my business, especially on small streams like the Cimarron. Even my own brother complained that I ruined the Cimarron. I explained to him that it would have happened whether I existed or not, which is true, but the Cimarron will never be the way it was when we were kids. The same holds true for most quality fisheries. It's all relative, of course, and each generation's perception of "the good old days" will always be better than current conditions.

Knowing that I couldn't turn back the clock, as an outfitter and guide I started looking for quality private waters to reduce my use and dependency on public waters, where I had no control over the regulations or angling pressure. At least on private waters I could better manage the fishery and regulate the pressure.

Even though private waters aren't the same as virgin waters with fish that have never been caught, in some cases, they are as close as you can get. Many private fishery owners carefully manage and regulate the pressure, while others don't. Generally, though, you are paying for quality, exclusivity, and solitude when fishing private water. By directing anglers who would otherwise be fishing on public waters to private waters, pressure on the public waters is more widely distributed, thus aiding those fisheries and improving the overall angling experience for everyone.

Because private sections are off limits to campers, bait throwers, and trespassers they tend to be cleaner and more attractive from an environmental standpoint. Indeed, most landowners seek out lease arrangements because professional guides and river masters make it their business to look after the overall health of the watershed. The end result is a better fishery with significantly larger fish, a greater trout population per mile, and a more appealing river.

Admittedly, private waters are not for everyone due to the high price anglers have to pay to gain access. On many private waters (including my own leases) you must hire a guide in addition to paying a hefty rod fee. Sometimes, you must stay at a lodge or cabins in order to fish. Other waters are controlled by nonprofit flyfishing clubs, and members can fish for considerably less than they would elsewhere.

Regardless, private water opens up water that was previously off limits. It also helps the landowner supplement his income and increase the value of his property at a time when cattle ranching is not very profitable, thus reducing the likelihood of the land being developed. It helps the economy in rural areas by bringing in tourist dollars to guides, outfitters, fly shops, motels, inns, and guest ranches near private fisheries. That money stays in the local communities and gets recycled. In my own case, by leasing several miles of private water, I attract anglers that otherwise might go somewhere else to fish. But they spend their dollars here instead because they can get quality flyfishing without the crowds.

For better or worse, private fisheries play an important role in New Mexico, so let's look at what some of the best have to offer.

Vermejo Park

Vermejo Park, located near the Colorado border in northeast New Mexico, offers an unparalleled opportunity to flyfish in one of the last large tracts that still resembles what the West was before we altered it almost beyond recognition in the last century.

On this enormous ranch of over half a million acres, you will still see large herds of elk, deer, antelope, and bison, along with bear and mountain lion. In addition, managers are working to bring back species that once made the ranch their home, such as Rocky Mountain bighorn sheep, black-footed ferrets, and wolves. They are also working hard to better protect the indigenous Rio Grande cutthroat trout, plus restocking their lakes with significant numbers of rainbow, brook, and brown trout for your fishing pleasure.

Not only is Vermejo Park a unique place to enjoy and interact with the natural world, it's also known for its excellent service. The quality of the food, lodging, and hospitality match the beautiful environment. Their great staff can design a trip for large or small groups of anglers interested in fishing the ranch's numerous lakes and streams.

Twenty-one well-stocked lakes provide impressive fishing for rainbow, brown, brook, and cutthroat trout. Most fish average 2 to 3 pounds, but many 4- to 8-pound fish are caught each year. Some brookies in the 5-pound range have been caught here. And the lakes provide unequaled opportunities to catch trophy trout in a magnificent alpine setting. The lakes range in size from 4 to 80 acres, with high glacial lakes that require a hike and man-made lakes you can drive right up to and launch a boat (provided by ranch) or float-tube. Adams, Bartlett, and Munn Lakes are the most popular, but large fish are caught in all the lakes. It doesn't matter where you fish because there are never crowds; you'll likely be alone.

The lower man-made lakes have the usual smorgasbord of aquatic bugs. From late June through mid-August damsels and caddis are prevalent, but there are great Callibaetis hatches, too. Ants, beetles, termites, and even hoppers can be found around some of the lakes. Of course, midges are always present and important, especially in May and late August. While late May weather may be unpredictable, lake fishing is superb with subsurface patterns like damsels and Woolly Buggers.

Float-tubers will find Vermejo a stillwater paradise. All the lakes are large enough to float-tube and all have a good variety of structure to fish around. There are weed beds, shelves, deadfall trees and brush, inlets, outlets, and coves, and early in the year there can be backwaters where rising lake levels move into vegetation, logjams, and forested areas.

For anglers who prefer moving water, some 30 to 40 miles of small to medium-sized streams traverse Vermejo. Plentiful populations of brook, rainbow, and cutthroat trout inhabit these waters, providing unsurpassed enjoyment for the beginner and experienced angler alike.

The Rio Costilla has two forks that feed Costilla Reservoir, known as Rio Costilla #1 and #2. Both tributaries are small and have excellent habitat for tons of small trout. Some parts are brushy, but there are many open meadows where casting is easy. Vermejo's streams offer some of the last remaining refuges for the Rio Grande cutthroat. An ongoing project is underway to continue expanding the habitat for these rare cutthroat trout so that this species will forever prosper.

Rio Costilla #1 has a man-made barrier that prevents non-native trout from coming upstream. Fairly pure Rio Grande cutthroats thrive above the barrier, while cuttbows swim below it. Rio Costilla #2 has cutts and some nice brook trout. Both tributaries have the potential to produce big fish near their inlets to Costilla Reservoir.

There is a brand new 5-star Silver Leed Certified lodge near the reservoir called Costilla Lodge for anglers looking to fish the creeks. It's more removed and quiet than the main lodge and few guests fish the streams, so you probably won't see anyone else on the stream, especially during the week. The lodge has 8 rooms with double queen beds and sleeps up to 16 people.

The Vermejo River is also an excellent stream on Vermejo Park, and it's a little larger than the Costilla. It has 15 to 20 miles of fishable water, much of it running through meadows, although some of it is very brushy. Several headwater tributaries also offer splendid dry-fly fishing and magnificent mountain scenery. The Vermejo River has brookies and native Rio Grande cutthroats.

On all the streams in Vermejo, regular hatches of stoneflies, caddis, and mayflies from late June through July send trout into feeding frenzies. August sees more mayfly hatches and caddis begin tapering off, but hoppers are present into September. Except during heavy rainstorms, which can cause the streams to get murky, attractors like Stimulators, Humpies, H&L Variants, Royal Wulffs, and Parachute Hoppers will produce trout all day long. It's not uncommon for a good angler to catch and release over 50 trout a day here, all on dries. The ranch's fishing season runs from late May to mid-September. Optimum stream flows usually start in late June or early July.

Guides are not required to fish on Vermejo Park, but if it's your first visit it might be a good idea to get one so you can quickly learn the best methods and places to fish while you're there. The ranch is enormous, and just getting to know a small part of it requires a few days. Once you go to Vermejo, it's a given that you'll want to return again and again.

Current Vermejo Park Fishing Rates

Headquarters
- $550 per person per day (includes room and board, fishing, horseback riding, skeet, sporting clays, boat and trolling motor - guides are extra, see below).
- Children 6 to 12: $175 per day.

Costilla Lodge
- $6,900 per day for groups up to 12 people, each additional person is an additional $575 (includes room & board, fishing, horseback riding, skeet, sporting clays, boat and trolling motor). Guides are extra.

Guides
- $425 per day (full day only).

Vehicle Rental
- $275 per day.
- Call 575-445-3097 for reservations
- Vermejo Park, P.O. Drawer E, Raton, New Mexico 87740; 505-445-2718, www.vermejo.com

CULEBRA CREEK AND THE TRINCHERA RANCH

Culebra Creek and the Trinchera Ranch are actually located just over the New Mexico border in south-central Colorado, but in recent years they have become important fisheries for visitors and residents in the vicinity of Taos, New Mexico.

The Culebra is located just across the border, about an hour north of Taos, and offers excellent flyfishing for large rainbows and browns in a valley surrounded by 14,000-foot peaks.

The Blanca Peaks are the most impressive, and they are just part of the vast Trinchera Ranch (formerly Forbes Trinchera Ranch). Individuals, corporate groups, family groups, flyfishing clubs, or just a group of fishing buddies are all at home at the ranch, which offers accommodations with all the amenities and access to more high mountain streams than you can possibly shake a stick (fly rod) at. Many of my clients and members of my private flyfishing club stay at the Trinchera Ranch and fish both the ranch and other club waters including Culebra Creek, which is just 20 minutes from the lodge.

Culebra Creek

Culebra (Snake) Creek is a medium-sized tailwater stream located just across the northern New Mexico border, in the southern end of the spacious San Luis Valley of Colorado. Many anglers come to Taos just to fish this little jewel, knowing they will have an opportunity to catch large trout on a fly in a relatively small stream without competition from other anglers. The entire stream is private, from its headwaters to

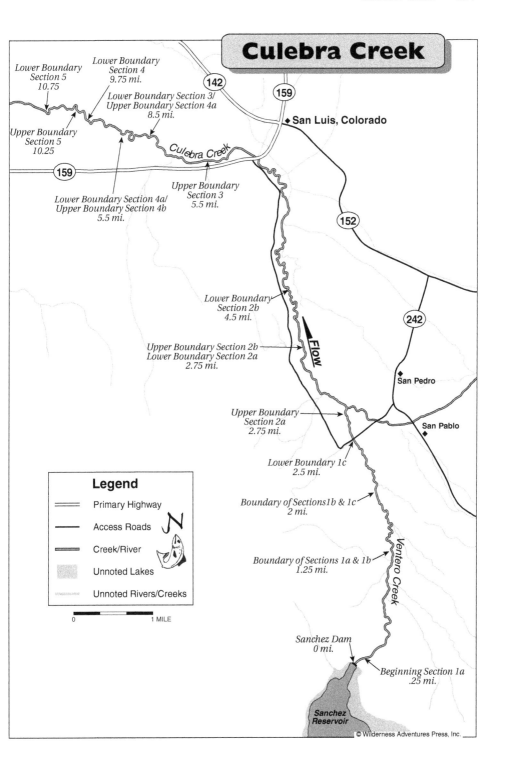

where it dries up in the sagebrush prairie. Most of the headwaters run through a huge private ranch in the Sangre de Cristo Mountains that is closed to the public. The lower Culebra below Sanchez Reservoir flows through about 12 miles of private pastureland in the San Luis Valley. About 10 miles of it is available to the public for a fee through my company, The Solitary Angler, located in Taos, New Mexico.

The first time I fished the Culebra I asked a rancher for permission to fish on his land. I drove my girlfriend, mother, and father down the rancher's rugged dirt road to the edge of the stream. The water was high and a little murky, and my dad wasn't too sure about it all, but we decided to give it a try anyway. Looking at the small size of the creek I reasoned that my 7½-foot, 2-weight Sage Light-Line rod would be a perfect match.

I decided to start with nymphs, as I usually do on a new stream unless I see a good hatch and fish rising. I tied on some 5X tippet and two old stand-bys—a Double Hackle Peacock on top and a Hare's Ear Nymph on the bottom—and twisted on some lead just above my top fly. For a depth indicator I rolled on a small piece of foam tape about 5 feet above the lead. After rigging my mother's rod with a black Woolly Bugger, we dropped her off with her chair and a good book in a deep hole near the car, then walked about a half-mile downstream to fish our way back up.

The first hole I came to was 4 or 5 feet deep on a nice bend about 50 feet long. The outside bank along the bend was covered with overhanging alders and willows whose branches and roots extending several feet over and into the river. The top of the bend was open, and a nice broad riffle dropped into the head of the pool where an old truck tire was lodged in a ball of roots and branches. The riffle tapered into the bend, funneling into a foam line along the edge of the brush. This was perfect brown trout water, and I knew there had to be at least a 16-inch trophy in there.

I started from the bottom, methodically hi-sticking the entire hole, with emphasis on the foam line. Cast after cast I anticipated a strike that didn't come. Finally, near the top of the run, my drift abruptly stopped and I set the hook, but it turned out to be the tire. I got it loose and tried again, and again my drift stopped and I set the hook. But nothing moved so I started jerking, trying to pull the fly free. After a couple of jerks with the light rod a half decomposed rainbow about 10 inches long came floating to the top. I thought, "What the hell is that?"

I lifted my rod tip, assuming I must have hooked an old snag that a fish had used to wrap up a previous angler's line. I could feel a strong vibration, so I yelled to my girlfriend "Look! I've got a big one!"

She looked up and said, "Right," and about that time my snag started moving downstream. All I could see was a brown tail about 6 inches wide, so I shouted, "No shit, I'm not kidding!" For the next 20 minutes I wrestled the giant brown, keeping him on a short leash with my rod bent over double, just like walking a big dog. Every time he moved downstream, I'd run down below him, keeping him facing upstream as much as possible. I did this pool after pool for about a quarter-mile before coming to a fence across the river, where I couldn't go any farther.

Luckily, he was getting tired, so I started forcing the big buck to the edge. I was able to slide him over a shallow sandbar into a small puddle about a foot deep, where I tackled the 29-inch beast. He had taken the old reliable Double Hackle Peacock. I was shaking and soaking wet as my girlfriend snapped off a couple of photos with my father watching. The 9-pound leviathan was at least 2 pounds heavier than my father's largest brown ever and 3 pounds heavier than my personal best. I took my time reviving the monster, and as he swam back into a deep undercut, I said to my dad, "I hope he finds another 10-inch rainbow to eat tonight, he needs it after that."

This was my first fish from the Culebra, and to this day, it's the largest brown I've ever caught. We proceeded to catch about 15 more browns that day over 16 inches. Many of them were caught on dries after the sun went down and caddis started hatching. On our return to the car my mother said that the largest fish she'd ever seen took her Woolly Bugger and snapped her off soon after we left. It was truly the best day of fishing I'd ever had, catching my record brown while fishing with my favorite fishing partner, Dad.

After about 3 years of keeping the Culebra to myself, one of the landowners, knowing I was a flyfishing outfitter and fly shop owner, asked me if I wanted to lease his water. Of course I did. He introduced me to the other landowners, and within a couple of years I had leased most of the lower Culebra. I was fortunate enough to purchase one of the properties in 2005. Currently, I own a couple of miles and lease over 8 miles of the magnificent tailwater. It's divided into ten sections and only one group of one to three anglers per day can fish each section. Each stretch receives at least two days of rest per week.

The beautiful scenery and water, open banks, and privacy are reason enough to fish the Culebra, but what sets the stream apart from other fisheries in the region is the average size of the trout. It's managed as a catch-and-release, flyfishing-only fishery so trout can grow to maximum size. There are wild browns and cuttbows and some stocked rainbows that average 14 to 18 inches, with some to 24 inches and occasional lunkers larger than that. Just below the dam are some wild brookies that average 8 to 12 inches, but I've

The author with a nice brown from Section 1-B on the upper Culebra.

caught them up to 18 inches. The growth rate is astonishing for such a small stream, due in part to the rich water flowing from the bottom of reservoir.

The Culebra exists because of the Sanchez Reservoir and Dam, constructed over 100 years ago without machinery, which provides much needed water for the ranchers that settled in the lower part of the Culebra Valley. Since the dam's completion, the Culebra has been a non-tributary of the Rio Grande because virtually all the water rights are granted and used up or stored by users in the valley before it runs into the Rio Grande. The good news is that the majority of the users are downstream of where the best fishing is.

From mid-April through mid-October the San Luis Ditch Company runs water for downstream irrigators. Sometimes it's high, up to the banks, and in between cuttings of alfalfa and hay—mid- to late July—they turn it down low. But usually it's just about right. During high flows the upper three sections fish better, and the lower three sections get a little murky. During low flows the upper three sections are tough to fish because the trout are spooky, while the lower three sections have good-flowing, clear water and excellent fishing. Section 2, in the middle, is referred to as the neutral zone because it tends to fish well at all levels.

They turn the river off after irrigation season, and the only water source is from leaks and springs that emanate from the base of the dam. A couple of small tributaries add some water just downstream, and about 3 miles below the dam (on Section 2), the main Culebra joins the creek, adding significant flow. Two other tributaries add more water near the town of San Luis, about 8 miles below the dam. During the winter

Another hefty brown caught in Section 5 on the lower creek.

months, the first three sections below the dam provide some great midge fishing, except when temperatures drop below zero for too long.

Pant or chest waders are recommended when water is running, but when it's shut off hip waders are sufficient. The river bottom ranges from sand, silt, and clay in Section 1-A to small pebbles, bedrock, and small boulders in the other sections. During summer and fall the weeds can be quite thick, particularly close to the dam, where the Culebra is like a spring creek.

The creek is 20 to 40 feet wide when it's running and about 10 to 20 feet wide when shut off. As its name suggests, the Culebra snakes its way through pastures in the upper sections and willows, cottonwoods, and alders in the lower sections before disappearing into a series irrigation ditches and stabilization reservoirs. There are many deep holes and undercut banks near the bends and several nice, shallow riffles that drop into long, deep pools. Submerged snags, bushes, and boulders provide excellent winter habitat for large trout, and gravel bars at the base of the pools are well suited for spawning trout.

While grazing has caused erosion on some of the streambanks, most are in good shape and others are being rehabilitated with help from the landowners. Prescription and reduced grazing techniques and riparian fencing are already helping to rejuvenate damaged streambanks. Current and future plantings of willows, alders, and cottonwoods will further enhance this quality fishery.

I stopped grazing my property in 2005 and started rehabilitating it. Within a year I had a much healthier riparian zone, and with willows and cottonwoods now taking hold, I have narrowed and deepened the channel and created more overhang and undercutting of banks. All this helps keep the water cooler, provides wind protection and produces more terrestrials for trout thus improving the dry-fly fishing considerably.

I recommend an 8- to 9-foot, 4- or 5-weight rod that can delicately handle the large trout on fine tippet, yet "horse" and turn a fish when necessary. There isn't enough room to let a fish run without losing it so you must keep it on a short line, steering it where you want it to go until it begins to tire out. If the fish runs downstream you have to go with it. Landing these large fish in such a small stream is what fishing the Culebra is all about.

The same cool, rich water that enables trout to stay active 12 months a year also provides a rich aquatic diet year-round. Spring starts the season with a fading midge hatch and a building Blue-Winged Olive hatch. This is a good time for dry-fly fishing on all sections, especially when Baetis are on the water. Large trout can be found sipping insects in the foam lines of pools, riffles, and back eddies. I match them with a BWO parachute or hair-wing imitation on a size 18 to 20 hook. If they refuse it, I switch to a Lawson's No-Hackle in the same size.

By the time the water goes up in May the big browns and cuttbows are already gorging on the ever-abundant cranefly larvae, perhaps the most important food source in the lower sections. The larvae live on and under rocks and are in a constant state of drift, especially when flows are high. It's not uncommon to see huge trout at the heads of deep holes flashing as they feed on drifting and swimming craneflies, some as big as your pinky.

Traditional cranefly patterns work, but I prefer a dark gray Bunny Leech because of its swimming action. I use a hi-stick technique so I can hold the fly up on the shelves and then let it drop off into the holes as it drifts downstream. Sometimes I give it a slight jigging action as it drifts, mimicking the swimming larvae. Another good imitation is Taylor Streit's Poundmeister, which many local anglers use. (Taylor is a famous flyfishing outfitter, guide, and fly tier based in Taos.) Craneflies are good producers through September.

By June, small Golden Stoneflies and caddis are in full swing, and fish will come to the top for them. Trailing a small beadhead stonefly nymph, size 14 to 16, underneath a Stimulator of the same size works best during the day when stoneflies are on the water. If they aren't, a double-nymph rig with a stonefly on top and a small caddis larva or dark Hare's Ear on the bottom will generally produce some nice fish.

Over 80 percent of a trout's diet is under the surface on this stream, but during the peak of a good hatch fish will rise consistently. Fishing a large dry can usually produce some strikes any time there is good flow. Evening caddis hatches can bring some great fish to the surface once the sun leaves the water. The strikes are usually vicious and unmistakable, and the fat browns tend to jump a lot, despite their reputation for heading deep.

August Trico hatches also provide challenging dry-fly opportunities, but you have to be on the water early to find trout rising to them. Nymphing is usually better, although rises can be found if the river is low enough to have foam lines. At these times, a black and gray thorax-style mayfly, black parachute, or black spent-wing spinner pattern, size 20 to 24, would be a good choice.

Most fish in the Culebra are caught on small nymphs like dark Flashback Hare's Ears, Pheasant Tails, and micro-mayflies, size 16 to 20, and red or green midge larvae, dark midge pupae, and emergers, size 18 to 24. Of course, San Juan Worms, Orange and Olive Scuds, micro-eggs, and Woolly Buggers are all good producers, especially during high flows.

After they turn the water off in the fall, Baetis start hatching and continue through November some years. This can be fun fishing. The low water, small flies, fine tippet, good hatches, and large fish feeding on top combine for a memorable day. Small pods of 16- to 20-inch trout can be found in the riffles and foam lines, sipping on the conveyor belt of emerging Blue-Winged Olives drifting endlessly down the river.

Of course, not every day is like this, but there are enough to make going to the Culebra well worth it. The worst thing that could happen is that you'd have to drift a dry-dropper or nymph instead. The fish are there and they eat every day. It's just a matter of whether they are rising or not. If the winds are light or it's calm, there will usually be a hatch and rising fish at some point in the day. Add some clouds and it could be one of those great days.

Match the Baetis with an Olive Parachute with blue dun hackle, size 18 to 22, and start with 5X tippet. If you're putting fish down despite good drifts, go to 6X or 7X and use fluorocarbon material, if possible. Don't cast blind; wait until you spot a rising fish then carefully pull out the right amount of line and false cast away from the water until your delivery cast. Try to make the fly land no more than a foot above the sipping trout, right in its feeding lane.

Winter brings the midges out. Now we're talking small flies, low, cold water, and spooky trout. Only the top three sections are fishable in most years, but during mild winters like we've had the last few years all the sections can be good. I use a 10- to 12-foot, 6X leader with a double-nymph rig. I put a red or green midge larva, size 18 to 22, on top and a tiny beadhead midge pupa, size 20 to 24, on the bottom, with a very small poly-yarn strike indicator about 2 or 3 feet above the top fly. I sneak up to the bottom of the pool where several trout tend to stack during low winter flows. One or two casts are all you get before spooking every fish in the pool, so make the first one count. Gently set the hook on the slightest bump and get your slack up quickly once the trout is hooked.

To fish the Culebra, you must hire a guide and pay a rod fee through The Solitary Angler, or you must be a member (or a member's guest) of the Solitary Angling Club. Most visiting anglers hire a guide because they are only fishing for a day or two and were going to hire a guide anyway, so the extra rod fee for exclusive rights to fish their own "beat" on a blue-ribbon stream is fine with them. Those that return to fish more often because they can't get enough of it sometimes end up getting a membership to the club, which allows them and their guests to fish all the waters I lease as often as they like. For details on the club and the fishing go to www.thesolitaryangler.com.

Beautiful but small Culebra Creek turns out some enormous trout.

CULEBRA CREEK MAJOR HATCHES

Insect	J	F	M	A	M	J	J	A	S	O	N	D	Time	Flies
Caddis						■	■	■	■				M/A/E	Green & olive caddis larva #12–#16; Double Hackle Peacock #12–#16; Van's Rag Pupa or LaFontaine's Pupa #10–#18; green or dark olive Green Weenie #12–#18; olive, tan & gray Elk Hair Caddis #12–#20; olive, gray & peacock Fluttering Caddis #10–#18
Craneflies						■	■	■	■				M/A/E	Cranefly larva peacock, gray or dark olive #6–#16; Taylor Streit's Poundmeister #6–#14; Double Hackle Peacock #6–#16; Foam Body Cranefly #6–#16
Midges	■	■	■	■	■	■	■	■	■	■	■	■	M/E	Red & olive midge larva #16–#20; olive, gray, black and zebra midge pupa #18–#24; Pheasant Tail #16–#22; Disco Midge #18–#24; Mating Midge #14–#20; black & gray Midge Clusters #10–#16; Griffith's Gnat #16–#22; Snowfly #16–#26
Ginger, Gray, Yellow & Mahogany Duns					■	■							M/E/SF	Light, dark & olive Hare's Ear Nymph #10–#18; Pheasant Tail Nymph #12–#18; light, dark, pink & ginger PW or Hair-Wing Duns or Cahills #12–#18 or the same in parachutes; Ginger, Red & Blue Quills #12–#18
Baetis				■	■					■	■		M/A/SF	Dark olive Hare's Ear Nymph #16–#22; Pheasant Tail #16–#22; Van's Rag Fly Nymph #16–#22; Lawson's Olive Fan-Wing Emerger #16–#22 Olive Parachute #16–#22; Olive Comparadun #16–#22

Hatch Time Code: M = Morning; A = Afternoon; E = Evening; D = Dark; SF = Spinner Fall

CULEBRA CREEK MAJOR HATCHES (cont.)

Insect	J	F	M	A	M	J	J	A	S	O	N	D	Time	Flies
Golden Stonefly, Yellow Sally							▉	▉					M/A	Black & brown stonefly nymph #4–#10; Golden Stone Nymph #10–#14; Elk Hair Salmonfly #4–#8; Orange & Gold Stimulators #4–#14; Terminator #12–#16
PMDs, PEDs					▉	▉							M/SF	Light Hare's Ear Nymph #12–#18; Pheasant Tail #12–#20; Van's Rag Fly Nymph light olive #14–#20; Hair-Wing, PW or Para Ginger or Light Olive Dun #14–#20
Terrestrials					▉	▉	▉	▉	▉				M/A	Para-hoppers tan, yellow #8–#14; red w/ black underwing Desert Hopper #6–#14 Bees #12–#14; Elk Hair Aquatic Moths #8–#14; beetles & ants #12–#18
Scuds	▉	▉	▉	▉	▉	▉	▉	▉	▉	▉	▉	▉	M/E	Orange, ginger & olive scuds #14–#16
Minnows	▉	▉	▉	▉	▉	▉	▉	▉	▉	▉	▉	▉	M/E	Assorted colors of Soft-Hackle Streamers, Woolly Buggers #2–#12

Hatch Time Code: M = Morning; A = Afternoon; E = Evening; D = Dark; SF = Spinner Fall

Stream Facts: Culebra Creek

Season
- Year-round.

Special Regulations
- Catch-and-release, flyfishing-only water, with only single barbless hooks allowed.
-      Guests must accompany a guide from the Solitary Angler or a Member of the Solitary Angling Club to fish .

Rates
- Guide $350 per day – 2 people per guide (plus rod fee)
- Rod fee per day - $75 per person
- Membership to the Solitary Angling Club – Contact Solitary Angler 1-866-502-1700 or www.thesolitaryangler.com

Trout
- Wild browns, cuttbows, and stocked rainbows that average 14 to 18 inches, some to 24, a few larger; brook trout 8 to 12 inches, some to 18 inches and now, Rio Grande cutthroat trout.

River Characteristics
- Medium-sized tailwater flowing from the bottom of Sanchez Reservoir. The first 2 miles are much like a spring creek, while the lower sections have more water with freestone characteristics. The entire river has riffles, pools, deep holes, and seriously undercut banks.

River Flows
- Winter, early spring, and late fall: 18 to 35 cfs
- Late spring through mid-fall: 35 to 120 cfs, with an average flow of 60 to 90 cfs

Maps
- *Colorado Atlas & Gazetteer,* page 91; USGS Quadrangle Maps: Sanchez Reservoir, San Luis

Outfitters
- The Solitary Angler, 204B North Pueblo Road, Taos, NM 87529; 1-866-502-1700, www.thesolitaryangler.com

The Trinchera Ranch

The magnificent Trinchera Ranch sprawls over 180,000 acres of some of the most spectacular mountains in the Rockies. It's the largest ranch in Colorado. Part of the enchanting Sangre de Cristo Range, the ranch varies in elevation from the valley at 8,000 feet to the top of several peaks above 14,000 feet, including Blanca Peak, the second highest in Colorado.

Three major watersheds with over 80 miles of streams and creeks combined with several ponds and a couple of high-country glacier lakes provide anglers the opportunity to explore and flyfish unspoiled and pristine waters. It's possible to catch wild browns, rainbows, brookies, and a pure strain of Rio Grande cutthroats, as well as cuttbows, without ever tying on a nymph or matching a hatch. Herds of elk, deer, and bighorn sheep also share the 250 square miles of this private paradise in the Rockies.

Acquired by Malcolm Forbes in 1969, the ranch was a place where he could savor the tranquil, wide-open spaces. He loved sharing the ranch with everyone from heads of state to motorcyclists to the captains of industry regularly chronicled in *Forbes* magazine. His children expanded on this tradition, and made the ranch available for selected groups from June through August and for hunters September through April.

In 2008 the Forbes family sold the ranch and the new owner is a bow hunter and environmentalist with an interest in rehabilitating the streams and wildlife habitat. Most of the ranch is in fine shape already and it won't take a lot to make the fisheries better. My company, The Solitary Angler, Inc. is working closely with the management and we are currently providing their commercial guide service and much of their angling clientele. Mostly, the streams just need to be pruned back in areas to make them more fishable.

The Trinchera Ranch is one of the most beautiful spreads in the country.

Headquarters, including the main lodge and state-of-the-art conference facilities, are situated in the Trinchera Valley. The lodge itself originally had only a few rooms but now up to 50 guests can be accommodated in 25 bedrooms and suites. It is specially suited for corporate groups, clubs and organizations, family reunions or just a couple of guys wanting to fish for a few days.

Activities are tailored to individual groups. Over the years, men and women have come to fish, hunt, skeet-shoot, hike, game-spot, and horseback ride. When I first started guiding on the ranch back in 1986, hardly anyone was staying there or fishing. The lodge was brand new and much smaller, and the angling groups that my partner, Jack Woolley, and I brought were usually the only ones there. At the time, they had plenty of customers for their hunts, but they were looking to start expanding into fishing during the summer months. It was like having your own lodge and hundreds of square miles of wilderness all to yourself. Even though the lodge has grown since then, it still feels that way today and usually, we're still the only ones there.

Dry-fly fishing on the crystal-clear creeks and streams of the ranch is nothing short of spectacular. All the trout in the streams are wild and colorful, although a large fish is 16 inches. It's not uncommon for even an inexperienced angler to land over 30 trout a day, and I've seen days when virtually every cast produced a strike. It can get ridiculous. Even avid anglers like fishing here at least once, just to experience what it must have been like before major angling pressure came to virtually every part of the West.

It's the perfect place for families, clubs, and corporate groups because everyone has success, especially if they pay attention to the experienced guide/instructor helping them. Most of the groups we take usually consist of beginner to novice anglers, and the guide's help ensures a great time and a successful trip. For those in

This is one of the last strongholds for pure Rio Grande cutthroat trout.

the group that don't fish, there are plenty of other activities to enjoy, including just kicking back and taking in the dramatic scenery that surrounds the lodge.

There are three main streams, each with its own unique qualities. All the headwaters and most of the main stem of each are within the boundaries of the ranch since it extends from the tops of the peaks to the bottoms of the valleys. There are hatches of caddis, mayflies, and midges, but the fish are opportunists and will usually eat any buggy-looking fly. Morning water temperatures can be quite cool, so fishing is usually best from midmorning through sundown, particularly on Ute Creek, which heads way up on the Blanca peaks. All three streams have good access via dirt roads or, in the case of Sangre de Cristo Creek, a highway. A guide is invaluable and required just to get you around the massive ranch.

You'll need a short, light rod for the streams and a 9-foot, 5-weight rod for the lakes. The streams are small, and rarely will you have to wade over your knees. Hip waders are all you'll need.

Trinchera Creek

Trinchera Creek is the southernmost stream on the ranch, originating at the base of Trinchera Peak and two other peaks. It flows down through the mountains into the Trinchera Valley right next to Forbes Trinchera Lodge and finally into Mountain Home Reservoir. In its lower reaches it's about 10 to 20 feet wide, winding through a combination of pastures and willows.

From just above the lodge downstream to Mountain Home Reservoir there are browns, rainbows, cuttbows, and brookies averaging 8 to 12 inches, some larger. A few miles above the lodge a diversion dam creates a barrier so non-native fish can't get upstream to where there is a fairly pure strain of Rio Grande cutthroats. From the barrier to the reservoir the creek has been channelized and dikes put up so the new owner is in the process of completely rehabilitating it. Once complete it will likely offer some of the finest fishing on the ranch. In the 1980s and '90s the ranch and Colorado Division of Wildlife attempted to eradicate brook trout and other non-native trout from the upper Trinchera with some degree of success. The catch rate dropped drastically, since the majority of fish were brookies, but the upper Trinchera is on the road to recovery. Angling for Rio Grande cutthroats is improving every year.

The creek splits into two forks at the top of the Trinchera Valley, and the grade becomes steep and the creeks narrow and brushy, making flyfishing difficult. The main Trinchera opens up into a meadow near the top, and I've caught some cutthroats up to 18 inches here.

Sangre de Cristo Creek

Sangre de Cristo Creek is a beautiful flyfishing stream in its lower reaches, where it meanders through stands of willows that form nice pools with undercut banks. This is prime habitat for cutthroat trout and beavers, both of which are abundant. Beaver ponds are scattered throughout the valley. There are mostly pure Rio Grande cutthroats in the creek, and I've caught them up to 16 inches, although they average 8 to 12 inches. The Colorado Division of Wildlife actually used the cutts from the headwaters of this creek to repopulate several other streams in the Rio Grande watershed. A few years ago there was a fire in the upper water shed followed by a flash flood that caused significant mortality. Small creeks like it usually bounce back quickly and already we are seeing many juvenile and some mature trout.

Despite its great fishing, few guest ever fish here because US 160 runs right next to the creek, detracting from the unspoiled and pristine nature of the rest of the ranch.

Upstream, the creek splits at the top of the valley. The main creek is followed by the highway, while Placer Creek heads north toward Iron Mountain. Placer offers excellent flyfishing for small cutthroats. It's only 3 or 4 feet wide in most places, but it slowly meanders through spotty meadows broken up by alders and willows. The open areas are fishable, and there are some deep little holes and undercut banks. It's easy to sneak up and spot the cutts before dabbling your fly in the water just above and then watching them slowly rise and gulp it down.

Ute Creek

Ute Creek's icy water flows out of the extremely high Blanca peaks, which make up the northern part of the ranch. This small freestone stream is the epitome of high-country flyfishing. The lower reaches run across a broad valley, meandering through cottonwoods, willows, and alders combined with open pastures. Jagged peaks tower overhead. The headwaters tumble down the steep side canyons, draining off the peaks and holding unbelievable numbers of trout.

The lower Ute is a delight to fish. The riffles, pools, pockets, and holes are broken by stretches of fast, shallow water. The water is very clear, and you can often spot the larger cuttbows and cast directly to them, reducing the risk of hooking a small brookie first. The cuttbows can get quite big—up to 18 inches—for such a cold stream with a short growing season. In between the big cuttbows, the Ute is filthy with 6- to 10-inch brookies and smaller cuttbows.

The water is usually very cold even in July and August, so the fishing doesn't get good until the sun has been up for awhile. Its heat brings fish out from their sheltering lies to warm their lethargic bodies and eat some food. Almost any good attractor will work, but if I get refusals I sometimes switch around until I find one they can't resist—or the one they won't hit. If you have a fly they like, the fish will move several feet to get it. This is visual fishing, watching trout feeding and then moving to your fly and devouring it. They can be spooky in low water years, necessitating more stealth and longer, more delicate casts. It's amazing how quickly a pool full of fish can suddenly seem barren when you aren't careful in your approach.

The upper Ute has two branches, and the Little Ute (also known as the West Fork) is the primary fishery. It's one of the most beautiful places I've ever fished. Tumbling down a steep canyon between Mount Blanca (14,345 feet) and Mount Lindsay (14,042 feet), the Little Ute heads at the Winchell Lakes, a couple of glacier lakes at the base of Mount Blanca. From its confluence with Ute Creek upstream for 3 miles the creek is very brushy, with continuous gin-clear pockets and small pools loaded with 6- to 10-inch brookies, some to 14 inches. A short, light rod with a short leader is in order here, and the best technique for plucking brookies out of the protective, boulder-strewn pockets is just dabbling as you work upstream.

After this 3-mile stretch the grade becomes significantly steeper, and there are many deep plunge pools and several waterfalls that prevent the brookies from moving upstream. This stretch is known as the Falls, and has pure native Rio Grande cutthroats. A look into the deep pools at the base of the falls will reveal several brilliantly colored cutts from 8 to 14 inches. The water is so clear that the trout appear to be suspended in air, and you can see the spots and every other detail on them, not just a flash or a shadow.

Although fun to catch, the cutts don't fight very well this high up, where the water is cold and the season short. The water is so clean that it isn't nutrient-rich, but there is enough food present, and fish eat anything they can get their mouths on. One good cast is all it takes; after that, they spook and it's off to the next pool. Everyone I've ever taken to the Falls has told me it's one of the finest outdoor experiences they've ever had.

Stillwaters

In addition to the splendid stream fishing on the ranch, there are some fine stillwaters to explore. Several man-made ponds have wild and stocked trout for anglers looking for some larger fish. Most are small enough that they can be effectively fished from shore with a 9-foot rod.

The usual stillwater flies work well here, and the fisheries get so little pressure that unless you're using midges you can get away with 3X or 4X tippet. I like to strip damsel nymphs unless fish are rising. If fish are on top, they're probably feeding on morning Callibaetis or evening midges. Watch cruisers working the banks for duns, then cast your fly in their path and wait for a fish to see it. Look for the slow gulp before setting the hook.

Ranch Facts: Trinchera Ranch

Availability

- The Trinchera Ranch is available for reservations from just after run-off, usually early June through October.

Reservations

- Reservations can be made by contacting the Solitary Angler at 1-866-502-1700 or www.thesolitaryangler.com.
- Day-use-only available with a guide from the Solitary Angler

Special Regulations

- Catch and release on all streams except that you may keep brook trout if you want to eat them for dinner or breakfast.

Trout

- Brook, brown, rainbow, cuttbow, and Rio Grande cutthroat trout.

Rates
- Trinchera Lodge - $250. per person per day (includes deluxe rooms and all meals)
- Guide and Rod Fee (two anglers per guide) - 1 angler $425 per day; 2 anglers $550 per day

- Call or email for information on group or multi-day rates or to make reservations

Location
- Alamosa Airport is a 45-minute drive from the ranch, Colorado Springs is two and a half hours, and Pueblo two hours. (Alamosa can handle all private planes up to and including a Boeing 727. There is regular commercial service via Denver on United Express, and helicopters are more than welcome on Trinchera itself.) The Trinchera staff will pick you up from Alamosa Airport. The easiest way to get there is to call 719-379-3263 and allow the staff to arrange the best way for you.
- If you'd like to know more about Trinchera, contact the Solitary Angler, 204B North Pueblo Road, Taos, NM 87529; 1-866-502-1700, www.thesolitaryangler.com

Maps
- *Colorado Atlas & Gazetteer*, pages 81, 82, 91, 92; USGS Quadrangle Maps: Ft. Garland, Trinchera Ranch, Twin Peaks, Blanca Peak, Russell, La Veta Pass

Outfitters
- The Solitary Angler, 204B North Pueblo Road, Taos, NM 87529; 1-866-502-1700, www.thesolitaryangler.com

CIMARRON RIVER—THE HOLY WATER

The Holy Water includes the first two-thirds mile of the Cimarron River below Eagle Nest Dam, and it's owned by the C. S. Cattle Company, the former owners of Eagle Nest Lake. The C. S. Ranch is one of the largest working ranches in America, and it's been in the same family for at least four generations. (See the Cimarron River on page 222 in the Northeast Region for a map and information on fishing the rest of the river.)

The Holy Water is enriched with nutrients from the bottom of the lake. Resembling a spring creek, the riverbed is full of weeds that harbor scuds, snails, water boatmen, midges, and a variety of mayflies, micro-caddis, and small stoneflies. Suckers, chubs, and other fish in Eagle Nest Lake also get sucked through the gate, and they are flushed into the stilling basin just below the dam, where they become food for large browns (over 20 inches).

The top end of the Holy Water has broad riffles, large pools, undercut banks, and channels, while the bottom third is mostly composed of abandoned beaver ponds with plenty of structure and nice riffles at the inlets. The browns and rainbows that inhabit this stretch of water are larger, partly due to the richer water but mostly because it's managed as a catch-and-release fishery. In fact, the Holy Water used to be, without a doubt, the best two-thirds mile of brown trout fly water in the state. Unfortunately, after the recent drought, leaks in the dam were fixed and a stopper on the valve (that kept 2.5 cfs flowing all the time) was removed. Now the state shuts the river off at the dam all winter long. This has drastically affected this stretch, although it is still far better than the public water, partly because fish from downstream move in each spring, once the water is turned back up.

In the spring, the state increases the flow coming out of the bottom of Eagle Nest Lake as downstream users call for water, and the initial surge wakes the trout up and dislodges scuds and nymphs for the ravenous fish to fatten up on. A Ginger or Olive Scud, size 14 to 18, and a dark Flashback Hare's Ear, size 16 to 20, are guaranteed to produce some nice trout during the first month or two after the gates open up.

By mid-May hatches are heavy, with PMDs in the morning followed by BWOs midday and midges in the evening. My favorite dry fly at this time is a Ginger Dun, size 16 to 20. It's tied with a light tail of elk hair, a tapered ginger Hareline Dubbin body, a split and divided elk-hair wing, and a ginger hackle spun fore and aft of the wing. It's basically a Ginger Wulff. Sometimes a parachute or thorax version works better.

Move slowly when fishing the Holy Water, carefully covering all the water. There are tons of browns and a few hefty rainbows, and they can be anywhere, as you will notice when you spook them. When they're feeding you may find some large browns in unlikely shallow riffles or quiet backwaters, so be patient and observant. During a hatch browns will sometimes stack in the heads of riffles. If you play your cards right you could land several browns over 16 inches on dries.

June brings Golden Stones and caddis, as well as sporadic hatches of Western Drakes, Blue Duns, and Ginger Duns. Dry-fly fishing can be fabulous all day long, and evening frenzies are sometimes downright ridiculous, with fish rising everywhere. Even though there is only about two-thirds mile of water, two anglers would be hard pressed to fish it all when the action is good, which is most of the time.

The old beaver ponds are also chock full of browns, including some over 20 inches, but they are picky. The best time to fish them is before sunrise and after sunset or on cloudy days when the browns tend to feed more readily on the surface. Evening midge hatches can be quite heavy, and big browns will sip emergers in the surface film. Sometimes they'll take a dry, but usually a midge pupa, size 20 to 24, fished in the surface film works better. Use at least 6X (preferably fluorocarbon) and grease the tippet to within about 4 inches of the pupa. Throw it slightly above the rise and watch closely for the sip. If you can't see the fly, just set the hook if you see a rise where you think the fly is or if your leader and line tighten up. Avoid strike indicators because they tend to spook the wily browns.

Fall on the Holy Water is fabulous, as browns feed aggressively on the remaining hatches to gain mass before spawning and enduring another winter with very little water. Baetis, midges, and some caddis hatch through mid-November, when the state usually shuts the river off at the dam. Parachute Blue-Winged Olives and small Pheasant Tail Nymphs are good producers at this time, but Orange Scuds and Woolly Buggers are also top producers.

At the lower boundary of the Holy Water the Cimarron River enters Colin Neblett Wildlife Area, where it's joined by Tolby Creek, just before the US 64 crossing. Tolby Campground is located just below the bridge in the cottonwoods next to the Cimarron River. It's a nice campground with good bathrooms, and the Special Trout Water starts less than 100 yards below. There is a cabin and two bunk houses on the Holy Water available to guests of the Solitary Angler and members of the Solitary Angling Club.

To fish the Holy Water you must be a member of the Solitary Angler Club or hire a guide through The Solitary Angler in Taos.

Stream Facts: Cimarron River—The Holy Water

Season
- April through November (water flows permitting).

Special Regulations
- Catch-and-release flyfishing with single barbless hooks; must be a member of the Solitary Angling Club or hire a guide from the Solitary Angler, 204B North Pueblo Road, Taos, NM 87529; 1-866-502-1700, www.thesolitaryangler.com.

Rates
Guide and Rod Fee (two anglers per guide)
- 1 angler $425 per day   2 anglers $550 per day
- Call or email for information on group and multi-day rates or to make reservations

Cabin on the Holy Water – Reservations –
- The Solitary Angler, 204B North Pueblo Road, Taos, NM 87529; 1-866-502-1700, www.thesolitaryangler.com
- 1 or 2 people per night $125   Each additional person $50

Trout
- Wild browns in abundance and some wild rainbows that average 12 to 16 inches, some bigger.

River Characteristics
- Medium-sized tailwater below Eagle Nest Dam with spring creek–like qualities. Riffles, pools, and holes with lots of brush and a slick, rocky bottom in the upper two-thirds; beaver ponds with channels, waterfalls, and nice riffles at the inlets and outlets and a silty bottom in the lower third.

River Flows
- Late fall, winter, and early spring: 0.5 to 5 cfs
- Late spring, summer, and early fall: 10 to 90 cfs, average flow is usually between 25 and 50 cfs

Campgrounds
- Tolby Campground, located 0.2 miles below the lower Holy Water boundary

Maps
- *New Mexico Atlas & Gazetteer,* page 17; Carson National Forest Map; BLM Map: Wheeler Peak; USGS Quadrangle Maps: Eagle Nest

Outfitters
- The Solitary Angler, 204B North Pueblo Road, Taos, NM 87571; 1-866-502-1700, www.thesolitaryangler.com

The Holy Water offers perhaps the finest two-thirds mile of brown trout flyfishing in New Mexico.

There are more and larger browns here, on average, than in the Colin Neblett Wildlife Area just below.

PECOS RIVER

The Pecos is the largest and most popular stream originating in the Sangre de Cristo Mountains. It has a diverse fishery with easy access in the lower reaches, where wild brown and stocked rainbows are plentiful. In the middle reaches, narrow and deep canyons make access more difficult and wild browns more plentiful. High, rugged mountain peaks collect snow nine months out of the year, providing an ample volume of clean, clear, cold water in the headwaters, which are only accessible by hiking. The headwater lakes and streams have wild Rio Grande cutthroats in addition to wild browns and cuttbows. (See the Pecos River on page 146 in the Northeast Region for a map and information on fishing the rest of the river.)

Perhaps the best fishing on the Pecos is on the private water controlled by the High Desert Angler and the Santa Fe Flyfishers. The properties are carefully managed to provide quality flyfishing without the crowds, just minutes from Santa Fe.

High Desert Anglers' Private Water
(Contributed by Jarrett Sasser)

High Desert Angler, a leading fly shop in Santa Fe, has access to roughly 4 miles of leased water on the Pecos Rover above the town of Pecos. Made up of three separate leases, the High Desert Angler segments are available on a first-come, first-served basis, and often are booked up to a year or more in advance. It's occasionally possible to gain access on the spur of the moment during peak times, but I wouldn't count on it.

The private stretches are broken up into beats numbered 1 through 5, and anglers must be accompanied by authorized guides when fishing here. There is a maximum of two anglers per guide, and the rule is strictly enforced. A full- or half-day rate is available on all beats, as many anglers prefer to fish the public water for a half day before hitting the private water. Time on the public water allows for a more complete experience, which often includes a tour of the unique canyons.

The private stretches can offer a surprising variety of conditions and opportunities. Among the High Desert Angler beats, for example, anglers will find that while all sections offer a shot at large trout, each beat is also unique.

Some beats have ponds for practice casting, and it's possible to catch a really big rainbow. Beat #1 is fairly typical. A side channel of the river feeds the pond, so it becomes near ideal habitat for fish to grow to trophy size, sometimes exceeding 20 inches. The pond is located roughly in the middle of the beat, which allows an angler to fish the pond for a while, try his or her skills on the river, and then return to the pond. At least one of the other beats offers two ponds.

In a typical beat, anglers will find long, slow-moving runs that can be more than 2 feet deep. An accurate cast and a stealthy approach are important. With help from a guide, most fish are sighted and stalked, providing some challenging flyfishing. Elsewhere, anglers can find numerous large and small pools, long and short riffles, tailouts, pocket water of all sizes, and endless opportunities to pick up fish holding in the shallow water along the banks.

All beats have major pools, some ranging from 7 to 10 feet deep. In many of these pools, long, accurate casts are necessary to avoid spooking the big residents of the underwater structure. Depending on the time of year, stream conditions, the season, time of day, water clarity, and a variety of other things, anglers may need to adjust their offerings. One pool might be ideal for dry flies and offer lots of exciting surface action. Another may call for deep nymphing with stonefly or mayfly imitations. Or your guide may rig you with the best of both—a dry-dropper combination. Other conditions, or hatches, may call for tiny midges, either on the surface or underneath. Whatever challenge a flyfisher is seeking, it can be found in the High Desert Angler private waters of the Pecos.

All of this is just a short, beautiful drive from Santa Fe. As noted elsewhere, an angler can be on the water and fishing in less than an hour. High Desert Angler, the oldest fly shop in Santa Fe, also offers New Mexico fishing and hunting licenses, booking for the above private waters, help with accommodations, guides, and, of course, top-notch gear. Visit the High Desert Angler at 460 Cerrillos Road in Santa Fe or call 1-888-988-7688 (www.highdesertangler.com). They're a one-stop full service fly shop and guide service.

High Desert Angler has the most water under lease on the Pecos River. However, a few other outfitters also have private water. These include another fly shop in Santa Fe, and the Reel Life,. A handful of individuals have lease arrangements, too, but most of these aren't available to the public. Here's a few that are.

Pecos River Ranch

(Contributed by Norman Maktima)

As the Pecos River descends out of the coniferous forests and granite rocks of the Sangre de Cristo mountains, it begins to slow its pace and meander through sandstone canyons and hills covered with pinon and juniper trees. Most of the river here runs through private property, however Pecos River Ranch is your opportunity to experience this unique stretch of river as several guide services have leases to fish this section.

The ranch is downstream of Pecos near the Pecos/Rowe exit on I-25. It is about as far downstream as you can go and still find good trout fishing. Here you will find brown trout and rainbow trout, but don't be surprised to hook a few chubs in the process. Being a lower elevation tertiary river, the forage for trout is greatly varied.

Stoneflies, mayflies, caddis, and midges all hatch here, as well as good abundance of terrestrials. The chubs also provide a great food base for the large trout that inhabit this stretch. The quality of trout here is remarkable. They are hearty, ranging from 10 inches to over 20 inches. Most of your bigger fish inhabit the pools, while the smaller ones will occupy the riffles and pocket water.

Fly selection here is not crucial as long as you pick patterns that go along with what is hatching that time of year. The pressure is not heavy here so they are eager to eat patterns one to two sizes bigger. Nymphs, dry flies, and streamers all work of course depending on time of year and time of day.

The best times of the year to fish are in the spring just as the daytime temperatures begin to rise and before runoff begins. Also, right after runoff when the river is still flowing full. Because the river slows and is exposed to the sun, the river becomes susceptible to extreme fluctuations in temperatures especially during the summer. In the summer when the water levels drop, temperatures rise, and rainstorms muddy the river, fish become stressed and fishing slows down. However, in the fall as temperatures drop the fish rejuvenate and fishing can be awesome.

To fish this unique section of the Pecos, contact Pecos River Ranch at www.pecosriverranch.com or Pam Sawyer at 505-690-9058

The High Desert Angler, The Reel Life and other outfitters also guide there.

COW CREEK RANCH

(Contributed by Lanier Watson, owner)

Imagine sneaking away to the seclusion of a cool high mountain valley to fish an undiscovered stream surrounded by willows, lush riparian habitat and tall pines. Then imagine working your way up the riffles of a rock-bottomed mountain stream to discover deep hidden pools, one after another, thriving with trout. All this and more awaits at Cow Creek Ranch.

This historic flyfishing guest ranch in the mountains of Pecos is one and a half hours outside of Santa Fe.

Cow Creek Ranch has four and a half miles of Cow Creek and seven high mountain lakes with trophy rainbows, browns, brookies and cutthroats—all within walking distance from the lodge. A natural fishery, the private waters yield trout measuring 16 to 20 inches and occasionally more. Experienced guides offer careful instruction to guests of all skill levels.

To book a day or a week with or without a guide and for directions contact, Lanier Watson at 505-757-2107 or www.cowcreekranch.com.

PECOS NATIONAL HISTORICAL PARK

Once it was part of a large ranch called Forked Lightning, and it was owned by movie actress Greer Garson. Now it's the Pecos National Historical Park, and you—as a U.S. taxpayer—own it. Welcome to three miles of fly-fishing water that's open to the public.

Technically still called a "pilot fishing program" by the Pecos National Historical Park (PNHP) authorities, the park opened its three miles of the Pecos River to the public for fishing in 2007 after more than 20 years of being closed to anglers. The water is divided into three "beats", each about a mile in length. PNHP usually opens its stretch of water to fishing early in the season, before the river becomes swollen by

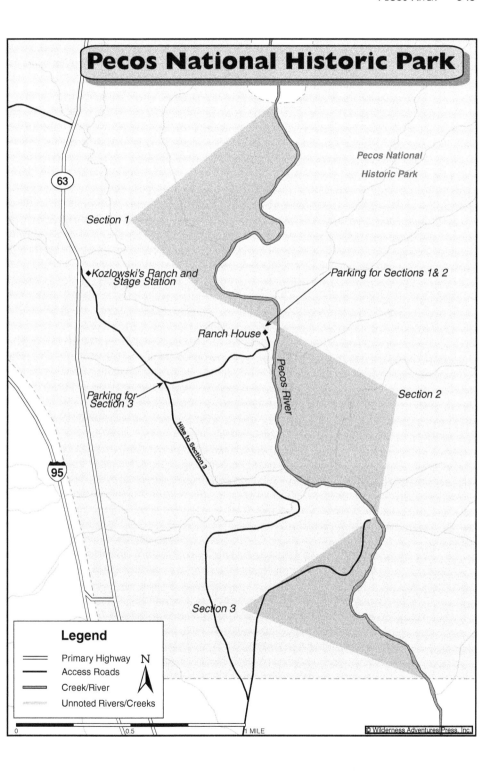

Pecos National Historic Park

Pecos National
Historic Park

63

Section 1

◆Kozlowski's Ranch and
Stage Station

Parking for Sections 1& 2

Ranch House ◆

Pecos River

Parking for
Section 3

Section 2

Hike to Section 3

Section 3

Legend

Primary Highway   N
Access Roads
Creek/River
Unnoted Rivers/Creeks

0   0.5   1 MILE

© Wilderness Adventures Press, Inc.

runoff, closes it during the runoff period, then reopens, usually in late June. It closes for the season late in October.

The headwaters of the Pecos River are high in the Sangre de Cristo mountains, approximately 25 miles north of the park. After flowing through the Village of Pecos, the river enters PNHP, where it winds through a pinion-juniper pine forest. The upper two miles form an isolated stretch of river shaded by trees and bordered by grassy banks fairly open for casting. The lower mile flows through more open country, offering braided flows, willow thickets and stands of cottonwoods.

The park's fishing program offers each angler the opportunity to make a reservation for a mile-long stretch of stream. Anglers may fish their beat alone or with up to two guests for the day. One of the three beats is reserved each day for walk-in anglers on a first-come basis. Expect to catch both rainbows and browns, usually up to about 14 inches. On rare occasions, anglers may find larger rainbows that have found their way into the park from privately stocked water.

Assuming PNHP authorities follow past practice, the river is available for fishing Thursday through Monday; the water rests Tuesday and Wednesday of each week. There is a rod fee of $35 per rod and guides are not allowed. For more information, visit www.nps.gov/peco to reserve a spot on the PNHP water, call 505-757-7272.

THE LODGE AT CHAMA

One of the premier outdoor sporting destination resorts in the country, the Lodge at Chama, formerly known as The Chama Land and Cattle Company, is a 36,000-acre ranch nestled in the magnificent San Juan Mountains of northern New Mexico. Their resource management strategies emphasize exclusivity, quality, and ecosystem stability to ensure that this unique environment is preserved for future generations. Anglers come from all over the world to enjoy this truly one-of-a-kind hideaway. (See the Rio Chama in the Northwest Region for a map and information on fishing the rest of the river.)

The ranch has earned, and maintains, a reputation for fishing excellence that is second to none. I guided on the ranch off and on for about 15 years during the late 1980s and 90s, and I can tell you that it offers some of the finest lake fishing anywhere, and their section of the Rio de Los Brazos is like fishing the spring creeks in Yellowstone country without the crowds.

They have over a dozen pristine alpine lakes from which to choose. You'll marvel at the behemoth rainbow, brook, and cutthroat trout that leave your arms weak by the end of the day. Some lakes are reserved exclusively for catch-and-release enthusiasts. Otherwise, there is a limit of four trout per person per day (under 18 inches, non-cumulative) for those who wish to retain fish. Some clients elect to catch their own dinner for the lodge's executive chef to prepare.

Daily hatches abound from mid-June to mid-September. The chance of landing a trophy trout here is as good as it gets, with the larger trout weighing in the 8- to 12-pound class.

If stream fishing is more your style, the Lodge provides miles of crystal-clear water on the pristine Rio de Los Brazos, which teems with powerful-fighting brook and rainbow trout, and Poso Creek, which has native Rio Grande cutthroat trout and brookies. You will find countless pools, runs, riffles, and pockets in front of the beautiful backdrop of this unspoiled ranch.

The Lakes

Within one hour of the Lodge at Chama are 14 lakes ranging from 2 to 8 surface acres. The lower lakes, such as Iron Springs and Pine, are situated near the Chama Valley floor around 7,800 to 8,000 feet in elevation, and they're usually fishable by early May. The mid-level and high lakes are usually fishable between early and late June, depending on how much snowpack there is. The lower lakes have cuttbows, rainbows, and rare leftover browns from earlier stockings (browns have been hard to get commercially lately). The upper lakes all have rainbows and cuttbows, and some— like North, Gary's, Charlie's, and Poso—have cutthroats. Poso also has brookies.

The Lodge provides all equipment in their package price or you can bring your own. As you might imagine, they are well equipped with rods, reels, terminal tackle, flies, waders, float tubes, and boats with small electric trolling motors. The guide picks you up at the lodge and takes you to the lake of your choice. They only offer guided fishing, but they do allow day-use (see below).

Once you leave the lodge and start up the dusty, rugged four-wheel-drive-only roads, it gets as wild as anywhere I've been in the Rockies. On your way to and from

An angler strips a damselfly nymph during the spring on one of the Lodge's lower lakes.

your destination, and while fishing, it's not uncommon to see deer, elk, beaver, raptors, and occasionally bear or mountain lions. The scenery is spectacular, with panoramic views of beautiful valleys, forests, and mountain peaks.

All the lakes harbor huge trout, and the average is around 3 pounds. Every year trout up to 10 pounds are caught here, and 5-pound fish are common. The trout are big for two reasons. The Lodge stocks big fish over 2 pounds every year, and the abundant aquatic habitat provides the food to keep the fast-growing trout fat and healthy. Most of the fish caught are released, but anglers wanting to eat fresh trout don't need to worry about wiping out the fishery by keeping a fish or two. These lakes are managed intensely to produce plenty of big trout for the light pressure they receive.

Frank Simms has been the ranch manager since before the acquisition by the Jicarilla Indian Reservation, although it's not part of the Reservation. When Frank first became manager, the hunting program was the main source of income for the ranch. The fishing program was insignificant, just a side activity. Frank brought the fishery into the 21st century, enticing flyfishers from all over the world to come experience this unique fishing paradise.

The lower lakes are usually free of ice by May, and the trout become active as the

Jack Woolley with a trophy rainbow.

water warms from the spring sun's brilliant rays. Any Woolly Bugger, damsel nymph, or swimming nymph will work, and midges often hatch, bringing hungry 'bows to the top. Fathead minnows are abundant in all the lakes, providing good protein for the large trout even when there are no hatches.

By June, the damsels are hatching, and a damsel nymph stripped near weed beds—with a 2-foot strip followed by a 2-second pause—can yield some unbelievable trout. The strikes are unmistakable, and these early-season fish are full of spunk. Dry damsels will also produce some vicious strikes near shore and along the edge of weed beds. By mid-June, Callibaetis and Blue Duns are hatching, continuing through August. Hoppers, termites, and ants are abundant in July and August; a terrestrial pattern with a nymph dropper can be deadly.

The mid-level and high lakes have the same hatches, but everything is about a month behind the lower lakes. They have good vegetation and forest along the banks, so terrestrials work better. Pat Carpenter is a top guide at the Lodge at Chama and he told me ants are extremely productive in July and August on many of the lakes. He also likes hoppers and Parachute Adams, but if fish won't come to the top he likes to use what he calls a "hinging" nymph. Put a round foam strike indicator on the leader about 10 to 15 feet above the first nymph and place a small split shot about 10 inches above the nymph. Then add a dropper of 12 to 18 inches, along with another nymph, larva, or scud. This setup allows you to fish deep along the edge of weed beds, shelves, and drops. Scuds are another favorite of Pat's, especially in high lakes like Bobo and Poso.

If you're fishing with a group it's nice to rendezvous at one of the lakes and let the staff of the Lodge cook up a shore-side lunch for everyone. I've guided several corporate groups at the Lodge over the years and I can tell you they sure know how to do it right.

Rio de Los Brazos at the Lodge

With all the fantastic lake fishing on the ranch the stream fishing is often overlooked by guests of the Lodge at Chama, but make no mistake, the Rio de Los Brazos is in a class by itself. Between the East and West Forks of the Brazos on the ranch and the additional water on the main stem of the Brazos available through Frank Simms, personally, there are over 8 miles of splendid fly water.

The Brazos and the two forks run through high alpine meadows in a beautiful valley reminiscent of Yellowstone National Park, and the fishing is every bit as good. You won't find any crowds here, though. It's a little over an hour's drive on rugged roads from the Lodge to the Brazos and it's all on private land. You will encounter wildlife all along the way, with elk often grazing on the hillsides above the river.

The two forks are about half the size of the main stem, and rainbows average 14 to 18 inches. They're also loaded with brook trout larger than any stream-bred brookies I've seen in water this size—12 to 16 inches on average. Dry-fly fishing on the forks is superb. A hopper or Stimulator will usually do the trick, but if there is a hatch of caddis or mayflies you may have to match the size, shape, and color of the insect to catch the 'bows, and sometimes even the more gullible brookies.

Pat Carpenter's fly of choice is often a yellow Dave's Hopper, but when there's a hatch of Gray Duns he likes to use a Parachute Adams, size 14 to 16. Also, he likes anything black, especially ants in August and September. During early-morning Trico hatches in August and September he uses small Parachute Tricos, size 18 to 22. If fish aren't looking up he uses a Stimulator or hopper on top and a dropper with a Hare's Ear or Prince Nymph.

To fish the two forks or the main stem you must have a guide from the Lodge or from an outfitter that works with them.

Poso Creek

Poso Creek is a much smaller creek than the Brazos, but it adds 4 more miles of open meadow flyfishing for wild brookies that average 6 to 10 inches, with some larger. The Lodge has restored the upper part of Poso Creek with Rio Grande cutthroats. These cutts are the only fish above Bobo Lake, and they are usually willing to strike almost any good attractor with enthusiasm. If you like beauty and solitude and don't care how big the trout are, have your guide bring you here for part of a day.

Flyfishing Schools

The Lodge at Chama also offers flyfishing schools, held at the beginning of each month in the summer. The schools include three days of fishing instruction covering all aspects of angling. You will learn about insect recognition, reading the water, proper casting methods, and catch-and-release techniques, among other things. Classes are limited to only four students per session. Make sure to call early to guarantee your reservation.

Services at the Lodge

The Lodge at Chama is over 16,000 square feet with 21 rooms. It has professional guides that are dedicated to making your trip the fishing experience of a lifetime. Delicious gourmet meals are prepared for you daily by the Lodge's executive chef and kitchen staff using only the best ingredients. The accommodations include all your meals and they are delicious. Start your day off with a steaming breakfast buffet with a scrumptious selection of fresh-baked pastries. Gourmet picnic baskets are prepared fresh each morning for you to take along on your flyfishing adventure. Guests choose from a selection of gourmet entrees for the evening meal, complemented by a selection of fine wines and highlighted by unsurpassed service and personal attention. The dining area showcases panoramic views of the beautiful San Juan Mountains.

Getting to the Lodge at Chama

The Lodge at Chama is located in Chama, New Mexico, an hour and a half northwest of Taos and two hours north of Santa Fe. From Taos, take US 64 west for 89 miles to the turnoff on your right (just before you reach the village of Chama) that is well marked. Just follow the signs from there.

Private or chartered aircraft up to King Air may land on their 6,000-foot air strip at Pagosa Springs or Alamosa, Colorado, or at the Taos or Santa Fe airports.

Fishing Facts: Lodge at Chama

Lodging (check their website for current prices)
- $275 per person per day (double occupancy), includes three meals a day.
- $575 per person per day (double occupancy), includes full use of lodge and spa facility, three meals a day, and any of the following guided activities: fishing, sporting clays, hiking ranch tours, and wildlife viewing and photography. They offer no unguided activities.
- $100 extra per day (single occupancy), in addition to regular lodging fees.

Guided Ranch Day Fishing (no lodging)
- $425 per person with a two-client minimum, guided fishing includes lunch.

Flyfishing School
- $2,250, includes 4 nights and 3 days of fishing (subject to availability).

Contact Information
- The Lodge at Chama, Frank Simms (President and General Manager), P.O. Box 127, Chama, NM 87520; 575-756-2133, www.lodgeatchama.com

RIO DE LOS BRAZOS

The Rio de Los Brazos is a surprisingly high-quality, medium-sized stream located in north-central New Mexico. A major tributary of the immense Rio Chama, the Brazos runs exclusively on private land. There is about a mile or two of public access near the bottom of the drainage, just downstream of the old Brazos Lodge near the village of Brazos.

The headwaters and the upper main stem of the Brazos meander through a gorgeous highland extension of the San Juan Mountains known as the Brazos Meadows. The river then literally falls off the edge of this meadow into the magnificent Brazos Box, a prominent geological feature in the region. The contrast between the Meadows and the Box is startling; they're like two completely different rivers.

There are several private ranches from top to bottom and some have commercial fishing operations. I am lucky to know most of the owners or the management, and some of them allow my guide service, The Solitary Angler, to guide clients on their prime waters. Some of them also have their own guides and fishing programs. Wherever you fish on the Brazos, you will find some of the best flyfishing you've ever had, in addition to spectacular scenery and solitude.

The Brazos Meadows

The Brazos Meadows includes about 10 miles of the East and West Forks of the Brazos and about 15 miles of the main stem of the Brazos. The forks, along with 8 miles of the main stem, are accessed through the Lodge at Chama. (See the Lodge at Chama description on page 378 for full details on their water.) Another 2 miles of the main stem can be accessed through the Brazos River Ranch.

The Brazos has brookies that average an astonishing 12 to 16 inches, and even the tributaries will yield a nice fish once in a while. A few brookies will grow to 19 or 20 inches, which is remarkable for a wild, stream-bred brookie. There are also wild rainbows, cuttbows, and occasional Rio Grande cutthroats, as well as some great holdover stocked rainbows that average 16 to 20 inches.

The reason for the larger-than-average fish in this mountain stream is the nutrient-rich environment. Even though it's considered a freestone stream, the river is enhanced by many spring-fed tributaries in the headwaters and by the fertile, grassy meadows below. The meadows provide nutrients and host numerous bends with deep holes, long pools, and severely undercut banks where fish can feed under cover and hold, even in winter. The river bottom has a good mix of gravel, round bedrock, and silt, providing good habitat for a wide variety of aquatic insects.

Although it's a hatch-oriented stream, the Brazos receives so little angling pressure that a large attractor will often work as well as anything. The meadows usually become fishable by mid-June, and large Salmonflies and Golden Stoneflies are already hatching by then. Try matching them with a Lawson's Salmonfly, size 4 to 8, and a Bird's Stonefly, size 8 to 14.

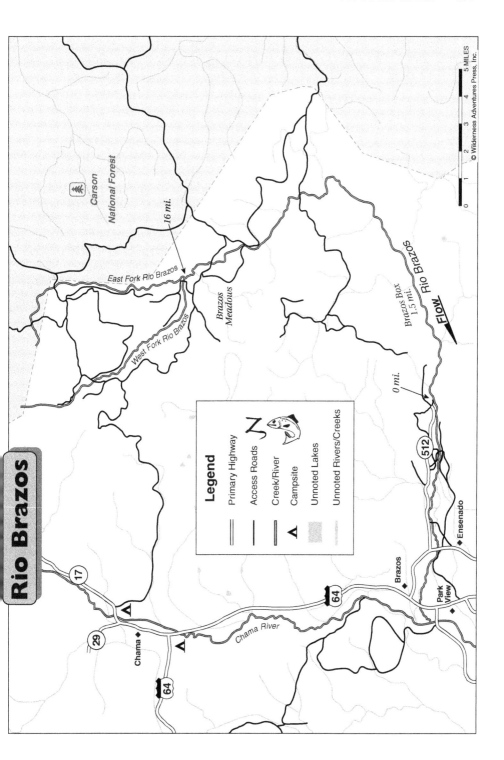

Rio Brazos

Legend

Primary Highway
Access Roads
Creek/River
Campsite
Unnoted Lakes
Unnoted Rivers/Creeks

Carson National Forest

East Fork Rio Brazos

16 mi.

West Fork Rio Brazos

Brazos Meadows

Brazos Box
1.5 mi.

Rio Brazos

FLOW

0 mi.

512

Ensenado

Brazos

Park View

Chama River

Chama

64

29

17

64

© Wilderness Adventures Press, Inc.

0 1 2 3 4 5 MILES

Caddis are abundant from mid-June through September, and a standard Elk Hair Caddis in olive, gray, or tan, size 14 to 18, will usually do the trick. There's a large orange sedge in July, which can be matched with a Bucktail Caddis, size 10 to 14, on top and an orange beadhead caddis pupa, size 12 to 14, on the dropper.

Sporadic and sparse hatches of Green Drakes come off in July and August, but fish will still eagerly smack a Green Drake Wulff, size 12 to 14. They hatch midday, especially if it's cool or cloudy, providing some great dry-fly fishing when fish would otherwise be down. Another hatch that is inconsistent but exciting is the Trico hatch. You must be on the water early in the day in August and September if you want to catch it. Other mayflies hatch, as well, including PMDs, PEDs, Blue Duns, Gray Duns, large and small Ginger Duns, Mahogany Duns, and, of course, Blue-Winged Olive (Baetis).

With all the grass in the meadows, there is an abundance of hoppers and other terrestrials. Try a yellow, tan, or green Parachute Hopper, size 8 to 16. In June and July there are often billions of tiny baby hoppers in addition to the adults. They are more easily blown into the water, so a small hopper can be deadly, particularly on windy days.

Hip boots are suitable for most wading, but breathable pant or chest waders aren't overkill. I like rubber soles for wading back and forth across the river at the bottom of the bends. Since felt carries foreign spores, weeds, etc, it is not recommended due to the pristine nature of the Brazos Meadows, which is whirling disease- and noxious weed-free. An 8- to 9-foot, 4- or 5-weight rod is recommended to fight the hefty trout and cast in the wind.

The Rio Brazos in the Brazos Meadows is one of the finest dry-fly streams in the state.

The Brazos River Ranch

Located at 10,000 feet, this section of the upper Brazos River produces large, robust rainbow, brook, and, occasionally, cutthroat trout. Elk, mule deer, black bear, pronghorn antelope, and golden eagles are common sights in this primitive setting. The riverbanks are completely unobstructed and wading is easy; the trails along the river are smooth to moderate.

With over 4,100 acres, the Brazos River Ranch has almost 2 miles of the Brazos River and over 2 miles of small tributaries loaded with brookies. The ranch's upper boundary on the Brazos is right at the confluence of the East and West Forks, and the river meanders from there downstream through the upper Brazos Meadows. The ranch joins the Carson National Forest and Cruces Basin Wilderness making a front yard of 354,000 acres uninhabited timberland, sitting on top of a high plateau from 8,000 to nearly 11,000 feet in elevation. Open meadows, rich in wild flowers, are interspersed with stands of pine, spruce, fir and aspen.

According to Bo Prieskorn, owner and manager of the ranch, they only stock a few rainbows every couple of years because the rainbows and cuttbows are spawning and successfully reproducing, evidenced by the number of rainbow fingerlings present.

The rainbows here grow fast and average 16 to 20 inches, with some to 24 inches. The ranch only allows catch-and-release flyfishing with a single barbless hook. They also require anglers to wear rubber soles disinfect their waders with a Clorox and water mixture, which they provide, to prevent the spread of whirling disease.

The hatches on the ranch are the same as for the rest of the meadows, but Bo told me that black Mormon crickets are thick some years and that a black foam or standard cricket pattern can be deadly. Black is a top producer on the Brazos during the summer months, so black ants, beetles, and crickets should always be in your box.

Except for a few old customers and friends of the Prieskorn's, a guide is required when you fish the Brazos River Ranch; and you must be staying at the ranch to fish the property. Mr. Prieskorn will provide a guide or recommend some independent guides that he works with. For the the most par, only one party at a time of two to six anglers is allowed to fish, ensuring solitude and exclusive access.

Even though it's remote and rustic, the ranch is clean, comfortable and Bo provides everything including the meals. The accommodations include six rustic and comfortable cabins. A solar-powered system was installed so there is electricity and wi-fi. There is propane heat, a refrigerator, lights, and a separate bathhouse with hot and cold water. There are also covered outside facilities for cooking, campfires, lounging, and viewing wildlife. There's even an outdoor wood-fired hot tub. The best part of all is that it's just you and your party on the entire ranch.

To get to the Brazos River Ranch from Taos, take US 64 west about 27 miles to its junction with US 285, then go north (right) for 11 miles and turn west (left) on FR 87 towards Lagunitas. Stay on the gravel and dirt road for 29 miles to just past Lagunitas and the intersection with FR 87F. Veer left onto FR 87F and go about a half-mile to the gate, which is marked with a Brazos River Ranch sign. A ranch staff member will meet you there and take you to the river and your cabin. A high-clearance vehicle is required for FR 87, and four-wheel drive is recommended but not required.

The current fees for fishing and accommodations are as follows (always check with the ranch for up-to-date rates):

All Inclusive Packages

$650.00 per person per night two-night minimum (double occupancy).
Children 6-12: $300.00 per day
Children Under 5: No Charge
Package includes: Private cabin, access to wood fired hot tub, full meals provided by their in-house chef, fly fishing guides, all flies and tippet material along with rods, reels and waders/wading boots if needed, access to all water and horseback rides (subject to availability of horses and wranglers).

A la Carte

Cabin Rental: $350.00 per person, per day, two-night minimum (double occupancy). Rental includes: Private cabin, access to wood fired hot tub, full meals provided by our in-house chef.

Guided Full Day Fly Fishing: 1 Person $450; 2 People $800; 3 People $1125; Maximum 3 people per guide. Includes lunch riverside, all flies and tippet material along with rods, reels and waders/wading boots if needed.

Fly Fishing School : $2250.00 per person, 2 person min. up to 6 people (limited availability); three days and nights of private instruction will teach all the fundamentals of fly fishing with practical on-stream experience, utilizing our private waters.

For additional information or to book a trip contact: Brazos River Ranch, LLC, PO Box 867, Las Vegas, New Mexico 87701, 505-453-1212. E-mail: brazoselk@yahoo.com.

The Brazos Meadows are famous for large wild brookies.

Brazos Box—Corkins Lodge

Corkins Lodge is located at the mouth of the Brazos Box near the bottom of the drainage and the Chama River confluence. From Chama, go south on US 64/84 for 9 miles to the village of Brazos and turn left on NM 512, then follow it for 8 miles to Corkins Lodge at the end of the road. Drive carefully and watch out for wildlife, as turkey, deer, and even bear frequent the canyon, especially near the mouth of the Box.

Corkins really isn't a lodge, but they have 12 rustic but nice cabins that can accommodate 2 to 8 people per cabin. They are building a new group cabin, which will be more modern, for corporate groups, fishing clubs, family reunions, etc. Corkins has been serving sportsmen since 1930 and has been catering to anglers longer than practically any lodge in New Mexico. Over 75 percent of their clientele return year after year, and they're usually booked up from Memorial Day to Labor Day. Luckily for the flyfisher, most of their guests are families that do most of their fishing on the man-made ponds. Most of the anglers never make it to the actual Brazos Box, about 1½ miles upstream.

Corkins sprawls over 3,000 acres of rugged canyon and steep forest and includes 2½ miles of the Brazos. The first 1½ miles is in a steep canyon, but it's still fairly open compared to the Box. The pools are long, wide, and fairly deep. Between the pools are boulder-strewn pockets and shallow riffles. The banks are brushy, but wading in pant or chest waders is pretty easy. Fishing the banks, especially during midday, can be productive because the larger browns and rainbows seek the shade of overhanging brush. The river bottom consists of gravel, bedrock, and bowling ball–sized boulders, with occasional larger boulders. Nasty logjams provide cover and create good pools above and below.

There are three trails into the river from Corkins: a ¼-mile trail, a 1-mile trail, and the Box trail. Each leads you deeper into the Box and farther from other people. The farther upstream you go, the narrower and deeper the river gets and the more big browns there are. The actual Box starts about 1½ miles above Corkins at the confluence of Encinado Creek and continues for about 4½ miles to the Brazos Falls. Above the falls are the Brazos Meadows, which are accessed via other private ranches.

You have to wade in the Box because in some places the river runs next to the towering Brazos Cliffs. This is one of the most beautiful places you'll ever fish, and the water is perfect, with deep holes, long pools, dark pockets, and broad riffles. The water is crystal clear except after a heavy rainstorm, and even then it clears up quickly because the watershed is in great shape in the headwaters. (Most of the landowners manage their properties for fish and wildlife instead of overgrazing with cattle.)

There are plenty of nice trout, too. Wild browns, rainbows, and cuttbows, as well as some stocked rainbows, average 12 to 15 inches, with several to 18 inches. Occasional brook trout are found near the top of the Box, most likely drifting down from the Brazos Meadows. The farther upstream you get, the more browns there are. Browns up to 20 inches can be caught in the upper portion of the Box.

The Brazos Box is a hatch-oriented stream, starting with a strong Salmonfly hatch in June. Unfortunately, the hatch takes place during spring runoff, although you can often catch the end of it when the river becomes fishable in mid- to late June. You can fish the entire hatch in a dry year. Before runoff in April you can have great success nymph fishing with giant brown or black stonefly nymphs, size 4 to 8, and olive caddis larvae, size 12 to 16. This is also a good time to fish because there is very little angling pressure at Corkins until Memorial Day.

Don't worry if you miss the Salmonflies, the Golden Stonefly hatches right after the big orange bugs. In late June, you'll sometimes find both hatching at the same time. I use a large Lawson's Salmonfly, size 6 to 10, to imitate the big bugs and a Bird's Golden Stone or Gold Stimulator, size 8 to 14, for the smaller stoneflies. A healthy PMD hatch also kicks off in late June, and this brings pods of fish to the surface at the tails of riffles and pools. My favorite imitation is a ginger thorax-style dun with a cream poly or blond elk wing, size 16 to 18. If you see fish sipping rather than splashing, they're probably keyed in on PMDs. Lone rising fish that make large splashes are probably taking stoneflies or caddis.

Various caddis hatches provide superb evening dry-fly action all summer long. An olive Elk Hair Caddis, size 14 to 18, with an olive or green beadhead caddis pupa or a Beadhead Prince Nymph for a dropper can be deadly when the sun gets low. Large pine moths are also very abundant and easily imitated with a large cream caddis or, my favorite, a Terminator, size 10 to 12. This fly also works well as a White Miller imitation. These insects hatch in massive numbers just before dark in July and August, bringing large browns to the surface.

Once, back when you could legally access the Box from the south side of the river, I walked 3 miles upstream to make sure I was alone and started fishing with a large Terminator. The first cast I made was into a boiling pocket below a huge tree root that was wedged between two large boulders. The fly hit the water and I immediately raised my rod tip, removing all the slack so the fly just sat there in the pocket, barely moving with the gentle swirls below the boil.

After about four or five seconds, a large brown shadow ascended to the surface, then a massive white mouth sucked in my fly. I lifted my rod tip and felt the surge of power as the 20-inch trout tried to take me under the log. But I pumped the rod, bending it almost double before he finally turned and came downstream where I could handle him. A couple of minutes later he gave in and I gently grasped the butter-colored buck and removed the barbless hook.

The same fly worked all day long before it was finally shredded from catching so many fish. I'd had a rare, spectacular day and decided to start back before it got too dark, but I couldn't resist casting into the pool near where I was parked just one last time. I cast the ragged fly up into the head of the pool, and no sooner did it hit the water than there was an aggressive, slashing rise. I set the hook, and sure enough it was mine. After several runs I landed the only rainbow of the day, a colorful 18-inch hen that I quickly released. Ever since that day I always carry a full row or two of Terminators (developed by guide Eddie Adams) in my caddis box.

In the summer months terrestrials also work well, including hoppers, ants, moths, and beetles. Anything black and buggy will do well, especially in August.

The Rio de Los Brazos just below the Brazos Box (shown in the background) produces large wild browns and rainbows.

Fishing the banks, under overhanging brush, with a black ant can produce some fine browns during the dog days of July and August.

When they won't take dries, try fishing the deep holes, pools, and riffles with a standard double-nymph rig; use enough weight to bump the bottom. Try a light or dark Hare's Ear for the top nymph and a green caddis larva or an olive cranefly larva on the bottom. Stripping a Woolly Bugger through the deep holes and pockets can also get the attention of trout, often when nothing else is working.

After Labor Day you can have most of the river to yourself, and the fall fishing can be quite good. Baetis hatch through October and into November, and fishing a Parachute Adams or an Olive Gulper at the tails of pools and near the banks can yield some nice trout. The lower river, below the mouth of the Box, is best during this hatch. Holdover rainbows up to 18 inches will readily take small dries. By October the browns are getting ready to spawn, and they feed freely in order to fatten up before starting their mating ritual. Woolly Buggers and other streamers can produce some nice browns in October and November. It usually gets too cold to successfully fish the Brazos by late November.

A guide is not required at Corkins, but it's highly recommended. You can contact my company, The Solitary Angler, for guide service on the Brazos while staying at Corkins. If you don't want to cook your own meals, you can eat at the Cliff View Restaurant overlooking the river. Corkins also has additional hiking trails, fishing ponds, a swimming pool, and sauna. The cabins start at around $180 for two and go up to to $640 for 10 people and that includes the fishing.

For current pricing, contact Corkin's Lodge, P.O. Box 396, Chama, NM 87520; 1-800-548-7688 or 505-588-7261, www.corkinslodge.com. The Solitary Angler in Taos also provides guide service here, contact them at 1-866-502-1700 or www.thesolitaryangler.com.

A beautiful rainbow taken in the Brazos Meadows.

Stream Facts: Rio de Los Brazos Private Water

Season
- Before runoff in April and after runoff mid-June through October.

Special Regulations
- The Lodge at Chama: catch-and-release flyfishing only.
- The Brazos River Ranch: catch-and-release flyfishing only with a single barbless hook.
- Corkins: general regulations apply for about the first mile, above that it's catch and release only.

Trout
- Brazos Meadows: brookies 12 to 16 inches, some bigger; rainbows, cuttbows, and some cutthroats 16 to 20 inches, some bigger.
- Brazos Box: browns and rainbows 12 to 15 inches, some bigger.

River Miles
- Corkins Lodge—0
- Beginning of the Brazos Box—1.5
- Brazos Falls—6
- Lower end of Brazos Meadows—10
- Lower boundary of Brazos River Ranch—14
- Confluence of East and West Forks/upper boundary of Brazos River Ranch/lower boundary of the Lodge at Chama property—16

River Characteristics
- Brazos Meadows: a medium to small freestone stream enhanced by springs and meandering through high alpine meadows at elevations ranging from 9,000 to 10,000 feet. There are deep holes, undercut banks, and long foam lines.
- Brazos Box: a medium freestone stream running through a tight box canyon in the upper 4.5 miles and a more open canyon near the bottom. Numerous deep holes, long pools, shallow riffles, boulder-strewn pockets.

River Flows
- Winter, summer, and fall: 25 to 70 cfs
- Spring runoff: 50 to 600 cfs

Maps
- *New Mexico Atlas & Gazetteer,* page 15; Carson National Forest Map; BLM Map: Chama; USGS Quadrangle Maps: Tierra Amarilla, Penasco Amarilla, Lagunitas Creek, West Fork Rio Brazos

Outfitters
- The Lodge at Chama and the Brazos River Ranch have their own guides or can recommend one. For a guide at Corkins Lodge contact the Solitary Angler in Taos.

RIO DE LOS BRAZOS MAJOR HATCHES

Insect	J	F	M	A	M	J	J	A	S	O	N	D	Time	Flies
Caddis									█				M/A/E	Green & olive caddis larva #12–#16; Double Hackle Peacock #12–#16; Van's Rag Pupa or LaFontaine's Sparkle Pupa #10–#18; green or dark olive Green Weenie #12–#18; olive, tan & gray Elk Hair Caddis #12–#20; olive, gray & peacock Fluttering Caddis #10–#18
Craneflies										█			M/A/E	Cranefly larva, peacock, gray, or dark olive #6–#16; Taylor Streit's Poundmeister #6–#14; Double Hackle Peacock #6–#16; foam-body cranefly #6–#16
Green, Gray Drake								█					M/A/SF	Olive Hare's Ear #10–#14; Van's Rag Fly dark olive #10–#14; Green & Gray Drake Hair Wing (Wulff style) #10–#14; Green & Gray Paradrake #10–#14; Green Drake spinner #12–#14
Ginger, Blue & Mahogany Duns					█								M/E/SF	Light, dark & olive Hare's Ear #10–#18; Pheasant Tail #12–#18; light, dark, pink & ginger Hair Wing Duns or Cahills #12–#18 or the same in parachutes; Ginger, Red & Blue Quills; Royal Wulff, Rio Grande King, or Rio Grande Trude #12–#18; H&L Variant #12–#18
Baetis				█									M/A/SF	Dark olive Hare's Ear #16–#22; Pheasant Tail #16–#22; Van's Rag Fly dark olive #16–#22; Lawson's BWO Fan-Wing Emerger #16–#22; Olive Parachute #16–#22; Olive Comparadun #16–#22

Hatch Time Code: M = Morning; A = Afternoon; E = Evening; D = Dark; SF = Spinner Fall

RIO DE LOS BRAZOS MAJOR HATCHES (cont.)

Insect	J	F	M	A	M	J	J	A	S	O	N	D	Time	Flies
Salmonfly, Large and Medium Golden Stonefly						▓	▓	▓	▓				M/A	Black & brown stonefly nymph #4–#10; Golden Stone Nymph #10–#14; Elk Hair Salmonfly #4–#8; Orange & Gold Stimulators #4–#14; Terminator #12–#16
PMDs, PEDs				▓	▓	▓	▓	▓					M/SF	Light Hare's Ear #12–#18; Pheasant Tail #12–#20; Van's Rag Fly light olive #14–#20; light olive Lawson's Fan-Wing Emerger #14–#22; PMD, PED #14–#20; Ginger or Light Olive Dun #14–#20
Terrestrials					▓	▓	▓	▓	▓	▓			M/A	Para-hoppers tan, yellow #8–#14; Bees #12–#14; Elk Hair Pine Moths #8–#14 beetles, lady bugs & ants #12–#18

Hatch Time Code: M = Morning; A = Afternoon; E = Evening; D = Dark; SF = Spinner Fall

JICARILLA APACHE RESERVATION

The Navajo River and seven clear mountain lakes, from 30 to 400 acres in size, grace the landscape on the Jicarilla Reservation in northwest New Mexico. Access to the lakes and the Navajo River is via Dulce, the main village on the Reservation. To get there from Chama, take US 64 west towards Farmington for about 24 miles to Dulce, which has gas stations, grocery stores, and accommodations. Camping is allowed at the lakes.

Permits can be purchased at the Jicarilla Game and Fish Department, at the Best Western Jicarilla Inn 24 hours a day, in Albuquerque at Charlie's Sporting Goods, in Santa Fe at High Desert Angler and the Reel Life in Taos at the Solitary Angler, and at other select sporting goods and fly shops in New Mexico. There is a list of vendors on the Reservation website. Permits can be purchased for the entire season or daily, and special discounts are available for children, vets, and senior citizens. No state permit is required. Check with the Jicarilla Game and Fish Department for current prices and conditions.

Navajo River

The Navajo River is marginal for flyfishing, except during the fall when the river finally clears up and browns begin moving upstream from the San Juan River and Navajo Reservoir.

To get to the Navajo River from Dulce, turn right off US 64 onto Hawks Drive and go about three-quarters of a mile, then turn right on River Hill Road, actually J2, and go about 2 miles to the J2 bridge. Follow J2, a dirt road, downstream about 5 miles to its junction with J9 and continue downstream for 10 more miles on J9. Turning left on J9 will return you to Dulce. The top 6 miles of river—between the J9 and J2 bridges—offer the best fishing. There's good roadside access throughout the 15 miles of water, with several pullouts and three campgrounds.

Fishing pressure on the river is light at best, partially due to the turbidity of the river caused by erosion and sediment loading, both natural and unnatural, and irrigation by farmers and ranchers. According to Kevin Terry, Jicarilla Fisheries Biologist, there aren't very many trout per mile, probably less than 250, especially in the lower 9 miles. Most are 10- to 14-inch browns, with a few rainbows scattered about.

The discolored water and warm summer temperatures, combined with a lack of suitable spawning habitat, keep the numbers of trout down except during the fall, when browns up to 30 inches migrate upstream from the San Juan River and Navajo Reservoir. The water clears up and cools off after irrigation ends, and migrating and resident fish can be very active.

During this time, large Woolly Buggers and other streamer patterns work well, as do golden egg patterns and small mayfly nymphs, size 14 to 18. For dries, try standard attractors unless there's a fall Baetis hatch. Match these flies with a size 18 parachute with an olive or gray body. Look for larger fish before approaching a riffle or pool, and throw to them first. With streamers, throw above and beyond the fish and strip the fly in front of its nose.

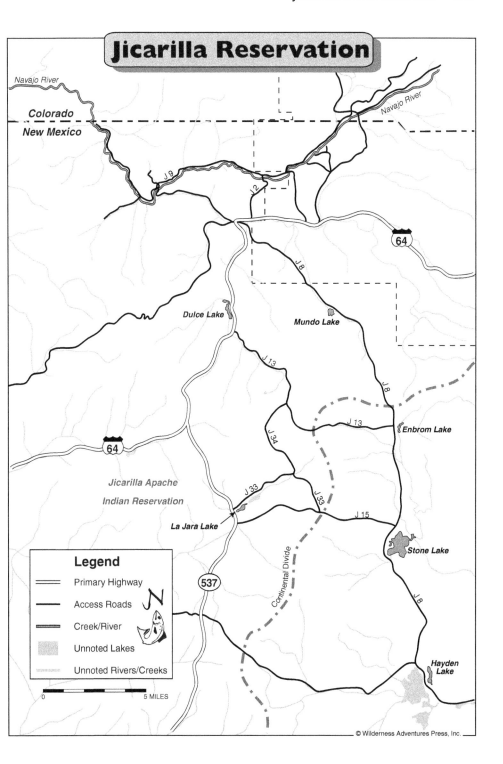

Jicarilla Reservation

Navajo River

Navajo River

Colorado
New Mexico

J 9

J 2

64

J 8

Dulce Lake

Mundo Lake

J 13

64

J 8

J 34

J 13

Enbrom Lake

Jicarilla Apache

Indian Reservation

J 33

J 33

La Jara Lake

J 15

Stone Lake

Continental Divide

Legend

— Primary Highway

— Access Roads

— Creek/River

Unnoted Lakes

Unnoted Rivers/Creeks

537

J 8

Hayden
Lake

0   5 MILES

© Wilderness Adventures Press, Inc.

When nymphing I use a golden egg, size 16 (shrimp hook), for my top fly and a beadhead flashback dark Hare's Ear for my bottom fly, about 12 to 18 inches below. With low fall water conditions, I opt to use a hi-stick nymphing technique, which involves using a tiny strike (or depth) indicator about 1½ feet higher than the average depth of the water you're fishing. Stand below the fish at about a 45-degree angle and cast 5 to 10 feet above the fish. Keep the line tight by taking up slack and keep the rod tip up and out over the line, indicator, and fly, letting the weight bump along the bottom and following it with your rod tip.

When it approaches the fish you're targeting, watch for the trout to flash while keeping an eye on the indicator. Also, feel for a strike with your line/rod hand. Strikes can be subtle, but they're usually detectible. If you're spooking fish, go to a standard nymphing technique with a floating indicator and make longer casts.

Jicarilla Lakes

The Jicarilla Reservation currently has seven lakes that hold trout. All the lakes are significant to flyfishers, except during drought conditions, when they can suffer from weed overgrowth, warm temperatures, and elevated pH levels. Winterkill can also be a problem in low-water years, as the weeds decay and cause fish suffocation by noxious gas.

The Jicarilla Lakes host large trout and are fishable from April through November.

The good news is that the Jicarilla Game and Fish Department (JGFD) maintains an excellent fish-stocking program. They generally stock rainbows between 6 and 8 inches, and the fish grow at an astonishing rate—an inch or more a month during spring, summer, and fall. There are also still a few wild browns hanging on from previous stockings.

The same weeds that kill fish also produce tons of nourishment in the form of aquatic insects, crustaceans, and minnows. When there's plenty of water the trout can live for several years and grow to enormous size. The JGFD has a weed-control program that involves cutting weeds and stocking grass carp in some of the lakes. Before the current drought, Stone, La Jara, and Dulce Lakes all produced 5-plus-pound fish on a regular basis. But it's very difficult to control weeds, and impossible to control water temperatures, during severe drought. Check with the JGFD for current conditions before going fishing or go to their website at www.jicarillahunt.com for a current fishing report.

Spring and fall fishing is superb for all species. Small boats (trolling speeds only) and float tubes are popular with many fishermen, and redwood fishing docks are present at several lakes for shore fishermen. All seven lakes are accessible by vehicle and are in close enough proximity to permit fishing several lakes in a day. Good fishing is always available; just move to the next lake.

Dulce Lake

Dulce Lake is the third largest Jicarilla lake, around 75 acres when full, and it holds a good population of rainbows and some cutthroats and browns that average 12 to 16 inches, some to 20 inches or more. Unfortunately, Dulce Lake was drained back in 1997 and has never sufficiently refilled due to the recent drought of the late 1990s and early 2000s. Plans to build a pump station on the Navajo River to provide water for Dulce Lake fell through so if the lake doesn't fill naturally from runoff it will remain a catfish lake at best. It's unfortunate because it offered easy access and fished well from shore as large trout cruised the weedbeds foraging for nymphs, scuds, snails and minnows. Pray for moisture!

La Jara Lake and Hayden Lake

Unfortunately La Jara and Hayden Lakes both died out during the last drought and met the same demise as Dulce Lake. They will be closed indefinitely.

Stone Lake

From La Jara Lake, continue south on NM 537 for about a quarter-mile, then turn east on J15 and go another 5 miles or so to J8, where you turn right. Stone Lake is on your left. There are developed and undeveloped campsites, picnic tables, toilets, and boat launching areas.

Stone Lake is the largest reservation lake, about 440 acres, and the most popular over the years. But it's not without problems. Formerly one of New Mexico's best lakes for large rainbows, the fishery diminished when someone fishing illegally with carp minnows dumped their minnow bucket in the lake and the carp took over. In recent years, attempts to eradicate the carp have helped, and the fishery has recovered well especially since the end of the last drought.

Now managed as an "artificials only" fishery, the reservation stocks over 100,000 6-inch rainbows per year. The lake grows rainbows quickly, over an inch per month, and they get quite large; many weigh over 5 pounds. The standard damsels, midges, Callibaetis, and micro-caddis patterns work well here, but most anglers strip large dragonfly nymphs, locally called hellgrammites, along the weed beds.

A special retrieve that I developed while fishing here back in the 1970s works well. Keep the rod tip an inch off the water for direct contact and make 2-foot-long strips in 2 seconds with a 2-second pause in between strips. Wiggle your stripping finger rapidly as you strip, giving the nymph a realistic swimming motion. Make sure your hellgrammite is tied with a marabou tail to impart the best swimming action.

Fishing can be tough here because the fish are so over-stuffed that they don't have to eat when you want them to. They tend to lay deep, feeding on an abundance of small stuff, where most flyfishers don't get to very effectively. If you aren't having success with traditional techniques go with a full-sinking line and use small midge larva, scuds and nymphs and strip them very slowly right along the bottom. When the line starts to tighten, just lift to set the hook. The fish will already be running at this point so be ready to let it have the reel. Avoid letting them run into the weeds by pumping the rod.

Enbom Lake

From Stone Lake, go north on J8 about 5.5 miles to Enbom Lake. This is a small but beautiful lake of around 30 acres sitting on top of the Continental Divide, with excellent views of the San Juan Mountains. Camping is limited and primitive and there are plenty of weeds in the summer, making bank fishing very difficult. The JGFD harvests the weeds, but the lake is shallow so it usually suffers from winterkill.

The reservation stocks over 10,000 8-inch rainbows per year and an additional 2,000 pounds of 16 to 22 inch bows to offset the winterkill. They put on the weight fast so fish in the 5-pound range are common.

Float-tubing can produce great results early and late in the year, although summer fishing is limited to very early morning and late evening. The water is clear, so it's easy to spot the cutts and rainbows that cruise the weed beds in search of nymphs, snails, and scuds. The usual patterns work well at Enbom Lake.

Mundo Lake

From Enbom Lake, continue north on J8 about 6 miles to Mundo. Or from Dulce, go south on J8 about 5.3 miles. This 60-acre lake is relatively new, so it has fewer weeds than the other lakes. It was designed for easy bank fishing, which makes it popular with baitfishers. There are campsites, picnic tables, toilets, and a pier. Mundo has nice rainbows, cutts, and browns, and some browns over 24 inches have been caught here. The reservation stocks over 30,000 8-inch rainbows every year and over 2,000 pounds of 16- to 22-inch bows. At the turn of the century, largemouth bass and bluegill were also stocked and have taken hold, and channel catfish are present, too.

Add large crayfish to your list of patterns here. Use a brown or dingy-orange crayfish imitation and fish it deep. Let the fly settle to the bottom, then make three long, quick strips while rotating the rod to one side. Then let it settle on the bottom again and repeat, rotating the rod to the other side, thus mimicking the erratic motion of a fleeing crayfish. Don't be surprised if you catch every species of fish with this fly. In the evening, if there's no wind, trout freely rise to midges, which I imitate with a Griffith's Gnat, size 14 to 18, or a black and gray Midge Cluster.

Lakes Facts: Jicarilla Lakes

Season
- Open year-round, but flyfishing is possible only from ice-out through October.

Special Regulations
- Daily bag limit is six trout.
- Privately owned by the Jicarilla Indian Reservation; permit required. Obtain current information, prices, and permits from the JGFD at 575-759-3255 or www.jicarillahunt.com or at any of the vendors listed on their website.
- New Mexico fishing license not required.
- Stone Lake season is April 1 through November 30. Only artificial flies and lures with barbless hooks may be used.
- Mundo Lake: five trout and only one bass over 15 inches.

Trout
- Rainbow trout all lakes; Mundo Lake has browns; Mundo Lake also has bass, bluegill, and catfish.

Permit Fees
- Daily permit – Adults $11 / Kids 12 and under $5 / vets and seniors $6
- Annual permit – Adults $60 / Kids 12 and under, vets and seniors $30

Lake Characteristics
- The lakes range in size from 30 to 400 surface acres at elevations ranging from 7,200 to 7,800 feet. Weeds are a main feature on most lakes. Spring and fall are best. In summer, try early morning and late evening. In hot, dry years it may become difficult or impossible to launch boats after midsummer.

Campgrounds
- Camping is allowed at all the lakes except Horse Lake. Camping is free with the purchase of a fishing permit.

Maps
- BLM Map, Chama; *New Mexico Atlas & Gazetteer,* page 14; Jicarilla Indian Reservation Map (available online at www.jicarillahunt.com); USGS Quadrangle Maps: Wirt Canyon, Dulce, Cordova Canyon, Cedar Canyon, Apache Mesa, Horse Lake

Agencies
- Direct fishing inquiries to Kevin Terry, Fisheries Biologist; on the web at www.jicarillahunt.com
- Jicarilla Game and Fish Department, P.O. Box 313, Dulce, NM 87528; 505-759-3255
- Stuart Perea, Acting Director of Jicarilla Game and Fish Department; sperea@jicarillahunt.com

JICARILLA LAKES MAJOR HATCHES

Insect	J	F	M	A	M	J	J	A	S	O	N	D	Time	Flies
Blue Damselfly										▮			M/E	Olive Marabou Damsel #8–#14; Extended Body Parachute Blue Damsel #8–#14
Midges											▮		M/E	Red & olive midge larva #16–#20; olive, gray, black and zebra midge pupa #18–#24; Pheasant Tail #16–#22; Disco Midge #18–#24; Mating Midge #14–#20; black & gray Midge Clusters #10–#16; Griffith's Gnat #16–#22; Snowfly #16–#26
Scuds											▮		M/E	Olive & light orange scuds #14–#20
Callibaetis									▮	▮			M/A/SF	Dark olive Hare's Ear #14–#18; Parachute Adams #14–#18; Blue Quill #14–#18; Speckled-wing Dun #14–#18; Callibaetis Spinner #16–#20
Caddis									▮				M/E	Olive & orange Elk Hair Sedge #8–#14; dark olive micro-caddis #18–#22
Minnows											▮		M/E	Soft-Hackle Streamer or Woolly Buggers in assorted colors #4–#14
Roe (Trout Eggs)						▮							M/E	Orange, Gold, Chartreuse, Peach Micro-Eggs #16–#18
Terrestrials									▮				M/E	Ants, termites, true flies, beetles, bees #12–#18; Dave's Hoppers, Parahoppers in yellow & tan #6–#14

Hatch Time Code: M = Morning; A = Afternoon; E = Evening; D = Dark; SF = Spinner Fall

Rio Penasco

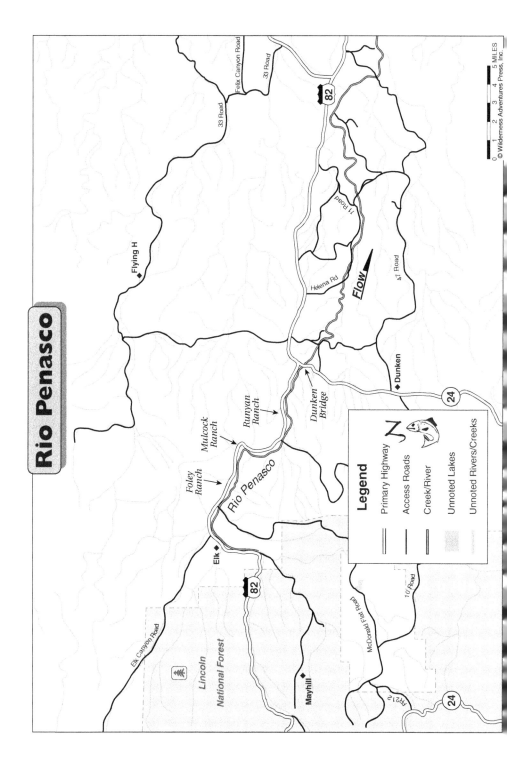

Legend

Primary Highway

Access Roads

Creek/River

Unnoted Lakes

Unnoted Rivers/Creeks

Felix Canyon Road

33 Road

33 Road

11 Road

A1 Road

Helena Rd

Flow

Flying H

Dunken

24

Runyan Ranch

Mulcock Ranch

Dunken Bridge

Foley Ranch

Rio Penasco

Elk

82

10 Road

Elk Canyon Road

Lincoln National Forest

82

McDonald Flat Road

Mayhill

RR212

24

N

0 1 2 3 4 5 MILES

© Wilderness Adventures Press, Inc.

THE RIO PENASCO

The Rio Penasco, located in southeast New Mexico about 36 miles east of Alamogordo and about 60 miles west of Artesia on US 82, is one of the only full-fledged spring creeks in the state. Unlike most streams in New Mexico, which get much of their water from runoff, the Rio Penasco gets virtually all its flow from springs spewing out of the Sacramento Mountains. Spring and summer rains add to the flow and melting winter snow seeps into the ground, replenishing the aquifer.

In a desert region that has very little in the way of coldwater trout streams, the Rio Penasco stands out like a shining oasis. In fact, it's one of the finest flyfishing streams in the state and the majority of it flows through private property, yet it can be accessed in a variety of ways.

From where it begins as several seeps, the Penasco flows east—paralleled by FR 164 for 11 miles—gaining water from small springs. NM 130 follows it for 9 more miles to Mayhill. From Mayhill, US 82 parallels it for about 20 to 25 miles before it becomes unsuitable for trout.

Although there are trout from the headwaters all the way to the Dunken Bridge on US 82, the main fishery doesn't start until about a mile below the town of Elk. Above there, the Penasco isn't much more than an irrigation ditch in most places, and the water is often used up before reaching Elk. There are some nice browns in the upper Penasco, along with a limited population of wild cuttbows, but it's almost all private so you must get permission to fish. The big springs enter the river below Elk, and this is where great flyfishing begins.

For about 10 miles downstream from Elk, the Penasco runs through a series of private ranches, each with different fishing policies. This section of the Rio Penasco is clean, clear, and cold. It exhibits many different water types, from open meadows with deep, undercut banks and numerous weed beds to narrow box canyons with waterfalls, pool drops, deep holes, and boulder pockets.

I swear there are holes over 15 feet deep and channels between watercress beds over 10 feet deep. The water temperature averages between 52 degrees in the dead of winter to only 60 degrees under the sweltering heat of summer. The river is from 5 to 20 feet wide and has a bottom that varies from gravel, watercress, and weeds to small rock and silt. But there is also a hell of a lot of horrible, sticky, slimy, nasty clay, especially in the upper pastoral flows. Chest or pant waders are necessary unless you wade wet, but avoid the nasty clay stuff. I've seen cows so badly stuck in the stuff that they had to be pulled out with a tractor.

Needless to say, the river is extremely nutrient rich, and its abundant food sources grow stocked and wild rainbows, cuttbows, and browns rapidly. The trout, mostly wild browns, feast on a variety of hatches that occur year-round, as well as on scuds and minnows. Fish easily average 12 to 16 inches, with many up to 20 inches and some browns reaching 25 inches. I heard of a 29-inch brown that was caught on a Ginger Scud on the Mulcock Ranch a few years ago.

Guide Cory Marchison lands a fat rainbow on the Foley Ranch.

The extreme southern latitude and low elevation (between 5,500 and 6,000 feet) result in a very mild climate, but the cool spring water protects the fish from the sometimes sweltering heat in July and August. Except after heavy thundershowers, the Penasco can be fished year-round. Most anglers prefer flyfishing during the spring, winter, and fall when it's cool, although summer fishing is good, too.

Hatches of Baetis occur every morning year-round, and other hatches are long-lived, as well, including caddis, which hatch from March through October. Match the Baetis with an Olive or Adams Parachute, size 18 to 22. For a nymph, try a Pheasant Tail or dark olive Hare's Ear, size 18 to 22. Dry-droppers work well sometimes, but just a dry fly usually does the job if insects are on the water and fish are rising. The Baetis come off early (8:00 a.m. to noon) during the hot months and later (10:00 a.m. to 2:00 p.m.) when it's cold. There are numerous caddis species, and the larvae are present year-round. Match the caddis with the appropriate size and color of Elk Hair Caddis, but if they won't come to the surface try an olive, gray, or tan caddis larva with or without a bead. Fish them deep, using lead and a strike indicator.

According to the late, great Norm Mabie, a veteran angler on the Penasco and senior member of the Mesilla Valley Flyfishers, there are some tremendous micro-caddis hatches. He imitated these with a small black or gray micro-caddis, size 18 to 20. Norm says small Golden Stoneflies hatch off and on all year, especially during winter and spring. Match them with a Bird's Stonefly or Gold Stimulator, size 10 to 14.

Tricos hatch most mornings from March through September and the trout love them, especially the morning spinner fall, when pods of large trout can be seen sipping the tiny spinners in the slow-water foam lines and next to weed and watercress beds. Try a black and gray Trico Parachute, size 22, or a black Trico Spinner, size 20 to 22, if they're being fussy.

According to Norm, a large aquatic butterfly can hatch anytime, and the trout will devour them. Of course, midges are abundant, too, and when it gets cold in the winter they become an important food source. Imitate them with a Griffith's Gnat, size 18 to 24, or an individual Grizzly Midge (Snow Fly), size 20 to 26. Another good pattern is the Mating Midge, which is merely a stripped peacock-herl body on a hook shank with one grizzly hackle palmered at the bend and another at the eye, sometimes called a fore-and-aft pattern (like a Renegade or Double Hackle). Tie them on 1X hooks, size 18 to 22. Also, tiny red or olive midge larvae work extremely well when fished in the deep channels between the weeds and watercress.

As for terrestrials, well, they're long-lived too, starting in May and lasting into late November, and the fish like them a lot. Any good hopper pattern will work, especially if it has legs. Use them on windy days or when there's no hatch; try a hopper-dropper with a small beadhead nymph on the dropper. I like a yellow, brown, or tan Parahopper pattern. Pay close attention to the banks and water with overhanging vegetation. The hoppers are generally smaller in the spring and larger from midsummer through fall. Look for desert hoppers, which make a loud clicking sound when they fly. They are tan with a black and yellow underwing or black with a black and red underwing.

The Rio Penasco also has billions of scuds that thrive in the weedy bottom and edges of the creek. Try a standard olive, ginger, or tangerine scud, size 16 to 20, tied on a curved scud and larva hook. Fish your scud like a nymph between the weed beds and anywhere else you'd fish a nymph. Use a scud in conjunction with a dark olive Hare's Ear or caddis larva for the best results.

Baitfish, including chubs, are plentiful, and streamers are an excellent way to catch the big browns, especially in the fall during pre-spawn and spawning modes. My favorite pattern is a Soft-Hackle Streamer with chain-bead eyes, size 4 to 10. I tie it with a spun marabou body using three plumes of marabou with flexible stems in various colors. For the Penasco, I prefer a yellow-white-brown combination with a couple of strands of pearl Krystal Flash between each plume.

After tying on the chain-bead eyes, tie in the first plume about halfway down the shank. Palmer it like a soft hackle forward toward the eye, making tight wraps. After cinching it down, pull the excess and all the marabou herls back toward the bend and over-wrap with thread so the marabou flares back. Tie in a couple of strands of pearl Krystal Flash, pull back, and over-wrap with thread.

Tie in the next plume directly in front of the first and repeat the process, and then again with the next plume. After three plumes are tied in, the front of the body should be almost to the chain-bead eye. Tie in two small partridge feathers with the outside of the bend facing the hook shank and the tips pointing away from the body (to imitate the pectoral fins) and secure. Tie in a yellow mallard flank feather and palmer it forward with tight wraps to form a collar. Tie it off, pull back, and over-wrap with thread. Wrap the thread forward past the chain-bead eyes and whip finish.

Fish the streamer as you would any streamer—stripping, twitching, and jigging the fly, making it look alive but vulnerable. Try different techniques until you find one that works. Fish all likely areas, and pay close attention to the heads of riffles and tails of pools where big browns hang out during the pre-spawning and spawning season, which starts in late October and lasts until the end of December. Avoid fishing over or walking on redds in order to ensure successful reproduction.

The rainbows and browns also love to eat protein-rich trout eggs, and a golden or peach micro-egg, size 16 to 18, works well from November through March when the rainbows quit spawning. The rainbows spawn sporadically from December through March, but other trout, rainbows in particular, can hardly resist the temptation an egg presents. It's like candy to a baby.

Trout in the Rio Penasco can be fussy, more so now that more anglers are fishing its private waters and educating the fish. I recommend an 8- to 9-foot rod for a 4- or 5-weight line and long leaders (9 to 12 feet) with light tippets of 5X to 7X, except when fishing streamers. If possible, use fluorocarbon when fishing dries.

As with many spring creeks, the fish can be very selective, especially during hatches. Matching the size, shape, and color of the natural is very important and knowing what stage the hatch is in will help determine your technique and increase your chances of catching fish. First, look for flies on the surface or in the air. If there aren't many flies on the water and you don't see fish rising, then dry flies probably aren't your best choice.

Identifying the rise form is important in determining what stage the hatch is in. If you look deeper into the water you'll probably see fish flashing subsurface, which means they are feeding on freshly emerging nymphs at the beginning of a hatch. You should nymph fish or at least use a dry fly with the appropriate beadhead nymph on a dropper about 18 inches long. After a while, you'll usually start noticing subtle rises where you don't see the fish break water but you notice a ring after the rise. This means fish are feeding on helpless emergers stuck in the surface film. Remove the beadhead nymph and try an emerger or try the emerger by itself.

When fish start rising consistently, breaking the surface with their noses as they take flies and leaving a ring and the telltale air bubble behind, the hatch is in full swing and you can switch to an individual dry fly.

Be careful not to false cast over the feeding trout, lest you spook them. False cast to the side with a short line while watching the trout rise. Select one fish, wait for it to rise, then place your fly just above the rise in the same drift line it's feeding in. Keep repeating this until you get it right or put the fish down, then go to the next one. You must be very patient, observant, deliberate, and accurate to be successful on the Rio Penasco.

Several different ranches on this unique stretch of river offer access. Let's look at some of the best for flyfishers.

The Foley Ranch

The 3,200-acre Foley Ranch, owned by Mel Foley, is on the uppermost section of the Rio Penasco, located just below where perennial springs join to create a year-round spring creek. The flyfishing operation offers about 1.5 miles of private water, and it's considered by many expert anglers to be the best stretch on the Penasco.

There are nice riffles, pools, holes, undercut banks, and deep channels cut between weeds and watercress. Habitat and stream improvements have enhanced the fishery considerably, and angling use is very limited. Mel only allows four anglers at a time for only a few days a week, so the river gets plenty of rest, ensuring high-quality fishing year-round. There are plenty of plump rainbows and a few browns, including some whoppers up to 6 or 7 pounds. The water is usually gin-clear, making sight fishing possible for experienced fish-spotters.

In addition to superb flyfishing, Mr. Foley offer fine streamside, camp-style accommodations at a price that won't break the bank. There are two durable, hard-framed cabins, each with three beds and a heater. Bathroom facilities, with a shower, are located just outside the cabins. They run $50 per cabin.

They offer various packages—day-use rod fees; day-use and lodging. They also have private memberships available. For more information, pricing, or reservations, contact the Foleys at 575-687-2221.

Only artificial flies may be used, and all fish must be immediately returned to the water.

To get to the Foley Ranch from Cloudcroft on US 82, turn right at mile marker 50 and look for the Rio Penasco sign.

The Foley Ranch has cozy hard-framed wall tents with heat and cooking facilities. A bathhouse with hot running water is just yards away.

An angler tests his skills on the Mulcock Ranch's selective trout.

The Mulcock Ranch

The Mulcock Ranch is the showpiece of the Rio Penasco in terms of versatility for the flyfisher. It's located just downstream of the Foley Ranch on US 82 between mile markers 50 and 51. There are about 5 miles of water with three distinct sections.

The upper section has classic riffles, pools, and runs, and the pools are deep. Weeds and watercress sway in the current, revealing large trout lurking beneath them at the bottom of deep holes. There's room to cast to the selective pods of trout that can be found feeding in the larger pools during a hatch. Don't let the size of the Penasco fool you, the holes are deep, and stepping into them can get you in trouble. Wade only where there is gravel and where you can easily see the bottom, usually at the tails of pools and heads of riffles. Avoid the mud.

The middle section is more channelized, kind of like an old irrigation ditch, and most anglers avoid it. But some of the biggest fish in the Penasco are in this stretch. They hang under the watercress in the deep channel. There's also some seriously deceptive undercutting that provides excellent cover for huge browns. It's almost impossible (and unnecessary) to wade, but watch out for the mud along the bank, as you could easily slip and fall in the deep channel.

Once, back when the Mesilla Valley Flyfishers invited me up to give a clinic, I decided to fish this section because everyone else was working the upper stretch. I hooked over five fish in two hours that were too big to handle in the narrow, weedy channel. I caught several others up to 18 inches using an Orange Scud and a small, dark Hare's Ear. Hi-sticking allowed me to get down 5 to 9 feet where the big ones were.

Fishing a dry will usually yield all the 12- to 16-inch fish you want, but the big browns in this section usually stay down except during evening caddis hatches.

The lower section is my favorite because it's within a 60-foot-deep box canyon where 20- to 30-foot waterfalls plunge down to form deep holes. There are many pool drops and boulder-strewn pockets, as well. The Penasco drops over 350 feet in the lowest mile of the Mulcock Ranch, where the beauty is astounding. There's even a decent stonefly hatch here, mainly in the spring.

The first time I fished the Rio Penasco was in the mid-1980s, when Ron Smorynski invited me up to look at a piece of water he wanted the Mesilla Valley Flyfishers to lease. Since I lease private waters, Ron wanted to know what I thought and how much it was worth. Of course, I wanted to fish this virgin water pretty bad so I happily joined Ron for an afternoon on the Mulcock Ranch.

We went straight down from the bunkhouse to the first good hole in the upper part of the canyon. It was late fall and I knew browns must be lurking about so I tied on a large Soft-Hackle Streamer and cast it to the top of a deep pool, letting it sink for a second or two before starting to strip. I noticed Ron observing everything I was doing, and I remember thinking, "Is he watching me to learn my technique or is he observing to see if I really know what I'm doing?"

I was nervous for a moment, but on my second strip I saw a wake heading for my fly and instantly I was attached to a brown of 23 inches or so. I wore him down quickly with a bent rod and landed the beast, the first of several I took on streamers. I was scheduled to give a slide show on streamer fishing to the club the next night, and Ron was to introduce me. Needless to say, he gave a very favorable introduction to the club and a firm recommendation to lease the Mulcock Ranch, which they eventually did. They had the lease until September 1997, when it became a private fishing club run by the owner, Charlie Mulcock.

To fish the Mulcock Ranch, you must be a member or a member's guest, or, if you want to test it out before becoming a member, Charlie will let you in for a rod fee. If you're a member you can fish anytime without a reservation. A rustic bunkhouse overlooking the box canyon is available to members for a modest nightly fee. There's a miniature fly shop at the main ranch house, with terminal tackle and a few other odds and ends; just knock on the door.

If you're interested in becoming a member, just call Charlie Mulcock at 575-687-3352 and set up an appointment to look at and fish the Mulcock Ranch. He'll give you a tour of the place and show you some deep, dark holes where big trout reside.

The Runyan Ranch Lease

(Mesilla Valley Flyfishers)

Since the mid-1980s the Mesilla Valley Flyfishers have been very active in trying to lease, protect, enhance, and preserve sections of the Rio Penasco for members of their very active club based out of Las Cruces. Currently, the club has over 235 members, which is incredible for a town the size of Las Cruces, in a region with very little cold water. At one time, they had leases on two ranches just below Elk—the Bernard Cleve

Ranch and the Charles Mulcock Ranch. Now the Mulcock Ranch has its own private flyfishing club (see Mulcock Ranch above), and the Cleve Ranch, which is the first ranch below Elk, has dried up in recent years since most of the springs enter the river below there.

Right at the turn of the present century, the club was able to secure about 2 miles of water on the Runyan Ranch just below the Mulcock Ranch. You must be a member of the Mesilla Valley Flyfishers to fish here, which is easy to join and not very expensive. As of this writing, a regular membership is just $20 and a family membership is only $25. Members pay $25 per day to fish, and children under 18 fish for free.

To inquire about becoming a member and to obtain information about the fishing, contact Mesilla Valley Flyfishers, Inc., P.O. Box 2222, Las Cruces, NM 88004-2222, www.mvff.org or call 575-522-6325.

To get to the Runyan Ranch Lease, follow NM 82 east from Cloudcroft or west from Artesia. The turnoff to the lease is located on the right side of the road about 100 yards before mile marker 54 (coming from Cloudcroft) or 100 yards after mile marker 54 on the left (coming from Artesia).

There are good access areas, and the club has made it very user friendly, with good signage, while protecting the streambank. There are about 2 miles of water. The upper half is very brushy with some deep holes and pools, while the lower half is more open with riffles, runs, and pools. The club has done and continues to do some improvements and some grooming to make the upper section more fishable. It now has more habitat for big browns, and not as much heavy brush as it used to have.

The club stocks small rainbows occasionally, which grow to be nice fish in a short time, and there are holdover rainbows and wild browns up to 20 inches, some bigger. The regulations are catch-and-release flyfishing only, so there are plenty of fish. The dry-fly action can be great here, especially March through June, when there are multiple hatches.

The club doesn't allow guiding on the river, and members enjoy figuring things out and teaching each other. They also conduct flyfishing clinics at the ranch so members can learn new tricks from other experienced anglers. It's great that the club has worked hard to ensure there is an affordable private fishery for their members to enjoy in an otherwise vast, dry region with very few angling opportunities.

In addition to the streamside accommodations on the Foley and Mulcock Ranches, there are accommodations about 15 miles back toward Cloudcroft in the village of Mayhill at the Mayhill Inn and Cafe (575-687-3066). The Barn Door Restaurant (505-687-3662) is another good restaurant near Mayhill.

For more deluxe lodging, there's the Lodge at Cloudcroft, about 40 to 45 minutes from the private fishing on the Rio Penasco. Contact them at The Lodge at Cloudcroft, Lisa Thomassie, General Manager, #1 Corona Place/P.O. Box 497, Cloudcroft, NM 88317; info@thelodgeresort.com.

Stream Facts: Rio Penasco

Season
• Year-round.

Special Regulations
• Catch-and-release flyfishing only.

Trout
• Stocked and wild rainbows and wild browns and cuttbows that average 12 to 16 inches, several to 20 inches, a few to 24 inches, and a rare brown to 29 inches.

River Miles
• Mayhill—0
• Elk—12
• Foley Ranch upper boundary—14.5
• Foley Ranch lower boundary/Mulcock Ranch upper boundary—16
• Mulcock Ranch headquarters—16.8
• Mulcock bunkhouse—18.5
• Lower boundary Mulcock Ranch/Upper boundary Runyan Ranch—21
• Lower boundary Runyan Ranch—23

River Characteristics
• Spring creek, 5 to 20 feet wide, running through a high desert and exhibiting riffles, runs, pools, deep holes, undercut banks, waterfalls, plunge pools, boulder-strewn pockets, and deep channels between weed and watercress beds.

River Flows
• Winter, summer, and fall: 15 to 30 cfs
• Spring runoff: 30 to 60 cfs

Campgrounds
• There's a private campground in Mayhill and several Forest Service campgrounds in the Lincoln National Forest on US 82 between Mayhill and Cloudcroft.

Maps
• *New Mexico Atlas & Gazetteer,* pages 48 and 49; Lincoln National Forest Map; BLM Map: Alamogordo

RIO PENASCO MAJOR HATCHES

Insect	J	F	M	A	M	J	J	A	S	O	N	D	Time	Flies
Caddis					█	█	█	█					M/E	Green & olive caddis larva #12–#16; Double Hackle Peacock #12– #16; Van's Rag Pupa or LaFontaine's Pupa #10–#18; green or dark olive Green Weenie #12–#18; olive, tan & gray Elk Hair Caddis #12–#20; olive, gray & peacock Fluttering Caddis #10–#18
Midges	█	█	█	█	█	█	█	█	█	█	█	█	M/E	Red & olive midge larva #16–#20; olive, gray, black, and zebra midge pupa #18–#24; Pheasant Tail #16– #22; Disco Midge #18–#24; Mating Midge #14–#20; black & gray Midge Clusters #10–#16; Griffith's Gnat #16–#22; Snowfly #16–#26
March Brown & Mahogany Duns						█							M/E/SF	Light, dark & olive Hare's Ear #16–#20; Pheasant Tail #16–#20; light, dark, ginger Hair Wing Duns or Cahills #16–#20 or the same in parachutes; Ginger, Red & Blue Quills #12–#18
Baetis									█				M/A/SF	Dark olive Hare's Ear #16–#22; Pheasant Tail #16–#22; Van's Rag Fly dark olive #16–#22; olive Lawson's Fan-Wing Emerger #16–#22 Olive Parachute #16–#22; Olive Comparadun #16–#22
Golden Stonefly, Yellow Sally					█								M/A	Black & brown stonefly nymph #4– #10; Golden Stone Nymph #10–#14; Elk Hair Salmonfly #4–#8; Orange & Gold Stimulators #4–#14; Terminators #12–#16

Hatch Time Code: M = Morning; A = Afternoon; E = Evening; D = Dark; SF = Spinner Fall

RIO PENASCO MAJOR HATCHES (cont.)

Insect	J	F	M	A	M	J	J	A	S	O	N	D	Time	Flies
Little Brown Stonefly		▓	▓	▓								▓	M/A	Dark brown Hare's Ear #14–#16; brown Elk Hair Caddis #14–#16
PMDs, PEDs							▓	▓					M/SF	Light Hare's Ear #12–#18; Pheasant Tail #12–#20; Van's Rag Fly light olive #14–#20; Ginger or Light Olive Dun #14–#20
Terrestrials							▓	▓	▓	▓	▓		M/A	Para-hoppers tan, yellow #8–#14; red w/ black underwing Desert Hopper #6–#14; beetles, crickets & ants #12–#18
Roe (Eggs)	▓						▓	▓			▓	▓	M/A	Orange, Golden, Peach Micro-Eggs #16–#20
San Juan Worms	▓	▓	▓	▓	▓	▓	▓	▓	▓	▓	▓	▓	M/A	Ultra Chenille Worms in orange, cinnamon, sand, flesh, brown, wine & earthworm #12–#18
Scuds	▓	▓	▓	▓	▓	▓	▓	▓	▓	▓	▓	▓	M/E	Orange, ginger & olive scuds #14–#16
Minnows	▓	▓	▓	▓	▓	▓	▓	▓	▓	▓	▓	▓	M/E	Assorted Colors of Soft-Hackle Streamers, Woolly Buggers #2–#12

Hatch Time Code: M = Morning; A = Afternoon; E = Evening; D = Dark; SF = Spinner Fall

Hazards and Weather

New Mexico—the northern region, in particular—has to be one of the best places in the country to live in terms of minimal hazards and bad weather. We don't have earthquakes, tornadoes, hurricanes, major flooding, or any other natural disasters on a regular basis. We receive less moisture annually than any state except Arizona, so storms are infrequent. Nevertheless, there are some hazards, weather problems, and other natural elements to contend with.

The lack of water means that we have very low humidity and bright sun, both of which can present problems. Protect yourself from the blazing sun with sunscreen (even in winter), plenty of lip balm, a good wide-brim hat with UVA and UBV protection, and a long-sleeve shirt. Drink plenty of water or other fluids. In the summer and fall you should drink at least four liters per day and at least half that in the winter, and I'm not talking about beer and wine because they can dehydrate you. At the end of the day, dowse yourself in a good moisturizing lotion and then have your cocktails.

Another nasty thing that can sneak up on you here is a cloudburst or thundershower, which presents two problems. First and foremost is lightning, which is deadly, and New Mexico has more lightning deaths per capita than any state in the nation. It's our worst natural disaster, and of course it also causes forest fires, another potential danger. I've been hit once and have had several close calls—so many that I was nicknamed "lightning rod" by my peers.

I now go by the 12-second rule. When I see lightning I count to 12, if I don't hear the thunder before I finish, it's cool. If I hear it in less than 12 seconds I'm out of there. Take cover in a car or man-made shelter, if possible. Otherwise, take cover in the lowest bushes or trees you can find and never get under a tall or lone tree in an open area. Stay as far away from these as possible until the storm has passed. If you're on a lake it's even more important to pay attention to how close lightning is. When you're on a lake in a boat or float-tube you're the highest thing around and water is a conductor, as is your graphite rod.

Another problem with cloudbursts is that they can cause flash floods, resulting in fast, swollen rivers where there once was a creek or dry arroyo. If you're fishing in a box canyon or gorge this can be particularly dangerous. Always know how to get up and out if necessary, and don't get trapped. Get to high ground fast when the water rises quickly and gets murky.

Winter can be very unpredictable in New Mexico. It might be bright and sunny and 45 degrees one minute and 25 degrees and snowing the next. Always wear layers, starting with good polypropylene or wool undergarments and socks and finishing with a Gore-Tex shell and a hat that protects your ears. I use a wool hat with a bill and earflaps that can be folded up, and, of course, fingerless wool gloves.

One more danger that exists here, especially in southern New Mexico, is poisonous snakes—rattlesnakes, in particular. The advice taught in first-aid classes is to avoid them by watching your step. Snakes don't want to hurt you, they want to get away from you. Dogs, on the other hand, can't resist messing with them the first time they encounter one, and I know of several individuals whose dogs have been bitten. None died, and now they leave snakes alone. If you do get bitten don't cut and suck, just get help and go to a doctor as soon as possible.

Mosquitoes are not a major problem in New Mexico because of our lack of humidity and moisture, but horseflies, deerflies, bullflies, and other hideous biting insects will get to you if you're not paying attention. Strong repellent with 99-percent DEET will help, but you really just have to watch them. They annoy you more than they actually bite.

PREPARING FOR YOUR TRIP AND GETTING HERE

For the traveling angler, New Mexico is very user friendly. Our roads are good and there is very little traffic, except right near Albuquerque and Santa Fe. Flying into Albuquerque International Airport is easy and stress-free, without the crowds of other major airports. Albuquerque is a great hub because it's centrally located so you can drive to any one of the four corners of New Mexico within four or five hours, and there is a great deal of good fishing within a couple of hours of the airport. There's also commuter air service from Albuquerque to Santa Fe, Taos, Farmington, Silver City, and Las Cruces.

With heightened security at airports, it's impossible to carry on fishing gear so plan on checking it in at the counter from the beginning and hope like hell it doesn't get lost. Travelers should have 3- or 4-piece travel rods that fit nicely into duffel or rod bags. Also, get to the airport early to make sure all bags get on the plane on time.

As far as planning your trip goes, I highly recommend using an experienced travel agent to book your flight or train (which is becoming more popular lately). Many people prefer planning their trips online, where they can check out everything from flights to accommodations, restaurants, fly shops and guide services, private ranches, maps, and even information on the fisheries themselves.

A simple phone call to one of the fly shops or outfitters in the region you're planning to visit will save you a lot of time and effort in planning your trip, as well. These businesses are listed in the hub city information at the end of each region.

In today's point-and-click, fast-paced world outfitters and guides are more important than ever for visiting anglers who want a quality experience in a limited amount of time. A guide can cut to the chase and help you with the techniques required on different waters. If you are an experienced flyfisher but have novice anglers in your group, a guide is invaluable. They can take over the task of instructing and guiding those individuals so you can enjoy the fishing. If you're like me, you know how hard it can be to teach your spouse, kids, or siblings to do anything. I guide all types of people with no problem, but I can't tell my own brother anything. Plus, guides automatically come with a little bit of authority on the subject so people pay more attention to them.

Studying maps, reading guidebooks, and asking questions about where you'll be fishing will enhance your trip and heighten your anticipation for the journey.

Things to Bring

When embarking on a flyfishing adventure, whether for an afternoon or a week, preparation is important if you want to have a problem-free trip. If you live in New Mexico and fish here regularly you should already have a system that works for you. Since I'm a guide, I'm always loaded and ready with enough stuff for two or three anglers to go fishing any time of the year, but the average person doesn't need quite so much gear.

A waterproof duffle or fishing bag is nice to have for carrying everything you might need. Your bad should have a loaded vest, rain jacket, extra reel(s), line, leaders, tippet, flies, fly boxes, floatant, lead, and indicator yarn. A back-up rod is also vital, whether in your car or your bag.

It's always best to prepare for the worst and hope for the best. Develop a comfortable system for loading your vest, packing your bag, and arranging your vehicle. This system will prevent you from misplacing or losing any of the gear involved with this fascinating sport.

When you load a new vest, chest pack, or tackle bag, put it on first and keep modifying it so that it works for you while fishing. Remember to keep hanging things like clippers, scissors, hemostats, and zingers out of the way so they don't hang up on anything or interfere with casting and stripping line. Put leaders, tippet, fly boxes, lead, indicators, floatant, and anything you use regularly in pockets that are easy to access. Put back-up stuff and flies you might need in the back pockets along with things like water, food, a small first-aid kit, a small patch kit, sunscreen, etc. Designate a zipper pocket for an extra car key that you only use in an emergency. Many people reserve a pocket just for fishing licenses, as well. This is always a good idea, especially if you fish multiple states regularly.

Arrange your vehicle so you can easily get at the things you use the most. If you fish a lot and have a vehicle just for fishing and other recreation, consider including a box or two just for your gear. Use one box for waders and wet things and another for your vest and back-up gear. You can take these in and out of the vehicle easily without reloading every time. Just throw the boxes in and go.

Rod racks mounted on the interior of the roof are great for carrying rods while fishing. You don't have to unrig or break the rods down, and they're safely stored out of the way. Also, make sure you have a toolbox, jumper cables, a good first-aid kit, shovel, and fire extinguisher in your vehicle. I also keep a roll-up table, folding chairs, a tent, blanket, and a couple of floor mats for putting on and taking off waders. All this, plus my fishing gear and a cooler, fit nicely in the back of my Isuzu Trooper, and I still have plenty of room for my client's gear.

Visiting anglers need to deal with far more than a local angler. If you're only able to fish a few days a year, you need to make sure you're fully prepared so something unexpected doesn't ruin your trip. Start with the right equipment. Not just any rod will do. If you're fishing the San Juan or Rio Grande you'll need a 9-foot, 5- or 6-weight rod with matching reel, but if you're fishing the smaller streams you'll need a shorter, lighter rod like an 8-foot, 4-weight.

The following checklists will help you to prepare for your trip.

Vest, Tackle Bag, or Chest Pack

_____Flies
_____Fly Boxes
_____Leaders, 7½ and 9 feet, 3X to 6X
_____Tippet material, 2X to 7X
_____Indicator yarn or strike indicators
_____Floatant and dry-fly powder
_____Larva lead or split shot
_____Thermometer
_____Seine
_____Clippers
_____Hemostats
_____Scissors
_____Sunscreen
_____Insect repellent
_____Water bottle
_____Miniature first-aid kit
_____Cigarette lighter
_____Head lamp with good batteries
_____Camera and film
_____Toilet paper and/or paper towels
_____Fishing license
_____Extra key
_____Catch-and-release landing net (optional)
_____Whisky flask (optional)
_____Cell phone if you have a signal (turn on for emergencies only)

Gear Bags or Boxes

_____Rods and reels
_____Extra flies and/or fly boxes
_____Extra leaders, tippet, lead, and indicator yarn
_____Extra fly lines
_____Extra clippers, hemostats, and scissors
_____Rain gear and jackets or sweaters
_____Fingerless gloves
_____Warm hat with a bill
_____First-aid kit
_____Flashlight
_____Cigarette lighter
_____Toilet paper or paper towels

_____Duct tape
_____Line cleaner
_____Extra film and batteries

Wader Bag

_____Hip, pant, and/or chest waders
_____Wading boots
_____Gravel guards
_____Wading belt
_____Patch kit
_____Floor mat (optional)
_____Extra bootlaces
_____Wading staff (optional)

Vehicle

_____*Flyfisher's Guide to New Mexico*
_____Appropriate maps
_____Cooler
_____Roll-up table
_____Folding chairs
_____Fire extinguisher and folding shovel
_____Jumper cables
_____Good toolbox
_____Spare key in magnetic key holder
_____Bottle opener and corkscrew
_____Small tent or sleeping bag for emergencies, especially during winter

Clothes

_____Wide-brim hat
_____Polarized tan or amber sunglasses
_____Long-sleeve shirt
_____Small pocketknife
_____Sunscreen
_____Reading glasses or flip-focals if needed

FLYFISHING ETIQUETTE

Fishing has traditionally been something we do to commune with nature, seek solitude, and until recently, put food on the table. But the recent explosion in the popularity of catch-and-release flyfishing across the West has resulted in too much pressure on many fisheries, making it difficult to find solitude and have a "wild" experience on many streams. As rivers and streams get more crowded with anglers, the standards of fishing etiquette have evolved. It has become more and more difficult to know what is good and bad form on some streams, even for me. What is acceptable on some streams is not acceptable on others. The old standards of stream etiquette are gone.

When I was a kid my father taught us never to fish anywhere near another angler. Depending on the size of the stream, we'd distance ourselves at least a mile or two from anyone else. We certainly didn't want to fish water that had already been fished so we were always searching for virgin water, and there was plenty to be had if you were willing to work at it a little.

Today, some streams in the West have so much pressure that if you tried to allow a mile of space per angler, you'd never be able to fish. In fact, the popular rivers have so many anglers that you're lucky to have a riffle or pool to yourself, much less a section of river. Sometimes on busy weekends, 50 to 100 feet between anglers is about as good as you can do. All this can get complicated, though, because if you pulled up and started fishing next to an angler on a river like the Rio Grande Gorge during the middle of the week when there is very little pressure, you'd probably get a very dirty look.

Proper etiquette is relative to the size and productivity of a stream combined with the amount of fishing pressure on any given day. If the stream you're fishing has a car parked at every pullout you'll have to park double somewhere. Make sure you don't get in the river above another angler that was already there. Instead, get in behind them, but not too close to anyone that may be fishing behind you. Of course, you can also do what I do in situations like this—go someplace else.

Fortunately, in New Mexico most of our streams aren't very famous, except the San Juan and a couple of others, but even on the San Juan you can usually find places away from the crowds. Weekends are by far the busiest times, especially on the streams that you can easily drive right up to. There are still many streams accessible on dirt or gravel roads or by hiking a little ways that provide solitude and good fishing. With a little forethought, weekdays could find you solo on almost any stream in the state.

So good stream etiquette is a judgment call based on how much pressure there is. Basically, respect an angler's space and give him or her as much room as possible under the circumstances. The smaller the stream, the more space you should allow. If someone else is fishing up to your favorite stretch of water, don't try to beat the angler to it; just try a different stretch.

A strange phenomenon has evolved as pressure increases. Anglers new to the sport see one or more anglers flyfishing and they want to fish with them, even though there is plenty of open water above and below. They evidently think that if another person is fishing there, then it must be the best water on the river. So they wade right in, and before you know it yet another person pulls over. Soon, you have a frenzy of anglers whipping the water up to a rich, creamy lather. Of course, they're lucky if any of them catch a fish because they've already spooked every fish in the river.

Meanwhile, a solitary angler a mile downstream is quietly working a stretch of water, catching a wild brown out of every pool. He's thankful they didn't spot him first. You see, it's always better to fish water that no one else is fishing. I guarantee that if you're fishing behind me or any other experienced angler your chances of success will drop significantly.

When hiking into remote areas you're less likely to encounter other anglers, but if you do remember that they were there first and they essentially "own" the stretch of water they're fishing. Go way above or below them. If your paths cross, try to strike up a little trout talk and find out where they've fished and where they're planning to fish so you can go elsewhere, out of their way. They'll usually be grateful for your polite communication.

On many rivers and streams today you'll see professional guides with clients. If you run into a guide while they're working it's not polite to ask too many questions or to stop and observe for too long. It puts the guide in a difficult situation because the clients are paying a lot of money for information you're trying to get for free. Instead, ask the guide for a card and wish them luck. You can always call them later and ask your questions or book a trip. Of course, if you see a guide just out fishing, it's okay to talk as long as they're willing.

Sometimes, you can't escape the crowds on certain waters like the San Juan River on a busy weekend. You may be sharing the same hole with 15 to 20 other anglers and a couple of boats. If you enter a pool like this, wade slow and yield as much space as possible to others before casting. If a nearby angler hooks a fish get your line up and out of the way. The anglers stack up because there are so many fish that even with this much pressure, everyone can catch fish if they cooperate. I usually opt to go find a side channel or move downstream where there are less fish and less people. If you decide to bypass a pool or run that someone is fishing make sure to walk way around them and the pool to avoid spooking fish or putting down rising trout.

Fishing partners also need to practice good etiquette with each other. One of the most common mistakes I see partners make is not realizing that they are spooking fish in front of the other angler all day long. As a guide, I have to contend with this on a daily basis. If you're fishing a small or medium-sized stream with one or more anglers you must first come up with a plan of action. You can't fish next to each other in the same small pools because there simply isn't enough room and you'll end up tangled. One person usually gets in front and the other fishes the same water just behind. This is the worst possible scenario, as the angler in front catches all the fish and the angler in back is fishing a desert. Each angler needs his or her own water, so if you must fish together use one of two methods.

The first method is to alternate fishing, letting one angler fish while the other acts as a guide, fish spotter, or photographer. After three missed strikes or one catch, you alternate. This can be a lot of fun, especially for beginners, although you only get in half as much fishing.

The second method is called leapfrogging, which allows you to stay close to each other but fish separate water. Usually, you'll be close enough to get to each other for a photo, if necessary. When you leapfrog it's very important that you stay far enough away from the stream to avoid being spotted by the trout, thus spooking them before your partner moves up. And make sure your partner knows you're passing and can see where you start fishing so he or she doesn't fish the same water.

If you just want to fish and don't care if you see each other for a few hours, the best method is for each of you to fish your own stretch of water. Drop one person off and then drive or walk up beyond that stretch before starting to fish. Your partner should have prior knowledge of where you're going to start; otherwise, you'll need to mark where you begin fishing with a flag on a stick or by where you park the vehicle. This is the best way to fish small to medium-sized streams because you spook less fish and you're both fishing nearly the entire time.

So observe the following rules of fishing etiquette and pass them on to your angling friends:

- The first person on a stretch of water owns that stretch until they're done.
- Do not crowd another angler.
- If you come upon an angler fishing slower than you, get out and go around if you can do it without spooking fish. Don't get back in until you are a reasonable distance above the other angler.
- An angler fishing upstream has the right of way over one coming downstream.
- In crowded conditions, yield to other anglers when they hook fish.
- If you're wading and a boat is drifting down, yield to the boat and let it pass.
- If you're floating and you come upon a wading angler, pull to the side and wait for the angler to yield, then pass quietly without fishing his/her water. Keep moving.
- Respect private property. Always get permission first.
- Pick up trash left by less thoughtful anglers.
- When fishing with a partner, don't just race to the river's edge and start thrashing. Instead, formulate a strategy that is good for both of you.
- Enjoy flyfishing for all it has to offer, not just the size and number of fish.

NEW MEXICO GAME FISH

New Mexico has a wide variety of cold and warmwater game fish that flyfishers can pursue, ranging from the normal trout species to cuttbow hybrids, kokanee salmon, striped bass, walleye, and even catfish. The NMDGF regulations booklet gives a description of each of these, but most flyfishers concentrate on the few species listed below.

Rainbow Trout (*Oncorhynchus mykiss*)
The rainbow trout takes its name from the pinkish-red band along the midline of its flanks. This band may be heavy or almost nonexistent, leaving the fish a silvery color. The fish is marked across its head, back, and upper flanks with many small, irregular black spots that are concentrated most heavily on its squarish tail.

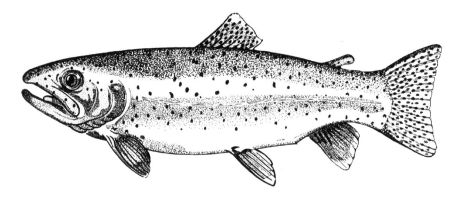

Rainbow Trout (*Oncorhynchus mykiss*)

Brown Trout (*Salmo trutta*)
The brown trout's basic coloration is golden-brown, with the back ranging from dark-brown to greenish-brown and its sides and belly ranging from light tan to lemon-yellow or white. The back and flanks are marked with many large black or brown spots. The few red spots on the lower flanks are surrounded by light blue-gray halos. There are few or no spots on its squarish tail.

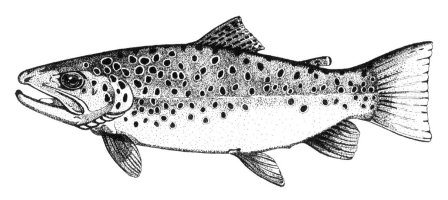

Brown Trout (*Salmo trutta*)

Rio Grande Cutthroat Trout (*Oncorhynchus clarki virginalis*)
Although not quite as brilliantly colored as cutthroat subspecies like the greenback or Colorado River, the Rio Grande is a beautiful trout native to New Mexico's waters. The Rio Grande has the famous red/orange gill plates that mark all cutthroats and a colorful body. It has spots that are clustered primarily at the back of the body near the tail. Small spots are also distributed sparsely along the back. Several other cutthroat subspecies have been introduced into state waters, often mixing with rainbow trout (cuttbows). Efforts are now underway to restore Rio Grandes to as much of their native range as possible.

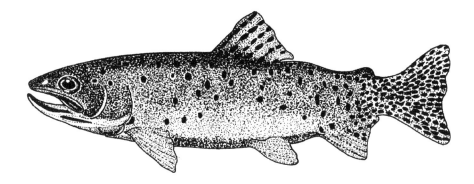

Rio Grande Cutthroat Trout (*Oncorhynchus clarki virginalis*)

Brook Trout (*Salvelinus fontinalis*)
The most distinctive markings on a brook trout are the white and black edges on the front of the lower fins, the wavy or wormlike markings on the back, and scattered red spots surrounded by blue halos on the flanks. Brook trout are dark green or blue-black on the back to white on the belly. The belly and lower fins turn brilliant red on spawning males in the fall. The tail is square.

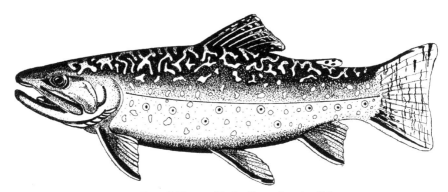

Brook Trout (*Salvelinus fontinalis*)

Smallmouth Bass (*Micropterus dolomieui*)
The smallmouth bass, often called bronze bass in New Mexico, is dark olive to brown on the back, with bronze flanks and a white belly. It has dark ventricle bands on the flanks. Its eyes are reddish, and the upper jaw ends in front of the eye. There is a shallow notch in the dorsal fin.

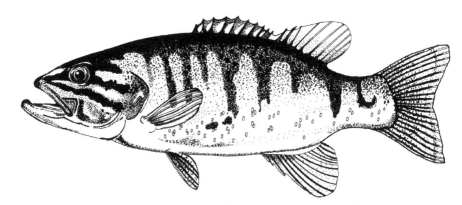

Smallmouth Bass (*Micropterus dolomieui*)

Top Trout Flies for New Mexico

1. RABBIT HAIR LEECH

2. VAN'S SOFT HACKLE STREAMER

3. VAN'S RAG FLY

4. GREEN WEENIE

5. SAN JUAN WORM

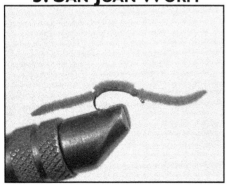

6. GINGER DUN

7. DOUBLE HACKLE PEACOCK

8. TERMINATOR

9. THOMPSON'S AF HOPPER

10. GLOW IN THE ASS CADDIS

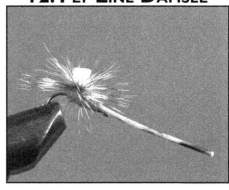

11. POUND-MEISTER

12. FLY LINE DAMSEL

Fly Recipes

1. Rabbit Hair Leech

HOOK: 1x or 2x long #8-#14
THREAD: 6/0 black
TAIL: Tuft of natural or brown hare fur with guard hairs
BODY: Natural or brown hare fur dubbing
WING: long tuft of natural or brown hare's fur
HEAD: Two strands of peacock hearl

Tie in the tail so that it extends past the bend of the hook a distance equal to the shaft of the hook. Dub fur forward ¾ of the way to the eye. Tie down the front wing so that the tips extend almost to the end of the tail. Tie in two strands of peacock and wrap forward to the eye and bind with several wraps and whip finish.

2. Van's Soft Hackle Streamer

HOOK: 3x or 4x long #2-#8
THREAD: 6/0 black or brown or match to color of fly
BODY: Three (any color) thin stemmed marabou (in this case yellow, brown and white) feathers with a hint of krystal flash.
EYES: Two chain bead eyes (color – match to body)
PECTORAL FIN: Two partridge flank feathers
HACKLE: Grizzly or mallard flank feathers

Tie in just four to six strands of krystal flash near the bend of the hook. Then secure the tip of a thin-stemmed marabou feather just a little forward of the bend of the hook and palmer it forward making tight wraps and tie it off, then pull the marabou fibers back towards the bend of the hook and make several wraps back toward the bend and then back. This gives the fly a tapered minnow like appearance when it gets wet. Tie in a couple of more strands and repeat this process with other colors of marabou, winding them forward and tying them off near the eye.

Add the chain bead eyes right at the eye of the hook using figure-eight wraps to secure. Wrap back to the initial marabou and tie in the two partridge feather tips, with outside curve facing the hook. Tie in the grizzly hackle or mallard flank feather and palmer forward to the eye and secure. Wind thread forward to the eye and whip finish.

3. VAN'S RAG FLY (BEADHEAD FLASHBACK)

This fly can be tied in any color, standard nymph or beadhead, flashback or not. It is simple to tie, represents a multitude of mayflies, midges and small stoneflies. It is symmetric so it looks real from any angle. I've caught more fish on this fly than any other by far. Of course I use it more than any other fly. Use ultra-translucent dubbing for this fly and dub it loosely, like a rag, so it captures water and air, giving it a realistic look.

HOOK: Dai Riki 135 size #12-#22
THREAD: Black 6/0 or 8/0 for small sizes
TAIL: Moose body hair or mane for large sizes
ABDOMEN: Medium hare's ear (or match to the natural)
THORAX: Dark hare's ear (or one shade darker than the abdomen)
WING CASE: Pearl flashabou or other tinsel (flash back only, otherwise no wing case)

Bead the hook (if you choose). Wrap the thread back to the bend and tie in the tail. Dub medium hare's ear and wrap forward ¾ of the way to the eye, tapering it so that it forms the abdomen and tie in the tensile. Dub the dark hare' ear loosely on the thread and wrap it forward forming a thorax that is thicker than the abdomen. Whip finish and trim.

4. GREEN WEENIE (BEAD HEAD)

The green weenie was developed by a local Taoseno to imitate the abundant free-living caddis larva in the Rio Grande Gorge, near Taos. He used it exclusively at times, catching more fish than anyone at times. Try it anywhere caddis are present.

HOOK: Mustad 3906 or similar hook
THREAD: 6/0 green
BEAD: Gold bead (optional)
BODY: Caddis green
TAIL: Moose body hair

Bead the fly and wind thread back to bend and back to the head. Lay the moose hair down the entire length of the hook with the tips extending past the bend equal to the gap of the hook. Dub the thread and wrap forward, tapering it. Secure, whip finish and trim.

5. SAN JUAN WORM

The San Juan Worm was developed right here on the San Juan River. About 100 people claim to have invented it but it started as just orange thread on a hook and evolved into various forms of ultra-chenille tied on a hook. This is the basic version that has worked on every tailwater in America for a quarter century. This is one of the easiest flies to tie in the entire world and one of the most effective!

HOOK: Dai Riki 135 size #10-#18 (Do not use limerick bend hooks as the gouge out the eyes of trout)
THREAD: Red or match the color of the worm
BODY: Various colors of ultra-chenille

Cut chenille to desired length. Slightly burn the ends so that they taper using a candle or a lighter. Lay a bed of thread on the hook winding to the bend. Tie in the chenille so that equal amounts extend beyond the bend and the eye of the hook and secure. Wrap the thread forward to the eye then lay the remaining chenille down on top of the hook and secure it at the eye. Make several wraps and whip finish and trim.

6. GINGER DUN

I developed this fly to imitate a fly that hatches in abundance on streams in the southwest. It's a mid-day and evening mayfly that that is ginger in color. It also imitates the Pale Morning Duns and Pale Evening Duns in light ginger.

HOOK: Any standard dry fly hook size #12 to #20
THREAD: Ginger
TAIL: Light elk body hair or ginger hackle fibers
BODY: Ginger hare line dubbing with guard hares
WING: White or opaque poly yarn
HACKLE: Ginger neck or saddle

Tie in a bed of thread to the bend and back ¾ of the way to the eye. Tie in the poly wing with the base of the wing extending back close to the bend, clip off the excess and wrap over to the bend, securing the wing tightly. Tie in the elk hair tail so that the tips extend past the bend equal to the length of the shank; the base of the tail should butt up against the base of the wing. Wrap forward to the wing, split and divide the wing using several figure eights and several wraps in front of the wings so that they are propped upright when finished.

Wrap back to the tail and dub the thread and taper the body forward to the base of the wing. Tie in the hackle and wind thread forward to the eye. Wrap the hackle three or four times in back of the wing and then three or four wraps in front and secure. Whip finish and trim.

7. DOUBLE HACKLE PEACOCK

This fly has been around forever and I'm still not sure exactly what it represents or why it works. But is one of the best flies I've ever used and it has worked for me anywhere there's trout. It can be used dry, wet or as a nymph and really works anywhere there are caddis or crane fly larva.

> **HOOK**: 1 or 2x long size #6 to #18
> **THREAD**: Black, 6/0 or 8/0 in small sizes
> **BODY**: Peacock hearl
> **HACKLE**: Fore and aft – brown saddle

Lay a bed of thread to the bend. Tie in the butt of the first hackle and make four or five tight wraps forward, tie off and trim. With butts facing the eye, tie in the peacock so that the butts are facing the eye, then wrap the peacock forward ¾ of the way to the eye, secure and trim. Tie in the second hackle and wind thread forward to the eye. Make several tight wraps with the hackle, secure and trim. Whip finish and trim.

8. TERMINATOR

This fly was devised by guide Eddie Adams back in the 1980s and has been used successfully as a small golden stone, yellow sally, caddis, pine moth and other moths ever since. It is irresistible to trout whenever those bugs are present.

> **HOOK**: Standard dry fly hook #12 - #18
> **THREAD**: Light yellow or golden stone
> **BUTT (EGG SACK)**: Amber or ginger dubbing ball
> **BODY**: Yellow or golden stone dubbing
> **HACKLE**: Grizzly saddle hackle
> **WING**: Light elk body fur w/o guard hairs

Lay a bed of thread to bend of hook. Dub a small amount of amber or ginger dubbing on the thread and form a small ball at the bend of the hook. Tie in the butt of the grizzly hackle in front of the butt. Wrap the yellow dubbed thread forward ¾ of the way to the eye. Palmer the hackle forward to the same point and tie off and trim. Tie in the elk hair (caddis style) so that the tips extend just barely past the bend of the hook. Clip the butts at the eye so that they form a small head. Whip finish and trim.

9. Thompson's AF Hopper

Designed and tied by Doc Thompson in 2000
Available through Orvis

HOOK: TMC 200R size 10-14 or similar hook
THREAD: 6/0 in tan, brown, olive or color to match
BODY: 2mm foam in tan, brown, olive or color to match
UNDERWING: 2mm foam in tan, brown, olive or color to match
WING: Elk Hair in natural, brown or bleached
LEGS: Round Rubber Legs or Barred Crazy Legs color to match
HACKLE: Brown, tan, grizzly or color to match

10. Glow In The Ass Caddis

Designed and Tied By Doc Thompson in 2003
Available through Orvis

HOOK: TMC 100 size 12-16 or similar dry fly hook
THREAD: 6/0 in tan, olive or color to match
BUTT (EGG SAC): Small glass bead in orange or olive
BODY: 2mm foam in tan, olive or color to match
WING: Elk hair in natural, gray or brown
HACKLE: Brown, grizzly brown or color to match

11. Pound-Meister

Designed and developed by angler, guide and author Taylor Streit, this is one of the best crane fly patterns around. Use them anywhere that crane flies are found.

HOOK: Dai Riki 135, #4-#10
THREAD: Gray 3/0
BODY: Wide, gray or pale olive chenille
HACKLE: Blue dun hackle
CASE: Four strands of peacock
RIB: Copper wire
HEAD: Peacock, bead (optional)

Lay a bed of thread from head to bend of hook followed by tying in the chenille through the length of the hook, ending at the bend. Attach the copper wire and then the hackle and chenille all at the bend of the hook. Wrap the thread forward ¾ of the way up the hook, then the chenille and tie it off. Palmer the hackle forward and tie it off. Pull the peacock over the top of the fly creating a peacock stripe down the back and tie it down. Do not clip the excess peacock. Wind the copper wire forward ribbing it between the hackle and tie it off. Wrap the thread forward to the eye, then wrap the excess peacock forward to the eye, forming a head slightly thicker than the body. Secure, whip finish and trim.

12. Fly Line Damsel

Designed and developed by Taylor Streit

As the body is extended over the eye of the hook a much higher percentage of hook-ups occur. Extended bodies tied over the rear of the hook are pushed away as a fish engulfs the fly and fish are either missed or just barely hooked.

HOOK: Tiemco 2487 or equivalent #8-#14
THREAD: White 6/0
BODY: Thin, white fly line (running line from WF- F 3-5 wt. running line.
THORAX: White dubbing
HACKLE: Long grizzly saddle or neck hackle tied parachute style around a foam post
PAINT: Blue or tan

Lay a bed of thread to almost the bend of the hook then attach the fly line so that it extends over the eye of the hook about 2.5 times the length of the hook. Add dubbing, wrapping it forward to the head and back to the middle of the hook. Tie in a small, white foam post then attach the hackle and wind it on the post parachute style and tie off and trim the hackle. Wrap thread forward to the head. Whip finish and trim. Paint the fly line and dubbing blue, brown, rust or yellowish brown with a magic marker.

FLY SHOPS, OUTFITTERS & SPORTING GOOD STORES

Albuquerque

Big 5 Sporting Goods, 1915 Juan Tabo Blvd Ne, Albuquerque, NM 87112; 505-275-4990; www.big5sportinggoods.com

Big 5 Sporting Goods, 3140 Coors Boulevard NW, Albuquerque, NM; 505-836-6555; www.big5sportinggoods.com

Big 5 Sporting Goods, 2720 San Mateo Blvd Ne, Albuquerque, NM 87110; 505-884-5026; www.big5sportinggoods.com

Big 5 Sporting Goods; 9391 Coors Blvd. N.W., Albuquerque, NM; 505-890-5121; www.big5sportinggoods.com

Big 5 Sporting Goods, 8102 Wyoming Blvd. NE, Albuquerque, NM; 505-797-8705; www.big5sportinggoods.com

Charlie's Sporting Goods, 8908 Menaul Boulevard NE, Albuquerque, NM 87112; 505-275-3006

Los Pinos Fly Shop, 2820 Richmond Dr. NE, Albuquerque, NM 87107; 505-884-7501

Los Ranchos Gun & Tackle, 6542 4th St., NW, Albuquerque, NM 87107; 505-345-4276

Mountain States Sporting Goods, 1102 Mountain Road, Albuquerque, NM 87125; 505-243-7623

Play it Again Sports, 3301 Coors NW; Landera Shopping Center; Albuquerque, NM; 87120; 505-890-7041; www.playitagainsports.com

Play it Again Sports, 7401 Menaul Blvd NE; Albuquerque, NM 87110; 505-881-0551; www.playitagainsports.com

REI, 1550 Mercantile Avenue NE, Albuquerque, NM; 505-247-1191; www.rei.com

Sports Authority, 4720 Alexander Blvd. NE, Albuquerque, NM 87109; 505-344-9001; www.sportsauthority.com

Sports Authority, 2100 Louisana Blvd. NE, Albuquerque, NM 87110; 505-881-8082; www.sportsauthority.com

Sportsman's Warehouse, 1450 Renaissance Boulevard NE, Albuquerque, NM 87107-7008; 505-761-9900; www.sportsmanswarehouse.com

Abiquiu

Bode's General Merchandise, US 84, Abiquiu, NM 87510; 505-685-4886

Alamagordo

Big 5 Sporting Goods, 3312 North White Sands Boulevard, Alamogordo, NM; 575-434-0320; www.big5sportinggoods.com

Angel Fire

Mountain Sports, 3375 Highway 434, Angel Fire, NM; 575-377-3490

Antonito (Colorado)

Fox Creek Store, 26573 Hwy. 17, Antonito, CO 81120; 719-376-5881; www.foxcreekstore.com

Aztec

Frontier Sports, 108 N. Main Avenue, Aztec, NM 87410; 505-334-0009
Sandstone Anglers, John and Monica Tavenner, 83 CR 2929, Aztec, NM 87410; 888-339-9789; www.sandstoneanglers.com

Bloomfield

Soaring Eagle Lodge & Fly Shop, 50 Road 4370, Bloomfield, NM 87413; 505-632-3721; full-service fly shop; www.soaringeaglelodge.net

Clayton

Knotts Sportsman Supply, 1015 South 1st St., Clayton, NM 88415; 575-374-8361

Deming

D&M Sporting Goods, 616 W Pine St #2B, Deming, NM 88030; 575-546-9767
Hibbett Sports, 707 East Pine Street, Deming, NM; 575-546-4689; www.hibbett.com

Durango (Colorado)

Adventures Beyond, Inc., 4140 County Road 234, Durango, CO 81301-8208; 970-385-7656
Animas Valley Anglers, 264 West 22nd Street, Durango, CO; 970-259-0484; www.gottrout.com
Apple Orchard Inn, 7758 County Road 203, Durango, CO 81301; 970-247-0751; www.appleorchardinn.com
Back Country Experience, 1205 Camino Del Rio, Durango CO 81301; 970-247-5830, 800-648-8519; www.bcexp.com
Big 5 Sporting Goods, 400 South Camino Del Rio, Durango, CO; 970-247-1588; www.big5sportinggoods.com
D Bar G Outfitters, 4748 County Road 243, Durango, CO 81301; 970-385-6888
The Caddis Company, 600 Main Avenue, Durango, CO 81301; 970-382-9978; www.caddiscompany.com
Duranglers Flies & Supplies, 923 Main Ave., Durango, CO 81301; 970-385-4081; www.duranglers.com
Gardenswartz Sporting Goods, 863 Main Avenue, Durango, CO; 970-247-2660
Pine Needle Mountaineering, 835 Main Avenue, Durango, CO; 970-247-8728; www.pineneedle.com

Eagle Nest

Dos Amigos Anglers, 247 East Therma Street, Eagle Nest, NM 87718; 575-377-6226

Espanola

Known World Guide Service, Inc., 702 CR 57; 800-983-7756;
www.knownworldguides.com
Toby's Sports, 1105 North Riverside Drive, Espanola, NM 87532; 505-753-6083

Farmington

Big 5 Sporting Goods, 910 E Main St, Farmington, NM 87401; 505-326-1805;
www.big5sportinggoods.com
East Main Trading Center, 5925 East Main Street, Farmington, NM; 505-326-7474
Zia Sporting Goods, Inc., 500 E. Main St., Farmington, NM 87401; 505-327-6004;
www.ziasportinggoods.net

Glenwood

Leah Jones Gila Wilderness Ventures, P.O. Box 280, Glenwood, NM 88039;
505-539-2800; www.gilawildernessventures.com

Hesperus (Colorado)

Anasazi Angler Inc, 12895 Highway 140, Hesperus, CO; 970-385-4665;
www.sanjuanguides.com
Blue Lake Ranch, 16919 Hwy. 140, Hesperus, CO 81326; 1-888-258-3525;
www.bluelakeranch.com

Las Cruces

Big 5 Sporting Goods, 3060 E Lohman Ave., Las Cruces, NM 88011; 575-522-0555;
www.big5sportinggoods.com
Dive Quest Scuba, 2005 Del Mar Avenue, Las Cruces, NM 88001; 575-525-3483
Fly Fish New Mexico, 811 2nd Street, Las Cruces, NM 88005-2248; 575-525-1015
Hibbett Sports, 700 South Telshor Boulevard, Las Cruces, NM; 575-532-0466;
www.hibbett.com
Sportsman's Elite, 7500 North Mesa Street, El Paso, TX 79912; 915-587-4867;
www.sportsmanseliteep.com

Las Vegas

Hibbett Sports, 2500 7th Street, Las Vegas, NM; 505-454-9162; www.hibbett.com

Mancos (Colorado)

Lost Canyon Lake Lodge, 15472 County Road 35.3, Mancos, CO 81328;
970-882-7871; www.lostcanyonlakelodge.com

Navajo Dam

Abe's Motel & Fly Shop, 1791 Highway 173, Navajo Dam, NM 87419-9712;
505-632-2194; full-service Orvis dealer, www.sanjuanriver.com
Fishheads of the San Juan River, 1796 Hwy 173, Navajo Dam, NM 87419;
505-634-0463; www.fisheadsofthesanjuan.com

Float N' Fish, 4 Road 4251, Navajo Dam, NM 87419; 505-632-5385
Rainbow Lodge and Resolution Guide Service, Chris Guiekema, Navajo Dam, NM; 1-888-328-1858; www.sanjuanfishing.com
Rise N Fly Guide Services, 1003 Highway 511, Navajo Dam; 505-632-1740
Rocky Mountain Anglers, Rick Hooley, Navajo Dam, NM; 505-632-0445
Soaring Eagle Lodge and Fly Shop, P.O. Box 6340, #48 CR 4370, Navajo Dam, NM 87419; 1-800-866-2719; www.soaringeaglelodge.net
Sportsman Inn Fly Shop, 1808 Highway 173, Navajo Dam, NM 87415; 505-632-0283

Pecos

Adelo's Town & Country Store, P.O. Box 517, Pecos, NM 87552; 505-757-8565
Cow Creek Ranch, P.O. Box 487, Pecos, NM 87552; 505-757-2107; www.cowcreek-ranch.com

Questa

Ed Adams Flyfishing, P.O. Box 428, Questa, NM 87556; 575-586-1512; www.edadamsflyfishing.com

Raton

Sports Arena, 113 N 2nd, Raton, NM; 505-445-3108
Vermejo Park Ranch, P.O. Drawer E, Raton, NM 87740; 505-445-3097; www.vermejoparkranch.com

Red River

Crazy Mountain Sports, 416 Main Street, Red River, NM; 575-754-6183
Williams Trading Post, 306 E. High Street, Red River, NM; 505-754-2217; fishing and camping supplies, fishing licenses

Santa Fe

Active Endeavors, 328 South Guadalupe Street, Santa Fe, NM 87501-2682; 505-984-8221; www.shopactiveendeavors.com
Big 5 Sporting Goods, 2860 Cerrillos Rd., Santa Fe, NM; 505-474-4260; www.big5sportinggoods.com
High Desert Angler, 460 Cerrillos Road St., Santa Fe, NM 87501; 505-988-7688; guide service, equipment sales and rental, flyfishing supplies and information, licenses; www.highdesertangler.com
New Wave Rafting Company, Rt. 5 Box 302 A, Santa Fe, NM; 1-800-984-1444, 505-984-1444; rafting trips; www.newwaverafting.com
The Reel Life, Sanbusco Market Center, 500 Montezuma Ave., Santa Fe, NM 87501; 505-995-8114, 1-877-733-5543; guide service, classes, lessons, flyfishing equipment sales and rental, licenses; www.thereellife.com

Sangre de Cristo Mountain Works, 328 S. Guadalupe, Santa Fe, NM; 505-984-8221; camping, backpacking, backcountry skiing, and climbing equipment; www. sdcmountainworks.com

Sports Authority, Santa Fe Place/Villa Linda Mall, 4250 Cerrillos Road, #1404, Santa Fe , NM 87505; 505-473-3555; www.sportsauthority.com

Taos

Cottam's Ski & Outdoor, 207 Paseo Del Pueblo Sur, Taos, NM 87571; 800-322-8267; www.cottamsoutdoor.com

Mudd-n-Flood Mountain Shop, 134 Bent St., Taos, NM 87571; 505-751-9100

Solitary Angler, 204B Paseo del Pueblo N, Taos, NM; 505-758-5653, 1-866-502-1700; www.thesolitaryangler.com

Taos Mountain Outfitters, 114 S. Plaza, Taos, NM 87571; 505-758-9292; www.taosmountainoutfitters.com

Taylor Streit Fly Fishing Service, P.O. Box 2759, Taos, NM 87571; 505-751-1312; www.streitflyfishing.com

Wild Rivers on the Fly, 106 Sutton Place, Taos Ski Valley, NM 87525; 505-715-6773; www.wildriversonthefly.com

Tererro

Santa Fe Flyfishers School and Guide Service, P.O. Box 5A, Tererro, NM 87573; 800-555-7707, 505-757-3294; guide service, classes, private water

Truth or Consequences

Lil Abners, HC 31 Box 112, Highway 187 Marker 23.2, Caballo, NM 87931; 505-743-0153; www.lilabners.com

Ute Park

Doc Thompson's High Country Anglers, P.O. Box 52, Ute Park, NM 87749; 505-376-9220; www.flyfishnewmexico.com

INDEX